Springer Series on Social Work

Albert R. Roberts, D.S.W., Series Editor

Graduate School of Social Work, Rutgers, The State University of New Jersey

Advisory Board: Joseph D. Anderson, D.S.W., Barbara Berkman, D.S.W., Paul H. Ephross, Ph.D., Sheldon R. Gelman, Ph.D., Nancy A. Humphreys, D.S.W., Sheldon Siegel, Ph.D., and Julia Watkins, Ph.D.

Terri Combs-Orme, Ph.D., is an assistant professor at the School of Social Work and Community Planning and in the Division of Pediatrics, University of Maryland at Baltimore. Her previous academic positions include Louisiana State University (School of Social Work), Northwestern University (Center for Health Services and Policy Research), and Washington University (Department of Psychiatry). She earned her Ph.D. in social work from the George Warren Brown School of Social Work, Washington University, in 1982.

Dr. Combs-Orme received her M.S.S.W. from the University of Texas at Arlington, and her B.A. in social work and sociology from Baylor University in Waco, Texas. Her social work practice experience includes positions in child welfare and mental health.

Social Work Practice in Maternal and Child Health

Terri Combs-Orme, Ph.D.

Springer Publishing Company
New York

Springer Publishing Company, Inc.
536 Broadway
New York, NY 10012

90 91 92 93 94 / 5 4 3 2 1

Printed in the United States of America

Library of Congress Cataloging-in-Publication Data

Combs-Orme, Terri.
    Social work practice in maternal and child health / Terri Combs
-Orme.
        p.   cm.—(Springer series on social work : vol. 15)
    Includes bibliographical references (p.   ).
    ISBN 0-8261-6370-X
    1. Maternal and infant welfare—United States. 2. Child health
services—United States. 3. Teenage pregnancy—United States.
4. Birth control—United States. I. Title. II.Series: Springer
series on social work : v. 15.
    HV699.C535 1990
    362.1'9892—dc20   89-26218
                                                                    CIP

To Charlie, Who made it real

Contents

Acknowledgments

It is difficult to know where to start in acknowledging those who helped me with this effort. My husband, John, provided the support and encouragement I needed to continue when I wondered if I had made a mistake in starting this book. Probably more important, he generously understood the time I took to work that should have been spent fulfilling other responsibilities. Finally, he is a model of the active, involved father whose full participation is so important to mothers and children.

Several persons provided assistance on all or much of the book. My friend and research assistant Jean Bettencourtt doggedly pursued references long past her responsibility and nagged me to pay attention to detail when I was sometimes inclined not to do so. Christina Risley Curtiss assisted me with such tasks in the final, agonizing weeks; in particular, she provided valuable comments on prenatal care and family planning. Sandy Wilson was a careful reader of the manuscript when that was just what I needed. Three administrators provided needed time and resources for me to accomplish this work: Dean James Midgley of Louisiana State University, and Dean Ruth Young and Assistant Dean Lily Gold of the University of Maryland. Bob Nevin's insightful review led to a helpful and important reorganization of several sections. I am also indebted to my series editor, Al Roberts, for his wisdom and patience in this long process.

Because I drew on the writing of many social work scholars and other professionals, I want to thank all those professionals who have taken the considerable time and effort to share their knowledge and experience. Their efforts have been valuable to me, all social workers, and those in other professions, because they allow us to build on existing knowledge to learn more about how we can be most effective with our clients.

Readers of the manuscript, all experts in their respective fields, provided comments and suggestions that carried me well beyond where I started. In particular, Mary Lou Ballasonne of the University of Washington went well beyond the call of duty in sharing her expertise on adolescent pregnancy and several other issues, and putting me in touch with other helpful experts.

Fred DiBlasio of the University of Maryland, Cecilia Runkle of Kaiser Permanente Health Group, and especially Frederic Reamer of Rhode Island College assisted me in the incredibly complex area of social work ethics. Beth Manning and Susan Eaton of Woman's Hospital in Baton Rouge, Louisiana, provided valuable insights from their practice regarding neonatal intensive care and infant death.

Ernestine Player and Gardenia Ruff, both of the South Carolina Department of Health, were particularly helpful in assisting me to describe and articulate the history of social work's role in MCH. Their important roles in that history particularly qualify them to offer criticism on the subject, and indeed South Carolina is a model progressive state for what social workers can do in MCH. Likewise, Elizabeth Watkins provided helpful comments from her extensive and distinguished experience, and I was inspired from reading her many excellent articles. Judy Barber also inspired me, both with her written material and with her discussion of what social workers are doing in Mississippi. Susan Varner of the California Department of Health Services was extremely helpful regarding family planning and particularly called my attention to the importance of the male role in family planning.

Dan Timmel of the Maryland SIDS Project provided important material and comments on the chapter on infant death. Deborah Stokes of the Ohio Department of Health led me to several important conference proceedings, provided valuable perspectives on primary health care for children, and in particular alerted me to some errors I originally made regarding federal programs. Lynn McDonald-Wikler alerted me to some important issues regarding developmental disabilities and facilitated my participation in the Carolina Conference on Personnel Preparation, from which I learned a great deal.

Finally, several persons were helpful in providing references. The Federal Office of Maternal and Child Health and the Clearinghouse on Maternal and Child Health Information were invaluable resources, as they have always been when I have called on them. Brice Freeman of Planned Parenthood located several important resources that I never could have found any other way. Sandra Chesborough of the North Central Florida Maternity and Infant Care Services provided information that led to several assessment tools. I am extremely grateful to Juanita Evans, chief social worker at the Office of Maternal and Child Health, for putting me in touch with several outstanding social work scholars whose help and perspectives have been invaluable to me.

In conclusion, I would like to give a special thanks to my parents, John Combs and Wanda Sheehan Combs. They not only raised me to have the self-confidence and belief in myself that are required to complete a project like this, but they are the kind of parents who reaffirm my belief in families.

Introduction and Overview

The purpose of this book is twofold. First, it is to describe and inform ourselves and others about what social work is doing to promote the health of mothers and infants in this country. Many social workers are "in the trenches" daily, providing services that probably have a positive impact on the health of mothers and babies. Lambert exhorted the profession to define its role in maternal and child health (MCH) in 1968 so that effectiveness could be assessed. The written literature still remains scattered and located where it may not be readily accessible to many social work practitioners and students, such as in conference proceedings (which although often excellent are frequently difficult to obtain) and in the literature of other professions. This book will attempt to synthesize this valuable material, as well as material from other areas of social work when it is appropriate, to describe what MCH social workers are doing and where it is being done.

A second and equally important purpose of this book is to begin to address the issue of the effectiveness of social work practice in MCH. This effort is a beginning, because much of our work is untested and difficult to measure with current limited methods. Some beginning effort must be made, however. These are times that demand accountability, and if social workers do not test themselves and their services, the profession will find that it is no longer needed. In keeping with this goal I have tried to identify gaps in knowledge, and to bring in material from other areas of social work and other professions, when such material may help bridge the gaps.

Several events make this book a timely and necessary addition to social work's knowledge base. First, the growth and proliferation of medical technology in the area have led to many new positions for social workers in this arena. The subspeciality of perinatal social work is a growing one, as demonstrated by membership in the National Association of Perinatal Social Workers, which stood at more than 400 in 1985 (National Association of Perinatal Social Workers, 1985). Moreover, the Maternal and Child Health and Social Work sections of the American Public Health Association remain vital components of that organization and include many MCH social workers.

Second, neonatal intensive care unit (NICU) technologies have resulted in the salvage of many infants who once would have died (McCormick, 1985), but in the process we have discovered new situations that physicians and their technologies cannot handle alone. Social workers have become an integral part of the modern team in the NICU and more generally in the modern obstetric-gynecologic setting. For example, social workers have for many years worked in prenatal clinics that draw the low-income, "reluctant" pregnant patient (e.g., Peoples & Siegel, 1983). As the outcomes of lack of prenatal care become more expensive and more apparent, social work expertise in these settings becomes more valuable, and it becomes more important that we demonstrate our skills.

An important result of the growth of medical technology is to show how little impact technology has overall. Even prenatal care, which is assumed to be effective and important in promoting positive outcomes of pregnancy, probably accounts for little of the variance in healthy birth (Gortmaker, 1979). Only minor progress has been made in the last 20 years in reducing the low birthweight (LBW) and postneonatal mortality rates in this country. Technology can do little to address these problems. The important variables that continue to threaten American children's lives are almost without exception social factors with which medicine traditionally has been little involved: race and inequality, poverty and its far-reaching effects, lack of education, and unmarried parenthood. These are traditional areas of social work practice, and as their critical role in health becomes clearer we are presented with a challenge to demonstrate the effectiveness of practice.

Finally, the timing of this book is crucial in that increasing evidence exists of both the potential for effectiveness of interventions to support and enhance the functioning of families, and more willingness on the parts of various government entities to fund such services (Weiss, 1988). Increasingly, MCH issues are being seen not as isolated factors (such as whether infants' immunization schedules are in compliance), but as complex multivariate factors related to the competence and abilities of families to care for themselves within the broader environment. Social work has an important place in such an approach to health.

ORGANIZATION OF THE BOOK

Each of the chapters of this book deals with one major topic area of MCH, although some overlap will frequently occur. In each chapter I will present an overview of the subject as well as unique social work practice roles and settings in each area. I discuss existing empirical evidence regarding effectiveness, and when no such evidence exists I describe the gaps in knowledge.

Each chapter also emphasizes relevant social policy issues. Social workers involved exclusively in the delivery of direct services need to be aware of and must operate within aspects of prevailing social policy, because such policy is significant in either enhancing or limiting what they can accomplish for and with their clients. Ideally we should also speak for our clients and work to create policy that promotes the health of mothers and children. Indeed, our Code of Ethics (both of the National Association of Social Workers and the National Association of Perinatal Social Workers) requires us to do this. First, however, we must be aware of the legislation and the programs within which we operate. This can be a formidable task.

It is unfortunate that the social work education process, which separates "practice" and "policy" into separate courses in many cases, does social workers and their clients a disservice; it often promotes a situation in which "clinical" social workers are unaware of the policy-making process and their responsibilities in that area. This situation is especially unfortunate because social workers in direct practice may enjoy excellent credibility for influencing the policy-making process, if they are aware of and active in that process. In MCH in particular, successful practice requires an understanding of a system that is often simply inadequate to protect the health of this nation's most precious resource. I hope that this book will contribute to the abilities and commitment of social workers to be professionally active in the tradition of many of our social work forebears.

In some cases I also will describe the professional, demographic, and social trends that seem likely to shape future directions and for which we must begin to prepare. Some events, however, appear so suddenly that they defy prediction. The current Acquired Immune Deficiency Syndrome (AIDS) crisis has been such an event. Helping professionals are reeling as they attempt to provide services for growing numbers of infected persons in a climate of uncertainty and lack of resources. In any case, it is important to look ahead to prepare the educational process and the service structure to meet future needs as well as possible.

The following is a brief overview of the chapters to come. It is important to note that although genetic social work is an important sub-specialty that is closely related to MCH, it is not covered in this book. The reader is referred to Schild and Black (1984) for an excellent source of information on this topic. I could contribute little to this excellent reference, so I have elected not to attempt to do so.

Chapter 1: Social Work Practice in Maternal and Child Health: An Orientation

Social workers who practice as part of the multidisciplinary MCH team should be conversant in the major terms and issues of the field, and also should be familiar with, at least, the most important statistics, the major threats to maternal and child health, and the range of current medical technologies. This chapter defines some of the major terms used in the broad field of MCH, and summarizes the current state of knowledge in the epidemiology, etiology, and treatment of LBW, prematurity, and child and infant health and mortality.

Chapter 2: Prenatal Care Services

This chapter describes briefly the rationale for and benefits of prenatal care, with emphasis on the activities in which social workers are involved. Increasingly it is being recognized that the determinants of pregnancy outcome lie less in medical procedures than they do in the environment and living situation of the mother and family. The practice skills of social workers that may contribute to good pregnancy outcomes include assessing, recruiting, and keeping the reluctant client in prenatal care, and obtaining needed services.

Chapter 3: High-Risk Infant Care

Perhaps in no area of MCH has medical technology so vastly changed practice as in the NICU, and yet nowhere are the human needs so evident. This chapter begins with a discussion of the special needs of families with infants in NICU, with attention to the basic research on attachment and bonding, and its relationship to the NICU experience. The social work practitioner's role in the NICU is discussed, along with the special skills required for being a part of the NICU team and the stresses the practitioner in this area may expect.

Chapter 4: Infant Death

The loss of a child at any age is an overwhelming tragedy for parents, and an enormous challenge for social workers. Whether the loss occurs even before conception (with infertility), after only a short pregnancy (miscarriage), during the last few weeks of pregnancy (stillbirth), shortly after the infant has been born (neonatal death), or during the first year of life because of Sudden Infant Death Syndrome (SIDS), no other loss affects parents so profoundly. This chapter deals first with grieving and what is known about normal behavior following a loss; then deals specifically with issues surrounding infant loss; and finally discusses separately the issues related to miscarriage, stillbirth, infant death in the NICU, SIDS, and infertility.

Chapter 5: Health Care Services for Young Children

Research shows consistently that children use primary health care resources less than any other age group in the United States, and that the poorest, least healthy children use fewer services than any other group. Social workers are involved in numerous programs designed to provide primary and preventive care to low-income children, including the Maternal and Child Health Block Grant programs. Assessment and screening during this period for child abuse and neglect, malnutrition, delayed development and learning disabilities, and other health problems are essential for both the protection of child health and the promotion of the health of future mothers and fathers. The special role of the family in a child's health is highlighted.

Chapter 6: Services for Children With Disabilities

Crippled Children's Services was one of the original Title V programs, and it continues under different names to provide services for thousands of children with disabilities today. This chapter describes the extraordinary service needs of these children and their families, the services provided under various programs, and the important roles social workers play in these programs. It also deals with the recent "empowerment" of families who have children with disabilities, and the need for social workers to work with parents as partners in the pursuit of services for these children and their families.

Chapter 7: Adolescent Sexuality and Pregnancy

No current issue evokes more concern or more controversy than teen-aged sexuality and pregnancy. Social workers have dealt professionally with adolescent pregnancy for many years, but many social workers find that health care-related practice with adolescents has changed enor-mously in the 1980s. The easy availability of contraception, possibility of affordable and confidential abortion, and acceptance of teenaged parent-ing make working with sexually active adolescents a new challenge today. Several innovative programs are attempting to meet these challenges, and social workers are in the forefront of these programs.

Chapter 8: Family Planning Services

At one time family planning was a source of great concern as well as controversy within the profession. The right of all families to limit the number and spacing of their children is taken for granted now, although as the reader will see, the right and capabilities do not always come together. This chapter discusses the provision of family planning services to low-income families and the continuing problems of access that some families face. It also discusses the related issues of abortion, sexually transmitted diseases, and AIDS.

Chapter 9: Ethical and Personal Values in the Practice of Maternal and Child Health Social Work

The practice of social work in MCH presents several ethical dilemmas to challenge the social worker. Abortion, parental rights to refuse treatment for their sick or deformed infants, and the provision of contraception to young adolescents are only some of the issues that may place the social worker in the position of dealing simultaneously with personal values and feelings, institutional obligations, and professional ethics. This chapter first explores some of the major philosophies of ethics to place social work ethics in context, and then attempts to define the current ethical climate. Various structures for decision making in this sensitive area are then provided.

An important note concerns the sticky (but important) issue of gen-der and language. No author who is sensitive to human rights can ignore the implictions of language—for example, the message that is conveyed by using male pronouns to refer to both men and women. Yet none of the available solutions to this problem is satisfying. I have elected not to say "his or her," in each case when a pronoun is required, because such language becomes awkward and difficult to read. Rather, when referring to parents or infants I alternate between the male and female gender. Because most social workers are women (especially in the MCH field), I use feminine pronouns when referring to social workers in most cases.

Male social workers have a special place in the field of MCH, because their presence affirms the belief that MCH is *not* a feminist issue, nor even a women's issue, as it is often cast. It is a family issue, and one that has equal importance and meaning to both men and women. Indeed, MCH is a misnomer. The subject of this book is family health, with emphasis on healthy reproduction and parenting.

1 Social Work Practice in Maternal and Child Health: An Orientation

Maternal and Child Health (MCH) is a multidisciplinary field dedicated to the improved health of mothers and children and composed primarily of the professions of medicine, nursing, public health, social work, and nutrition. MCH is generally understood to cover the preconceptional period to adolescence, and increasingly is seen as a family-centered service that should include fathers as well as mothers and children (Dott & Dott, 1985). Services include not only those provided by the major professions listed earlier, but also auxiliary services that would contribute to a healthy birth and childhood including dental care, health education, mental health services, and others. The orientation of MCH is both preventive and curative, both population based and individually centered, and avoids the common but false and meaningless distinction between health and welfare services.

Social work practice in MCH occurs within the multidisciplinary MCH team (Reichert, 1980; Watkins & Player, 1981). The team approach to MCH care was evident from the beginnings of the Progressive Era when social workers held positions of leadership at every level, but with the reforms of the 1960s the importance of the team approach was reaffirmed. The intentions of those reforms included the reduction of fragmentation of services (Kumabe, Nishida, O'Hara, & Woodruff, 1977) and the provision of comprehensive health care services to low-income mothers and children including primary, secondary, and tertiary services in the areas of mental health, dental care, health education, and social, nutrition, and physical therapy services (Kaufman & Watkins, 1981).

The importance of the multidisciplinary team derives from the fact that no single discipline encompasses all of the necessary skills and knowledge required to provide comprehensive services (Kumabe et al., 1977). Starfield (1982), herself a physician, says:

1

Regardless of the characteristics of the organization in which they may work, there are few physicians who are trained to deal effectively with the variety of other problems that complicate the care of the poor, including . . . crowded living conditions . . . inferior arrangements of heating, lighting, and refrigeration . . . less congenial neighborhoods . . . their greater difficulty in establishing rapport with health care providers because of differences in background, living styles and education; and their competing priorities for food and shelter which inevitably place healthful practices much lower on the scale of priorities. (p. 248)

The importance of these factors in health, and particularly in the health of children, mandates the involvement of social work in MCH.

The remainder of this chapter serves to orient the reader to the role played by social work on the MCH team through a discussion first of the knowledge base in social work for MCH practice including both theoretical orientations and basic practice skills and tasks. Next, a brief definition of the important terms in the broad field is presented. Finally, major epidemiologic risk factors for MCH are discussed.

KNOWLEDGE BASE FOR SOCIAL WORK IN MCH

One may characterize three aspects of the general knowledge base for MCH social work practice: (a) theoretical perspectives, which though not specific to MCH are claimed by the social work profession and are appropriate to clinical practice; (b) certain essential practice roles (outside the realm usually considered to be "clinical") that cut across various theoretical approaches to social work; and (c) knowledge specific to MCH (including epidemiology) and the practice setting.

Guiding Theoretical Perspectives for Practice

Public Health

Although no consensus exists for a prescribed model of clinical practice in MCH social work, the public health perspective guides many MCH social workers. Public health is a distinguished discipline that itself is multidisciplinary, including primarily physicians and nurses, and that has contributed perhaps more than any other profession to the significant improvements in American health during this century (Winslow, 1923). Public health improvements in hygiene and sanitation, milk and water purity, and food storage, in conjunction with mass vaccinations and immunizations, have reduced infectious disease as the major killer of children and young people to a fairly rare cause of death for this age group in this country today. The approach used by public health in these great campaigns has always been one directed toward the community or population group rather than the individual and toward primary prevention rather than "treatment."

Social work's historical link with public health is a strong one, growing first from medical social work (Bartlett, 1954). Public health departments used hospital social workers to do needs assessment and counseling with bereaved families in the 1918 influenza epidemic (Kerson, 1982). The public health link was most evident in the great reforms of the Progressive Era and the Social Security Act (Mantell, 1984). Because most of these federal programs mandated social work involvement, after 1935 state public health departments began expanding their social work staffs, strengthening the bond between the two professions. Then in the 1950s public health was publicly recognized as a specialty within the social work profession (Mantell, 1984). Public health social workers continue to identify themselves as a specialty group and have progressed toward operationalization and refinement of their professional skills (see Gitterman, Black, & Stein, 1985).

Public health social work is defined by Mantell (1984) as more than the practice of social work in public health settings. "Social workers who address the preventive health needs of groups are practicing public health social work" (p. 218), she says. The public health social worker thus possesses both the traditional one-to-one skills of the social worker, evidenced by the M.S.W. degree, and the epidemiologic perspective and broader approach of the public health professional, which may be (but is not always) evidenced by the M.P.H. degree (Miller, 1986). As Watkins (1985) and others conceptualize the methods of the public health social worker, those methods include casework, advocacy for social reform, program planning, and research.

As early as 1954, Bartlett dealt with the dual function of the public health social worker. How is casework, the *sin qua non* of social work, combined with the community approach of public health? She answered this question in part by noting, "In public health social work the consultant's objective is always services to individuals, but the emphasis is, appropriately, more on development of program, on building a program of services to people" (p. 23). Rice (1959) further clarified that the public health social worker spent less time on individually oriented services, concentrating on preventive casework. For example, she noted that social workers may engage in anticipatory guidance, teaching young mothers about and preparing for infants' developmental milestones. Individual casework is still important to the public health social worker, but its emphasis is slightly changed.

Other aspects of public health have not been widely claimed by public health social workers. Mantell (1984) notes that public health social workers are involved only nominally in assessment of community needs, program planning, structural reform, legislative lobbying, and health policy development. She asserts:

> Social work practice in public health, however, must move beyond individually-oriented preventive interventions in hospital settings and revive its focus on the community. As part of its policy to expand and diversify practice, social work needs to participate in large-scale epidemiologic surveys which examine the psychosocial health problems of communities. (p. 252)

The major tool of public health is epidemiology. Lilienfeld and Lilienfeld (1980) define and explain the role of epidemiology in public health:

> Epidemiology is concerned with the patterns of disease occurrence in human populations and of the factors that influence these patterns. The epidemiologist is primarily interested in the occurrence of disease by time, place, and persons. He tries to determine whether there has been an increase or decrease of the disease over the years; whether one geographical area has a higher frequency of the disease than another; and whether the characteristics of persons with a particular disease or condition distinguish them from those without it. (p. 3).

Thus the descriptive and analytical information provided by epidemiologic research enables the public health professional to determine and attack the causes of the disease or social problems at the community level. Epidemiology also indicates which groups in the community are at risk for certain diseases or problems, based either on sociodemographic characteristics or behavior. Such information is essential to primary prevention.

The prevention focus of public health social work is evident in the list of functions of the public health social worker, as listed in the *Standards for Social Work in Health Care Settings* published by the National Association of Social Workers (1981). The functions include the promotion of healthy behaviors, the assessment of the health needs of populations, and implementation of interventions designed to improve health. Interventions may focus on reducing social stress, increasing social supports, and improving access to health care and social services by the disadvantaged (Watkins, 1985).

Family-centered/Developmental Approach

Kumabe et al.'s (1977) discussion of the knowledge base of social work in community health settings emphasizes knowledge of the family life cycle as the fundamental component of that knowledge base. "As the source of the individual's primary relationships, the family provides the most important social context within which health is maintained, illness occurs and is resolved" (p. 25). Although the MCH setting is somewhat different from that of the community health agency because it concentrates less on illness and more on prevention, knowledge of the family is equally important for MCH practitioners. Indeed, a family orientation is a distinguishing feature of the social work profession.

The family's experiences during pregnancy and delivery, or during the illness and treatment of an infant, may have long-term consequences for the quality of parenting and family relationships (Klaus & Kennell, 1982). Moreover, it is possible to have a positive impact on the family's development during these times that may go well beyond the immediate situation. Klaus and Kennell's (1982) work has had some positive effects on medical procedures and policies (such as more humane visitation policies in NICUs, but it has not been developed into a comprehensive, operationalized model of service delivery.

The approach articulated by Klaus and Kennell (1982), however, has much in common with the family-centered focus of health care that has been emphasized recently (Ross, 1982a; Shelton, Jeppson, & Johnson, 1987). The greatest influence on the health of any individual, but particularly the health of a child, is the family and the circumstances in which the family lives (Kumabe et al., 1977). Indeed, despite great progress in medicine during the last century, medicine, when compared with social and environmental factors, has a relatively small influence on children's health (Select Panel for the Promotion of Child Health, 1979).

The greatest access to these important social and environmental factors in a child's life is in the family. The family is the location of the formation of health attitudes and beliefs as well as the formation of early health-related behaviors. The influences of the family are evident at many possible intervention points; for example, education of mothers on child care, nutrition, discipline, and other elements may have a tremendous impact on a child's health (George, 1979). The capabilities, attitudes, and resources of parents determine their utilization of health care services when services are available, and health-related personal behaviors are modeled and learned within the family.

Likewise, certain aspects of the situation of the family are directly related to access to health care services, such as clinic hours and employ-

ment conflicts, health insurance, transportation, and child care arrangements. Most health care is available only during those hours that many
parents must work, especially low-income parents who may have less job
flexibility than other families. Waiting times may be long, and transportation may be difficult for many families to find or arrange. An individual-
centered, isolated approach to health care that does not consider these
factors can have little impact on the health of either an individual child,
or on large groups such as minority or underprivileged children.

What does family-centered health care entail? Shelton et al. (1987)
emphasize that the first principle of family-centered care is "recognizing
that parents play a central role in their child's life" and "valuing their
judgment and respecting the unique contributions that they make." Because parents are the only ones who see their child in all settings, they
really are the "experts," and their observations and recommendations
must be taken seriously if the health care plan is to be "family centered"
(pp. 3–4).

Second, family-centered primary care means the assessment of the
social circumstances of the family that might affect the child's health
status—for example, low income, young maternal age, the quality of the
relationship between mother and father, and so forth (Shelton et al.,
1987). These factors might fall within the general category of "family
stress" or functioning. It may be useful for MCH social workers to use a
standardized measure of family functioning because such measures provide the advantage of an easily administered, objective indicator of problems that may be combined with clinical judgment to produce a more
sensitive indicator of the need for intervention. (Assessment tools are
discussed later in this book.)

Because of the importance of the home and community to children's
health, it has been emphasized that assessment of the family's needs may
be incomplete without the complete picture of the family's environment
that can come from a home visit only (Select Panel for the Promotion of
Child Health, 1981). In reviewing the available studies from other nations
where home visitors are an integral part of the health care system,
Roghmann (1985) found that substantial anecdotal, if not empirical, support exists for the usefulness of home visitors in preventing low
birthweight (through recruitment of women into prenatal care), SIDS,
accidents, and possibly other health problems in children. The extent to
which social workers are able to do home visits is unclear, but public
health nurses frequently perform such visits and appear to be effective in
this capacity (Combs-Orme, Reis, & Ward, 1985).

A third aspect of family-centered care concerns culture and race.
Culture and race are believed to influence health, in part through attitudes toward health care and use patterns (Bullough, 1972). Moreover,

different cultural groups use different problem-solving orientations, have different perceptions of appropriate help-seeking behavior, and set different priorities on self versus family needs (Okazaki, 1981).

For example, the special health care problems and needs of migrant and undocumented alien children must be understood by social workers in communities where these families reside (Young, Hall, & Collins, 1979). For instance, Hispanic extended families are active in problem solving when children have difficulties; the extended family may even include close friends who are instrumental in helping the family deal with adversity (Anderson, 1981). Social workers in areas serving large immigrant populations should be familiar with the relevant traditions and problems, if not the language, of those groups. No MCH social worker can provide sensitive, effective services without an understanding of the cultural and racial factors that are specific to the clientele being served.

Other aspects of a family focus as they relate to specific service areas are included in the remaining chapters of this book. The essential principle is that affirmed by social work's "person-in-situation" emphasis—that is, the client's need can only be understood when viewed in the perspective of the major systems in which the client lives (Hartman, 1981). For children, the major system that affects health and other aspects of functioning is the family.

Crisis Theory

Crisis theory may be particularly relevant to certain settings in MCH social work. Kumabe et al. (1977) note several assumptions made by crisis theory that are pertinent. First, crisis is not pathological. Second, crises are temporary and self-limiting. Third, crises proceed along a series of typical, identifiable stages. Fourth, the individual in crisis is amenable to help. Fifth, a small amount of help can enable the individual to cope well with the crisis. Finally, it is assumed that effectively dealing with a crisis can enable an individual to cope more effectively in future crises.

Normal pregnancy and birth are considered a family crisis because of the inherent psychological and emotional changes associated with childbirth and childrearing (Bibring & Valenstein, 1976; Kumabe et al., 1977). When all does not proceed normally, such as when an infant is born with a malformation or dies, or at premature delivery and admission to a NICU, the crisis is more acute (Kaplan & Mason, 1960). Social workers in these settings may use crisis intervention to promote the coping (in the short-term) and growth (in the long-term) of the family (e.g., Hancock, 1976; Stevens, 1979).

Crisis intervention entails a short-term approach with clients who are experiencing the normal emotional effects of a crisis. Those normal emotional effects include extreme tension and anxiety, possibly confusion and disorganization rendering the client unable to make decisions or act, and sometimes depression. Different emotions predominate at various times during the crisis. The crisis may be a single catastrophic event, such as the death of a child, or the cumulative results of several experiences, such as the extended effects on families dealing with disabled children.

In general, crisis intervention is aimed at both assisting the client in marshaling his or her usual coping resources to deal with the immediate situation, and using the crisis to learn and generalize to other aspects of life. A guiding principle of crisis theory is that a crisis situation is particularly conducive to facilitating learning and growth. Failure to resolve a crisis successfully is thought to place the individual at risk for other types of malfunctioning in the future.

In discussing the techniques of crisis intervention, Golan (1987) emphasizes both "psychosocial tasks," in dealing with emotional issues, and "material-arrangemental" tasks, such as provision of material resources and tangible services. Because they so often deal with crises around the life cycle (e.g., pregnancy, birth, and death), MCH social workers may find crisis theory to be an important part of their knowledge base even if they use some other model of intervention in their daily work.

Other Important Practice Roles

Advocacy

Whatever one's job or theoretical orientation to practice, it is impossible to ignore the importance of policy in practice. In MCH, federal policy determines what kinds of health care, related services, and income are available to low-income mothers and children. Serious budgetary restraints in the 1980s have led to curtailment of many important programs and services for families. Perhaps at no time since the 1930s, when the Social Security Act was enacted, has it been more crucial for social workers to advocate for the services that are needed by their clients (Mack, 1985).

Advocacy may entail both case advocacy (working to obtain rights and services for individual clients) and class advocacy (working to obtain those rights and services for groups of individuals) (Weinrich, 1987). Social workers are probably more accustomed to working for individual clients than they are to working for client groups, but current funding realities demonstrate that class advocacy will be increasingly important as essential programs face continued cuts.

Although advocacy has long been declared a "core activity" of social work, little is known about advocacy styles and strategies, and "almost nothing is known about what methods are most effective" (Sosin & Caulum, 1983, p. 12). Advocacy as defined as "an attempt, having a greater than zero probability of success, by an individual or group to influence another individual or group to make a decision that would not have been made otherwise and that concerns the welfare or interests of a third party who is in a less powerful status than the decision maker" (Sosin & Caulum, 1983, p. 13).

In an attempt to clarify how advocacy works in practice, Sosin and Caulum (1983) propose a typology that includes two elements: contexts of advocacy and methods of advocacy. The issue of context revolves around the degree of social influence the social worker has over the decision maker or the degree of agreement between the two. Thus the social worker and the decision maker may be allies (e.g., when the NICU social worker speaks on behalf of families to the nursery director), neutral (e.g., when the social worker functions as an expert witness before the hospital ethics committee), or adversarial (e.g., when the prenatal care clinic social worker speaks with a hostile landlord on behalf of a pregnant client who has been evicted).

Advocacy methods may be individual, administrative, or policy based (Sosin & Caulum, 1983). Individual methods are undertaken on behalf of a single client for one, concrete situation. The purpose of administratively based actions is a change in the application of regulations, such as a change in the process of setting fees for prenatal services. Finally, policy-based interventions seek to alter basic rules or laws on behalf of client groups. Judy Barber, of the Office of Maternal and Child Health in Mississippi, provides an excellent example of such policy-based advocacy. She meets monthly with an interdisciplinary group of MCH providers to discuss the clients seeking perinatal services and related policy implications. That group, and Barber in particular, has been instrumental in making important changes that have extended services to many indigent women and children.

The advocate may take general conceptual approaches ("strategies") that may be coercive, utilitarian (e.g., bargaining or negotiation), or normative (e.g., moral arguments). Strategies are determined in part by the context of advocacy; an alliance situation calls for normative strategies, neutrality calls for bargaining, and adversarial contexts call for coercive strategies.

Van Gheluwe and Barber (1986) demonstrated an effective advocacy effort on behalf of mothers and children in Mississippi, which was carried out by a coalition including the Mississippi chapter of the National Association of Social Workers. This group formed a task force whose purpose was to convince the state legislature of the necessity of enacting legislation to extend Medicaid coverage without regard to marital status to provide prenatal, delivery, and outpatient pediatric care to members of poor, intact families.

The strategies used in this case included gathering information and doing research; educating the public, professionals, and the legislature; soliciting support from organizations and the public at large; "networking," or cooperating and communicating among many varied groups and individuals; and monitoring the status and location of the bill in the legislature at all times. It should be noted that these advocates' familiarity with the entire legislative process included knowledge of where bills are introduced, how bills go to committee, who the chairs were in committees to which the bill was sent, and what individual legislators thought about the legislation. Despite some problems and necessary compromises in the bill, the advocates were successful, extending Medicaid coverage to at least 3,600 additional births and 18,000 additional children.

For social workers who want to learn more about being good advocates, Barber (1988) suggests methods ranging from the complex and sophisticated to the simple ones that require only dedication:

> In our group, we pool our talents, those who have experience in working with the media, those who will talk on the telephone or write letters, those with important personal relationships (perhaps developed during work on a political campaign), and those of us who are good at folding, collating, and stapling. Some of us can use our xerox machines without a counter and others can provide stamps or paper or important information. (p. 7)

Further discussion of advocacy and specific examples of effective advocacy by social workers, are included in each chapter. The ethical issues surrounding the responsibility to engage in advocacy are also discussed in Chapter 9.

Consultation

Often social workers act as conveyers of information that is within their expertise to other members of the MCH team. Such activities are called "consultation" and involve educating other team members (physicians, nurses, and others) about the psychosocial aspects of clients' lives (Fairley, 1979). Rice (1959) defined consultation as

> that process whereby the social worker, when requested, contributes his social work knowledge and skill to help others in meeting the problems presented. . . . The consultant's authority is the authority of knowledge or

skill. He has no administrative or technical responsibilities to the individual or group served. The individual or group has the right to choose to utilize or not the ideas growing out of the consultation. (p. 84)

Consultation was an early social work function that developed within the specialty of medical social work. It began as explaining to physicians the psychological and social effects of illness and hospitalization on patients (U.S. Department of Health, Education, and Welfare, 1953).

Consultation may take several forms. First, it may entail the provision of specific client-related information by social workers to other members of the MCH team. For example, the social worker often will have information on a client's social history, situation, or emotional state that is important to the plan of care. The provision of such information is essential if the client is to receive services that are appropriate to her circumstances.

Consultation may also involve the provision of more general information about the nature of social problems to other members of the MCH team (Rice, 1959). For example, social workers may inform medical and nursing personnel about the extent of homelessness in the community and its relationship to the health care needs of the client population, or about changes in Medicaid eligibility regulations. This type of consultation takes the form of education, much as physicians might educate other members of the team about the effects of high blood pressure on pregnancy outcomes.

Finally, program consultation, the most frequent form of consultation, is used by agencies to obtain expertise that is not found within the organization (White, 1981). Consultation is provided on a contractual basis, without obligation to implement the consultant's recommendations. For example, a prenatal care clinic might hire a consultant to suggest changes in scheduling to enhance use by their client population.

Program Planning and Administration

Social workers have been active in program planning in MCH since the enactment of Title V, which established federal policy requiring states to employ social workers in their Crippled Children and other MCH programs (Insley, 1980). Many states retain the policy of having social workers in planning positions in their state-level offices (Watkins, 1979).

Rice (1959) articulated the basis for social work involvement in program planning when she said:

> The more the social worker sees beyond the patient to the total group
> served and the more he evaluates the meaning of the experiences to the
> patient, the greater a contribution he can make to the formulation of policies
> and planning with others for the agency's program. (p. 86)

The Children's Bureau intended that the MCH programs created in the
1960s and 1970s and funded by Title V would include a planning element
by social workers (Insley, 1966). Today many state MCH agencies include
social work administrative positions that are written to include a planning
function (Watkins, 1980).

Moroney (1987) provides a brief overview of the steps in program
planning. Planning begins with a problem analysis or needs assessment—
that is, "who needs what where." This analysis also must consider the
political environment. The tools for such analysis come first from epidemiology, which identifies the population, the nature of the problem, and
the causes of the problem. More sophisticated tools based on mathemati-
cal and linear programming also may be used to project future needs.

Needs assessments follow and include attention to several types of
needs. First, Delgado (1981) defines normative needs as the "extent to
which a condition deviates from professionally accepted standards"
(p. 40). Normative needs may be determined, for example, by consulting
local obstetricians and public health nurses about the MCH problems
they observe in their patients.

Perceived needs are derived from surveys and public forums in
which consumers express their own ideas about what they need. One
might determine the perceived needs of pregnant women and mothers in
a neighborhood by asking them what services they would like but cannot
find or use. Delgado (1981) refers to these as "felt needs" and emphasizes
that felt needs do not have to result in expressed needs.

Expressed needs refer to the demand for services and are based on
the assumption that individuals do not demand services unless they need
them (Delgado, 1981). One may determine expressed needs by polling
medical and social agencies to determine which clients they are unable to
serve and what needs they see that they cannot fill. For example, a child
health clinic might indicate that its inability to provide services to clients
older than 15 years of age results in many adolescents not obtaining
primary medical care.

Relative needs consider not only the preceding factors but also such
issues as the available resources, the needs of other communities, and
equity concerns. For example, a community might determine where to
put scarce resources by weighing the relative need for a free pediatric
clinic against the need for a shelter for the homeless. Delgado's (1981)

reminder that all planning endeavors are based on values is relevant to considerations of relative needs.

Part of the needs assessment process is setting operationalized objectives that follow from the needs identified earlier (Levey-Mickens, 1987). Objectives should be reasonable and should be related directly to the proposed services. For example, the free pediatric clinic in the previous example might acknowledge that half of the children in the community are not immunized and might select as a first-year objective to improve the community's rate of immunization by 20%.

Decision making follows needs assessment in the planning process, focusing on how limited resources are allocated (Moroney, 1987). Although economic rationality has been touted as the sole basis for decision making, some situations require other bases (Moroney, 1987). In particular, issues such as social costs and benefits may not "fit" into models based on economic rationality. For example, it might be more "rational" for a community with limited resources to invest in drawing new industries to the community, rather than to provide immunizations to a few children when their risk of actually contracting the diseases is quite low.

Finally, Moroney (1987) emphasizes that all planning activities must include an evaluation component. Evaluation is a highly political process, as poor outcomes can threaten jobs and reputations. Moreover, pressure often exists to evaluate quickly, before it is reasonable to expect observable effects. Nonetheless, evaluation remains important, and new technologies are becoming increasingly available to make it a viable component of planning. Evaluation should be a key component of planning from the beginning, not added as an afterthought when it is too late to collect important data, and should address directly the specific objectives of the program (Levey-Mickens, 1987).

Despite agreement that program planning is an appropriate function for MCH social workers (Moroney, 1987; Watkins, 1980), limited evidence exists that many social workers engage in this activity in a significant way. Watkins (1979) reasoned that to be effective in planning regional perinatal systems, social workers would have to be involved in three aspects: planning the overall network of services, developing social work programs within that network, and developing supportive services to be provided by other agencies. She surveyed perinatal social workers in eight states and found little such planning activity (Watkins, 1980).

The consequences of lack of social work involvement in program planning can be serious. For example, Watkins (1979) noted that the weakness of the social work component of the Improved Pregnancy Outcome programs was due to the absence of social workers on the planning teams of each state when the overall programs were planned. Non-social work administrators of the programs were unaware of the importance of social work services to the projects.

Conversely, planning by social workers can result in enhanced program effectiveness. Benford and Stokes (1988) demonstrated how use of the Maternal and Child Health Information Network has enabled social workers in the Ohio Department of Health to maintain a computerized data base that contributes to the planning of social work services for mothers and children in that state. Funded by a Special Project of Regional and National Significance grant, this project involved computerizing data from multiple MCH programs including birth certificates, matched birth and death records, family planning data, and data from numerous other categorical programs. Matching of the data permits longitudinal follow-up and planning based on comprehensive data.

Research

Contributing to the body of knowledge through research is acknowledged as a professional and ethical responsibility of social workers (e.g., National Association of Social Workers, 1980). Each area of social work practice can point to many unanswered questions about client needs, the most effective methods of delivering services, and other areas. MCH is certainly no exception, as all the indicators show that a great deal remains to be done to protect the health of mothers and children. More information is needed about the needs of client groups and the outcomes of social work services as well as basic information for purposes of program planning, legislative lobbying, budget justification, staffing patterns, and so forth (Insley, 1981a). Despite Rice's (1959) comment that "It is now trite to say that social work has a responsibility to study its own practice" (p. 87), Watkins (1981) noted that social workers are still relying on "practice wisdom" in MCH limiting the profession's knowledge to biased and narrow observations.

The responsibility to conduct research may be met by MCH social workers in many ways. Because of their daily "front line" experiences with human and social problems, some social workers may engage in the kind of basic epidemiologic research that is reminiscent of the early work of the Children's Bureau. Results of this type of research tell us what the problems are, who has those problems, and some of the causes of those problems (Watkins, 1981). Without such information, services cannot reach those in need. For example, Young, Berkman, and Rehr (1973) described women who sought abortions at a time when the Supreme Court's *Roe v. Wade* decision was expected to increase the demand for

abortion services. Such information was vital as service providers prepared to meet the need.

Research on health policy and the organization of health services is
of particular concern to MCH social workers (Watkins, 1981). Policy
changes such as those that change eligibility standards for public assistance or Medicaid can have profound effects on MCH clients, as can
changes in administrative policy. Documentation of those effects through
research constitutes an important part of advocacy. For example, Balassone (1987) described major problems in access to Medicaid based on her
analysis of policies in 18 western states.

Other social workers may conduct intervention or evaluation research designed to assess the effectiveness of particular methods of service delivery (Watkins, 1981). Evaluation studies are particularly difficult
to do, because they are expensive if done well, and the methodological
pitfalls are many. Yet without evaluation research it is impossible to
conclude that services are effective or even to be sure that services are
not harmful in some unexpected ways. Moreover, evaluation research that
documents the process of program design and implementation is necessary if successful programs and methods are to be replicated in other
areas and with other clients, and if practitioners are to understand which
components of service yield the most productive results (Weiss, 1988).
The program of research by Schinke and colleagues (e.g., Schinke, 1978),
which is discussed in Chapter 7, has demonstrated the utility of a skills
training approach in preventing adolescent pregnancy.

The single-subject design has been advocated as an appropriate research design for social workers in MCH (Appel, 1981; Coulton, 1979).
Single-subject designs enable practitioners to test their own practice by
monitoring the status of a client's problems at different stages of implementation of the intervention. The designs are simple to implement and
are particularly useful for identifying the necessity for change in the
intervention when it appears to be unsuccessful. Extensive knowledge of
statistics and experimental design is not required for the use of single-
subject designs.

Other social workers may contribute to knowledge through case
studies or the synthesis of available literature. Chilman's (1979) summary
of the extensive research on adolescent pregnancy provided a good overview of the voluminous amount of work on that subject. Shapiro's (1980)
case study on abortion provided a valuable illustration of the difficulties
for clients who experience unplanned pregnancy. These two types of
research provide vastly different perspectives on a problem. Each type
of research contributes immensely to the professional knowledge base of
social work.

EPIDEMIOLOGY OF MCH

Some Important Terms

A thorough discussion of MCH requires a definition of the major terms used in the field. *Infant mortality rates* refer to the number of deaths in the first 365 days of life per 1,000 live births. Infant mortality rates are frequently used as social indicators of the quality of life of a society and are usually shown as 10.5 per 1,000 or just 10.5. The inclusive term *infant mortality* includes neonatal mortality (deaths in the first 27 days of life) and postneonatal mortality (deaths on days 28 to 365), which are thought to have different etiologies.

A *spontaneous abortion* (or miscarriage) is defined as the nondeliberate interruption of a pregnancy before 20 weeks after the last menstrual period. *Fetal deaths* are those that occur in utero after 20 weeks of gestation with no signs of life at delivery. Some states use a birthweight of 500 or 1,000 g, rather than weeks of gestation, to distinguish a fetal death from an abortion.

Several factors make some of these definitions problematic. Uncertainty about the length of gestation (which is not uncommon, especially among those at risk for low birthweight) could result in differing definitions of an event and could affect these mortality rates. Second, some hospitals and health professions may be more conservative in perceiving signs of life than others, and this is complicated by the development of technologies that can save smaller and smaller infants. Physicians may be more likely to define a birth as a live one if they think heroic measures might save the infant.

The term *perinatal mortality* refers to the period just before and after birth and varies somewhat. It usually encompasses infant deaths from 20 (or sometimes 28) weeks of gestation through the first 7 days of life. The perinatal death rate is computed by dividing the number of fetal deaths at and above the designated gestation plus the number of deaths in the first week of life, by the number of fetal deaths plus the total number of live births. The term is generally of interest in discussions of obstetric interventions and their effects on mortality, because many of the same factors are related to death just before and after birth.

Other important terms that are often used concern birthweight. *LBW* refers to infants born weighing less than 2,500 g (about 5.5 lb), whereas *normal birthweight* usually means infants weighing 2,500 g or more. *Very low birthweight* (VLBW) refers to birthweight of less than 1,500 g. The average U.S. birthweight is about 3,400 g (Valadian, 1982). Approximately 6.8% of all U.S. births (12.4% of black births) are LBW

(Miller, 1985). LBW is increasingly being used as the hallmark measure of the health status of infants rather than infant mortality, because as mortality becomes increasingly more rare it becomes less and less sensitive to the major economic, social, and medical factors that influence infant health (Kotelchuck, 1984).

Premature birth is usually the cause of LBW and refers to delivery after less than 37 weeks of gestation (World Health Organization, 1975). (Normal gestational length is from 38 to 40 weeks.) Because knowledge of the length of gestation is based on the timing of the last menstrual period (LMP), information that many women cannot provide precisely, LBW (which is discussed later) is usually used as an indicator of prematurity. The difficulty of obtaining accurate data on length of gestation is especially pertinent regarding research based on birth certificate data, because missing data on LMP occurs disproportionately among the same groups who are at high risk of LBW: unmarried women, young mothers, and those of low income (David, 1980). This bias has made it difficult to determine the proportion of LBW that is due to prematurity versus the proportion resulting from intrauterine growth retardation (IUGR), which may be due to inadequate weight gain or medical problems in the mother or to certain kinds of fetal malformations. The appropriate methods of prevention and intervention vary considerably when LBW is due to prematurity as opposed to IUGR, although some babies suffer from both problems.

Maternal mortality is a complex term, meaning death in the period following delivery (within 42 days) from several directly related conditions that are specified in the International Classification of Diseases (World Health Organization, 1975). Maternal mortality in the United States is rare, even allowing for probable measurement error, and probably ranged from 9.6 to 12.1 per 100,000 births in 1978 (Smith, Hughes, Pekow, & Rochat, 1984). Maternal mortality remains a concern, however, in part because black women suffer 3 to 4 times the rate of maternal mortality as white women (Children's Defense Fund, 1988). Moreover, between 1983 and 1985 black and nonwhite maternal mortality rose by 11% and 10%, respectively, whereas white maternal mortality declined by 12% (Children's Defense Fund, 1988).

Risk Factors for Poor Maternal and Child Health

Another component of the effective MCH social worker is knowledge specific to MCH (Kumabe et al., 1977): risk factors for poor MCH and mortality, the etiology of common medical problems and diseases in his or her specialty area, a basic understanding of the treatments and technologies used to remediate those conditions, the economics of the health care system, genetics, and child development issues. A brief discussion of the epidemiology of MCH follows, with the other components listed earlier discussed in detail in later chapters specific to the various MCH settings.

Research has identified several risk factors for infant mortality and morbidity, maternal mortality, and other indicators of poor MCH. Most of these factors occur in constellations, sometimes making it difficult to pinpoint those factors that exercise independent effects.

Low Birthweight

LBW is the most powerful predictor of infant mortality; two thirds of all neonatal mortality occurs among LBW infants (Harris, Keeler, & Michnich, 1977). In fact, LBW is the mediating factor by which many of the other risk factors operate to increase the risk of mortality and morbidity for infants. LBW infants remain at risk of mortality through the first year of life, and may be at risk for numerous childhood problems including rehospitalization (Combs-Orme, Fishbein, & Summerville, 1987; Hack, DeMonterice, Merkatz, Jones & Fanaroff, 1981), diminished cognitive and language abilities (Crnic, Ragozin, Greenberg, Robinson, & Basham, 1983), and developmental delays (Ross, Lipper, & Auld, 1985).

Three conditions may operate to cause an infant to be born below optimum weight: premature birth (defined earlier), IUGR, or a combination of the two. IUGR may be due to several factors including small maternal size, poor maternal weight gain, chronic diseases, anemia, smoking, drug or alcohol use during pregnancy, abnormalities of the placenta or cord, multiple fetuses, fetal infection or abnormality, or prolonged pregnancy (Pritchard, MacDonald, & Gant, 1985). Although the causes of premature labor are not known in most cases, some that are known include spontaneous rupture of membranes, cervical incompetence, uterine or fetal abnormalities, problems with the placenta, and fetal death. In recent years, drug therapy has improved in its success at delaying delivery for some women in premature labor, although some risks are associated with those drugs (King, 1987).

Much remains to be learned about the causes of both IUGR and prematurity, but it is likely that more LBW is due to IUGR than previously has been thought (Kaltreider & Kohl, 1980). Low income has a significant effect on maternal nutrition and other chronic risk conditions among poor women (Rudolph & Borker, 1987), both of which are highly correlated with prematurity and IUGR as well.

Poverty

The tremendous risk that poverty poses to mothers and children has been well known since the Children's Bureau carried out its innovative cohort infant mortality studies early in this century (Lathrop, 1919). These studies, which were methodologically sophisticated for that time, established for the first time the serious risks to infants posed by poverty, ignorance, overcrowding, and maternal employment (Lathrop, 1919).

Although poverty is difficult to measure with absolute scientific precision, it is clear to most experts that it is the single largest risk factor for poor health in mothers and children (Miller, 1985). Research indicates over time and with many samples that poor women and children are less healthy on several measures and have higher mortality throughout life (e.g., Nersesian, Petit, Shaper, Lemieux, & Naor, 1985). The Children's Defense Fund (1987) estimates that 10,000 American children die each year from the effects of poverty.

Despite being less healthy, poor women are less likely to get good, early prenatal care (Institute of Medicine, 1985), and poor children are less likely to receive well-child and preventive care throughout childhood (Hoekelman, 1987). Although their reduced access to health care is certainly influential in the disadvantaged health status of the poor, medical care by itself is probably a minor factor in good health (Davis, Gold, & Makuc, 1981).

Inadequate income exerts many more subtle and difficult-to-measure influences on pregnancy and childhood: poor and unsafe housing, inadequate heat and light, chronic poor nutrition and health habits (such as dental and exercise behavior), and lack of hope for the future (most difficult to measure). Poverty is highly correlated with most of the following risk factors: The poor are more likely to be black and undereducated, to bear children outside marriage and the optimum childbearing age range, and possibly to have certain medical risks. It is also likely that the effects of poverty during several generations are cumulative.

Race

Black and other minority infants are nearly twice as likely to be born at less than optimal weight and to die in the first year of life (Miller, 1986). Despite improvements in both black and white mortality rates during many years, this ratio has held, and even increased somewhat, with passing time (Wegman, 1987). Comparisons with other nonwhite races (such as Hispanics and Asian Americans) are problematic because of relatively small numbers and inaccurate racial designations on Vital Statistics data, but in general it appears that other nonwhite races also have an increased risk of infant mortality. Black children also have more chronic and acute illnesses, and higher mortality in the early years of life than white children. Finally, as discussed earlier, black mothers continue to face a much higher risk of dying in childbirth and of childbirth-related causes than white mothers (Pratt, 1982).

Race is a proxy variable for income, education, and other indicators of socioeconomic status (SES). It is not clear whether after controlling for SES, race still exerts an independent effect on infant and maternal mortality. If so, such an effect would suggest a genetic effect of race. An independent effect for race is suggested by one anomaly: Among very tiny infants, blacks are more likely to survive than whites (Miller, 1985). If a genetic effect exists, though, it is small compared with the effects associated with poverty and disadvantage.

A final point about race is important to the reader of epidemiologic literature. It is standard practice in research on infant mortality to "standardize" for race—that is, to compare white rates with white rates and black rates with black rates. Although this practice is justified from the standpoint of making comparisons easier to understand (because the rates are so different, various racial distributions among different populations can obscure comparisons), it may suggest an acceptance of unalterable genetic differences that is not justified given available knowledge (Miller, 1985). The consistent ratio of black to white infant deaths during the last century of 2:1 must be unacceptable, and standardized rates should not lead to complacency about this shameful disparity.

Maternal Age

Young mothers (younger than 17 years of age) are at increased risk of infant mortality (Bakketeig, Hoffman, & Oakley, 1984), probably through increased risk of LBW. It is generally agreed now that most of the excess risk to adolescents (except perhaps to those younger than 15 years of age or so) can be mediated with good prenatal care. Good prenatal care would be expected to deal with the adolescent's poor eating habits and the consumption of harmful drugs (such as tobacco and alcohol) as well as to monitor her condition so that problems such as high blood pressure can be alleviated. Unfortunately, adolescents are less likely to get good prenatal care; therefore, as a group, they have less favorable pregnancy outcomes.

Although the increased risk is not as great as is sometimes assumed, mothers older than 35 years of age also have increased risk of infertility, miscarriage, premature labor, birth defects, and various complications of pregnancy (Daniels & Weingarten, 1979). It is important to recognize, however, that although the risks of these conditions increase with age, risks generally do remain low even into the 40s, with the possible exception of infertility.

Some older mothers face particular problems of concern to social workers that contribute to poor pregnancy outcomes. These include older women with many other children and those with social problems such as low income. In addition, the older woman who is pregnant with her first child is considered to be at higher medical risk.

Education

It is not clear how low levels of maternal education act independently to increase the risk of poor pregnancy outcomes and risk to infants and children, but the correlation between low levels of education and poor MCH has been replicated many times. Low education is correlated with being young, black, poor, and unmarried. In addition, however, lack of education may indicate inadequate knowledge regarding self-care, nutrition, infant care and parenting, and the proper use of health care facilities.

Marital Status

Marital status is much like education in that it is highly correlated with the other social factors that interact to increase the risk of infant mortality and morbidity. Unmarried women who give birth are more likely to be poor, uneducated, and black. They are also more likely to begin their prenatal care later in pregnancy and to have fewer prenatal visits during the course of pregnancy, perhaps because many are attempting to hide their condition (Kumabe et al., 1977).

In addition to this intercorrelation with other risk factors, however, being unmarried may act to increase the risk of poor health by increasing the stress of pregnancy and parenthood (Institute of Medicine, 1985). Being unmarried and pregnant may mean having less emotional support, having less help with daily and extraordinary tasks, and being more worried and anxious about finances and other matters related to being pregnant. For an infant or child, being born outside of marriage usually means less attention, stimulation, and supervision (one parent instead of two), less income and all the advantages that come with income, and other disadvantages.

Preventive Care

Research has demonstrated repeatedly a correlation between prenatal care and pregnancy outcome: Those who have fewer prenatal visits and who enter care later in pregnancy have less desirable outcomes on every dimension (Institute of Medicine, 1985). Other types of preventive care also are associated with favorable health status: "well-baby" care, preventive care for young children, immunizations, and family planning to name but a few. Continuity of care is a positive factor—that is, regular continuing care by a primary physician as opposed to episodic care at various facilities such as Emergency Rooms (Hoekelman, 1987).

Despite the well-known advantages of preventive care, the poor consistently use such care less frequently than those with more advantages. A major reason for this lack of use is inaccessibility. Poor communities tend to have fewer health care facilities (especially of the continuing care type) and fewer practitioners (Institute of Medicine, 1985). Rural communities in particular suffer from an inadequate number of health care providers (Schlesinger, 1985). Access is more difficult for the poor also because of limited hours and less flexibility associated with lower status jobs, poor public transportation, and lack of child care. Moreover, the high cost of health care may deter the poor from seeking care for anything but an acute problem.

Numerous studies have shown that when they do use the health care system, the poor are more likely for all of the preceding reasons to receive care from emergency departments and clinic facilities, generally considered of lower quality because of lack of continuity (Bazzoli, 1986). These acute care settings are not likely to emphasize the principles of preventive health care.

Attitudes also inhibit the use of preventive care by the poor (Institute of Medicine, 1985). For example, many women do not recognize the need for preventive care during pregnancy in the absence of apparent problems, especially if they have delivered safely before. Poor women may not trust medical personnel, especially if they have had unpleasant experiences before. In other cases, women whose life-styles are not conducive to healthy pregnancy (smokers, drug users, etc.) may not seek prenatal care because they realize that they will be urged to change their behavior. Numerous other attitudes and beliefs may impede poor and minority women from seeking preventive prenatal care.

Behavioral Factors

In recent years greater emphasis has been placed on the preventive aspects of health care. For example, the content of prenatal and well-baby care includes encouragement for parents to avoid drugs and alcohol, education about "safety proofing" homes for babies and toddlers, recognition of symptoms and appropriate response to illness, use of infant car seats, and other behaviors that may contribute to health. Attention to these factors is in recognition of the fact that as medical science has eliminated many of the health hazards of the past (such as contagious diseases), injuries and other preventable phenomena have become larger contributors to mortality and morbidity among children.

Evidence of increasing interest in prevention may be seen in the publication in 1979 of *Healthy People: The Surgeon General's Report on Health Promotion and Disease Prevention.* In this document, a number of goals for improvement of the health of the American people were set, to be achieved by 1990. In the area of maternal and child health, goals include the reduction of overall infant mortality to fewer than nine deaths per 1,000 live births. Subgoals under this objective include reducing LBW and birth defects. National prevention objectives also relate to reducing birth injuries, SIDS, childhood accidents, inadequate nutrition, and parental inadequacy. Achievement of these goals will be dependent not only on progress in medicine and social problems but also on behavioral changes.

A major target for behavior change is smoking, which is known to be harmful to the fetus during pregnancy (Institute of Medicine, 1985) and associated with several childhood illnesses as well (Dutton, 1985). Black and lower income women are more likely to smoke during pregnancy (Royer & Barth, 1984), and this difference may contribute to excess rates of LBW and prematurity among blacks.

Knowledge of epidemiology provides guidance to MCH professionals about "at-risk" groups to whom they may aim services, and also provides the ability to gauge the progress being made in improving MCH. It is important to remember, however, that such knowledge must be used not only to target individuals, groups, and neighborhoods for programs and services, but to target policies at the federal, state, and local levels for change. Epidemiology provides clues when policies prohibit or discourage preventive health care by the poor, make family planning inaccessible to sexually active teenagers, or erect barriers to quality primary health care for young children in the inner city. Solutions to all these problems appropriately lie at all levels.

2 Prenatal Care Services

Insofar . . . as poverty, slum housing, poor diet, poor education, multiple births spaced too closely, and out-of-wedlock pregnancy constitute social risk and affect the outcome of pregnancy, social work must share responsibility with the health professions in working toward prevention and control. Insofar as imperfect caretaking agents in the community affect the quality of care received by pregnant women, maternal and infant care is a legitimate and pressing social work concern. (Haselkorn, 1966, p. 9)

Prenatal care is considered to be an effective method of ensuring healthy birth, despite the fact that no universal consensus exists on its appropriate content nor on the mechanism by which prenatal care improves pregnancy outcomes. For the healthy woman, the American College of Obstetricians and Gynecologists (ACOG) and the American Academy of Pediatrics (AAP) (1983) recommend that prenatal care should begin in the first trimester, and that the woman visit an obstetrician or other provider once every 4 weeks until the 28th week of gestation, then once every 2 to 3 weeks until the 36th week, and once weekly thereafter. ACOG also recommends certain specific medical services to be provided including blood pressure and proteinuria testing, weight at each visit, and hemoglobin testing. From a medical perspective the most useful aspect of prenatal care may be simply to monitor for identification of certain potentially risky conditions so that they can be controlled until delivery (e.g., high blood pressure, diabetes, inadequate weight gain, or anemia) or so that labor can be stimulated early (when possible) to avoid fetal death (e.g., toxemia or maternal infection).

It is generally accepted, however, that some of the most important facets of prenatal care are not medical in nature (Barnard & Sumner, 1981). The ACOG and AAP guidelines (1983) state:

24

Socioeconomic factors are significant determinants of pregnancy outcome, and social workers should be members of perinatal teams. Perinatal services with a great many high-risk patients require full-time social workers with special skills in perinatal problem-solving. (p. 11)

In the clinic or hospital setting, prenatal care is most often provided using a team approach, including physicians, nurses (often public health nurses), social workers, nutritionists, dentists, and perhaps others (Watkins & Player, 1981). The setting where care is provided by a single private practitioner is probably less likely to provide social work services (Kaufman & Watkins, 1981). Social work services are a mandated part of care in several federal programs including the Maternal and Child Health Block Grant programs that grew out of the Maternity and Infant Care programs (Schmidt, 1982).

SOCIAL WORK FUNCTIONS

Social workers have been involved in prenatal care for many years. Early in her work with immigrants in Chicago, Grace Abbott decried the fact that poor women often had no prenatal and delivery services during childbirth except unsanitary and untrained midwives (Abbott, 1915). Under the leadership of great social workers such as Abbott and Julia Lathrop, the Children's Bureau not only advocated for services but also published numerous widely read materials that provided needed child care information for many Americans—for example, "Infant Care" (West, 1914) and "Prenatal Care" (West, 1915).

The social work role in prenatal care has been recognized at least since the 1940s, when during World War II the Emergency Maternity and Infancy Care (EMIC) program was created to provide free medical and auxiliary services to millions of military wives and children in the lower pay grades (Sinai & Anderson, 1948). Social work services were a mandated part of the EMIC program (Insley, 1971) which included prenatal care, delivery services, and pediatric medical care.

For the sake of simplicity, social work tasks in the provision of prenatal care services may be divided into assessment, service procurement and referral, coordination and consultation, supportive counseling, outreach services, educational tasks, and advocacy functions. The effort to compartmentalize and operationalize social workers' practice is a crucial one in efforts to improve the quality of practice, because effective education and evaluation depend on a thorough understanding of the particular elements of practice. In actuality it may be difficult to categorize what the worker is doing at any one time, because of the fact that the various aspects of practice are interrelated, and that practice seldom follows an orderly progression from beginning to end (Kumabe et al., 1977). Nonetheless, for the sake of simplicity, the following discussion will attempt to operationalize as specifically as possible the tasks of social workers in obstetric settings.

Assessment

Assessment is the most basic function of social work practice in any setting and yet often may be the most poorly accomplished. If social work services are to be valued as an essential part of prenatal care, the profession must develop innovative assessment methods that are specific to its professional role and that relate directly to the interventions to be provided. Without accurate assessment, both effective intervention and evaluation are impossible.

High-risk screening in the broad sense is an evolving technology in obstetrics that attempts to identify those women at high risk for a poor pregnancy outcome to concentrate scarce resources where they may have the most productive outcomes (Wallace, 1982). Indeed, assessment of high risk is the foundation of sophisticated regionalized perinatal care, because it is only through highly accurate assessment that women can be provided with appropriate levels of prenatal care (Rudolph & Borker, 1987).

While the physician monitors the pregnant woman for indications of developing medical problems, the social worker assesses the social and psychological condition of the pregnant woman. In both cases the risk factors for neonatal mortality (as opposed to postneonatal mortality) are emphasized during pregnancy; however, many of the same factors increase the risk of postneonatal mortality or other problems (especially with the social variables), such as poor parenting or child abuse and neglect.

Social work assessment "goes beyond the identification of a problem or illness and includes an appraisal of the inter-relation among biological, psychological, and sociocultural factors and an identification of positive motivations and capacities" (Northern, 1987, p. 172), however. Assessment is an ongoing process in prenatal care, with each profession bringing a unique perspective that is valuable (Cowin, 1968). For the obstetric social worker, assessment centers around identification of those social factors known to be associated with elevated risk of poor pregnancy outcome (an epidemiologic approach as advocated by Northern [1987] and others), so that high-risk women may receive more intensive services and additional auxiliary services when necessary, including referral to a regionalized perinatal center. Early identification of most problems is crucial if interventions are to be effective in preventing or reducing the impact of poor outcomes (Siefert, 1983). Early identification of pregnancy problems also is likely to prove more cost-effective (Bergman & Weissman, 1983).

Although social workers will be most interested in social risk factors, the tendency of risk factors to cluster means that they should understand the implications of certain medical risk factors for poor pregnancy outcomes. Important risk factors include high parity (especially in very young or older mothers), previous pregnancy problems or losses, certain maternal diseases (including diabetes, renal disease, blood Rh incompatibility, urinary infections, eclampsia and preeclampsia, and hypertension), and an interpregnancy interval of less than 1 year (Bakketeig et al., 1984).

Different methods are used to determine which patients are seen and assessed by the social worker. In some settings (especially public health clinics and other settings serving primarily low-income patients) all patients may be routinely seen by social workers—for example, in the Indian Health Service Maternal and Child Health program in Oklahoma. Hunt (1985) reports that up to 70% of the population of American Indian women in that program are considered at risk, however, and that MCH staff is inadequate to see everyone who is considered to be in need of services.

In other settings, clients see social workers only on a referral basis by medical personnel (Watkins & Player, 1981) or according to certain high-risk criteria (Collins, 1974). Referral of especially serious cases may be necessary in settings where the entire population is considered to be at risk for poor pregnancy outcome and staffing does not permit social work contact for all patients. Conversely, Rehr, Berkman, and Rosenberg (1980) caution against screening procedures that rely on referral by non–social workers, because these professionals may not be qualified to recognize the factors that call for social work intervention. They urge a "case finding" approach that includes screening of all potential clients by social workers.

Ruff (1985) described another approach to the role of social workers used in a demonstration program in South Carolina, in which social workers completed psychosocial assessments and plans of care on pregnant high-risk clients including, for example, teenagers and recipients of the Special Supplemental Nutrition Program for Women, Infants, and Children (WIC). The protocol for whom the social workers saw depended on specific program objectives. For example, in an effort to lengthen the short interconceptional periods of WIC recipients, social workers assessed and reviewed the contraceptive plans of some WIC recipients in prenatal care.

Fairley (1979) asserted that the most effective method of deciding whom social workers will see is self-referral, and that a high correlation exists between self-referral and effective work with the client. She suggested publicity (posters, pamphlets, and so forth) within the clinic, and information provided by nurses and other personnel about the social services offered, with the goal of encouraging clients to seek out social workers themselves.

In any case, during the assessment process the social worker is especially interested in several risk factors for LBW and other poor outcomes of pregnancy. These include poverty, poor nutrition, maternal age outside usual childbearing years, single marital status, isolation or lack of social support, inadequate transportation, inadequate knowledge, and negative feelings about the pregnancy. Each of these risk factors is discussed subsequently.

Poverty

It is clear that poverty is correlated with infant mortality (Miller, 1985). Poverty usually means poor nutrition and housing, inadequate access and reduced use of medical care, less desirable health care resources, and numerous other disadvantages. In some settings, all patients may be presumed to live on low incomes to one degree or another, and special circumstances may be required to determine those in the most need. For example, in some low-income neighborhoods, *not* receiving public assistance is considered an indicator of risk, because virtually the entire patient population is made up of unemployed single mothers. Other such special cases might occur in settings with large patient populations who are in need but who are ineligible for public assistance, such as illegal migrant workers and military families. In any case, the social worker examines the following areas with special care.

What is the patient's income level and source of income? If the mother is single and employed, has she made arrangements for taking time off after delivery, and how will she support herself? When the mother receives financial assistance (usually Aid to Families with Dependent Children), it is important to assess whether she understands the procedure for enrolling the new baby so that she will receive additional benefits for the baby's needs as soon as possible after delivery. If she does not receive financial assistance it is important to inform her of available assistance and to determine whether she should apply for benefits. In addition, many persons may not understand that a considerable lag occurs between applying for and receiving benefits, and the social worker should explore these issues with the client.

It is also necessary for the social worker to determine whether the mother currently has significant unmet needs, and whether other sources of assistance (such as family members or the baby's father) are available. A single mother's understanding of her legal right to child support from the father and the procedure for obtaining that assistance if the father does not volunteer to help might also be explored.

The low-income mother may also be unable to prepare adequately for the day she brings the baby home from the hospital. Some agencies routinely send out social workers or public health nurses to assess whether the mother is ready to receive the infant (e.g., Combs-Orme et al., 1985). In Mississippi, Medicaid provides reimbursement for social work services with maternity patients including psychosocial assessments, counseling, and home visits, according to Judy Barber of the Office of Maternal and Child Health in Mississippi. In settings where a home visit is not possible, social workers should determine whether the mother will have adequate and appropriate furniture and bedding for the baby; whether she has seasonally appropriate infant clothing; and whether she has bottles, formula, and sterilization equipment ready if she does not plan to breastfeed. If the mother is not prepared, the social worker should determine how and when she plans to obtain the needed items. These important questions are rarely asked by physicians.

Poor Nutrition

Poor nutrition goes hand in hand with low income, although a high income does not guarantee a good diet. Although research has not been conclusive, consensus is that the pregnant mother's nutritional status before conception and during pregnancy has a significant impact on the weight, length of gestation, and health status of the baby at birth (Jacobson, 1982). When the mother is young or has other problems, nutrition may be even more important (Cowell, 1985).

In many obstetric settings, a professional nutritionist or dietitian has the responsibility to advise and educate patients regarding their special dietary needs during pregnancy (Johnson, 1974). In such settings, the social worker's task may be primarily to help identify those at high risk for nutritional problems for referral to the dietitian. Dwyer (1974) notes that in many settings it is not possible (albeit desirable) to target all low-income women as automatically "at risk" nutritionally because virtually everyone would meet such a criterion. She points to several groups at very high risk for poor nutrition whom the social worker may identify for referral to the nutritionist. These include addicts (including those ad-

dicted to both drugs and alcohol), those with language barriers to following recommended dietary advice, those with unusual eating habits (such
as vegetarians or women with pica), mothers whose other children show
poor growth, and mothers with evidence of stress or emotional distur-
bance. Others might include retarded or illiterate women, illegal aliens,
heavy smokers, and those who lack food preparation facilities (such as
homeless or transient women). Teenagers also tend to have poor dietary
habits that place them at nutritional risk (Cowell, 1985).

In some cases, no staff nutritionist may exist. In such cases the social
worker should possess adequate knowledge of dietary needs during pregnancy to assist the pregnant woman in assessing her needs and making
outside referrals in extreme cases, and in helping her to plan well-
rounded menus in others. Workers might consult with medical personnel
to do this, using laboratory data such as hemoglobin analyses. The social
worker also may make general recommendations for shopping and planning on a limited budget (U.S. Department of Health, Education and
Welfare, 1975). In other cases the social worker may discuss vitamin use
with the patient. Often a physician recommends or prescribes vitamins to
a patient, but because the patient does not understand her special nutritional needs during pregnancy, she may not take the vitamins. In other
cases, a woman may not discuss with the physician her inability to buy
the prescribed vitamins.

Dwyer (1974) notes that the social worker can be especially helpful
in making appropriate referrals to the team nutritionist when barriers to
good nutrition include lack of knowledge about planning and preparation.
Because they may talk at length with clients, social workers may be the
most likely of anyone on the prenatal care team to recognize intellectual
or educational deficiencies that may affect a woman's ability to plan and
shop (especially on a limited budget), and to prepare food properly.

The nutritional assessment also should include information about
whether the client receives Food Stamps or WIC coupons. Regulations
regarding eligibility and benefits vary in each state, so the social worker
should be familiar with her state's programs.

Maternal Age

The ideal age for childbearing, in terms of positive outcomes, is between
20 and 24 years of age. Generally, for purposes of identifying women at
risk, those younger than 19 and older than 35 years of age are considered
at risk (Bakketeig et al., 1984), although interaction effects of maternal
age with parity and social class occur (Royer & Barth, 1984).

Teenagers who become pregnant also tend to be unmarried and less
educated, and come from homes with lower incomes than older pregnant

women. In addition they are more likely to receive inadequate prenatal care and begin that care later in pregnancy. Teenagers are also at elevated risk of poor nutrition and often feel less positive about pregnancy than older women. All of these factors are probably significant in their elevated risk of a poor pregnancy outcome. Physiological factors may play a part in the excess risk associated with pregnancies among young teenagers (those younger than 15 years of age).

Single Mothers

Although research has shown increased mortality among babies born to unmarried mothers, owing again to correlations among risk factors, it is not clear how marital status acts independently to increase the risk, if indeed it does. Not only is neonatal mortality higher among this group, but a greater risk for postneonatal mortality from SIDS, accidents, and child abuse exists. This fact suggests that having only one parent available often increases an infant's risk of inadequate supervision and parenting, decreases the support available to both mother and infant, and may place excess stress on the mother that increases the risk of abuse or poor parenting.

In addition to determining the marital status of the mother, however, the social worker should evaluate the relationship with the baby's father. In some cases the father may live with or near the mother and may provide both financial and emotional support (Fairley, 1979). In other cases he may be an additional source of stress. In others he may be totally absent. It would seem that it is not just marital status that is important, but the amount of support available to the mother and baby.

Stress and Lack of Social Support

Pregnancy is logically an inherently stressful time, owing both to the physical demands of pregnancy and the impending responsibilities of parenthood. Stressful life events have been found to have negative effects on pregnancy (Institute of Medicine, 1985), and the social worker should attempt to determine whether the pregnant client is under unusual stress. The American Nurses' Association (1987) has identified six common sources of stress for the pregnant woman that may constitute barriers to prenatal care and may require intervention:

- Stress related to basic needs such as food, shelter, and employment
- Stress related to living in a chronic state of crisis
- Stress related to fears about the pregnancy and birth
- Stress related to being single, alone, or supported

- Stress related to "ordinary" life events, such as moves, job changes, and family illness
- Stress related to employment conditions

Because social support may mitigate the effects of stress, it is also important to identify women who are at risk of the effects of stress because of lack of adequate social support. It is well known that lack of social support may be influential on physical and psychological health, and in particular lack of support has been linked with many parenting problems including child abuse and neglect (Kugler & Hansson, 1988). In addition to determining the woman's marital status and the nature of the relationship with the baby's father (especially if she is unmarried), the social worker should address the issue of social support by asking with whom the mother lives, whether family and friends are close by, the number of contacts per week with supportive persons, and other indicators of social isolation or lack of support. Fairley (1979) also suggests that a relationship with a spouse or boyfriend that diverts energy away from proper medical care or parenting may be a risk factor; Royer and Barth (1984) stress marital discord as a risk factor for poor pregnancy outcome that should be of special concern to social workers.

In recent years many measures of social support and isolation have become available and might be useful for the social worker in determining client need in this area, despite the fact that they have not been widely used in prenatal settings. The practitioner who selects such a measure, however, must be careful to select one with adequate reliability and validity. The whole area of high-risk assessment continues to suffer from inadequate levels of reliability and validity (Rudolph & Borker, 1987).

One measure that apparently is adequate is the Social Support Questionnaire (SSQ) (Sarason, Levine, Basham, & Sarason, 1983). The 17-item SSQ measures both the number of supportive individuals one has and satisfaction with them, and may be useful as a clinical tool for identifying socially isolated clients.

Transportation Problems

Lack of reliable transportation is a barrier to good health care that consistently receives inadequate attention (Insley, 1980; Lesser, 1966; Royer & Barth, 1984). In rural areas far from health care settings, and in dense urban areas with poor public transportation, some women may not receive adequate health care simply because they cannot get there (Robert Wood Johnson Foundation, 1987; American Nurses' Association, 1987). Other women may be able to negotiate some kind of transportation but face great practical difficulties because of the necessity of taking other (perhaps several) small children on uncomfortable, unsafe, public transportation, often in cold weather.

A basic piece of information that the social worker should elicit then is whether the mother has resources that she can rely on for transportation throughout her prenatal care course and for transportation to the hospital when labor begins. The social worker also may want to encourage the expectant mother to have an alternate plan for circumstances in the event that her main source of transportation becomes unavailable.

Inadequate Knowledge

It is important for the social worker to determine whether the mother has knowledge deficits in the area of pregnancy and parenting that may place her at risk for poor pregnancy outcome or for poor parenting. A basic question concerns the mother's understanding of the importance of following the recommended prenatal care schedule, even if she is having no problems. Lack of knowledge about child development also has for many years been thought to be a risk factor for poor parenting and child abuse and neglect, although it may be difficult for the social worker to assess the client's knowledge in this area (Orme & Hamilton, 1987).

To determine the woman's knowledge about pregnancy in general, the social worker may inquire about pregnancy history (because first-time mothers may be more likely to lack knowledge and experience) as well as other experience with infants, such as contact with siblings or those through baby-sitting. Other assessment issues might include whether the woman has had other sources of information such as home economics or Family Life Education classes in school. It is also important to determine whether the woman's mother is available as a source of information and support, especially with younger mothers, because in many cases the pregnant teenager's mother may take a major responsibility for infant care (Collins, 1974). Although this arrangement may have some disadvantages, the worker may feel more confident about the infant's safety and security in the early days of its life if an experienced grandmother is nearby and involved.

Many clinics distribute reading material about various subjects such as nutrition, smoking during pregnancy, and so forth. The social worker may determine the expectant mother's interest in such materials as well as her ability (regarding education and intelligence) to benefit from it.

Negative Feelings About Pregnancy

Ambivalence and anxiety about pregnancy are not uncommon (Klaus & Kennell, 1982), but practitioners may be concerned about pregnant women who express disgust or extreme unhappiness about being pregnant (Cheetham, 1977). Fairley (1979) includes on her list of risk factors clients who are emotionally rejecting, those who have no plans for their unborn children, and those who have requested and been denied termination of their pregnancies. Fairley (1979) and Collins (1974) both note a particular need to provide special attention and intensive services to women who are planning or considering relinquishment of their children.

In Cheetham's (1977) work on unintended pregnancy, she notes several situations to which the social worker should be alert and that would suggest the need for counseling. They are a referral late in pregnancy for medical or other help or a referral by a friend or relative; emotional flatness or lack of concern about the pregnancy, especially when problems are obvious; an apparent lack of interest in the progress of the pregnancy or the baby as an individual; a lack of interest in the baby's father; a rejection of contraception; and indications of contradiction between what parents say about the pregnancy and how they behave.

In some cases negative feelings about pregnancy are indicators of other problems such as financial need. Negative feelings may relate to the mother's negative or ambivalent relationship with baby's father, the unplanned nature of the pregnancy, or worry about her ability to provide for herself and the baby. In such cases supportive and other, tangible services may be helpful. Shoemaker (1966) makes a valid point:

> In giving service, it must be remembered that *concrete* services are needed for all socially disadvantaged pregnant women. Let us not underestimate the value of concrete services in their own right. We in social work have tended to deprecate such services—monetary assistance, nursing services, educational help—perhaps out of our own lack of appreciation for the effects of physical deprivation. (p. 106)

Assessment Instruments

A standardized measure that social workers could use across many situations with pregnant clients would be useful for various reasons including better precision in identifying clients and providing services to high-risk clients. In times of limited resources it is essential for those resources to be provided first to those in the greatest need. Such an instrument would also be useful for the profession's knowledge building, as quality research is essential for the development of better practice methods and for the profession's credibility.

Moreover, good practice is dependent on good assessment. Guendelman (1987) noted the importance of quality measurement instruments in the achievement of practice objectives and further noted: "If we are able to demonstrate that our services actually improve the health of the population we serve, we will be in a far more advantageous position to obtain funding for our services" (p. 86). Such a standardized tool also would have enormous usefulness in professional training and education.

The ideal social risk measure would be both standardized (to permit research across client populations) and flexible for use with different types of clients and problems, and would possess adequate reliability and validity. The instrument should also be sensitive (identify a large proportion of those truly at risk) and specific (not pick up a large proportion of those who are not at risk) (Gould, 1987). Social workers often have not been concerned with these concepts, and hence their instruments have had little usefulness for research or clinical practice.

Two reviews have examined the available instruments for assessing high-risk pregnancies. Chesborough (1987) reviewed several assessment instruments for the purpose of identifying pregnant women at high social risk of poor outcomes. Noting the difficulties of quantifying some variables believed to be important to pregnancy outcome, such as general anxiety and feelings about the pregnancy, she reviewed several instruments designed to assess pregnancy-related stresses and risks. Important areas of assessment based on accumulated research included socioeconomic factors, personal adjustment, and social support. Rudolph and Borker (1987) also reviewed the available instruments for high-risk assessment within the context of their importance for regionalized perinatal care. These authors provide an excellent discussion as well as appendixes detailing the individual variables, coding, and methods of scoring to determine level of risk.

Although none is widely accepted or without flaws, several instruments have been used to assess high risk, and several are reviewed here. The Perinatal Forum Psychosocial Tool (Selmar, 1987) is an instrument designed to assess social risk in pregnant women, which was developed by a team of social workers, nurses, and others who are part of this consortium of providers to low-income women. The instrument is rather lengthy, and its reliability and validity have yet to be demonstrated; however, it is a promising tool that examines many variables including obstetric history, feelings about the pregnancy, housing and employment, family structure, certain factors in the client's psychiatric history, and drug and alcohol use.

The Maternal Attitude to Pregnancy Instrument (Blau, Welkowitz, & Cohen, 1964) is a self-administered instrument (available in both English and Spanish) that measures several general attitudes and feelings about pregnancy (e.g., "A woman looks her best during her pregnancy," "the delivery is a frightening part of pregnancy," and "most women are unprepared for having a baby"). Factor analyses on the two versions resulted in four factors with moderate reliability (coefficients ranging from 0.58 to 0.79), but differences require that the data be scored separately for English- and Spanish-speaking groups.

Although the Maternal Attitude to Pregnancy Instrument might be a promising method of identifying women whose attitudes toward pregnancy are negative, and it could be presumed that such negative attitudes might place them at risk of anxiety and thus poor pregnancy outcomes, a search of the literature reveals no evidence that the instrument does indeed have predictive validity, despite its use in several studies. Moreover, the instrument measures only general attitudes toward pregnancy, whereas increased risk is more likely to result from interactions among attitudes, and other social and medical factors.

The Maternal–Child Health Index (Nesbitt & Aubry, 1969) is a 30-item measure of several medical and social factors that have been shown previously to be related to poor perinatal outcome. The authors tested the method on a sample of relatively high-risk women who were "ward" patients (and thus lower SES) who registered for prenatal care relatively late in pregnancy and found the measure to predict several poor outcomes including preterm delivery, LBW, and maternal complications. The social factors by themselves were not predictive; however, as the authors themselves note, the interview method used to collect the data probably was not reliable enough to obtain sensitive measures. Moreover, social and medical circumstances are generally highly correlated.

Nuckolls, Cassel, and Kaplan (1971) developed the Adaptive Potential for Pregnancy Scale to measure self-esteem; feelings about pregnancy, partner, and family support; as well as a broad concept of "adjustment." They also used a measure of significant life events (Holmes & Rahe, 1967) and found an important interaction effect in predicting pregnancy complications among 253 married women. Although no first-order effects on pregnancy outcome were found for either measure, women with high "psychosocial assets" (high support, good self-esteem, and adjustment) who had experienced many life events believed to cause high stress had only one third as many pregnancy complications as those with low "psychosocial assets" and many life events. These results appear promising, and the measure merits further study; however, a search of the literature reveals few uses of the instrument since its original publication.

The Modified Life Events Inventory (Newton, Webster, Binu, Maskrey, & Phillips, 1979) is similar to the more general Life Events Inventory (Cochrane & Robertson, 1973), which was based on the Holmes and Rahe Life Schedule of Recent Experiences (SRE) (1967).

Each of these instruments measures stress owing to accumulated significant life events. The Modified Life Events Inventory was developed to apply specifically to pregnant women and includes 59 self-scored items. Although no reliability data were reported on the measure, predictive validity is suggested by the fact that women who delivered prematurely had experienced significantly more life events in the week preceding the onset of labor. Results were independent of social class.

Creasy's Risk of Preterm Delivery Sheet (Creasy, Gummer, & Liggins, 1980) incorporated several factors including SES (e.g., low SES, multiple children at home, maternal age, etc.), pregnancy history (e.g., number of abortions, interval since last birth, pregnancy problems), daily habits (e.g., smoking, heavy work), and complications of current pregnancy. The instrument predicted that 10% of patients would deliver prematurely but was more discriminating for multigravid than primigravid women. Although only one third of those found to be at risk by the instrument did actually deliver before term, this group accounted for two thirds of the total number of premature births. The authors reported that the instrument was more accurate when it was rescored at 26 to 28 weeks' gestation.

The usefulness of the Preterm Delivery Sheet would seem to lie in its multivariate approach to risk, because psychosocial risk factors do often occur in combination with other factors. Its limitations lie in its relative inaccuracy with first pregnancies and early in pregnancy. Ultimately the most effective screening and assessment would occur early in pregnancy, allowing comprehensive preventive services. Moreover, the report of the instrument seems to indicate that the instrument was designed specifically for use by obstetricians, who might not be expected to be competent in the assessment of social factors that are important in pregnancy outcome. Indeed, the measure might be more predictive with improved assessment of those social factors.

Both family functioning and social support are believed to be important factors in pregnancy outcome, despite difficulties in demonstrating the relationships empirically (Chesborough, 1987). Although several instruments are available to measure these concepts (e.g., see Corcoran & Fischer, 1987; Krauss, 1988), in general these concepts are complex and difficult to measure in meaningful ways that are still simple enough to have broad application. Moreover, social workers in MCH settings require instruments that are not only reliable and valid, but that are brief and easy to use for clients with various educational levels and skills. One promising measure that was developed for assessment of family functioning by family practice physicians is the Family APGAR (Smilkstein, 1978).

The Family APGAR is a simple qualitative measure of five components of family functioning: adaptation to crisis, partnership and sharing, growth of individual family members through mutual support and guidance, affection among family members, and sharing and commitment of family members to each other ("resolve"). For each area, individual family members score themselves 2 ("almost always"), 1 ("some of the time"), or 0 ("hardly ever"), and the scores are totaled. Scores of 7 to 10 indicate a functional family, 4 to 6 a moderately dysfunctional family, 0 to 3 a highly dysfunctional family. The authors claim that the measure is simple enough to be used with a wide range of clients, and testing indicates that it is highly reliable and probably valid in predicting pregnancy complications (Smilkstein, Ashworth, & Montano, 1982; Smilkstein, Helsper-Lucas, Ashworth, Montano, & Pagel, 1984). (It should be noted that predictive value is relative; no method of predicting poor pregnancy outcomes has been shown to predict a majority.)

Adequate measures of social support are more difficult to find, despite convincing evidence of the connection between social support and health (Cleary, 1988). "Social support" is difficult to define, and may include a broad range of issues such as the number of persons in one's network, the function of each support (e.g., material vs. emotional), availability vs. use of supports, and value to the individual (Cleary, 1988). Cleary (1988) notes that the sophisticated measures require too much time for respondents to use routinely, but that in some situations a single-item measure (e.g., asking women if they have someone they can call when they feel low, or if someone will be available to baby-sit when they need relief) may be appropriate. The Family Resource Scale (Dunst & Leet, 1987) contains items relevant to individuals' perceptions about social support resources, although the measure as a whole is designed for use with families with young children and thus may have no applicability to women who are pregnant with their first child.

In conclusion, few promising measures exist for predicting a fair proportion of poor pregnancy outcomes. The problems that remain in the technology for assessing women at high risk include the need to consider joint risk factors, assure the reliability and validity of such instruments, and improve the ability of such measures to detect high risk early enough in pregnancy so that preventive interventions are still possible. Social workers may find it most useful to use several measures to compensate for the weaknesses of individual measures.

Service Procurement and Referral

Assessment is the backbone of practice, but it is only a beginning. Social workers in prenatal care settings must be thoroughly familiar with community resources and how to obtain those resources if their assessments are to be helpful to clients. Many pregnant women, especially those of low income, require services that relate directly to the health and outcome of their pregnancies, and the social worker is generally considered the prenatal team "expert" regarding those resources. In recent years this social work function has fallen into disrepute, perhaps because as the profession seeks to enhance its professional status, it has sought to shed its "welfare" image. In actuality, however, an understanding of the various services available to clients and the way the system works is critically important in any area of social work practice. In perinatal social work it is especially difficult (but valuable) because the social worker must be facile in both the health care and social service (or welfare) systems. Both systems constantly change in response to fiscal and political trends at federal and local levels.

The most basic programs of concern to the perinatal social worker are the Aid to Families with Dependent Children (AFDC) and Medicaid programs. AFDC is a federal-state program, meaning that although federal funds and rules partly finance and govern the program, states administer the programs, and rules regarding eligibility and benefits vary. The amount of benefits varies by state, but grants are never more than subsistence level. All recipients of AFDC are automatically eligible for Medicaid in all states.

Medicaid is a program for reimbursement to health care providers for specific covered medical services. Some services are mandated including inpatient and outpatient hospital care, physician care, laboratory tests, radiographs, and family planning services. Others are permitted at the discretion of the states, such as nurse-midwife services. As with AFDC, Medicaid rules on eligibility, services covered, and reimbursement rates vary by state. In 1980 about 19% of all deliveries in this country were financed by Medicaid (Gold & Kenney, 1985), but changes in AFDC and Medicaid coverage since 1981 have reduced the numbers of mothers and children who are eligible, restricted the specific services that are covered, and reduced the amounts paid for services (Levitan, 1985).

Recent changes in the Medicaid program accomplished through the 1986 Consolidated Omnibus Reconciliation Act (COBRA, Public Law 99-272) and the Sixth Omnibus Budget Reconciliation Act (SOBRA, Public Law 99-509) will make health services available to more low-income women. Under these acts, Medicaid coverage has been broadened to include many more children (those younger than 5 years of age). The act accomplishes this goal in three ways (Rosenbaum, 1987): liberalizing income eligibility standards, permitting states the option of waiving asset criteria altogether for pregnant women and children younger than 5 years of age, and guaranteeing continuous Medicaid coverage for 2 months following the pregnancy for any woman who qualifies.

In addition to these changes, states now may temporarily (for a period of 45 days) enroll pregnant women who appear to be eligible for Medicaid in "presumptive eligibility" programs while the eligibility determination process is completed. These changes may not only qualify many more high-risk women for Medicaid coverage but may result in such women beginning prenatal care earlier in pregnancy, because in the past the lengthy and complex application process has delayed the beginning of prenatal care for many indigent women.

Balassone (1987) reviewed the Medicaid programs in 18 western states and demonstrated tremendous variation among those states in eligibility standards for Medicaid coverage. For example, the maximum qualifying income (for a family of four) for AFDC and Medicaid coverage in 1985 in Washington was $10,272 (34% of that state's median income) and in Missouri was $4,380 (17% of that state's median income). Other discrepancies among the states demonstrated by Gold and Kenney (1985) included whether pregnant women could be covered if they lived in a two-parent, unemployed household or in a home where the husband was employed in a low-income job; and whether the number of physician or outpatient visits was limited. Some states provide coverage to the "medically needy" that is, women whose high medical bills exceed their low incomes, whereas others do not.

Despite these problems, Davis and Schoen's (1978) evaluation demonstrated a positive effect of Medicaid and other programs in increasing access to health care for poor women and children. Corman and Grossman (1985) found that the availability of Medicaid was responsible for a significant portion of the decrease in white neonatal mortality between 1964 and 1977; Norris and Williams (1984) showed improvements in perinatal mortality in California to be associated with Medicaid. Some have made suggestions (e.g., Miller, 1985), which can only be demonstrated by time, that cuts since 1981 have begun to limit that increased access. (Recent changes in the Medicaid program designed to expand coverage for pregnant women and young children may restore some lost services. These changes are discussed in detail elsewhere in this book.)

Several other programs with which it is essential that prenatal social workers are familiar derive originally from Title V of the Social Security Act. The 1981 Omnibus Reconciliation Act combined many of these programs into the Maternal and Child Health Block Grant, although some programs are still known by their original names. The MIC programs were federally funded programs administered by states and directed specifically toward high-need areas with inadequate health care resources— for example, dense urban areas with high infant mortality and few obstetric providers. Some state and local public health departments administered clinics that were partially funded with MIC funds. These MIC clinics, now funded by the Maternal and Child Health Block Grant, are primary settings where social workers are part of the prenatal care team. Evaluations of the MIC programs have shown that they do increase the access to quality health care by low-income pregnant women and infants (e.g., Chabot, 1971), and that proportionately more of the benefit of MIC services accrues to those at high risk of a poor pregnancy outcome (Peoples & Siegel, 1983).

Two of the most important federally funded resources for the perinatal social worker's clients are the WIC and food stamps programs. WIC is a valuable resource that provides nutritional education and coupons for purchase of about $20 worth of specific, highly nutritious foods (such as milk, cereals, and cheese) per month for nutritionally high-risk pregnant and lactating women and children up to 5 years of age. In most areas, WIC sites are located in public health clinics because the program is considered a health program rather than a welfare benefit, and because such a link promotes greater participation in both services through referral (Institute of Medicine, 1985; Kotch & Whiteman, 1982). Despite numerous problems in evaluating WIC, a summary of studies during the years suggests that the program is effective in improving infant and child health (Barnard & Sumner, 1981). Corman and Grossman (1985) found in a large-scale study of the United States that WIC was one of several factors accounting for the reduction of infant mortality among whites between 1964 and 1977. In any case, most social workers would support providing nutritious foods to pregnant women and children based on values alone (Rush, 1982).

The Food Stamp program is a complicated federal-state program that is automatically available (although in differing amounts) to recipients of AFDC (Levitan, 1985). In some areas, low-income persons who are not recipients of public assistance also may qualify, and social workers should always discuss possible eligibility for Food Stamps with pregnant clients who are or may be at risk of nutritional deficiencies.

Other services recommended by the American Nurses' Association (1987) that may or may not be available, but that may be needed and valuable for the pregnant low-income woman include home visits, homemaker services, child care assistance, sanctuaries and shelters for battered women, respite care, and "hotline" services to provide information during hours when clinics are not open.

In some cases the worker does not have adequate resources to assist clients with identified problems. In such cases social workers should identify gaps in services (Cowin, 1968) for the purpose of reporting those gaps and advocating for services. In the meantime, innovation may be necessary. For example, in urban south Chicago a public health nurse organized a self-help group to aid low-income mothers to use their WIC coupons. WIC coupons require that food be purchased in bulk (for example, infant formula must be purchased by the case), and in this neighborhood, most small grocery stores did not accept WIC coupons. All of these AFDC mothers had one to four small children and no baby-sitting, resources or private transportation. Therefore, because the cold Chicago weather made it impossible to walk the long distance or to get their children out for the train ride to the supermarkets that did accept WIC, most had stopped using their coupons. The nurse organized five mothers to pool their money for a taxi to the supermarket every other week, while one mother stayed with all the children and the others shopped for her. Such innovation requires all of the skills for which social workers are trained including one-to-one casework, groupwork, and organizational skills.

However the social worker locates the needed resources, this contribution is one that should not be underestimated. An MIC project director described the social worker's role:

> She is out there with the bus tokens and the bus fare, arranging for transportation, arranging for home visits while the patient is in the hospital, taking care of all the problems that would upset maternity patients, seeing that they're put in proper programs, such as Aid to Families with Dependent Children, seeing whether they're eligible for welfare. To the patients the social worker represents someone who is giving them something tangible. . . . She is really putting it on the line and helping them. (U.S. Department of Health, Education and Welfare, 1975, p. 7)

Coordination and Consultation

In addition to understanding the network of available services, the social worker should be adept at coordination of those services (Watkins, 1979). In fact, case management is a function increasingly being cited as a high priority for perinatal social workers and other members of the prenatal care team (American Nurses' Association, 1987). The American Nurses' Association (1987) defines case management as "responsibility for the oversight of the woman's care; this responsibility is assumed by one professional member of the health team" (p. 17) and recommends that all pregnant patients be assigned a case manager. This same professional group also recommends that the determination of the case manager for specific clients should be made based on the woman's identified needs. For example, clients whose greatest needs involve health education might be managed by the health educator, whereas the woman who has multiple social problems might be managed by the social worker. The case manager is able to determine when additional services are needed, and may maintain a central file on the client's needs, agencies with which she has had contact and the results, and progress of the client's pregnancy.

Many of the clients seen in prenatal settings, as in other setings, may be termed "multi-problem families" who have contact with many different programs at various times (Cowin, 1968). Case management on behalf of these clients often may involve organizing case conferences among different agencies to avoid duplication or miscommunication. The case manager also must maintain relationships and contact with practitioners in various agencies to monitor referrals and the progress of mutual clients as well as to stay informed about changes in eligibility requirements and services. Watkins (1979) emphasizes the importance of building linkages among different services in a regionalized system of perinatal care, especially between ambulatory care centers and the hospital settings where women deliver. Sometimes this function may involve serving on state planning or advisory teams for establishing or monitoring regional systems of perinatal care (Goldenberg & Koski, 1984).

In many, if not most, cases one of the most important linkages for the prenatal social worker is with the local welfare or public assistance agency, such as the one between MIC workers and their local welfare agencies in Minneapolis and Cincinnati (Clark, 1968). Informing workers at the welfare department of the importance of maternity and pediatric care seemed necessary because most MIC patients were low income, and Clark reports that the relationship between the agencies has been helpful in the identification and planning of new services. A well-maintained relationship between the prenatal social worker and the local welfare agency might be expected to result in referrals in both directions, to the benefit of pregnant clients.

Social workers also may assist the pregnant client through linking her with self-help or support groups such as La Leche League for breast-feeding information and advice, community groups such as churches or clubs that provide services or resources such as birthing classes, or even other clients who may share certain concerns or who simply live nearby. In some cases the social worker may perceive the unmet need for such groups and provide leadership in starting them.

An important part of coordination of services, however, is sometimes conducted within the team itself through consultation. Consultation is an especially important function in the low-income prenatal care clinic. Physicians may not understand why clients do not take the vitamins that were ordered (they cannot afford to buy them), miss their appointments (one of the other children got sick and no baby-sitter could be found), or act fearful and tense during the examination (they are embarrassed about

being examined by a male physician). Rude, hostile, or insensitive staff
has been identified as a major barrier to access to prenatal care for many
high-risk women (American Nurses' Association, 1987), and through consultation the social worker may be effective in modifying other staff's
behavior in a positive manner so that clients do not discontinue care in
response to insensitivity.

Supportive Services

The supportive function of obstetric social work has not been well operationalized, but centers around the inherently stressful nature of pregnancy and the documented deleterious effects of stress on pregnancy
(Rudolph, 1985). Moreover, it is assumed that the reduction of anxiety
during pregnancy may promote a more positive relationship later between the mother and child (Cyr & Wattenberg, 1957). The Committee
to Study the Prevention of Low Birthweight (Institute of Medicine, 1985)
classified pregnancy-related stress into two categories: physical stress and
fatigue, and psychological distress resulting from maternal attitudes and
environmental factors. The social worker is most often concerned with
the latter.

The effects of psychological tension or anxiety are more difficult to
assess, owing mainly to inherent difficulties in the measurement of what
is called "stress." Normal pregnancy might provoke anxiety relating to the
responsibilities of impending parenthood, the financial demands of pregnancy and parenting, concern over the pain and risk associated with
delivery, or any number of other factors. These fears are experienced not
just by women but also by future fathers (Bernstein & Cyr, 1957), although much less attention is usually paid to their concerns. The clinic
setting itself may be stressful, especially for low-income and minority
clients who are unfamiliar with medical settings (Mathis, 1980).

For the low-income woman, pregnancy may present a special stress.
The Committee to Study the Prevention of Low Birthweight (Institute of
Medicine, 1985) suggests that psychological stress may be part of the
reason for the negative effects of poverty on pregnancy; poverty itself
creates psychological stress in daily survival issues in addition to its well-
documented effects on nutrition, medical care, and so forth. Unmarried
women may suffer stress related to their added financial burden and the
social stigma associated with being pregnant out of marriage (Miller,
1985). Whatever the reasons, the data do seem to indicate a relationship
between anxiety or poor maternal attitude and pregnancy outcome. (See
Wortman, 1982, for a review of the evidence on this point.)

Social workers who function as part of a team to reduce stress generally concentrate on several tasks. One way of reducing anxiety is the provision of information to allay stress that is related to fear of the unknown (e.g., "Will I be able to handle labor pain?" "How will I know if something is wrong, and what do I do?"). Some fear is related to lack of understanding of the birth process or medical procedures (American Nurses' Association, 1987). Clients may be embarrassed to ask questions, so the perceptive social worker should initiate a discussion with the obviously anxious client about the source of her anxieties.

Perhaps one of the most helpful things a social worker can do to reduce a pregnant woman's anxiety is to provide assistance in the form of needed resources ("How will I ever pay for my vitamins?") (Bernstein & Cyr, 1957). Many of the lower income woman's fears and anxieties are completely justified, and she may require information about obtaining the resources she needs. Simple verbal reassurance ("It's OK! Most women are afraid they won't be able to be good mothers right off—it takes some practice") also may be helpful, especially to women who may have no other source of emotional support.

Three authors have proposed the group format for providing supportive services to pregnant women. Everett (1980) suggested that the group method is the ideal one for alleviating pregnant women's natural anxieties. She asserted that groups could be a comfortable medium in which to educate patients about the normal course of pregnancy, provide the opportunity for natural peer support, and create a forum for discussing common fears and concerns. Mathis (1980) also used a group format with an Hispanic group leader to provide support and education for pregnant Latinas. George (1979) proposed supportive groups for pregnant teenagers and their significant others including their own parents and boyfriends. None of these authors presents an evaluation of the effectiveness of the groups.

The high-risk woman and her family have all the normal stresses of pregnancy, plus those associated with elevated risk status. These additional stresses include the constant fear of spontaneous abortion or premature labor, burdens associated with frequent medical appointments and tests that also serve to remind her constantly of her "abnormal status," and the physical problems associated with her condition and the treatment or management of it (Emery, 1985). In addition to the possible adverse effects of such stress on the pregnancy, it has been suggested that high-risk women may resist bonding with their unborn infants in an effort to protect themselves from grief should something happen, and that this lack of appropriate bonding may place the infant at risk later for poor parenting (Waldron & Asayama, 1985).

The reduction of anxiety in high-risk women is made especially diffi-cult by the very technology used to manage many obstetric problems. For example, amniocentesis and prenatal diagnosis, toxolytic management of premature labor (drugs that may stop premature labor), and even ultrasound testing all create a highly charged emotional atmosphere around the pregnant woman that is ever more highly changed if she has had previous problem pregnancies that resulted in poor outcomes. Waldron and Asayama (1985) examined the emotional stresses of 18 pa-tients who remained hospitalized in a maternal-fetal intensive care unit during the last few weeks of pregnancy because of the threat of prema-ture delivery. These women reported physical discomforts and feelings of helplessness, loss of control, and isolation.

Despite lack of operationalization of "supportive" techniques (e.g., Gallivan & Saunders, 1982), social workers generally understand such activities to include assisting patients in clarifying and verbalizing their fears and feelings (on the assumption that such expression provides re-lief), providing encouragement and reassurance that is nonetheless realis-tic in the face of the patient's condition and situation, and encouraging the use of natural support networks such as family.

Joyce, Diffenbacher, Greene, and Sorokin (1983) advocate social work support as a method of inducing women to remain in prenatal care when stress otherwise might lead them to discontinue it before delivery. Although supportive activities certainly possess face validity as useful activities, it is important to remember nonetheless that data do not exist to support their effectiveness in reducing patients' stress nor in improv-ing their pregnancy outcomes. Evaluation must determine how effective social workers are in the provision of support services to pregnant women and their families, and what the outcomes associated with support serv- ices are.

Outreach Services

One of the most difficult problems in the provision of prenatal care is that patients who need it most are least likely to seek it in a timely and consistent manner (Institute of Medicine, 1985). Low-income women, minority women, teenagers, and unmarried women receive less prenatal care and begin their care later than do women at lower risk for poor outcomes. The use of prenatal care parallels the use of health care by lower income persons in general. Research from numerous sources indi-cates that lower income persons use less health care than more advan-taged persons; that they tend to engage in more episodic, crisis-oriented care such as Emergency Room visits as opposed to regular visits to a primary care physician; and that the poor do not use preventive health care as often as the nonpoor because they do not value such care (e.g., see Kovar, 1982). All this is true despite the fact that lower income persons are less healthy than more advantaged ones.

For years health care programs have grappled with the difficulties of recruiting high-risk women into care and keeping them there until delivery. In the process of attempting to bring more women into care, health care providers and researchers have asked the following questions: What causes women not to seek care or to drop out from prenatal care before delivery? What barriers exist to the provision of prenatal care to those at highest risk for poor outcomes? How can these barriers best be overcome?

Three studies have addressed these questions by interviewing women who sought no prenatal care. Bernstein and Sauber (1960) interviewed 520 unmarried women who delivered in a probability sample of New York hospitals. Of this group, 17% sought little or no prenatal care and only 21% began care in the first trimester. Although their reasons for seeking no care varied somewhat by age and ethnicity, the major reasons were as follows: no need seen (20%); attempts to conceal the pregnancy as long as possible (18%); child care problems (16%); problems taking time off from employment (12%); failure to recognize the pregnancy (9%); fear of medical examination (9%); inability to pay for private care and lack of desire to visit a public clinic (7%); and public clinic rejected them as ineligible for services (6%). Lack of knowledge about available services was not cited as a factor. Although access and availability of public prenatal services have certainly changed since 1960, many of these same reasons probably still inhibit women from obtaining timely prenatal care.

Joyce et al. (1983) interviewed 70 patients who had given birth in a large metropolitan hospital without having had any prenatal care. Twenty-three percent of the total (including one third of teenagers) claimed external reasons such as inability to pay, lack of transportation and child care, inability to get an appointment, or excessive clinic waits. Forty-seven percent of the respondents attributed their lack of care to internal reasons such as depression, denial of the pregnancy, fear of physicians, and unplanned pregnancy. Thirty percent claimed they sought no care because they felt fine and saw no reason to do so.

Butler (1985) reported six barriers to prenatal care that social workers perceived in their local settings including religious fanaticism that precluded medical care, lack of intelligence, genetic and social isolation, miscegenation, life-style such as drugs and transience, and pica. In each case the social workers believed that it was crucial to use the natural support systems of family, neighbors, and friends to draw pregnant women into appropriate health care.

Other researchers have summarized major barriers to universal prenatal care as the cost of prenatal care (not high in an absolute sense but often out of reach to those who need it most) (Bernstein & Sauber, 1960; Hughes, 1985); the inaccessibility of health care services in many areas (Orr, Miller, & James, 1984); crowded, uncomfortable clinics and resulting long waits in many publicly funded facilities (Bernstein & Sauber, 1960; Lesser, 1966); and cultural and personal attitudes and values that are not conducive to using prenatal care (Joyce et al., 1983; Mathis, 1980).

Overcoming the barriers to prenatal care will require effective outreach, long touted as a social work function (Raymond, 1985; Watkins & Player, 1981) and increasingly recognized as essential to reaching the high-risk client (e.g., Barber, 1989). For example, if one reason women do not seek and continue in prenatal care is that they are unaware of the importance of consistent care, especially for a normal pregnancy (American Nurses' Association, 1987; Bernstein & Sauber, 1960; Everett, 1980), the social worker may be important in explaining the importance of care, establishing a personal relationship (however brief) that may reinforce the mother's taking what may be considerable trouble to continue her visits, and sometimes providing reminders before appointments and follow-up calls when visits are missed. In other cases social workers in other community settings may provide outreach to prenatal care through referrals made by agreements between agencies. For example, social workers in public welfare agencies may inquire of their pregnant clients whether they have begun prenatal care and may provide personal referrals and follow-up on those referrals.

A major reason that high-risk minority women may not seek timely prenatal care is cultural barriers that may include inability to speak English, cultural values regarding modesty and male physicians, cultural medical practices, and anxiety about the unfamiliar clinic atmosphere (e.g., see Everett, 1980; Martinez, 1985; Mathis, 1980; Raymond, 1985; Towbin, 1985). Certain cultural and ethnic groups may also lack information about resources because of language problems and undocumented status (Mathis, 1980). Social workers are professionally obligated to be knowledgeable about and sensitive to clients' cultural backgrounds and may be in the best position to work within the client's own system to enroll her in appropriate prenatal care. They may also educate other staff about patients' beliefs and customs to improve the general attitude toward and treatment of patients among staff (Everett, 1980).

Educational Tasks

The entire prenatal care team is involved in educational tasks from the beginning of prenatal care, yet George (1979) states that "the role of educator seems to be the one most frequently abdicated by social workers" (p. 34). Most women require information on issues such as the physiological process of pregnancy, and "normal" physical and emotional concerns. Some women require information on the importance of remaining in prenatal care until delivery, appearing for the postnatal examination and enrolling the baby in well-baby care on schedule; self-care, such as proper diet and exercise and avoidance of smoking, alcohol, and other drugs; the signs and symptoms of problems and appropriate responses; and parenting skills, especially infant care. Prenatal education also should include birth control information (American Nurses' Association, 1987), because this may be the best time to begin, especially if this pregnancy was unintended. (In some studies, state laws may preclude the social worker's mention of this issue, especially with teenagers.) In some settings the nurse is the primary health educator (Combs-Orme et al., 1985); the physician often gives advice or "orders," but rarely engages in the kind of discussion that is useful in providing such information.

Depending on the setting, the social worker may have responsibility (or may share responsibility with a nurse) for educating mothers in what to expect physically during pregnancy including what is normal (e.g., fatigue) and what is not (e.g., bleeding) (Everett, 1980). Early notice and appropriate action when danger signs appear may be significant in delaying labor and delivery (Institute of Medicine, 1985). The division of responsibility for patient education will depend on the particular practice setting, but in general education is a comprehensive task that may be shared by the entire prenatal care team. In fact, health education may be an effective method of allaying clients' anxiety and fear about the examination and prenatal care in general (Fairley, 1979).

In the last decade evidence has accumulated that smoking and ingestion of drugs and alcohol during pregnancy create a hazard for the developing fetus (e.g., Wright, 1981). In fact, it has been stated that if education could induce pregnant women to give up alcohol and smoking during pregnancy, LBW rates could be reduced by 25% (Goldenberg & Koski, 1984). Social workers, along with other health professionals, have joined in efforts to persuade pregnant women to abstain from or at least to decrease their consumption of these substances during pregnancy (e.g., Hare, 1985; Ouellette, 1985). Methods have included the distribution of written materials, group education techniques, and personal advice. Limited evidence suggests that pregnant women have responded in the desired direction (e.g., Ershoff, Aaronson, Danaher, & Wasserman, 1983).

Gallivan and Saunders (1982) reported on a program designed to provide specialized educational and support services to a population of high-risk (young, low-income, socially isolated) pregnant women in a military housing complex. Although several different types of services were provided (including transportation, facilitation of group self-help, and community referrals), a key component consisted of a series of 10 workshops to provide information on issues such as those described earlier. The qualitative, noncontrolled evaluation indicated that 75% of the women obtained useful information. Other important benefits of the program were continuation of the workshops by other community agencies, participation by fathers in those workshops, and improved community linkages among various resources.

Advocacy Roles for Social Workers

Several specific factors can be used as rallying points for advocacy by social workers on behalf of low-income expectant mothers. First, further cuts in AFDC, Medicaid, and Maternal and Child Health Block Grant programs must be stopped. Since 1981, thousands of poor women and children have been driven off AFDC and Medicaid rolls, limiting their access to quality health care and other essential services. Social workers were instrumental in enacting many of these programs (Combs-Orme, 1988); they must fight to preserve them.

Second, calls for universal prenatal care merit serious consideration. Congressional legislation has been developed that would provide prenatal care for all women regardless of ability to pay. Other nations routinely provide such care, and leading medical authorities assert that it would actually save public dollars (Institute of Medicine, 1985). In the past social work has acted collectively to advocate for MCH services (Combs-Orme, 1987; Siefert, 1983); such action needs to be taken now. Social workers can also act to increase public awareness and education about the potential economic and social benefits of prevention, although they should not promise unrealistic outcomes (Rudolph, 1985).

Perhaps most important, social workers must be cautious of the artificial division that is often drawn between health and welfare services. For the pregnant woman or young child, quality medical care may be defeated by poor nutrition, unsafe housing, and lack of education. Advocating for free prenatal care in the absence of an adequate diet or housing is self-defeating. Further, as Clark (1968) pointed out nearly 20 years ago, the problems of a low-income pregnant woman precede her pregnancy and go on long after it. Shlakman (1966) asked: "Can we expect to single out one episode in the life history of poverty and seek to neutralize its debilitating effects for the period of pregnancy, while leaving the larger condition unchanged?" (p. 80).

When prenatal care is but a brief interlude in an unhealthy life, it probably contributes little to the health of mothers and children. Although we must continue to advocate for quality prenatal and delivery care, we must not forget the overall impact it is likely to have in the absence of a decent standard of living. Watkins (1979) believes that to protect maternal health during pregnancy, social workers must work for "assurance of provision of adequate standard of living, optimal medical care, nutrition and alleviation of social stress for women of all income levels prior to pregnancy, so these women enter pregnancy in optimal social, emotional and physical health" (p. 9).

EVALUATIONS OF SOCIAL WORK PRENATAL CARE SERVICES

Few studies have examined the effectiveness of social workers in prenatal care settings, despite numerous and continuous calls for evaluation of social work in MCH (Combs-Orme, 1987; Lambert, 1968; Watkins, 1973). It appears that one reason for the neglect of this all-important question lies in the failure of the profession to define the purview of practice in prenatal care adequately, because it is not possible to evaluate the effectiveness of services unless one can operationalize those services. As the foregoing discussion should illustrate, defining and operationalizing practice are indeed formidable tasks. Nonetheless a few studies can be used to measure practice indirectly; most are evaluations of prenatal care in specific Title V programs that include nonmedical services. A few are nonempirical evaluations of nonoperationalized social work services in prenatal settings. In total they may provide only a suggestion that the types of services social workers provide can be important to pregnancy outcome for disadvantaged mothers and infants.

Chabot (1971) used Denver infant mortality rates in an attempt to demonstrate the effectiveness of a comprehensive neighborhood health program that included prenatal services provided by a broad array of professions including social workers, nutritionists, public health nurses, and others. Funded by MIC, Family Planning, the Office of Economic Opportunity Comprehensive Health Care Project, and Public Health Service Comprehensive Community Service grants, the program provided services in numerous locations around the city. Utilization data indicated that low-income participants replaced Emergency Room and hospital use with more appropriate clinic visits. Although infant mortality did decline with increased use of these services, it is important to recognize that other variables probably affected the rates. The city level is generally too small to provide statistically reliable results using infant mortality rates (Kleinman, 1976).

Olds, Henderson, Tatelbaum, and Chamberlin (1986) used a rigorous experimental design to evaluate the effects of home visits by nurses to high-risk pregnant women. Although the authors found no overall treatment effects on birthweight or gestation, several positive program effects suggest the usefulness of the intervention. First, women who received home visits improved their use of other community services and social support (e.g., more fathers were present at delivery) and suffered fewer kidney infections. Second, two especially high-risk groups (adolescents and smokers) showed small but significant improvements in birthweight and gestation, respectively.

Ruff (1985) described but did not evaluate South Carolina's efforts to reduce its high infant mortality rates. On a statewide level all hospitals were reviewed by an outside team, including a social worker, to assess and upgrade comprehensive prenatal services. Social workers contributed "a psychosocial perspective in addressing identified health problems of the MCH population" (p. 14).

Allison (1979) reported a collaborative (social workers, clinical and developmental psychologists, infant development specialists, community health nurses, and physicians) prevention project aimed at expectant mothers with apparent impaired nurturing abilities. The objective of the program was to modify the mothers' nurturing skills to reduce the chances of negative infant-mother interaction early in life, using concrete services, psychotherapy, individually designed infant development plans, and advocacy and consultation with other community agencies. Allison reported that mothers were identified using a maternal nurturing capacity scale developed for the project; no data were presented on the instrument. The key outcome measures of the intervention were the children's cognitive, social, and emotional development during the first 5 years of life. Data were not presented, but at the time Allison reported on the project, 35 infants had been served.

Rudolph and Borker (1987) provide a detailed description of the Central New York Regional Perinatal Program, which began in 1966. As part of the regionalized system, high-risk prenatal patients are referred by private physicians and local maternity clinics to receive intensive prenatal care. Referrals may be made on the basis of medical risk factors (often diabetes, hypertension, repeat cesarean sections, and multiple serious medical problems) or behavioral (such as substance abuse) or social problems (such as very young maternal age or a history of child abuse or neglect). Rudolph and Borker (1987) report that about 60% of the patients are referred for primarily medical reasons, 20% for social risks with medical problems, and about 20% for behavioral problems. Because of a feeling that medical care can do little for most of the social problems observed there, Rudolph and Borker (1987) report with some dismay that efforts were being made to reduce the number of referrals for social problems.

The pattern and type of services received by the prenatal patients of the New York program are dependent on the nature of their problems. All patients are seen by a nutritionist on their first visit, and referrals are made to the WIC program, a nutrition education program, or to a social worker, if poor nutrition is thought to be related to poor living conditions or financial status. The description of services appears to be consistent with the emphasis on medical risk factors. Although Rudolph and Borker (1987) do not formally evaluate the New York program, their data do demonstrate increasingly appropriate use of the regional system through increasing percentages of high-risk births in the regional hospital. Access to high-risk prenatal care for women in remote rural areas remains a problem.

In total the data do not conclusively establish the value of social work or other auxiliary prenatal care services, but neither do they indicate that these services are not effective. Haggerty (1980) reminds us that demonstrated effectiveness may not be the only important criterion in evaluating some programs when he says that

> we must be careful not to be caught in the trap of proving everything by cost-benefit analysis; there are humane aspects of human services that may not be cost-effective, yet should be done. Things like food for the hungry or affection for a lonely child, which have social and humane values, are difficult to quantify, but they are justified for their own sake. (p. 398)

CURRENT AND FUTURE TRENDS

Several current important trends may have a profound impact on practice in the next few years, and social workers' training in both individual and systems approaches places them in the best position to use that training to identify gaps in services and future program needs.

Experts recently have noted an apparent slowdown of the improvement in infant mortality that began a century ago (Wegman, 1987). Such a slowdown apparently occurred briefly in the 1950s, a period much like now in terms of the economy and the widening of the gaps between the poor and nonpoor. In fact, in the last few years the black:white ratios in mortality, LBW, and postneonatal mortality have all increased slightly despite improvements by all groups (e.g., Binkin, Williams, Hogue, & Chen, 1985; Starfield, 1985).

Why might this century's progress in infant mortality be deteriorating? It may relate in part to a reversal of the trend in the 1960s and 1970s of increasing access to and use of medical care by poor and minority women (Davis & Schoen, 1979; Schwarz, 1983). Evidence indicates that increased funding by AFDC and Medicaid, and increased resources authorized by MIC funds related to the war on poverty resulted in increases in women seeking prenatal care, particularly during the crucial first trimester of pregnancy (Davis & Schoen, 1979). Cuts in those same programs since 1981 have reduced access to care by the poor as well as restricted the range of available services under Medicaid (Levitan, 1985).

As access to care is restricted and care becomes more expensive, many have made increasing calls for containing health care costs, especially costs borne by the public. Such calls may further restrict prenatal services for the poor, or they may force a reevaluation of how health care dollars are spent. A rational response could increase the availability of services. The Institute of Medicine (1985) has estimated that for every $1 spent providing prenatal care to low-income women, more than $3 could be saved in caring for these women's prematurely born infants. A commitment to provision of prenatal care to all, regardless of ability to pay, could begin a new decline in infant mortality and could provide a major expansion of obstetric social work in perinatal settings.

At the same time as public care has been restricted, private care has become much more expensive. Lack of health insurance or inadequate coverage of pregnancy services probably deters many women from receiving early and adequate prenatal care; 17% of all women of childbearing age have no health insurance, whereas many others only have partial coverage (Alan Guttmacher Institute, 1987). At the current time no reason exists to expect a reversal in this situation.

Other events foretell problems for mothers and infants. The AIDS epidemic appears to be striking increasing numbers of infant victims who contract the disease in utero from their mothers. (More information on AIDS is located in Chapter 8.)

Recent media concern has focused on infants who are born addicted to heroin, methadone, or cocaine (Langone, 1988). Currently little is known about effective ways of influencing addicted pregnant women to curtail drug use, and few services exist for addicted mothers or their infants. Indeed, a severe shortage of overall services for drug dependence exists. This larger problem must be addressed if its distrastrous effects on MCH are to be mitigated.

Finally, although no figures are available about how many women are homeless, concern exists about the health care needs of these women (Bassuk, Rubin, & Lauriat, 1986). It is likely that pregnant homeless women are at high risk of poor pregnancy outcome. Currently the health care delivery system is not structured for finding pregnant homeless women and delivering the services they require, but as this problem increases it will be necessary to make provisions. Social workers are a logical group to assume leadership in the role of advocating for such services.

3 Care of High-Risk Infants

Birth and early life are safer for mothers and infants than they ever have been in this country. Dangerous complications occur in only a small proportion of births, and perinatal mortality is at an all-time low in this country (Bakketeig et al., 1984). Despite these significant improvements, however, thousands of families still experience complications associated with birth and early infancy, and for these families the crisis has tremendous consequences. Social workers practice in any number of settings where they would have contact with young parents and their newborns, but in two settings they are most likely to play a critical role: NICU and settings providing follow-up care for high risk, low-income infants.

In ancient times sick and premature infants were often destroyed. The beginning of "modern" treatment of premature and malformed infants is probably considered to be the turn of this century, when incubators were developed to maintain such infants' body temperature; however, for many years following this development, "treatment" of premature infants often consisted more of exhibition and experimentation than treatment (Gluck, 1974). Fear of infection also led to strict isolation of infants from everyone, including parents. Better understanding of the epidemiology of neonatal infection, which was found not to be airborn, now allows for more contact between parents and infants in the NICU.

Only since the 1960s has intensive care technology begun to make significant progress in reducing the mortality of extremely premature infants. The success of the technology that has evolved since that time probably lies largely in the improving success with Respiratory Distress Syndrome, the lung ailment due to immaturity that has presented the greatest danger for premature infants, being present in about 10% of all premature infants (Klaus & Fanaroff, 1979). Major contributors to the improvement in survival of very small infants include resuscitation equipment, special radiant warming isolettes, ventilated assistance, gavage feeding, apnea monitors, and laboratory tests for cardiac and respiratory functions (Rudolph & Borker, 1987).

NICU technology constantly improves the treatment of premature infants' other major problems involving temperature regulation, biochemical derangements, blood clotting deficiencies, sepsis and other infections, immature enzyme systems, gastrointestinal and feeding problems, and neuromuscular pathophysiology (Gold, 1982; Klaus & Fanaroff, 1979). Intraventricular hemorrhage, bleeding in the brain due to damage of immature blood vessels, is a major cause of death and disability among premature infants in the NICU (Ichord, 1986a). Intraventricular hemorrhage is graded from I (mild, little chance of permanent brain damage) to IV (life threatening, almost certainty of permanent damage).

In addition to improving survival rates, NICU technology appears to be reducing the morbidity of surviving infants. Despite fears to the contrary, and noting that it is difficult to determine exactly how many NICU graduates suffer ongoing handicaps, it appears that more and more very small infants are being discharged from the NICU to lead normal lives (Rudolph & Borker, 1987). For infants who do have handicaps, many services are now available to assist them to function at their maximum potential. (Follow-up services are discussed later in this chapter.)

Attention to the emotional needs of families with infants in NICU and to the long-term consequences of such care is more recent than the medical technology (Allison, 1979). The director of the first NICU in this country (at Yale) soon realized that the birth of a defective or premature baby constitutes a crisis and said: "This prompted us to seek a social worker who was willing to chart new areas of social service and to begin to establish lines of communication and aid that would help in this almost unbearable family crisis medicine" (Gluck, 1974, p. 73).

Moreover, because NICU care is so sophisticated and costly, it is not available in all hospitals. Coordinated regional perinatal systems generally provide routine care in community and local hospitals, with transfer to regional perinatal systems (which are usually associated with universities) when problems develop or are anticipated. Regional systems are designed to make high-level, quality care available to all, while keeping health care costs as low as possible (Rudolph & Borker, 1987). Regionalization results in additional stresses on families, however, because often their infants are hospitalized many miles from their home (Watkins, 1979). (For an excellent description of the history of regionalization and the organization of one such system, see Rudolph & Borker, 1987).

As NICU technology has improved and spread throughout the country, the needs of families have been recognized increasingly. Klaus and

Kennell (1976) documented that the separation of mother and infant during the NICU stay placed great stress on the family and damaged the formation of the maternal attachment. (This should not be interpreted to mean that most NICU infants are subsequently abused. Most NICU families will have satisfying family relationships.) Most NICUs now have policies designed to minimize the necessary separation of parents and infants, and to encourage the formation of the natural bond or attachment during these early days between parents and infants. (These policies are described in detail in a later section of this chapter.)

Indeed, the NICU family experiences a wide range of extremely stressful emotions in addition to practical day-to-day problems. Guilt is often mentioned as one of the most common emotions, especially in the presence of a congenital malformation or premature labor of unknown etiology. In addition the family must mourn the loss of the perfect baby they planned for (Mahan, Krueger & Schreiner, 1982; Sheridan & Johnson, 1976), even while they often resist getting too close to their tiny infant because they fear his or her imminent death. The physical surroundings of the NICU and the baby (who may be thin, unattractive, extremely fragile looking, and hooked up to numerous intravenous lines and monitors) and the precarious prognosis also induce tremendous anxiety in parents, who may understand little about the technical procedures.

Through all this, the mother most frequently suffers normal postpartum depression exacerbated by the premature delivery and her fear of the loss of her infant. She may also be physically weak from delivery, surgery, or medication. Often she (and perhaps the father, too) are in a location far from the regional center where the infant is hospitalized, so that they cannot even see the baby. The father may feel helpless to aid both his baby and his wife, for whom he may feel he needs to "be strong." The different manners of dealing with their feelings, and the various emotional paces of men and women may result in strain on their marriage at a time when they need each other a great deal. These complex emotions may be transitory for some parents, but lengthy and debilitating for others.

SOCIAL WORK ROLE

Social workers were a part of the NICU team almost from the beginning. When the Yale-New Haven Hospital opened the world's first Newborn Special Care Unit in 1960, social work services were provided on an on-call basis. In 1964 a full-time social worker was assigned to the unit (Breslin, 1974), and since that time many such units have included social work as a basic part of the services provided. The medical director of that unit charged the unit's social workers with their tasks in 1964:

> Families of infants admitted to the Unit also require special care: Design and maintain a program that will enable their needs to be identified, enlist and involve others within the medical team, in hospital or in community to meet these needs. As a teaching hospital we must provide totality of care if we are going to teach what is expected in comprehensive pediatrics. Good service is the basis of good teaching. (Breslin, 1974, p. 78)

Social workers in the NICU generally have approached practice from three perspectives, each of which has a great deal to contribute. These approaches include crisis theory, the long-term family developmental approach of NICU pioneers Klaus and Kennell, and the public health perspective. (These perspectives are discussed in greater detail in Chapter 1.)

Crisis theory (e.g., Dillard, Auerbach, & Showalter, 1980; Hancock, 1976; Mahan et al., 1982; Sheridan & Johnson, 1976; Stevens, 1979) is particularly relevant to social work practice in the NICU because premature delivery is by definition unexpected and presents unavoidable demands with which the person is unable to cope adequately (Caplan, Mason, & Kaplan, 1965). The social worker's task from this perspective would be to help the family respond adequately to the overwhelming demands of the situation, possibly learning new coping skills in the process.

The major tasks of the social worker in the NICU also should take a longer view, however, for as Klaus and Kennell's (1982) work dramatically demonstrates, the family's experience during NICU may have long-term consequences for the quality of parenting and family relationships, and it is possible to have a positive impact on the family's development during this time.

Finally, the public health perspective of the NICU social worker calls for both the traditional one-to-one skills of the social worker and the epidemiologic perspective and broader approach of the public health professional (Miller, 1986). For the NICU public health social worker, this broad approach would entail both working with individual families in dealing with this crisis, and working on behalf of their clients for humane and effective NICU policies at the hospital level and beyond.

Combining these perspectives, the tasks of the NICU social worker perhaps may be categorized most easily in chronologic order from delivery and admission to NICU through discharge and follow-up.

Admission to NICU

The first few hours following delivery and admission of the premature infant to the NICU certainly constitute a crisis period for the family. In some cases the infant has been transported to the NICU from a distant community hospital, and the mother must remain behind. Separation of the family, and the father's conflicts about whether to leave his wife to be with his sick infant may contribute to this stress. At this time the medical team is concentrating on the infant, and the family is the social worker's first priority (Breslin, 1974). Social workers' tasks during these first few hours and days may be categorized as follows.

Provision of Information

It is important that parents understand as much as possible about their infant's condition, the nature of the NICU, and the procedures that will be used to treat their infant. During the initial few days parents may be unable to absorb more than basic information about their baby, however. In many cases, the mother's physical condition will preclude her having a lengthy discussion with the social worker and medical staff, and the father will pass on the information later. Breslin (1974) reported that at the Yale-New Haven Hospital a social worker meets with the father of each infant transferred into the unit to provide an orientation.

A thorough explanation is essential before the parents enter the NICU, however, because the sight of the unit may be a great shock if they are unprepared (Newcomb, 1979). Although the physician may provide this explanation to the parents, the social worker also must have a thorough understanding of NICU procedures and equipment as well as each infant's basic medical problems before speaking with the parents (Breslin, 1974). The NICU also has its own language (Siegel, 1982), and it may be helpful to explain some common terms to the parents.

It is critical that the social worker (and others on the NICU team) be totally honest about the baby's prognosis, while being as optimistic as possible (Noble & Hamilton, 1981). Klaus and Kennell (1982) emphasize that NICU personnel should, in addition to noting the baby's problems, describe what is strong and normal about him or her so that parents have a balanced picture. They also believe that reactions of the staff to the infant at this time make a great impression on the parents; personal attention and kind remarks ("She has such sweet little hands," or "Doesn't he look alert?") may provide hope during this bleak time and may be long remembered. It would be helpful for the social worker to view the baby before meeting with the parents so that he or she can provide this feedback to the parents.

Sosnowitz's (1984) naturalistic observation of two NICUs suggests that NICU staff (including social workers) often are less than honest with parents, controlling the flow of information to parents based on the staff's assessment of the family's emotions. To consent to the medical treatment the staff thought necessary, the parents had to be in control of their emotions, so Sosnowitz maintains that parents who were distraught often were not provided full information. Moreover, staff interacted with parents more extensively when infants had a good prognosis, tending to avoid parents whose infants were expected to die. It is not possible to determine the validity or generalizability of the results of this study, however, because Sosnowitz did not provide an explication of her methods.

Mahan et al. (1982) suggested supplying a list of names and telephone numbers in the unit to the parents, so that they may call when they would like current information. Most units encourage calls (if not visits) anytime, and some provide toll-free numbers for long-distance parents (Siegel, 1982). This will be especially important if the infant must be transported to another hospital and the mother must remain behind, and in cases in which the parents' home is in a different city from the NICU. Breslin (1974) emphasized that a social worker must be available (either on duty or nearby on call) during off hours for parents whose visits and calls must take place during those times, and for emergencies.

Assessment of Parents' Needs

Soon after admission to the unit the social worker begins assessing the parents' abilities to cope with the crisis of NICU (Breslin, 1974; Dillard et al., 1980; Siegel, 1982). Potential areas for assessment include the parents' immediate emotional reactions, their intellectual capacity for understanding the situation, their relationship with each other, their own supportive resources such as extended family and close friends, their financial situation and any anxiety this may present for them, and perhaps their ways of coping with previous crises. The mother's physical condition and any limitations it places on her at this time (e.g., the mother may be taking pain medication following a cesarean section) should be discussed with the physician.

In some cases the social worker will only see NICU parents on referral. Stevens (1979) described factors used for determining those NICU parents who require social services at the Michael Reese Hospital in Chicago. Among the risk factors believed to require intervention by a social worker were poor visiting and telephone contacts, poor infant feeding skills by the parents, excess fear of holding or touching the infant, poor integration of medical information, evidence of drinking by parents when visiting the nursery, displacement of the mothering role on the grandparents, and a history of inadequate prenatal care.

York (1987) has identified a problem that is most appropriately handled by the NICU social worker. She noted that a fundamentalist family whose religious convictions are strong may be prone to deny the seriousness of their infant's condition and may refuse to consult with physicians about treatment decisions. In particular she discussed infants whose prognoses provided no hope for recovery, but whose parents refused to acknowledge the likelihood of death. York provided case examples demonstrating that social workers who are called into such cases early can assess such families' coping. When it is necessary, they can provide the support and respect that can enable these families to deal with their infants' situations more realistically.

No standardized measure exists for assessing the needs and coping skills of NICU families, despite the need for and usefulness of such a measure (Watkins, 1979). Several instruments that were developed for other, more global purposes may be useful. The Family APGAR (Smilkstein, 1978) (described in Chapter 2) is a qualitative measure of family functioning that has been shown to be reliable in a variety of situations. The Parent–Staff Interaction Guide (Cropley & Bloom, 1975) may be useful for identifying families who are not visiting their infants in the NICU, or for indicating situations in which families have inadequate contact with NICU personnel and thus may have questions or concerns that are not being addressed.

The Impact-on-Family Scale (Stein & Riessman, 1980) (described in Chapter 6) measures some of the relevant stresses on NICU families including economic burden, impact on social relations outside the family, impact on relationships within the family, and subjective distress. Because the instrument was designed to measure the impact of chronic illness of a child on the family, however, its focus is on chronic stress rather than the crisis-oriented type of stress experienced by NICU families; however, it may be useful in many cases.

The Family Resource Scale (Dunst & Leet, 1987) (described in Chapter 6) measures the physical and social resources of families with young children, and thus may be useful for identifying families whose lack of resources places them at a particular disadvantage when they have a child in the NICU. In particular, the instrument identifies families with inadequate income, transportation, and time. Again, however, the instrument does not measure some factors that may be relevant to the crisis of neonatal intensive care.

As in any area of social work, assessment should continue throughout the infant's hospitalization (Dillard et al., 1980), because families' coping abilities probably will change over time with shifts in the infants' condition and the families' specific situations.

Promotion of Parental Attachment

Even at this early period the social worker should encourage activities to promote the attachment of the parents with the tiny infant. Kohlstaat (1975) believes the separation of mother and sick infant to be one of the prime foci for social service attention at this time. Despite the necessary separation, several activities are known to be helpful for this purpose. First, it is recommended by all experts that parents visit the infant in the NICU as early and as much as possible. Years ago physicians believed that contact between parents and infant presented a danger of infection, and parents often were not permitted to enter the NICU at all. Now most units allow visitation on the unit 24 hours a day and encourage as much physical contact as the baby's condition permits, including holding the infant as soon as possible, especially before any necessary transfer that may make frequent contact impossible (Noble & Hamilton, 1981).

In some cases parents may be fearful of visiting their infant and may engage in "anticipatory grieving," believing that their infant will not survive. Indeed, anticipatory grieving and withdrawal from the relationship established with the infant during pregnancy is one of the psychological tasks that parents must complete in mastering the NICU crisis (Siegel, 1982). They fear that seeing their infant will only make losing him or her more painful. In these cases the social worker should encourage visitation as soon as the parents can do so, being as optimistic as possible and providing support, perhaps by visiting with the parents the first few times. Klaus and Kennell (1982) also believe that visiting will be helpful to the parents when the infant does not survive, and that their grief will be more difficult to resolve if contact has been minimal.

The social worker also might provide a Polaroid photograph of the infant for the parents, for this helps them to recognize the reality of their child (Dillard et al., 1980). Minton (1983) describes several other advantages of providing a photograph of the infant. First, it is a way of introducing oneself to the parents in a positive way and demonstrating the types of services social workers can provide. Second, the social worker may use it to point out some of the equipment and its uses to prepare the parents for their first visit to the NICU. Third, the photograph may be used by the parents to bond with their infant, as they may gaze at it much like parents usually gaze at their newborns (Robson, 1967). Finally, in the unfortunate event that the infant does not survive, the photograph will provide a tangible memory for the parents that will aid them in their grief.

Social workers may suggest other ways that the parents may feel closer to their NICU infant. If they are able, parents should be encouraged to name their infant as soon as possible. In some cases the mother may be able to breastfeed and should be encouraged to do so (Minde, 1984). The nutritional composition of the milk may be good for the infant, and it will enable the mother to keep lactating until the baby is discharged if she wishes to breastfeed him later. Another valuable asset of providing the breast milk to the infant is that this enables the mother to feel that she is doing something to help her baby recover at a time when she feels helpless.

Even when the baby cannot breastfeed because he is on the respirator or for some other reason, Beth Manning and Susan Eaton of Woman's Hospital in Baton Rouge, Louisiana encourage mothers to pump and freeze the milk to be given to the baby later by gavage feeding. La Leche League provides information, advice, and support to mothers regarding breastfeeding of premature infants (See chapter 6 of Brewster, 1979).

Siefert, Thompson, ten Bensel, and Hunt (1982) urge social workers to be especially cognizant of including the father at every step during this time, as he has been left out of many NICU procedures in the past. Healthy functioning of the family depends not only on the father's developing a relationship with his newly born infant but on his continued, healthy relationship with his wife. Even social workers often have been guilty of failing to consider the needs and potential of the father at this time (Player, 1979). The father often concentrates on the equipment, test results, and other less emotional aspects of the situation at this time. Social workers Beth Manning and Susan Eaton speculate that this may enable them to regain some sense of control of the situation.

Dealing With Other Family Members

In some cases the new mother and father may be confused about what to tell the extended family and their other children about the infant in the early days following delivery. If the prognosis is poor, they may not want to send out announcements and telephone the family to bring such news, and yet they are confused about how to inform others of the birth. Communicating with the extended family, however, provides contact and sets the stage for support from them that the family needs during the crisis. The social worker may assist the family in asking a relative or close friend to notify the extended family and other close friends. Although research in the area is lacking, it is also believed that siblings should be given as much information as they can understand at their ages (Mahan et al., 1982), and the social worker may suggest that the father talk with them as soon as possible. Some families may not be ready to handle this difficult task for a few days.

Long-Term NICU Care

In the first few days following the shock of premature delivery and admission to the NICU, the family may rejoice that the infant continues to survive and may note each passing day as a milestone in the baby's recovery. Soon, though, the emotional stress of daily "ups" and "downs" begins to take its toll, and the tasks for the social worker change with the family's changing needs. An infant may remain in the NICU for many months, and most families will go through many periods of crisis, especially until the prognosis for survival is clearly positive. Social workers Beth Manning and Susan Eaton note a common parental reaction to these daily changes: "If the baby has a good day I have a good day. If the baby has a bad day, so do I" (Manning & Eaton, 1988).

Promotion of Family Bond

Despite 24-hour visitation policies, as time drags on with little progress, it may become difficult both practically and emotionally for parents to continue frequent visits. The practical problems described later may become more serious and present barriers to visitation, and the continued separation may hinder the parents' desire. In addition, it is common for parents to see the NICU staff providing the complex technical care their infants require and to believe that they can never be as competent as the professionals in the unit (Klaus & Kennell, 1982). They may thus begin to feel superfluous on the unit and in their infants' lives.

To provide parents with the competence and confidence that are necessary for them to care for their infants later, many NICUs encourage the parents to assume aspects of the baby's care (e.g. feeding and diapering) as soon as the baby's condition permits (Newcomb, 1979). Such procedures have been found to increase the parents' sense of competence and confidence that they can care for their child on discharge, which are essential to their forming a satisfactory bond and are often central issues for social service (Kohlstaat, 1975). The social worker may be part of the team that teaches parents what to do and helps them to overcome their initial anxiety about caring for their infants.

Exploration of Feelings

Most parents have many irrational beliefs during this time about why the baby was premature ("I shouldn't have played tennis that day") or about his or her future ("He will certainly have brain damage, being so small") (Mahan et al., 1982). In addition, because men and women have been socialized to handle their feelings so differently, this crisis may result in unspoken resentments and strains on the marriage. Klaus and Kennell (1982) note the importance of discussing each parent's beliefs and feelings in joint sessions to be certain that false ideas are corrected, and that each partner understands how the other is feeling. They note, as do Siefert et al. (1982), that the relationship between the mother and father may be the most important factor in the future functioning of the family.

Availability of social support to the family with an infant in the NICU is thought to be critical to the functioning of the family during this stressful time (Benfield, Leib, & Reuter, 1976). Such support is necessary for the parents to move beyond their feelings of anger and grief, and to develop the confidence they need to bond with their infant and to care for him when he is discharged (Rudolph & Borker, 1987). Rudolph and Borker (1987) note that although little consensus exists about a definition of "social support," it is generally thought to include financial assistance, psychosocial counseling, and provision of material and other resources (such as child care assistance or transportation). Such support can be provided through either formal (agencies or institutions) or informal (friends and family) sources.

Rudolph and Borker (1987) found that among the 152 parents they studied, grandmothers, friends, and relatives were most often useful in providing support. Only one third of these families met with other parents to share concerns, whereas nearly two thirds of comparison normal parents shared concerns with other parents. Only about 20% of the NICU families reported having a professional case manager to assist them.

Philipp (1984) hypothesized that social support would facilitate parents' ability to cope with the NICU experience. Her findings supported the hypothesis, indicating that the availability of social supports both during and after hospitalization were related to "parental adjustment." Results of the study must be taken with caution because of severe methodological shortcomings of the study, including a small sample ($N = 24$), the likelihood of chance findings owing to multiple comparisons, the use of retrospective measurement instruments with unknown reliability and validity, and lack of clear definitions of major concepts such as "social support" and "adjustment." Nonetheless the findings are consistent with the widely held belief that the availability of social support is related to the quality of parenting (e.g., Kugler & Hansson, 1988).

Support groups for NICU parents are a resource that social workers have been active in promoting. Some parent support groups provide in-service training for parents as well as emotional support (Siegel, 1982).

Smith (1986) described a parent volunteer group organized and monitored by a social worker but essentially operated as a self-help group for NICU parents. Veteran NICU parents were trained to provide information and support to current NICU parents, with the social worker assessing and screening out those whose problems might interfere with group goals or who might benefit more from individual help. Reactions to the group were positive, but empirical evidence of effectiveness was not presented.

Dealing With Practical Problems

The most pressing problem at this time for many families is often finances. NICU care is tremendously expensive, frequently costing more than $1,000 a day, and sometimes lasting as long as 6 months. The average bill for care of Rudolph and Borker's (1987) sample of NICU infants was more than $26,000. Only families with high incomes or excellent private insurance can pay for such care easily. Some families may need assistance when their private insurance runs out, and many will require help either in attempting to qualify for Medicaid or the Medically Needy Medicaid program, or for services or assistance from the Crippled Children's Program (see Chapter 6) or other local programs. Some parents may benefit from financial counseling for the immediate future and for the child's special needs on discharge (Breslin, 1974). In some cases the social worker is called on to act as an advocate for the family with the hospital to work out a way of paying bills over time (Noble & Hamilton, 1981).

Rudolph and Borker (1987) found that families of NICU infants were more likely ($p < .10$) than families of normal infants to use several sources of assistance following discharge from the hospital. These included public health nurse visits, counseling, Medicaid, state aid, and WIC. Nonetheless, these families' relatively low use of some resources was surprising. For instance, they made little use of homemaker, respite, and day-care services. Similar findings by Rowe, Thomas, and Combs-Orme (1988) demonstrated lower rates of usage of social services than one might expect, given the circumstances and serious problems of low-income NICU families.

Rudolph and Borker (1987) suggest that the restrictions and burdens associated with caring for their infants may prevent these families from seeking additional supports. Another study of Rudolph and Porter's sample (1986) supports such a conclusion. In this study, several variables were entered into a stepwise multiple regression in an attempt to predict use of social services following discharge. The authors' model accounted for 32% of the variance in social service use, and contact with the perinatal social worker during hospitalization was a significant ($p < .01$) predictor. Higher use also was associated with older mothers, receipt of income support before birth, and congenital abnormalities.

Other practical problems include child care (if other children exist) and transportation to permit the parents to visit, especially if the infant is hospitalized for a long period. Because regionalized care means that some parents' homes will be many miles from the NICU, parents may have unusual difficulty in visiting (Rudolph & Borker, 1987; Siegel, 1982), and the parents may have problems getting time off from work to visit their infant. Siefert et al. (1982) emphasized the advocacy function of the social worker in obtaining community resources for the family such as transportation, housing close to the hospital, and assistance to allow the father paid leave from work. (The latter is an especially difficult task requiring the support and action of the entire profession, because the United States has yet to enact or even recognize the need for a humane maternity-paternity leave policy.) Rudolph and Porter's (1986) findings that contact with the perinatal social worker during hospitalization was a significant predictor of social service use following discharge also suggests that the social worker has a major role in connecting NICU parents to available community resources.

Siegel (1982) described the Family Care Program at Children's Hospital in Denver. Recognizing the particular difficulties for families who are separated by long distances from their infants, this program provides a booklet to all NICU families with information about inexpensive housing and restaurants near the hospital, and about a home near the hospital (established by a national corporation) that provides inexpensive accommodations to families. Families are referred to the March of Dimes and other local resources for extraordinary needs, and the hospital also provides free day care for siblings of NICU babies.

Discharge Planning

Discharge is another crisis period for families, for the homecoming of the infant will necessitate many changes and adjustments in the customary routine of the family (Weinstock, 1986). In addition, many infants may be discharged when they are still less than 5 lb (Combs-Orme et al., 1987), and the family may be anxious about whether they can provide proper care (Stevens, 1979). It is essential that the family be prepared to meet the baby's special needs, but with a minimum of anxiety that would interfere with their relationship with their child (Siegel, 1982).

Rudolph and Borker's (1987) study of 156 families of NICU graduates illustrates the problems in adjustment for these families in the first few months following discharge from the hospital. These parents described considerable nervousness about the proper care of their infants and about the use of special equipment such as monitors. The special feeding problems of premature infants also presented a problem for these parents as well as managing medications and being alert for symptoms of serious problems. Parents noted the restrictions on their lives owing to their infants' special needs and fears about the future as being stressful as well.

The social worker and the entire NICU staff should work from the beginning to prepare the family for discharge, because appropriate planning can assure that the family is ready to care for their child. Primarily, parents need education in any special tasks and procedures their child will need, such as an apnea monitor or ventilator assistance (Mahan et al., 1982). As discussed earlier, many units encourage parents to assume aspects of their infant's care as it becomes possible; some even have a mother "live in" during the last few days and assume child care completely while staff is present to answer questions and provide backup if needed (Klaus & Kennell, 1982).

Parents also require education during this time about their child's likely developmental course. Healthy NICU graduates who have suffered no major brain insult (e.g., resulting from intraventricular hemorrhage) will generally follow the same course of development as other children, although milestones may occur somewhat later—usually by about the amount of time they were premature (Ichord, 1986b). Less certainty exists about the course of development when significant brain damage has occurred. Parents who are informed about their particular child's likely course of development will be less likely to worry unduly and can help by watching for and reinforcing appropriate skills.

Other aspects of discharge planning may include making referrals to community and hospital (such as high-risk follow-up programs) resources that are needed (such as infant stimulation programs or home visits by public health nurses), and applying for any assistance that may be needed (such as Medicaid or WIC) (Rudolph & Borker, 1987). New York state law requires that public health nurses visit NICU infants' homes before discharge to assess the families' capability for caring for such high-risk infants (Rudolph & Borker, 1987). Coordinating the often complex follow-up services for high-risk infants is often a function of the social worker (Rudolph & Borker, 1987).

A home visit is often suggested to ensure that the infant will have adequate physical surroundings (heat, furniture, etc.). The social worker should be sure that the parents have an infant car seat to be used from the beginning (Rivara, 1985); many hospitals can provide an infant car seat free or at low cost. The seat, special medications, and some other items such as bottles and nipples, formula, and so forth may need to be purchased in special small sizes or strengths for the premature infant (George & Ahmann, 1986). Parents may be unprepared for their infants' discharge because of his or her unanticipated early delivery (Sheridan & Johnson, 1976).

In some cases a home visit or discussion with a parent may alert the social worker to potential danger to the child. For example, the home may be inadequate for the child's needs or physically unsafe, or parents may be seriously abusing drugs or alcohol to the extent that the social worker believes they will be unable to care for the child properly. Although such a situation presents a dilemma regarding confidentiality for the social worker, certainly the needs of the child would dictate a report to Child Protection in such cases (White, 1985).

Throughout hospitalization and at discharge the social worker should be especially alert for indications of lack of parental interest in continued follow-up because this may indicate either potential parenting problems (such as abuse or neglect), or misunderstanding about the necessity for continued follow-up for the baby. Although it is far from conclusive, some evidence suggests that NICU "graduates" are at increased risk of abuse and neglect (Searight & Handal, 1986) because the separation of parents and infant that occurs with NICU damages the parental bond, especially among families with unusual stress. Sheridan and Johnson (1976) cautioned that parents who have visited infrequently may be at increased risk of abuse or neglect, and should be assessed especially carefully.

It is important to remember, however, that the evidence linking abuse and separation owing to NICU is far from conclusive and may be due in part to the fact that low SES is associated both with prematurity (and thus NICU care), and with reported child abuse and neglect. Most parents whose infants are in the NICU will be competent, caring parents, although they require additional support in the beginning.

Other preparation may include discussions with siblings and other family members about the baby's homecoming and any special arrangements that may need to be made. Siblings should understand any special needs the baby will have and the part they will have to play in welcoming the baby home. The social worker also should remind the parents of the importance of spending adequate special time with their other children after the baby comes home, as the tendency may be to neglect them in favor of the seemingly fragile and especially needy infant. Such neglect could be harmful to the parents' relationships with their other children as well as to their children's sibling relationships.

Follow-up Care for High-Risk Clients

It is well known that the NICU graduate is at increased risk for both mortality and morbidity during infancy and perhaps beyond (McCormick, 1985), so specialized care of these infants should not end with discharge from the hospital (Minde, 1984). Specialized, multidisciplinary, follow-up teams for high-risk clients usually include pediatric, nursing, psychology, social work, audiology, and nutrition specialists, with frequent referrals to specialists in neurology, pulmonary disease, and ophthalmology (van Dyck, 1982).

Some follow-up services attempt to follow all high-risk graduates, at least until they are developing normally and enrolled in other primary care settings (e.g., Combs-Orme, Fishbein, Summerville, & Evans, 1988). The Central New York Perinatal Program requests that infants in certain categories be followed—that is, infants born at less than 1,750 g; those who were ventilated; and those with birth asphyxia (Rudolph & Borker, 1987). That program typically sees infants at 4, 8, and 12 months.

Follow-up services, which may continue until the infant is thought to be developing normally, vary with the specific child. Frequently they include treatment of the conditions that are common to NICU survivors including anemia, impaired hearing, retrolental fibroplasia, seizures, heart disease, lung problems, and other difficulties (Hurt, 1984). Other important medical services include screening for developmental delay (which affects about 15% of NICU survivors), vision, neurological, or hearing problems; and immunizations, the timing of which may differ for premature infants (Hurt, 1984).

In addition to the usual tests and examinations performed at "well-baby" appointments, it is common for visits to include evaluation of the family's resources with particular regard to the child's normal and extraordinary needs, the mental and emotional condition of the child and family, and any other factors that might affect the child's development. Research indicates that even in a group of medically high-risk infants, the quality of parenting and the social environment in which the infant grows up are the most important determinants of developmental course, especially in the longer term (Sameroff & Chandler, 1975; Wortis, Cutler, Rue, & Freedman, 1964).

Specialized follow-up clinics for high-risk clients often provide education to parents about their child's likely developmental course, training on how they can best teach and stimulate their infants, and sometimes special educational and activity programs for the children (Healy, Keesee, & Smith, 1985). An understanding of the child's limitations and potential is especially important to the parents of a premature or disabled child, because sometimes the peculiar responses of these children (because of neurological immaturity or damage) may be unfamiliar, possibly leading to withdrawal by the parents and subsequent damage to the relationship with the child.

In some cases younger, less educated, or less motivated parents might have to be prodded or even "threatened" with reports of child neglect to follow the prescribed course of treatment and follow-up for their children (Combs-Orme et al., 1988). In other cases parental reluctance may be due to feelings of inadequacy or depression about producing a less-than-perfect child, or to personal inadequacy of the parent in caring for an especially needy child. The ethics of aggressive follow-up with parents who are unenthusiastic or even hostile to service is a difficult issue, but in most cases the professional's behavior and sensitive communication skills should lead to a more productive cooperation between professional and parent. In all cases it is important to remember that it is to the advantage of both child and family to encourage parents to be independent, competent caregivers (Healy et al., 1985).

The social worker's role on the follow-up team for high-risk clients might include special attention to the parents' ability and motivation to stimulate the child appropriately; the parents' own relationship with each other and whether it is suffering because of any special needs of the child; the social support available to the family; and many of the other same factors considered during the NICU stay. More intensive services, such as "respite care" similar to that provided to parents of handicapped or chronically ill children, might be necessary for the family whose child is disabled, frequently ill, or especially slow in developing. (See Chapter 7 regarding services for children with disabilities.) This is particularly true in the case of children with cerebral palsy or other significant disabilities.

Phillips, Gorman, and Bodenheimer (1981) described a group for mothers and their infants up to 3 years of age who were at risk for any of several reasons. The group was designed to strengthen the mother-infant bond and to provide a health-oriented atmosphere where learning might occur. A social worker and teacher met weekly with four or five mother-infant pairs and used six intervention techniques: (a) providing nurturance for both mothers and infants; (b) supporting both including use of videotapes and praise of appropriate maternal-infant interaction; (c) modeling of appropriate disciplinary and play behavior with the children by the group leaders; (d) teaching alternative behaviors when mothers exhibited inappropriate behavior; (e) helping mothers identify their own problems; and (f) encouraging both mothers and children to request help when they encountered problems. The authors of this study described it as "successful," although they provided no empirical data.

OTHER TASKS OF THE NICU SOCIAL WORKER

Low-Income Families

The practical tasks of the NICU and follow-up social workers on behalf of the high-risk, low-income family have been neglected in the literature; few researchers have addressed in detail the special problems of poor families. This omission is surprising because low-income women are at greater risk of delivering babies who require NICU care and most vulnerable to the tremendous practical problems created by this situation. The poor family faces a tremendous burden in several areas.

First, a family (often a single mother) must qualify either for Medicaid or some other kind of public assistance to pay for NICU care and be prepared for the child's long-term health care needs. If the NICU infant qualifies for Supplemental Security Income because of disability or is an AFDC recipient, Medicaid eligibility is automatically established. In many cases the mother will already be receiving AFDC because she has other children and thus will be qualified for Medicaid when she becomes pregnant. If this baby is her first, however, or if she is married, in many states she will not be qualified for AFDC and Medicaid until the last trimester of pregnancy. (In states that do not have the Medically Needy option of Medicaid, the married woman may not qualify for Medicaid at all, regardless of her income. In other states assistance may be provided through the AFDC–Unborn Child provisions. The social worker must be aware of the eligibility requirements in her state.) Sensitive and competent help in completing the eligibility forms for Medicaid will be required following the trauma of the premature delivery.

Second, low-income families and especially single mothers may have difficulty finding transportation to the hospital during the baby's hospitalization (Rudolph & Borker, 1987). In many NICU units the staff may develop and communicate negative attitudes toward families who do not visit their infants frequently while they are hospitalized (Mahan et al., 1982); yet many low-income families may be unable to visit, especially if their homes are far from the regional center. A prime task for the social worker is assisting the family in obtaining transportation or a place to stay near the hospital (Siefert et al., 1982) and helping other NICU personnel to understand and sympathize with parents' problems in visiting frequently. Telephone communication may provide a means for the family to stay in touch, but it is especially important that the busy NICU staff be sensitive and helpful when communicating with families by telephone.

Third, early discharge may pose special problems for low-income families, especially as new prospective payment plans shorten lengthy of stays. Families may be ill prepared for discharge and for the infants' special needs, including special clothing, frequent transportation to the clinic for follow-up (perhaps necessitating public transportation or an infant car seat), ongoing medication and vitamins, and perhaps special formula. In some states Medicaid coverage includes transportation assistance to medical appointments (George & Ahmann, 1986). In other cases, social workers may help low-income families contact the Red Cross or another local program for such transportation. Although all infants need safe and comfortable housing with adequate heat, furniture, and food preparation facilities, these needs are especially critical for the tiny NICU graduate.

Other discharge needs may be especially overwhelming for the poor family, especially the young unmarried mother or the uneducated family. NICU graduates often require special care or may be discharged on special equipment such as apnea monitors or ventilators. It is critical that the parents fully understand and feel confident about their abilities to meet their infants' needs. The social worker is an important member of the team who must teach the parent and instill in him or her the confidence required to care for the tiny fragile infant including special procedures and the use of special equipment. Follow-up may provide needed support in the first few days and weeks following discharge.

Consultation and Advocacy

In many cases social workers may need to explain and interpret clients' problems to physicians and nurses on the NICU who are unaware of their problems (e.g., why they do not visit, why they appear to be hostile, etc.) (White, 1985). In this sense, consultation is undistinguishable from case advocacy and may result in more humane hospital policies concerning visitation, provision of information, and so forth.

The opposite is also true: The social worker often must explain to the parents why the NICU staff seem brisk or unconcerned, may have little time to talk, or do not explain their procedures more thoroughly. Social workers are the most logical links between parents and staff because of their training in dealing with clients and other professionals and the frequency with which a family may form a personal relationship with the social worker (White, 1985).

Advocacy also may take the NICU social worker outside the hospital. NICU social workers frequently may be called on to act as the advocates of individual clients with the public assistance system, and deal with discrimination and insensitivity, unclear or inconsistent regulations, and other barriers to services. Effective referral often will involve not just giving a client a telephone number, but making a personal contact or follow-up to facilitate the referral. For such actions to be effective, practitioners must be well acquainted with the system, which changes constantly.

NICU social workers also often also must act on a broader level on behalf of their clients as mandated by the ethics of the National Association of Social Workers and the National Association of Perinatal Social Workers. For example, Siefert et al. (1982) urged social workers to work for paid paternal employment leave so that fathers could be close to their sick infants. Watkins (1980) surveyed perinatal social workers in eight states, however, and found that social workers claimed to engage in little advocacy designed to change welfare policies for their clients, although they did report working with Departments of Public Welfare on behalf of individual clients.

Program Planning and Administration

Many aspects of NICU care could benefit from the values and skills of social workers, particularly the planning of humane NICU policies, and needs assessments of target populations for NICU. Social workers are particularly needed to examine the emotional and social needs of high-risk, target populations; assess effects of NICU services on families; and make recommendations and assist in planning programs for any needed changes. For example, an assessment of low-income families of infants in a regional NICU showed that most families either lived some distance from the hospital or did not have adequate resources to visit their infants frequently (Rowe et al., 1988). If service providers are interested in promoting a healthy relationship between NICU infants and their families, transportation assistance might be provided for such families.

Social workers were leaders in the planning of South Carolina's Perinatal Program, including selection of districts to receive funding, needs assessments, formulation of evaluation tools, personnel decisions, and budgeting procedures (Player & Oviatt, 1976). The state-level social worker also provided consultation to small, local projects that could not afford social work staff. Other states also have modern humane perinatal systems in part because of the influence of social workers.

One important part of planning in the regionalized system is communication between social workers in the regional NICU and those in community hospitals (Hall, 1979; Watkins, 1979). This linkage is useful for the mother who must remain in the community hospital where she gave birth (because of surgery or illness) while the baby is transferred, and in cases in which the infant will be transported back after his or her condition improves. The communication linkage can prepare the regional NICU social worker, especially when the social worker needs to make immediate contact on arrival of the infant. A site visit by NICU social workers to community hospitals might be useful to educate social workers there about the special needs of high-risk families, who may be seen less frequently in these hospitals (Hall, 1979).

Evaluation

Calls for evaluative research to document the outcomes of service can be heard in every area of the profession including perinatal social work. Process evaluation or evaluative research is not rare, and such research is important; however, the profession also must begin to document the outcomes of services. This is especially true for services that are well established, as social work services are becoming on NICU units. NICU care is extremely costly. As hospitals become increasingly concerned about costs, it will be incumbent on social workers to demonstrate that the cost of social work in the NICU is justified. The future of social work in the NICU cannot be secure in the absence of such documentation.

No less important is the fact that research evidence will provide the guidance that is needed for the further development and refinement of practice. Past experience has taught that NICU technology is constantly changing and improving, and the practice of social work on the NICU must do likewise.

4 Infant Death

No other tragedy is so overwhelming for parents as the death of a child. Nothing else seems quite so unfair, so against the "natural order" of things. It is a tragedy that changes the entire lives of parents, siblings, and grandparents. It leaves professionals feeling helpless to bring comfort, and struggling with their own grief and guilt. In many important ways it does not matter how a child is lost—through miscarriage, still-birth, after a time in the NICU, owing to SIDS, or even before conception—it is an overwhelming tragedy.

The American College of Obstetricians and Gynecologists and the American Academy of Pediatrics (1983) acknowledge that the emotional impact of these events has probably been underestimated in the past, and recommend that any family that experiences infant death should be offered counseling by a social worker or other staff member. Indeed, although many families have adequate intrafamilial and social supports for weathering nearly any crisis, the loss of a child may be one that almost always warrants outside intervention (Lang & Oppenheimer, 1968).

The role of social workers in birth tragedies grows in part from the inability of medical personnel to deal with families' grief. Generally physicians are not properly trained to assist families with grief and may fear death more than other persons because it represents professional failure (Knapp & Peppers, 1979). Indeed, physicians themselves experience grief and guilt when their infant patients die (Knapp & Peppers, 1979), and their own feelings may make it difficult for them to be helpful to the parents.

Extensive research on death and dying, highlighted by recent interest in Kübler-Ross's (1969) work, suggests that grief brings some predictable events and that intervention can be helpful to grieving individuals.

Application of these intervention methods to families of birth tragedies has been well accepted in social work. Mahan and Schreiner (1981) emphasize the importance of establishing a "protocol of care" for families of birth tragedies—that is, a specific set of established, effective procedures and techniques that can be easily invoked during this stressful time. "This implements the care philosophy . . . in a visible way and can insure consistent sensitivity to the family's reactions" (Mahan & Schreiner, 1981, p. 70). Indeed, social work with grieving families requires sensitivity and skill.

Several factors may influence the grief reactions of families who lose infants, among them the age of the infant. It is probably safe to say, however, that whenever families experience the tragedy, fewer differences than commonalities exist among the experiences of grieving families. In this chapter, issues common to the various types of infant death and the grief experienced by families will be discussed first, along with social workers' roles in helping grieving families. Then issues particularly related to miscarriage, stillbirth, neonatal death, child death by SIDS, and infertility will be discussed, along with specific social work roles and tasks. Finally, issues surrounding the stress suffered by social workers and other staff who work with birth tragedies and infertility will be discussed.

NO GREATER GRIEF

The death of a child is a profound loss to parents. (It is startling that until recently professionals concerned with perinatal loss have felt bound to provide evidence that grieving and mourning are natural and predictable reactions to perinatal loss.) The death of any family member is painful and should not be discounted, but the loss of an infant is particularly difficult for several reasons. First, one expects to outlive a parent and even perhaps a spouse, but one does not expect to bury a child, or an infant in particular. In this sense the death is unexpected and unprepared for generally; it is also usually unexpected in the immediate sense, occurring early in a hoped-for pregnancy, toward the end of an uneventful pregnancy, in the first year of a healthy child's life, or perhaps when a young couple is planning the conception and birth of their first child. Although some disagreement exists on this issue, empirical evidence demonstrates that the intensity of grief experienced by parents who lose children does not differ based on the length of the child's life or gestational period (Kennell, Slyter & Klaus, 1970; Peppers & Knapp, 1980).

In addition to the loss of the child, the death of a child represents the loss of many valuable intangibles for parents: extension of their family, hopes and dreams for the future, their own social roles as parents, even a part of the self (Mahlstedt, 1985; Palmer & Noble, 1986). Borg and Lasker (1981) note that parents are members of a "special club." When the child dies, "suddenly, instead of being members of the club, they stand outside it, pitied and isolated" (p. 14). Moreover, in the past most families were experienced with the death of a child because mortality was so high. With recent decreases in infant mortality, few parents have experienced or even witnessed infant death (Kennell & Trause, 1978). Nor do families and friends know how to react; often their inadequate responses serve to wound the grieving parents further.

Finally, the loss of an infant is particularly poignant because one can find no comfort in the belief that the individual "lived a full life," or enjoyed life to its fullest. The situation seems especially unfair because the child has had no chance to enjoy anything and was "so innocent" of any wrongdoing (Borg & Lasker, 1982).

Although both partners suffer effects of an infant loss, the meaning of the event may be different for the mother and father. The mother's experience is marked by physical reminders; she may have pain and recovery from delivery, and her engorged breasts may remind her of the breastfeeding she planned (Gilson, 1976; Woods, 1987). In the case of infertility she has a monthly menstrual period to remind her of her inability to conceive. She typically feels herself a failure as a woman and mother because she could not conceive or carry a healthy baby to term. Moreover, she may have quit a job or interrupted a career to assume the full-time role of "mother," and she suddenly finds herself with no meaningful role. She may sit alone in a decorated nursery, surrounded by baby shower gifts, wondering what to do. In the case of the death of an older infant (by SIDS, for instance), the mother often has invested a great deal of "emotional energy" in the child because of her greater involvement in child care (Williams & Nikolaisen, 1982) and thus feels particularly lost when she no longer has those child care tasks to perform.

The father may be intensely worried about his wife's health and recovery, perhaps having witnessed a difficult and painful delivery or miscarriage as he feared for his wife's life, or having waited for her through numerous episodes of testing and surgery. He may feel that he must "be strong" for his wife (Gilson, 1976), or that he should hide his grief and be cheerful for her sake (Ewy & Ewy, 1984). It is common for fathers to immerse themselves in the "business" of funeral arrangements or in their work following a death (Klaus & Kennell, 1982; Mandell, McAnulty, & Reece, 1980). The father's grief may be overlooked at this time by persons who show genuine concern for his wife (Ilse, 1982). Even some professionals who profess to be concerned with his problems may see the father primarily as "support" for his wife and not as a parent whose grief is as profound and as intense as the mother's, even if it is expressed differently (e.g., Tadmor, 1986). Indeed, the literature that purports to deal with parents' responses to perinatal death deals in reality almost exclusively with mothers, and often fails to even mention fathers' responses to the loss except in passing (e.g., Kennell et al., 1970).

Neglect of the father's grief may be due to the contention by some that the father's attachment to a fetus or infant is less intense than the mother's because he has not carried the child in utero as she has (Borg & Lasker, 1982), or because the father's attachment is based more on physical proximity following birth than the mother's (Greenberg & Morris, 1974). If this point is true, it is relevant that in some cases of death in the NICU the father may have more contact with the infant than the mother, either because the infant is transferred to a regional perinatal hospital or because the mother is too ill to see the infant. Intense paternal-infant attachments have been noted following such contact (Gilson, 1976). Conversely, the father's attachment also forms during pregnancy as he fantasizes about the baby and makes plans for the future (Borg & Lasker, 1981).

It is common to criticize fathers for grieving in ways that are presumed to be dysfunctional. Little evidence exists that male patterns of grief are problematic, although they do appear to differ from female patterns. Fathers may have more difficulty expressing their grief in socially acceptable ways (C. Rappaport, 1981), may tend to grieve silently (Schreiner, Gresham, & Green, 1979), or may grieve on a different "time-table" than mothers (Renne, 1977; C. H. Shapiro, 1982). In a small ($N = 83$) study of SIDS parents, Williams and Nikolaisen (1982) found fathers to be more "reality-oriented" than mothers regarding their child's death. Mandell et al.'s (1980) study of 28 SIDS fathers found that they experienced diminished self-worth, self-blame for not having been more involved with the infant, and a limited ability to ask for help.

The different experiences of the husband and wife and their frequent inability to talk about those experiences contribute to marital difficulties, which are common following infant death (Ewy & Ewy, 1984; Klaus & Kennell, 1976) and infertility (C. H. Shapiro, 1982). Rando (1985) asserts that bereaved parents have an excessive rate of divorce, although this remains a matter of controversy. Each parent may blame the other, and while seeking consolation from each other they may become angry because they do not get "enough" (Borg & Lasker, 1982). It is generally believed that satisfactory grieving requires good communication between the grieving parents (Kennell et al., 1970; Gilson, 1976).

Siblings also grieve the loss, even if they are quite young. Indeed, the "ideas that arise from a sibling's death may be devastating" (Klaus & Kennell, 1982, p. 276). They may not understand the meaning of death, but can see their parents' reactions and the concerns of others for their parents. Moreover, their reactions may be complicated by separation from the mother during her hospitalization and convalescence, and then her mourning (Price, Carter, Shelton, & Bendell, 1985). If they witnessed the pain and bleeding associated with a miscarriage, they may also fear for her safety (Borg & Lasker, 1981).

Typical concerns of siblings include whether they somehow caused the baby to die (especially if they did not want a baby brother or sister), fears for their own health and safety, and confusion about their parents' actions. Siblings also may interpret their parents' emotional distance as rejection (Gilson, 1976).

Grandparents (and other extended family members) also suffer from the loss of an infant (Matthews, 1987). In addition to the loss of their grandchild, they lose their expected roles as grandparents (or aunts, uncles, etc.), and they also suffer for the grieving parents (Borg & Lasker, 1981). For example, they make plans and talk about the expected baby with their friends (Ewy & Ewy, 1984). Grandparents also may feel guilty, particularly if genetic problems contributed to the infant's death. Social worker Dan Timmel of the Maryland SIDS Project has called grandparents the "forgotten grievers."

The grief literature, as well as references specific to infant loss, generally describe the grief process in several stages, although it is important to note that individuals do not all proceed through these "stages" in an orderly fashion as the word might imply. They may go back and forth among the various states, and the length of time any individual experiences these phenomena varies greatly. Variations should *not* be interpreted as pathological.

Immediate Grief Reactions

The first stage of grief, which generally lasts a few hours up to a few days, is marked by shock and emotional numbness (Borg & Lasker, 1985). It is generally believed that this stage, which is characterized by a physiological slowdown of the body, is a protection mechanism that enables an individual to gather resources before dealing with the reality of the death (Borg & Lasker, 1982). Sometimes the denial associated with this period is so total that it may appear that the parents are "taking it well" or that the event is not that significant to the parents, but this denial will usually abate within a short time.

The mother's adjustment in the early days following an infant death may be complicated by her physical condition, particularly if she is on medication (Gilson, 1976). Although in the past the mother was often heavily sedated, it is generally recognized now that unnecessary medication should be withheld to facilitate normal grieving (Klaus & Kennell, 1982; Tadmor, 1986). Kennell and Trause (1978) recommend withholding tranquilizers, with the exception of a sedative solely at bedtime when needed.

Single and adolescent mothers are especially vulnerable during this period of grief. In particular, Hawkins (1980) notes that their immaturity, guilt, inadequate financial resources, and poor health may accentuate their grief. In addition, they may have inadequate emotional supports and may have been ambivalent about the pregnancy (Mahan & Schreiner, 1981), thereby increasing their feelings of guilt. Gilson (1976) suggests that the single mother's own mother may be an important resource.

Disorganization and confusion may follow shock (Tadmor, 1987). Simos (1987) notes that grief makes the bereaved appear disturbed, and indeed it is common for parents to exhibit bizarre behavior following the shock of an infant loss. The social worker must be knowledgeable about the grief process to avoid making a misdiagnosis that may cause further pain and lead to increased fears of the grieving parent that he or she is "going crazy." Moreover, parents often cannot make decisions competently or may not think to ask for what they would like (Borg & Lasker, 1981). They also may not hear all the pertinent information that is given to them because they are so overwhelmed (Klaus & Kennell, 1982); therefore, information may need to be conveyed again at a later time (C. Rappaport, 1981).

Social Work Tasks

The major tasks of the social worker during the time immediately following the birth tragedy are both practical and supportive. First, the social worker should be present when the physician informs parents of the death, especially if the social worker and family have formed a relationship during hospitalization (Mahan & Schreiner, 1981). The parents should be together when they are informed of their infant's death (Knapp & Peppers, 1979; Mahan & Schreiner, 1981), but if this is not possible (perhaps because the infant was moved to another hospital and the mother remained in the hospital of birth), additional staff known to the family and friends should be called on to be with them when they are told.

In the practical arena, numerous arrangements must be made following a death, and the social worker may assist families in dealing with these arrangements (Mahan & Schreiner, 1981). Arrangements must be made to complete birth and death certificates (depending on state laws and practices), and to arrange for burial of the infant, as well as any memorial service. Some families wish to make arrangements for themselves and may find these tasks helpful ways of taking control of a situation that is out of control. Other families are overwhelmed and need a good deal of assistance at this time.

In many cases of miscarriage and stillbirth, the hospital frequently offers to "take care of things" or in unfortunate terminology, to "dispose of the remains." Ilse (1982) suggests that parents should not rush the decision about burial but should wait until they can think more clearly. When they do, most parents would prefer to make their own arrangements for burial and funeral services (Stringham, Riley, & Ross, 1982; Tadmor, 1986). Social worker Dan Timmel advises that all families should be protected from staff, family, or friends trying to impose decisions on them at this time about important matters that may have lifelong implications for them (e.g., not having a funeral).

Indeed, it may be wise to discourage the parents from making important or irreversible decisions at once (Borg & Lasker, 1981), such as a decision to cremate their infant or to forego an autopsy. Most such decisions can wait a few hours or even days (Ilse, 1982), but the social worker may need to act as the parents' advocate with medical staff, who may be anxious to complete those arrangements. In many cases, for example, physicians request permission to perform an autopsy to determine the cause of death. Some families will welcome the opportunity to obtain added information, but others may find the idea repugnant ("he has suffered enough") or against their religious or ethical beliefs (C. Rapport, 1981). Many others need a few days to decide.

The social worker's responsibility is to be sure that the family understands the options (Mahan & Schreiner, 1981), perhaps including an explanation of the autopsy procedures to the family in as humane a way as possible. The social worker should volunteer her services as soon possible to spare the family anxiety and discomfort about asking (Borg & Lasker, 1981). If they understand the procedure and its importance in providing information about why their baby died, most families will consent to autopsy, especially if they are approached properly and not too soon following the death (Woods, 1987). Some families may object based on religious convictions or other reasons, however. It is the social worker's role to support the family members in their decision about the autopsy, whether or not the medical staff is in agreement (C. Rappaport, 1981).

Dan Timmel encourages social workers to overcome personal reactions to graphic discussion about the autopsy and become informed about the subject. Discussions may include the family's concerns about the types of incisions that are made, how much they show, and whether an autopsy will delay the funeral (Mahan & Schreiner, 1981). Families also are concerned about whether the autopsy will disfigure their child as well as what kind of information might be obtained by the procedure (Woods, 1987). Social workers should understand the value of the autopsy as potentially assisting families in their final understanding of the cause of death and should not feel apologetic for dealing with this topic. Similarly, parents should not be shielded from considering organ donation, because many have later expressed feelings that such a donation would have provided some meaning to the death.

Because parents' energy is low at this time, they may need to be encouraged by the hospital staff to discuss the death with their children (Mahan & Schreiner, 1981), and they also may benefit from advice on how to handle the situation (C. Rappaport, 1981). It is now generally held that young children should receive as much information about a sibling's death as is appropriate for their age (National Institute of Mental Health, 1979; Tadmor, 1986), but clearly this is an extremely painful task for the parents.

In general, children should be told directly and gently that their sibling has died, using the word "death" rather than confusing euphemisms. They should be told what the cause of death was (in simple terms they can understand), and that no one is to blame. They should also be told that it is normal and expected that everyone will feel bad about this loss for a while, that "Mommy and Daddy might cry and be sad for a time," and that their sister's or brother's death does not mean that anyone else in the family also will die soon. Dan Timmel finds it helpful to have a trusted adult to help with the siblings while the parents are preoccupied.

Children do mourn, and their grief, guilt, and anxiety should be acknowledged by the parents; they should be reassured specifically that neither they nor anyone else "caused" the baby to die (Borg & Lasker, 1981; C. Rappaport, 1981). For many children it may be beneficial to attend the funeral or to be part of some family ritual, depending on their age (C. Rappaport, 1981). Few children have difficulties with funerals or viewings of the body, but they should never be forced to attend. In any case, it is neither desirable nor possible to "protect" a child from the pain of losing a sibling. For example, the practice of sending children away to stay with relatives until the parents feel better able to cope should be avoided (Borg & Lasker, 1981; National Institute of Mental Health, 1979).

The entire family grieves, and grieving together can be a source of comfort to every family member.

It might be useful for social workers to provide written material that parents can refer to as often as necessary. The National Institute of Mental Health publishes a booklet entitled *Talking to Children About Death*,* which is part of their Caring About Kids series (National Institute of Mental Health, 1979). Borg and Lasker's (1981) chapter on the needs of the other children also is particularly good. Most public libraries also have books to read to children that explain death and grief, and these books may be helpful to families.

Grandparents may be helpful in comforting both their other grandchildren (Borg & Lasker, 1981) and the grieving parents (Borg & Lasker, 1981; Kennell & Trause, 1978; Mahan & Schreiner, 1981), if they are handling their own distress. Indeed, a major role for the social worker at this time is not trying to meet all of the parents' needs for support but rather assisting them in mobilizing their natural supports for that purpose. For instance, a social worker may call friends, family, or clergy to inform them that the infant has died and the family requires assistance.

Other important practical tasks may include dealing with the hospital's discharge or accounting office regarding bills and other official business. In many cities a local funeral director provides low-cost infant funerals and burials (Stringham et al., 1982). The social worker should be able to refer families to such resources and to assist them in making arrangements for the burial. In fact, because of his or her contact with the family at a particularly crucial time and because of his role at this time, the funeral director can be a valuable member of the team with whom the social worker should work on behalf of the family (Troyer, 1987).

The literature recounts several important ways that social workers can facilitate the family's grief. First, it is important to provide information about grief and what parents are likely to experience in the first few days (C. Rappaport, 1981). Such information may assure parents that their grief is normal (they are not "going crazy"), and that it is time limited. Parents should be prepared specifically for some strange, but completely normal, symptoms that may occur, such as imagining the baby's crying in another room or feeling its kicks (Kirkley-Best & Kellner, 1982; Mahan & Schreiner, 1981). Weinberg's (1985) study of 155 persons who had recently experienced the death of a close family member found one of the

---

*Single free copies may be obtained by writing to the agency at 5600 Fishers Lane, Rockville, MD 20857. The publication may be duplicated freely as there is no copyright.

most helpful functions performed by social workers was reassurance of the normality of grief.

The literature documents the importance of allowing each parent to mourn in his or her own way. It is well documented that men and women express grief differently (see earlier), and the social worker should not attempt to convince the parents to mourn according to a preconceived agenda. This will involve listening sympathetically and assuring the parents that they are free to express themselves. Encouraging them to talk with each other is helpful, but it should not be forced. Ewy and Ewy (1984) suggest telling parents that neither can do some things for the other, but that just talking about the baby is therapeutic in itself. Mahan and Schreiner (1981) state: "The importance of fostering good communication between parents cannot be overemphasized" (p. 71).

Opportunity to Say Good-Bye

Although it is unclear when it should be done, several experienced practitioners (Klaus & Kennell, 1982; Mahan & Schreiner, 1981) encourage parents to see and hold their baby to say good-bye, believing that this practice helps parents to recognize the reality of the death and thus to mourn (Kirkley-Best & Kellner, 1982). In the past it was feared that holding their dead child would be too upsetting for parents or the medical staff (Klaus & Kennell, 1982), but it is now standard practice in most hospitals to offer parents this opportunity.

Several suggestions have been made to make the experience of holding their dead infant a less difficult one for the parents. First, parents can be prepared for the experience of holding the body and specifically for any deformities the child had (Gilson, 1976). For instance, they might be told about the temperature and texture of the infant's skin. Some parents will be frightened of seeing the infant, especially if the child had deformities, so preparation is important to making the visit a comforting one. Gilson (1976) reports that even when deformities exist, parents usually concentrate on their child's positive qualities and tend to remember those in the future.

Second, experts advise that the family be offered a quiet, private place for as long as they wish to remain with the infant (Stringham et al., 1982). The social worker (or other professional) should offer either to remain with the parents or to leave them alone. Klaus and Kennell (1982) recommend that as many family members as possible should see the dead infant to facilitate discussing and sharing memories and feelings about the baby that are important to the grief process. Similarly, Matthews (1987) recommends that older siblings see their dead brother and sister so that they may share in the family's grieving. These authors note the rapidity with which all evidence of a stillborn baby is removed following birth and the difficulty this may present for grieving parents as they strive to believe that the child was real.

Finally, how the staff treats the infant is important to the parents' experience of holding their dead child. Certainly the body should be treated gently (Woods, 1987; Zahourek & Jensen, 1973) and with dignity, perhaps wrapping the baby in a colorful blanket. Mahan and Schreiner (1981) and Woods (1987) suggest emphasizing the normal aspects of the child to the parents, calling the baby by name in the process.

When parents decline the opportunity to see their child, it is the practice in some hospitals to make the offer again later that day or the following day, when they may have changed their minds (Tadmor, 1986). Batterman (1985) interviewed a father who still regretted not having seen his stillborn infant many years before, and Kennell and Trause (1978) have spoken with many parents of infants who died perinatally who regretted never having had contact with them. Stringham et al.'s (1982) study of 20 mothers who had experienced stillbirth found that 11 mothers could not remember being offered the option of seeing their dead infants. Of the six who did see their babies, none had regrets except that they did not spend more time with their infants.

If parents still do not wish to see the infant, many social workers and other professionals take photographs to be kept in the file in case the parents later express the desire to see them (Borg & Lasker, 1981). A photograph may be the only memento a family has of their child and may facilitate satisfactory resolution of their grief in the future (Minton, 1983). When a photograph is taken, Woods (1987) recommends that it be taken with the baby in a blanket, in as normal and lifelike a position as possible. (For example, any deformities should be hidden or de-emphasized in the photograph.)

Other important supportive tasks include encouraging parents to have a funeral or memorial service (Kennell & Trause, 1978; Mahan & Schreiner, 1981), and to bury the infant rather than allowing the hospital to "dispose of the remains" as they frequently offer. The burial spot serves as an important place where the family can go together in the future to recount their memories (Kennell & Trause, 1978). When the family does choose to have the hospital take care of the body, the physician (or social worker) should find out the location of the burial spot. This information should be included in the file in case the parents inquire later (Matthews, 1987).

Social workers also may help parents by encouraging them to name the baby if they have not done so before his or her death (C. Rappaport, 1981; Stringham et al., 1982). Even in cases of an early miscarriage, naming the child provides the family with indications that the child and his or her death were real, and enables them to reminisce about and mourn for a real child (Kennell & Trause, 1978).

Middle Stages of Grief

As denial is overcome and the family is confronted with the reality of their child's death, overwhelming sadness, despair (Zahourek & Jensen, 1973), anger and guilt usually occur, perhaps intermittently (C. Rappaport, 1981). Parents also may become preoccupied with determining why their infant died. Somatic complaints also are common during the months following loss, such as sighing, weeping, shortness of breath, insomnia, or loss of appetite (C. Rappaport, 1981). These symptoms may be frightening to the parents, who should be assured immediately of their normality in this situation (Weinberg, 1985). Because the symptoms of grief are similar to depression at this time, in the past they were often considered evidence of a pathological reaction to loss.

Some describe a "search" for or idealization of the deceased as part of the middle stages of grief (Kirkley-Best & Kellner, 1982). This may involve visiting the hospital nursery or looking in crowds for infants that resemble the dead infant. Idealization frequently involves going over details of the infant's appearance and personality. Repeated reminiscing about the infant is common and may be upsetting to others around the parents, but it is quite normal. Parents who did not see their infant and who do not have a picture or other memorabilia may have particular difficulty with this phase (Kirkley-Best & Kellner, 1982).

As families acknowledge that their infant has died, anger is common—at themselves, their partner, friends with healthy children, God, and even the baby for "not being stronger." Anger at the doctor, nurse, hospital, and the social worker is also common (Klaus & Kennell, 1982). Borg and Lasker (1982) note that men express the anger before women do, as they are more accustomed to expressing this emotion than many others. Although anger is a normal part of grief, in some cases objective, justifiable reasons will also exist for parents' anger, such as when they are treated insensitively or when their infants' care is not adequate (Borg & Lasker, 1981). Although their anger should always be understood and accepted as a normal part of grieving, such objective reasons for anger also should be considered and responded to with respect.

Running throughout the process of grief, sometimes most predominantly following anger, is the parents' search for information. Why did the baby die? Could anything else have been done? How can this be prevented in future pregnancies? Pathology or autopsy results can help allay parents' guilt, but results often require a lengthy wait. Any information that is obtained should be communicated to the parents promptly by the physician or someone who is able to help them interpret the findings (Gilson, 1979). The search for information may appear to be an obsession, but it is a normal part of grieving. "The very effort of trying to make sense of the event, to find a meaning in disaster, can strengthen the bereaved parents" (Borg & Lasker, 1982, p. 25).

Guilt

An almost universal experience for parents whose infants die is guilt. They question whether they did something that caused the tragedy, especially if they were ambivalent about the pregnancy in the beginning. Most parents review everything they did before the death happened, perhaps focusing on the glass of wine at a party, an aerobics class, sexual relations, a delay between the onset of symptoms and seeking medical treatment, or failure to check on the infant during the night (Borg & Lasker, 1982). Physicians emphasize, however, that in most cases parents' actions are unrelated to the miscarriage, premature labor, or even SIDS, and that once symptoms appear, it is almost never possible to stop them. Guilt may be especially intense if the child died of an illness, because the parents agonize about not having sought medical attention sooner. This may be true even if the parents sought medical treatment immediately (C. Rappaport, 1981).

In some cases the parents' guilt is intensified because they have involuntarily elected abortion of a wanted child. Involuntary abortion may occur either when the mother develops a serious medical condition that threatens her life if the pregnancy continues, or when prenatal genetic testing indicates a serious deformity in the fetus that suggests the need for abortion. In either case the emotional consequences of the loss are similar to those that occur with a spontaneous abortion, but the parents also must deal with the guilt brought on by the act of selecting or consenting to abortion (Borg & Lasker, 1981). The guilt may be exacerbated by isolation if the couple feel that they cannot discuss the abortion with family and friends (Hager, 1987).

The involuntary abortion often occurs following the diagnosis of abnormalities by amniocentesis. Because the procedure cannot be done until the second trimester and results require some time, the abortion may not occur until after quickening or after the parents have seen the fetus on ultrasound imaging, events that may have strengthened the developing attachment to the child. Waiting for the results of the amniocentesis (which take 2 to 3 weeks), and then if the results indicate a problem, deciding whether to have an abortion are stressful for parents

(Borg & Lasker, 1981). In these cases the parents' grief is exacerbated by guilt because the abortion was chosen rather than spontaneous. In addition, others may question the parents' decision and may make comments that exacerbate the parents' feelings. Even hospital staff may give the impression of not approving of the family's decision by avoiding the woman during her hospitalization for the procedure.

Social Work Tasks

Again, social workers may help parents during this period in both supportive and practical ways. Supportive tasks include first the recognition that the infant's death is a terrible loss, regardless of whether it occurred early in pregnancy, at birth, or several months later (Borg & Lasker, 1981). Families have dreamed and planned for the child. The mother has grown to know him through her pregnancy, and the father perhaps through touching her abdomen and making plans for the baby. The social worker should offer a forum that validates the family's feelings and allows their full expression. Others, including friends and family, may avoid the subject or make insensitive remarks ("It's all for the best," being the commonest), so the family will need support that validates their grief. In his work with the Maryland SIDS Project, Dan Timmel emphasizes the important role of the social worker in these situations:

> The social worker may be the only person in the family's environment sending the clear message that she will hear the most 'inappropriate' rage, the 'pettiest' details, the obsessions and nagging questions like what happens to the body in the grave.

In addition to allowing the family to express their feelings, the social worker's making appropriate comments is also important during this time. Social workers should openly express their grief and sympathy (C. Rappaport, 1981), using the infant's name when it is known (Schreiner et al., 1979), avoiding platitudes or "easy" comments such as "It was probably for the best because she would not have had an easy life." Caregivers' reactions are extremely important to parents in this situation, as they may act as role models for the expression of grief (Tadmor, 1986). Moreover, what they say to parents about the baby may become one of the few memories the parents have of their child's short life (Stringham et al., 1982).

It is not uncommon for professionals to be uncomfortable about talking about death (Palmer & Noble, 1986). In addition, sympathetic social workers may find the intensity of parents' grief to be almost overwhelming at times, and it may remind them of their own losses or cause them to fear such losses. Nonetheless it is critical for the social worker to allow the parents adequate time to grieve and to do so in their own way (Simos, 1987).

Because isolation is one of the most difficult aspects of parents' grieving for an infant, social workers should emphasize to the parents the possible benefits of sharing with each other and with other family members and close friends how they feel during this time (Klaus & Kennell, 1982). As discussed earlier, many couples have difficulty communicating with each other as well as with others. It may be helpful to encourage them to talk about their feelings and to reassure them it is normal to want to do so. Conversely, some individuals may grieve in a more introverted way, and little evidence exists that such a style is pathological. In some cases when one parent feels a greater need to talk than the other, it may be helpful to refer that parent to a support group.

It may be particularly helpful to assist the family in anticipating and dealing with the reactions of others, who may make insensitive comments in an effort to comfort the parents (Klaus & Kennell, 1982). Conversely, friends or family may sometimes avoid the topic altogether in an effort to "spare" the parents (Borg & Lasker, 1981).

In some cases social workers may be especially effective in the role of bringing comfort to the family by linking them with community and self-help resources, such as support groups of parents (e.g., Compassionate Friends, Support for Prenatal Decision, or Parents Experiencing Neonatal Death*) who have experienced similar losses. Videka-Sherman (1982) found involvement in Compassionate Friends to facilitate adjustment for some bereaved parents. Her study of 194 parents who had lost a child within the previous 18 months revealed that helping other bereaved parents and assuming a new role (e.g., taking a new job) were correlated with lower depression. She pointed out that effective coping skills may predict involvement in a self-help group in addition to such involvement facilitating effective coping.

The social worker may have to organize such a group in her community if it does not already exist and should be aware of all such resources in the surrounding area. This may be difficult if she works in a regional perinatal center that covers a wide area, but it is important to be informed and to make contact with these groups.

The delivery of information of various types is the most important practical task at this time. It is important that the family be given all medical information that is available as it becomes available (Gilson, 1976) in terminology that they can understand. Families may ask the

---

*Compassionate Friends can be contacted at P.O. Box 3247, Hialeah, FL 33013. Support for Prenatal Decision, a self-help group for parents undergoing involuntary selective abortion, may be contacted at P.O. Box 1745, San Pedro, CA 90733.

same questions and receive the same answers repeatedly, but social workers should recognize that grieving families often do not hear the answers and must receive the same information again to understand it (Hawkins, 1980). Sosnowitz (1984) explains that NICU staff often provide little information to parents because they are busy. Moreover, staff are under a great deal of emotional stress because of the constant crises on the unit and may lack sufficient emotional energy for dealing with parents.

Some families have noted great difficulty in obtaining autopsy and pathology reports (Stringham et al., 1982). In some cases the social worker may act as an advocate by obtaining the autopsy results for parents. In other cases, when families do not actively seek the autopsy results, they should be invited to discuss them as part of the follow-up services (Tadmor, 1986). (Follow-up services are discussed later.)

It may be useful for the social worker to meet with the parents and the physician regarding the possibilities of future successful pregnancies. Certainly this task is more difficult when multiple miscarriages have occurred or when the prognosis is poor for future pregnancies. The social worker should meet with the physician in advance to be sure that she understands the material before the family is present. At some point, families may want to discuss other options, such as adoption or reproductive technology. The social worker should know the basic facts and have sources for referral on more detailed information. It is generally advised to encourage parents to make no decisions about pregnancy or adoption at this time but to wait at least 6 months to a year until this infant has been mourned (Klaus & Kennell, 1982). (Decision making about subsequent pregnancies is discussed in greater detail later.)

Resolution and Beyond

The basis of grief work with families is that "normal grief under favorable conditions and with opportunities for restitution can lead not only to recovery but also to growth and greater integration of the personality" (Simos, 1987, p. 75). Resolution can take many years, and some families may never feel that they have recovered from the loss of their child (Palmer & Noble, 1986; Valentine, 1986). Some emotional changes such as lack of self-confidence may never be resolved (Borg & Lasker, 1981). Rubin (1984-85) asserts that no "end point" of grieving exists.

Experts assert that grief generally lasts from 6 to 24 months but is seldom resolved before 1 year (C. Rappaport, 1981; Stringham et al., 1982). Indeed, for many parents the grief may last much longer without being called "pathological." Holidays and anniversaries of the death may be especially difficult for many years (Borg & Lasker, 1982), but such events are a part of the healing process (Hawkins, 1980).

Valentine (1986) makes an excellent point when she asks what is meant by "resolution" of grief in the case of infertility. As she notes, resolution is not forgetting or putting the pain aside. Rather, C. H. Shapiro (1982) operationalizes resolution of grief as getting on with life. In the case of loss of children through infertility, resolution means that the couple is no longer preoccupied with their infertility and can begin to pursue other parts of their lives such as careers and their marriage, and can begin decision making about alternative means of parenting, if desired. The same may be true of parents who have experienced birth tragedies. The child is not forgotten nor the pain completely ended, but gradually the parents begin to be able to involve themselves in their other roles and to gain satisfaction from them (Borg & Lasker, 1981).

For many families who have miscarried or lost an infant, the issue of another pregnancy is one that arises as part of their recovery. Some families feel that they can never recover until they have another child (Klaus & Kennell, 1982), whereas others agonize about whether to attempt another pregnancy, perhaps even electing sterilization to spare themselves another loss (Wolff, Nielson, & Schiller, 1970). For other families grief is complicated by a history of miscarriages or losses, or by infertility. These families must grieve not only for the infant that has just died, but perhaps for previous and future infants (C. Rappaport, 1981). Their resolution may involve decision making regarding alternative means of parenting.

Simos (1987) notes that the important psychological task of mourning is that of breaking the emotional tie with the lost child and reinvesting those energies in relationships with others. It is generally believed that until grief for one child (or for all biologic children, in the case of infertility) is resolved, it is unwise to attempt another pregnancy or to seek adoption (Renne, 1977). Parents are often thus encouraged to give themselves some time before making this decision (C. Rappaport, 1981), although one has no way of knowing how long is long enough. If the parents do not bring up this topic, it may be broached by professionals either at discharge from the hospital (Tadmor, 1986) or at follow-up (C. Rappaport, 1981).

Follow-up

It is critical that the parents of birth tragedies not be sent home and forgotten; yet grieving parents may be unable to seek the follow-up care that they often need. Social workers have been the most active profession in extending follow-up services to bereaved parents (Matthews, 1987).

C. Rappaport (1981) notes that social workers must reach out to families because they will rarely call or return for follow-up services. This does not indicate that parents would not like or could not use such services, for when Clyman, Green, Mikkelson, Rowe, and Ataide (1979) offered follow-up care to parents, 76% accepted that offer.

Experience suggests that follow-up services should take several forms. First, one individual should be responsible for contacting parents and offering services. Schreiner et al. (1979) found that although follow-up was a part of their protocol, many parents were "lost" or missed in the follow-up process. Few parents took advantage of follow-up services until a social worker was given the responsibility of outreach. Thereafter, most parents accepted the offer of services.

Both Mahan and Schreiner (1981) and C. Rappaport (1981) advocate a telephone call to parents within a few days of the infant's death, followed by one or two visits, either in the home or the office. The agenda at these visits calls for four items. First, the social worker should review what the parents understand about grief and how they have been experiencing it personally (Mahan & Schreiner, 1981). She should reemphasize the normality of some seemingly bizarre reactions (Simos, 1987), such as hearing cries or feeling kicks (C. Rappaport, 1981).

Second, the social worker should inquire whether the family has all the information they need. Perhaps they have questions about their baby's death, the autopsy or pathology report, and so forth (C. Rappaport, 1981). Some families may have unresolved questions but are unwilling or afraid to make contact for the purpose of asking. In other cases families may want information about contacting Compassionate Friends or other support groups, even if they declined this offer earlier (Mahan & Schreiner, 1981). (Compassionate Friends, headquartered in Oak Brook, Illinois, has many chapters throughout the country, and the social worker should be able to provide a telephone contact if the family wishes to investigate the group.)

Third, because the evidence is clear that marital problems are common following infant loss, the social worker should inquire about how well the parents are communicating with each other, and should reemphasize the importance of their sharing their grief (Mahan & Schreiner, 1981). If they indicate that they have a problem in this area they may want to discuss this with the social worker, or they may benefit from a referral for marital counseling. In particular, resumption of sexual intercourse is difficult for all bereaved parents (Ewy & Ewy, 1984). One partner may desire the comfort provided by sexual intimacy, whereas the other may feel guilty about engaging in a pleasurable activity at such a time. At follow-up the social worker should assess whether both parents are comfortable with their current sexual activity to determine whether additional services are indicated to prevent long-term marital problems.

Mahan, Schreiner, and Green (1983) investigated the usefulness of bibliotherapy with parents whose infants died on the NICU. They sent letters and a copy of *The Bereaved Parent* (Schiff, 1977) to 132 parents a short time after their infant died (70% within 1 to 4 weeks of the death). Only 39 families responded, with 36 mothers, 4 fathers, and 7 significant others reporting that they had actually read the book. More than 90% of this small group reported that they found the book to be helpful. The authors note that the sample who responded to the questionnaire was somewhat older and more highly educated than the entire population of NICU parents. Thus the results must be taken with caution. Nonetheless this study does suggest that for some parents, written material might be helpful.

Several books may be useful for social workers who wish to provide them to their clients. *Empty Arms* (Ilse, 1982) and *Miscarriage: A Shattered Dream* (Ilse & Burns, 1985) are short and easy to read books that answer common questions parents may have and provide reassurance about the normal grieving process.* *When Pregnancy Fails* (Borg & Lasker, 1981) is somewhat longer and addresses a broad array of issues related to miscarriage, stillbirth, and neonatal death. Chapters concern prenatal diagnosis and selective abortion, single mothers, legal issues, and environmental causes of perinatal death. This book may be too involved for many parents, but it is a valuable resource for some.

Pathological Grief

Finally, the social worker's approach to working with bereaved families should be one focused on the crisis of perinatal loss and the process of normal grieving. Some individuals may develop more pathological grief reactions, however. Certainly individuals with mental health problems can become infertile or lose infants, and persons who are vulnerable to emotional problems may develop extreme responses to the stress of infant loss. Proper assessment should indicate when such persons require other types of assistance.

Social workers may observe several indications of "pathological grief," which is more likely in cases of previous emotional or psychological problems (Kay, 1987). The most often discussed type of pathological grief reaction is an apparent lack of grief—that is, behavior that suggests the parent is avoiding the reality of the death (Kay, 1987). Such parents may

*Copies of both are available from Wintergreen Press, P.O. Box 165, Long Lake, MN 55356.

seem unduly cheerful, unwilling to take care of necessary arrangements (such as the funeral or signing the death certificate), and may want to return to their normal routine immediately. Conversely, they may experience heightened irritability and tension, along with somatic complaints (Kay, 1987).

In other cases, parents may experience what Rubin (1984-85) calls the "freezing" of the grief process in which the mourner remains preoccupied with the deceased in maladaptive ways including frequent intense reveries or prolonged (during many years) thoughts of the dead child (Kay, 1987). In other cases, parents may abuse drugs or alcohol, or appear not to be based in reality (Batterman, 1985).

The Perinatal Grief Scale (PGS) (Toedter, Lasker, & Alhadeff, 1988) is an 84-item scale designed to measure the nature and extent of perinatal grief. The scale was based on a thorough review of the literature and measures the dimensions thought to be related to grief in general and grief regarding perinatal loss in particular. The scale has good internal consistency (α = .97) and acceptable item-total correlations ranging from .22 to .78 (mean = .52).

Factor analysis of the PGS revealed that three major factors of perinatal grief are active grief (crying, thinking about the baby), difficulty coping (keeping up normal activities, making decisions), and despair (self-esteem, worthlessness). Although the PGS score was correlated with depression, grief was found to be more than depression as only about half of the PGS score was explained by depression. Further, greater grief was correlated (for mothers) with older gestational age, poor mental and physical health, poor marital relationship, and the possibility of having more living children in the future.

The PGS is a promising measure of grief specific to perinatal loss. Its utility as a clinical measure, or as an outcome measure for interventions with grieving parents, has yet to be demonstrated, but testing of the measure is continuing.

SPECIFIC TYPES OF LOSS AND SPECIAL NEEDS

Miscarriage

A *miscarriage* (or "spontaneous abortion") is defined as the delivery of a fetus before 20 weeks of gestation (or less than 500 g) and before the fetus can live outside the uterine environment (Pritchard et al., 1985). Most miscarriages occur within the first 12 weeks of pregnancy (Borg & Lasker, 1981). It has been estimated that many conceptions end in miscarriage, often before the woman is aware that she has conceived, but difficulties in detecting early pregnancy prevent estimates of the true incidence of spontaneous abortion (Pritchard et al., 1985). Although they are rare, ectopic pregnancies (pregnancies that occur outside the uterus) also may occur and always result in induced abortion to save the life of the mother. Hager (1987) notes that the parents' grief is similar to that of parents who miscarry.

The causes of miscarriage are often not known, but causes include an abnormal fetus, abnormal or defective implantation of the fetus in the uterus, an abnormal uterus or cervix, or disease or infection in the mother (Pritchard et al., 1985). The frustration of not knowing the cause of a miscarriage often makes the emotional impact more painful (Ilse & Burns, 1985).

Unique Pain

Several factors are unique to miscarriage that make it a difficult experience for prospective parents. First, it may occur before the parents have had time to consider the possibility that it could happen, sometimes just when they are becoming excited about being parents. In some cases they have not even announced the pregnancy. Conversely, miscarriage may be even more unexpected if it occurs after the first trimester. Because 75% of miscarriages occur during the first 3 months, many couples feel they are "safe" after this time (Borg & Lasker, 1982).

Second, the actual experience of a spontaneous abortion is different from what many people expect, and it can be frightening. Pain usually occurs (sometimes quite intense and lasting longer than expected) and possibly profuse bleeding. In many cases the mother is alone throughout the process of the abortion (Hager, 1987), which may occur during several hours. Conversely, the symptoms of a miscarriage sometimes can be so ambiguous that the natural tendency to deny it is happening is confirmed (Borg & Lasker, 1982). The mother usually is not admitted to the hospital and thus may have no contact with a professional who can provide emotional support (Ilse, 1982).

Perhaps most difficult for the bereaved parents of a miscarriage is the fact that no baby was known, so people often underestimate or ignore the parents' grief. Even when the pregnancy lasted but a few days, the child usually has become real to the parents through their fantasies, wishes, and dreams for the child. Others do not understand that the baby was a known person to the parents, and may minimize the parents' grief, denying them the social sanction that is so important to mourning (Stringham et al., 1982; Simos, 1986). Even medical personnel often make insensitive remarks such as "it might have been deformed anyway" or they may fail to provide enough accurate information to the parents (Borg & Lasker, 1982), as if the miscarriage is not worth the effort.

Finally, miscarriage almost always results in fears about another pregnancy or infertility, especially if repeated miscarriages have occurred or if the parents are older (Borg & Lasker, 1982). A woman who has had one miscarriage runs no greater risk of another miscarriage. If more than one has occurred, the physician may begin to suspect a genetic or physical abnormality, but she still has a good chance of carrying subsequent pregnancies successfully (Pritchard et al., 1985).

Victims of ectopic pregnancy may suffer from additional isolation and lack of understanding. Physicians and others often concentrate on the medical emergency of ectopic pregnancy (which often results in hemorrhage and can be fatal if not treated promptly) to the exclusion of the meaning of the lost pregnancy (Hager, 1987).

Social Work Tasks

The appropriate social work tasks with parents who suffer miscarriage include those described earlier in this chapter. Particular attention should be paid to sanctioning miscarriage as a loss for the parents and preparing them for the grief they will experience. When the miscarriage has occurred early in pregnancy, many couples may not realize that they "have a right" to mourn and may fear that they are "going crazy" (Ilse & Burns, 1985). This task may include encouraging the parents to discuss with each other and with significant others what has happened to them, even if they had not previously announced the pregnancy.

Stillbirth

Stillbirth is defined as the birth of a dead infant of more than 20 weeks' gestation or one weighing more than 500 g. About 1 in 100 pregnancies ends in stillbirth (Lewis, 1979). Death usually occurs before the start of labor, but some deaths occur during delivery. The causes of stillbirth include umbilical cord accidents including a prolapsed cord or a twisted or knotted cord (Ewy & Ewy, 1984). Because the cord carries oxygen and nourishment to the fetus, such accidents cause death by anoxia.

Other major causes of stillbirth include placenta abruptio, a condition in which the placenta separates from the implantation site in the uterus, and placenta previa, in which the placenta precedes the baby in the birth canal. In each case the baby's oxygen is cut off, and the mother is in danger of a fatal hemorrhage. Other less common causes include genetic abnormalities and maternal illness. In about half of all stillbirths, the cause is never known (Ewy & Ewy, 1984).

Special Type of Loss

Like those who have suffered miscarriage, parents who experience a stillbirth may be unsupported in their loss (Stringham et al., 1982). Mourning a stillbirth has been called "silent mourning" because others commonly avoid discussing the event in a futile effort to spare the parents pain, and because no memories exist to provide a basis for conversation and mutual mourning (Lewis, 1979). Lewis (1979) notes:

> Memory facilitates the normal mourning processes essential for recovery. With other bereavements there is much to remember. These memories can be shared and cried over with family and friends. Not so with stillbirth—there is no one to talk about and no one to talk about it. (p. 304)

When a stillbirth has occurred, the parents are often in a state of anxiety as they undergo tests to confirm that the death has occurred. Often the expectant mother has visited her obstetrician because she has felt no fetal activity for a time, or sometimes the death is diagnosed at a regular prenatal appointment (Woods, 1987).

When the death is confirmed, it is important that appropriate action be taken. The parents should be told in privacy and together, if possible. If the mother has come alone to the office or hospital, she should not be allowed to leave alone after learning that her baby is dead. Rather the husband or another close support person should be called to the office. Woods (1987) recommends that a social worker be brought into the case as soon as possible when the diagnosis is made.

When fetal death is confirmed by the obstetrician a decision must be made about whether to induce labor or to allow it to start naturally. Usually labor will proceed within 2 weeks of the death (Ewy & Ewy, 1984), although the mother's condition or wishes may dictate inducing labor before that time. Some parents find this time useful as anticipatory grieving and in their preparation for arrangements (Stringham et al., 1982). Others find it more painful to wait while carrying a dead baby and prefer immediate induction. This is an important decision that should be made by the parents and the physician, with attention to all the relevant factors. It is especially important that the father and mother be together during labor and delivery when it is known that the infant is dead (Klaus & Kennell, 1982).

Several events following the initial shock are extremely difficult for parents. First, the mother's stay in the hospital following the birth may be excruciating if she remains on the obstetric ward where she can see and hear other mothers and their babies. It is the practice in many hospitals to move the mother to another floor or to offer her that option (Borg & Lasker). Social workers should be certain in these cases that the mother is informed of her options. The same is true of the option of the husband's remaining at the hospital with his wife overnight; many hospitals provide a cot in the mother's room because of the importance of their remaining together (Klaus & Kennell, 1982), and parents should be informed of this option.

Leaving the hospital without a baby is described by most parents as particularly difficult. Other particularly stressful events following discharge from the hospital may include going home to view a prepared nursery with baby clothes everywhere, or the mother's milk coming in (Borg & Lasker, 1982; Gilson, 1976). It may help families to be prepared for these events, and they should make their own decisions about what they wish to do. For example, social worker Dan Timmel has observed well-meaning friends who attempt to dismantle the nursery and leave the parents without a way of slowly disengaging from the baby and the parental role.

Dealing with the reactions of others after a stillbirth is stressful for many families. They may welcome advice and discussion regarding such issues as sending out announcements or calling friends and family to let them know the stillbirth has occurred. Some anticipatory guidance may also be helpful regarding the tendency of others to ignore the subject or to make remarks that are meant to be helpful, such as "It was probably for the best." If families understand that others really are trying to be helpful, they may be able to respond in ways that assist them in their grief.

Again, the appropriate social work tasks for working with parents of the stillborn baby are discussed earlier in this chapter. Particular attention should be paid to informing parents of the options they have while in the hospital (such as the mother's moving to another floor, and the father's remaining overnight with the mother in the hospital), and regarding their infant's body (e.g., funeral, burial, etc.). Like parents of miscarriage, these parents may benefit from anticipatory guidance about others' reactions to their loss.

Neonatal Death

Infant death on the NICU may occur after only a few moments or after several agonizing months of intensive treatment. Parents may have endured many periods of hopefulness, followed by medical emergencies and dashed hopes. They may have spent many hours beside their infant's incubator, sharing in his care and becoming intimately acquainted with his unfolding personality, or they may have avoided the NICU and the pain of a relationship they feared would only end with the baby's death. Thus parents may face their neonate's death extremely fatigued from months of intensive care or still in shock about his premature birth; they may have expected his death and begun anticipatory mourning, or the death may have been totally unanticipated; they may have formed a deep attachment to their child or avoided such an attachment as much as possible.

Good social work with families whose infants die on the NICU begins immediately after the infant's birth. That is, those tasks that the social worker performs to aid the family whose infant is in the NICU are also helpful in the event that the infant does not survive. For example, the social worker can be of greater help to a family when she has established a relationship with the family before the death occurs (C. Rappaport, 1981). The reader is referred to Chapter 3 for details on this subject; however, two points deserve special mention here.

First, some (e.g., see Tadmor, 1986) recommend that when an infant's death is inevitable, the family should be encouraged to engage in anticipatory grieving. According to the literature on death and dying, anticipatory grieving may be helpful for healthy resolution of grief. The second point to be emphasized is the importance of encouraging the family to form an attachment to their infant. Formation of such an attachment is thought to contribute to the healthy resolution of grief (Klaus & Kennell, 1982), although it may make the grief more intense (Kennell, Slyter & Klaus, 1970). Social workers may assist here by encouraging the family to name the infant, to visit and hold him, to assist in his care when possible, and to take and keep photographs. Doing these things provides memories of the child, which are essential to grieving. Minton (1983) also advocates having tangible items that may be saved, such as locks of hair or small toys placed in the infant's crib (Minton, 1983).

In some cases, however, death will occur before parents have had time to prepare in these ways. In some cases the infant dies immediately after admission to the NICU, perhaps after transfer from another hospital or immediately after birth. The social worker can still be of assistance to the family in many of the ways discussed early in this chapter. For example, families may be linked with local NICU support groups for bereaved parents. Many hospitals sponsor such organizations within the unit, whereas others serve as a referral source.

Many families require assistance in dealing with the hospital accounting department about bills and funeral arrangements. Families may not be able to concentrate enough to deal with payment schedules or insurance forms at this time, and accounting departments may not be sensitive to the family's loss. The social worker's skills as advocate and liaison may be particularly helpful in this area. Borg and Lasker (1981) note that parents may be fearful of bringing up financial issues because they are afraid that others may criticize them for thinking of money "at a time like this" (Borg & Lasker, 1981). Social workers should anticipate this fear and initiate the discussion.

SIDS

SIDS ("cot death" or "crib death") is defined as the unexpected death of an apparently healthy infant, usually during sleep, and for whom no other cause of death can be established (Peterson, 1984). Although exact figures are problematic because of difficulties and inconsistencies in definition and diagnosis, approximately 10,000 SIDS deaths occur annually in the United States, making it the largest single cause of death in the postneonatal period (Beckwith, 1979). Following the first week of life, SIDS is the leading cause of death until 1 year of age, with the incidence peaking between 2 and 4 months of age (Hawkins, 1980).

"Crib death" was noted in the Bible and in the Middle Ages, but until the 1900s so many entities caused young infants to die that a SIDS death often went unrecognized (Barnett & Hunter, 1983). When it was recognized, accidental suffocation often was blamed, thought to be due to overlying or entanglement in bed clothes (Johnson & Hufbauer, 1982). Neglect or infanticide often was suspected. Suspicion that SIDS was not due to suffocation began in the mid-1930s, followed by a focus on a virus as the possible cause of SIDS in the 1940s.

Federal concern about SIDS began in 1963 owing in large part to pressure from organized SIDS parents. That year the National Institute of Child Health and Human Development sponsored a conference to discuss and encourage SIDS research. Considering the magnitude of the problem, SIDS research never received adequate attention, however, until mounting pressure by parents led to a planning workshop in 1971 and a Congressional hearing in 1972 (Johnson & Hufbauer, 1982). The Sudden Infant Death Syndrome Act of 1974 (Public Law 93-270) provided funding both for research regarding the etiology of SIDS and for services for bereaved families. Moreover, the 1978 amendments to Title IX of the Public Health Service Act authorized the SIDS program, which is administered by the Office for Maternal and Child Health, to fund various projects to collect data on SIDS, to conduct educational programs about SIDS, and to provide services to parents who have experienced a SIDS death. The program is now included in the Maternal and Child Health Block Grant.

Etiology of SIDS

Despite extensive research and speculation, the etiology of SIDS remains a mystery. During the years several factors have been hypothesized as responsible for SIDS including infanticide, suffocation, hypothermia, scurvy, various types of infection, and numerous types of anatomic neurological abnormalities. None has adequate evidence to be considered plausible. SIDS is not a cause of death but a syndrome. This point means that the etiology and pathogenesis are unknown (Hawkins, 1980). Indeed, a defining feature of the SIDS diagnosis is that no more specific cause of death can be discerned on autopsy (Bass, Kravath, & Glass, 1986).

Several social and psychological correlates of SIDS have suggested psychogenic origins. SIDS is commoner among babies of mothers who are nonwhite, poor, unmarried, undereducated, and among those who live in poor housing (Biering-Sorenson, Jorgensen, & Hilden, 1979). In addition, twins, premature babies, and male infants are at increased risk (Beckwith, 1979). Behavioral risk factors include smoking, taking illicit drugs, and receiving inadequate prenatal care (Peterson, 1984). SIDS parents continue to suffer from the suspicion that bad parenting or outright neglect led to the death. Some have suggested (in the absence of empirical evidence) that SIDS is an infant response to anxiety (Cranshaw, 1978), or even that SIDS is the infant's effort to regress back to the womb by cessation of breathing (Friedlander & Shaw, 1975).

Research in the last decade suggested that although SIDS may be the end point of a complex process, various types of chronic or recurrent respiratory problems do seem commoner in infants who die of SIDS (Hoppenbrouwers & Hodgman, 1983). In particular, SIDS had been linked with sleep apnea, or periods of cessation of breathing during sleep (Barnett & Hunter, 1983), but current thinking casts some doubt on this connection (Brooks, 1987). Several other areas of research implicate brain stem dysfunctions or chemical imbalances (Barnett & Hunter, 1983).

Shock and Pain

Several factors make SIDS unique among types of infant death. First, SIDS is especially unexpected because it occurs in healthy babies with no sign of illness (May & Breme, 1982-83). The shock often is exacerbated by the mother's finding the infant's lifeless body in the morning or after a nap (Gyulay, 1976; Lowman, 1979).

Second, although all parents who lose children feel guilty because they have not fulfilled the basic protective function of parents (Rando, 1985), guilt and anxiety are even more pronounced with SIDS because of its mysterious nature. The suspicion of "foul play" has diminished in recent years, but still may be evident particularly when police and medical examiners encounter SIDS cases in lower income or single-parent families. Because parents themselves feel guilty and confused, this suspicion by others is especially painful. Szybist (1988), a nurse and mother of a SIDS baby wrote to her dead infant:

> I didn't need a judge and jury to indict me for your death. I was only too willing to do it to myself. Pneumonia. That has a cure, or symptoms. I must have missed something. It must have been my fault. Babies are little, vulnerable, dependent. They couldn't do anything to themselves, only their caretakers, their parents could. Lack of information is such a fertile environment for doubt and guilt. (p. 34)

Indeed, parents of SIDS victims often become preoccupied with the search for the cause of their baby's death and may be rebuffed by medical personnel because of their "obsession" (Johnson & Hufbauer, 1982). In fact, it was the drive of parents to "do something" and to find out why their infants died that led to the current government investment in SIDS.

Social Work Tasks

Working with a family who has experienced a SIDS death requires great sensitivity and skill. In many cases because an infant is transported to the hospital on discovery, it is the nurse and not the social worker who works with the family (Gyulay, 1976). In other cases, emergency department social workers may have first contact with SIDS families. Prompt recognition of the SIDS family and their unique needs in the emergency department may reduce the family's trauma (May & Breme, 1982-83). The first contact should consist of a private interview in which the parents are provided all available information, advised of the procedures in SIDS cases (e.g., involvement of the Medical Examiner's office), and told the importance of an autopsy (Gyulay, 1976). Much of what is said may have to be repeated later, because parents are in shock and may be unable to assimilate all the information.

Successful alleviation of the family's inappropriate guilt is the prime purpose of intervention with SIDS families. To this end, the chief tool of the counselor is knowledge about SIDS and about the particular case, which should be imparted in detail to the family as soon as it is available. It is not necessary to wait for confirmation of the diagnosis by autopsy, as long as parents are aware that the information is provisional. Provision of written material about SIDS also may be helpful to some parents. Kotch and Cohen (1985-86) provide a copy of the autopsy report to parents. (Graphic detail in autopsy reports could be upsetting to many parents, however.) Social workers may contact the National Sudden Infant Death Syndrome Clearinghouse* for written material and a list of other organizations that provide material about SIDS.

Unfortunately, little information is available about the long-term needs of families who experience SIDS. It is logical to assume that these families may suffer additional stress and may require a longer period to resolve their grief than families who lose infants to other causes. Szybist (1988) noted that she still grieved for more than 20 years after her son's SIDS death. These families also may suffer great anxiety about the possibility of SIDS with subsequent infants, particularly because the risk is somewhat greater for siblings of SIDS infants (Peterson, 1984).

Price et al. (1985) stress the importance of social support in the long-term recovery of SIDS families. These authors and Williams and Nikolaisen (1982) noted unusually high proportions of SIDS families relocating in the year following the death, and suggest that moving may be a form of coping. It also exacerbates the need for social support, which may be lacking when friends and family engage in avoidance owing to discomfort or their own sadness. Families might be discouraged from moving, and encouraged to reach out to their friends and family. Some may benefit from self-help groups to which the social worker can refer them.

May and Breme (1982) provided an assessment tool for adjustment, the SIDS Family Adjustment Scale. Although they provided no empirical data on the reliability or validity of the instrument, it appears to be a promising tool for clinical use. Elements measured by this scale include ability to communicate about the death, resumption of the daily routine, perception and use of social supports, belief that the SIDS death was preventable, issues regarding future children, religious values and practices, symptoms and illnesses since the death, emotional dysfunction, and degree of emotional closeness of the family members. Further research is needed to validate the instrument as a predictor of maladjustment.

Infertility

Infertility is defined as a failure to achieve pregnancy during at least 1 year of regular, unprotected intercourse. ("Primary" infertility indicates that a woman has never achieved pregnancy, and "secondary" infertility indicates that there has been at least one pregnancy.) According to this definition, approximately 20% of American couples are infertile (Behrman & Patton, 1988).

---

*The address for this organization is 8201 Greensboro Drive, Suite 600, McLean, VA 22102.

Infertility is caused by several problems, approximately 40% of which are due to problems in the woman, 40% to problems in the man, and the remainder either to problems in both or to unknown factors (Schoysman-Deboeck, Van Roosendaal, & Schoysman, 1988). Medical progress in treating infertility has been impressive in the last few years. Not all infertile couples seek medical services, but of those who do, approximately 50% will eventually conceive (Menning, 1977).

Recent evidence suggests that the prevalence of infertility is increasing (Aral & Cates, 1982; U.S. Department of Health and Human Services, 1982). The increases are thought to result primarily from delayed childbearing and changes in sexual and contraceptive behavior that have resulted in the increased prevalence of sexually transmitted diseases (STDs) associated with infertility through pelvic inflammatory disease. Increased exposure to environmental toxins also may play a part.

Need for Social Work

Two factors make infertility a concern for social workers. First, social work's long history in adoption provides a rationale for involvement with infertile couples, because social workers understand the intense desire childless couples have for children (Batterman, 1985; Renne, 1977). Second, the emotional consequences of infertility are similar to those of miscarriage or stillbirth; infertility is a "crisis" within the domain of crisis theory (Valentine, 1986). Would-be parents have hoped for and dreamed of a child, perhaps delaying the start of their families until they were professionally or financially secure. When it becomes apparent that pregnancy may not be possible, individuals go through the same grief process for the wished-for child as do parents who lose a child after conception (Shapiro, 1982). In this case, however, the couple must mourn for all children who might have been (Mahlstedt, 1985; Shapiro, 1982).

Mahlstedt (1985) explains clinical depression by describing the losses entailed that are part of infertility. Indeed, she notes that infertility involves all of the different types of loss (e.g., loss of health, loss of important roles) that are important to the etiology of depression. Others (e.g., Batterman, 1985) review the stages of classical grief and illustrate their connection to infertility.

In some ways couples experience infertility just as couples who lose children who have already been conceived or born. Like others who lose children, infertile couples suffer from the unexpected nature of their problems. Most individuals grow up expecting to have a family and never believing anything could go wrong with that plan (Mahlstedt, 1985). Years of faithful contraception have acted to reinforce their feelings of control over their reproduction (Batterman, 1985). Moreover, many of those in their 30s and 40s are individuals who have been professionally and personally successful, planning and achieving consistently in their lives. It is a blow to discover that this important and basic human function is out of the reach of their best planning.

Also like those who experience miscarriage and stillbirth (which may be part of infertility in some cases), infertile couples may be denied the social sanction to grieve. After all, no child has been known, so no loss is recognized (Mahlstedt, 1985; Valentine, 1986). In some cases others may assume that the couple "can always adopt," or that they do not really want children. Couples may find themselves grieving alone, perhaps avoiding their friends with children and increasingly isolating themselves (Batterman, 1985).

In some other ways the grieving of infertile couples is unique. Infertility threatens the self-esteem and sexual self-identity of its victims, who may equate their reproductive failure with failure of their sexuality (Batterman, 1985). The medical process further damages the couple's sexual relationship with its emphasis on the timing of sexual intercourse, which is intrusive and destructive of spontaneity (Mahlstedt, 1985). Virtually every reference reviewed for this chapter mentioned the infertile couple's (especially the woman's) "preoccupation" or "obsession" with infertility and the mechanics of sex and treatment (e.g., Greenfeld, Diamond, Breslin, & DeCherney, 1986; Shapiro, 1982; Valentine, 1986). This damage to the sexual relationship is also damaging to the marital relationship, robbing the couple of an important way of being close just at the time they need it most.

Guilt may also be especially salient for the infertile couple, as they go back over past indiscretions, agonizing over premarital sex, previous abortions, or STD (Batterman, 1985; Renne, 1977). The guilt of the partner who has the medical problem is especially painful, and it is not uncommon for the "guilty partner" to suggest or seek divorce as a means of mediating that guilt (Mahlstedt, 1985).

The damage to sexuality and the guilt experienced by couples are complicated by the difficulties of communicating that are typical for couples experiencing infertility (Renne, 1977). Men and women have different means of expressing grief, although Renne (1977) maintains that men suffer as deeply as women. Women tend to talk about their feelings, whereas men tend to cope with their pain silently, by focusing on their wives' grief (Mahlstedt, 1985). The silence that often results from these differences may lead to misinterpretation of each other's feelings and consequently a deeper rift between the couple (Batterman, 1985).

The process of the medical examinations, tests, surgery, and various treatments involve their own stresses and problems, and further complicate the grieving process. Batterman (1985) describes the frequent visits to physicians, daily temperatures and charting, collection of semen and cervical mucus specimens, radiographs, surgery under general anesthesia, and the use of drugs with potentially dangerous side effects that are typical of the medical procedure. Most procedures can only be done at a certain point in the woman's menstrual cycle, so it can require months to proceed through the list. Indeed, infertility testing and treatment may last for years, alternately preserving and dashing hopes month after month and rarely indicating conclusively that continued treatment is futile (Mahlstedt, 1985). In addition, the treatment process is invasive, humiliating, expensive, and often painful (Mahlstedt, 1985).

As progress has been made in the treatment of infertility, physicians have discovered that they are unprepared to treat the emotional turmoil that is involved (Mahlstedt, 1985; Renne, 1977). Increasingly, physicians and clinics are using social workers, psychologists, and other trained professionals to assist families with the emotional problems they typically experience. In addition, a national self-help group, Resolve, now provides support and group counseling to thousands of couples nationwide.

In addition to helping infertile couples deal with grief described earlier, the social worker engages in counseling and support, education and advocacy, referral, and decision making. The counseling and support recommended for infertile couples is similar to that used with other grieving couples, with emphasis on allowing them to express their feelings (Batterman, 1985). As in the other cases, a crisis and grieving approach is used rather than a pathology-oriented one. This distinction is an important one. For many years, the responses of infertile couples were interpreted as pathological. The early psychiatric literature attributed half of all infertility to psychological factors (Greenfeld et al., 1986). Indeed, many still interpret the anxiety and frustration that are consequences of infertility and its treatment as the causes of the condition. (Few infertile couples are unable to recall several people telling them to "relax and you'll get pregnant," or "adopt and then you're sure to get pregnant.") A basic early function in working with infertile couples is to assure them that they are not "going crazy" but are experiencing normal grief.

Supportive work by the social worker should encourage the couple to use their natural support systems by enhancing marital communication and contacts with family and close friends. In many cases it will be helpful to encourage them to attend a meeting of Resolve if they desire to seek companionship with others experiencing infertility (Shapiro, 1982). The self-help group is not for everyone, however. For example, Valentine (1986) reported on a small sample of infertile men who indicated that talking about their problems exacerbated their stress rather than lowering it.

An important part of the support offered by the social worker may involve assisting the parents in dealing with rude and insensitive comments by others, who either may discount their loss or are awkwardly trying to comfort the couple. Assertiveness training may be helpful in this regard. Couples may even find it helpful to engage in behavior rehearsal. Because loss of control is such a strong component of infertility, couples may find it helpful to feel confident about what they say to others whose comments elicit anger in them (Batterman, 1985; Shapiro, 1982).

Special Procedures

"Heroic" treatment procedures may call for specialized procedures by the social worker. For example, artificial insemination—donor is a procedure that is used in cases when the male's sperm is absent or inadequate, in cases of hereditary disease in the husband, or in some cases of incompatibility between the man and woman (Schoysman-DeBoeck et al., 1988). The relatively easy procedure involves placing donor sperm in the mouth of the woman's cervix.

In general, this procedure is a relatively simple medically, but it presents some issues that couples should consider before proceeding. Special concerns for couples include the husband's ability to accept the child as "his own" or the husband's acceptance of the procedure only to assuage his "guilt" about being the cause of the couple's inability to conceive (Schoysman-DeBoeck et al., 1988). In addition, the couple may feel some embarrassment and concern about privacy, and may have legal questions about the paternal rights of the donor. The most recent concern about this procedure concerns the possibility of the mother's or the infant's contracting AIDS through the donor sperm (Daniels, 1986).

In the course of discussion, the social worker should address the husband's feelings about not being the biologic father of the child born through this procedure. If the husband cannot deal with this issue or if he is agreeing to it out of guilt about his infertility, the social worker may advise against the procedure at this time. Further discussion may enable the couple to deal with the problem satisfactorily so that they can go ahead with the procedure.

A more complex and controversial procedure is in vitro fertilization, (IVF), which is indicated for tubal disease or semen irregularities (Jones, 1988). Since the first successful IVF procedure was performed in 1978, much publicity has surrounded "test tube baby" technology. Success rates are low overall, about 15%, although rates may be improving recently (Jones, 1988).

IVF is a safe but relatively involved procedure. The woman may be injected with daily doses of a fertility drug from the beginning of her cycle to promote ovulation. She may be monitored continuously to watch the growth of the developing ova. When ultrasound imaging indicates that the ova are mature and just before ovulation, a laparoscopy is performed to "harvest" the eggs. The ova are then fertilized in the laboratory with a sample of the husband's sperm, and the embryo(s) are implanted back in the woman's cervix. Reimplanatation is performed in an office procedure that, though safe and simple, is somewhat uncomfortable. Pregnancy tests are then administered every few days until a positive result is obtained or until menses begin. Needleman (1987) describes the procedure in detail.

IVF is an extremely stressful procedure for several reasons. First, many couples regard it as their "last chance" to have a child (Greenfeld et al., 1986) after years of treatments and disappointments (Needleman, 1987). They have probably tried every other procedure without success and may be older. Some couples may be too old to adopt through most agencies, so this procedure may be their last chance to parent an infant. Moreover, the procedure is expensive (about $5,000 per cycle) (Greenfeld et al., 1986), and many insurance companies do not pay for it (Greenfeld, 1986). For the woman it involves using a strong drug with frequent side effects, daily testing, and minor surgery with all the attendant unpleasantness.

Some programs employ social workers for the purpose of assessing couples' abilities to withstand the stress of IVF (Greenfeld et al., 1986; Needleman, 1987). Greenfeld et al. (1986) reported that the social worker's assessment that a couple is not prepared to handle the stress might result in denial or delay of the procedure, whereas Needleman (1987) specifically stated that this was not the case in her program.

Social workers can assist families in reducing their anxiety (Needleman, 1987) and in decision making about the number of unsuccessful cycles that will be tried before alternative means of parenting are pursued. Finally, social workers have important roles to play with families who are unsuccessful in conceiving by this method (Needleman, 1987). Sometimes additional support from the social worker is needed by those couples who are successful and go on to a stressful, high-risk pregnancy (Shapiro, 1986). For some of these "successful" couples, the 9 months of pregnancy may involve extreme anxiety that interferes with their ability to begin forming an attachment with their infant (C. H. Shapiro, 1986).

The role of educator is an important one for some social workers in infertility settings. All infertile couples probably can benefit from information about infertility and normal grieving (Batterman, 1985). Many physicians provide none of this information to their infertile patients, so couples may be confused and frightened about what is happening to them. Moreover, many physicians do not take adequate time to provide detailed information to patients about their diagnosis, the treatments being used, and their alternatives. Greenfeld et al. (1986) say this can be an important task for the social worker.

The educator also may serve as a referral source for couples. Resolve* may be an excellent resource for couples. If no local chapter exists social workers may work to start one or may obtain written materials that may be helpful to couples.

Finally, social workers may engage in a task that is often not done well, that of assisting couples with the complex decision making that is required of them (Greenfeld et al., 1986). Couples often must select a physician based on little information and when their decision can have profound outcomes. They must balance the odds of success with certain treatments that they do not fully understand against the time required to complete those treatments (which may prevent the use of other treatments).

At some point prospective parents must decide when they are ready to discontinue medical treatment and pursue other options of parenting, such as adoption. Discontinuing treatment may be difficult for couples who need to feel that they have done everything possible to conceive a child. In many cases the couple may need "permission" or encouragement to discontinue treatment, and "It is often with a sigh of relief that patients hear physicians state that they have used all their skills without success" (Schoysman-DeBoeck et al., 1988, p. 733).

In the past these crucial decisions for the most part have been left to the physician, but increasingly it is being recognized that such decisions should be made largely by the couples themselves. These couples are likely to require assistance in making such important decisions, however. Renne (1977) notes the importance, for instance, of couples' reaching a point of "resolution" about their infertility before pursuing adoption. A need also exists to discuss their feelings concerning the importance of reproduction vs. parenting. For some couples, the experience of pregnancy and birth is so important that adoption may be unacceptable. For these parents the social worker may discuss "child-free" living or other means of channeling their desire to nurture, such as foster parenting (Batterman, 1985; Shapiro, 1982).

Renne (1977) notes that many times physicians refer couples to adoption agencies without assessing their readiness for this step. Social workers are the best prepared professionals to assist families with grieving and

*The address for this organization is P.O. Box 474, Belmont, MA 02178.

proceeding to consider adoption, and they have a long history of doing so.

STRESSES ON PROFESSIONALS

Although it is frequently not recognized, social workers and other professionals who work with grieving families suffer significant stress associated with their work (Palmer & Noble, 1986). For example, NICU nurses may become attached to specific infants on the unit and experience frequent grieving when those infants die. Social workers are more likely to form close relationships with the families on NICU units rather than the infants (Sosnowitz, 1984), and it is particularly draining emotionally to work with families who have lost infants. Moreover, the ethical dilemmas frequently experienced on the NICU may cause strain for the physicians, nurses, and social workers (Kornblum & Marshall, 1981).

Professionals handle the stress of frequent infant death in different ways. NICU nurses have described personal coping strategies such as attending the funerals, weeping, transferring out of the NICU, and attending group sessions (Palmer & Noble, 1986). Others may begin bringing in toys for "special" infants and thinking of them as their own children (Borg & Lasker, 1981). Physicians manage their pain by treating physical symptoms while avoiding discussion of their feelings (Gilson, 1976). Both nurses and physicians may begin avoiding families as a way of coping (Sosnowitz, 1984). Indeed, Klaus and Kennell (1982) noted that they hold frequent NICU meetings because staff have difficulty functioning properly unless they "air their feelings" regularly.

Mahan and Schreiner (1981) note that the process of educating and training staff about death and dying through case conferences, in-service training programs, and informal encounters can be useful for professionals to exchange the emotional support that is required of individuals who experience infant death so frequently.

In many cases social workers function as consultants with NICU staff, perhaps by leading groups designed to permit the expression of feelings (White, 1985). Kornblum and Marshall (1981) described the role of a social worker in providing such a service to NICU nurses. On other units this function may be filled by a physician or nurse (Beardslee & DeMaso, 1982). Groups are designed not as therapy groups but as meetings to encourage discussion of feelings and problem solving. Beardslee and DeMaso (1982) noted that the staff groups in one pediatric hospital were essential to the successful provision of care. They provided no empirical data to this effect, however. Research is needed to suggest how NICU staff may be helped to deal more adequately with the stresses of their work.

It is not possible to "spare" parents the grief they experience when an infant dies. Rather, social workers may hope to bring some comfort and support, and to assist families in gathering the resources they need to enable them to resolve their grief satisfactorily. The tasks of the social worker are based on the premise that effective work with bereaved families can help them to grow from their experiences and to function more adequately in the future than they would have without such assistance.

5 Health Care Services for Young Children

Childhood is the healthiest time of life and is healthier now than it has ever been before (Select Panel for the Promotion of Child Health, 1981). With the public health advances of this century and the virtual end of diphtheria, cholera, poliomyelitis, tetanus, pertussis, and other scourges, childhood mortality rates for children 1 to 4 years of age have dropped 10-fold since 1925 to a rate of about 60 per 100,000 (Kovar & Meny, 1981). This does not mean, however, that no unmet health needs exist among this generally healthy group. Three facts demonstrate that health care for children continues to be an area in which great improvements could be made.

First, great disparity exists between the health of children who are disadvantaged and those whose families have adequate resources. Mortality from all causes (and particularly from causes related to social factors such as accidents and homicide) and morbidity are significantly greater and have more serious consequences for poor and minority children (Starfield & Budetti, 1985).

The second fact that suggests the continued need for efforts to improve the health of children is that despite the fact that poor children are less healthy than their more advantaged counterparts (Newacheck & Halfon, 1986), they receive less health care (e.g., Meyer & Lewin, 1986; Orr et al., 1984). Poor children whose health is described as "poor" or "fair" are least likely to see a physician regularly (Newacheck & Halfon, 1986), least likely to be able to see a physician when they need one, and less likely to have a medical home (Select Panel for the Promotion of Child Health, 1981). Moreover, the health care they do obtain may be of lower quality, because disadvantaged children tend to receive episodic care from many providers rather than the more highly prized continuous care (Wilson & White, 1977). A review of the impact of federal policy on health care received by the poor indicates that poor children are less often immunized and are less likely to receive regular well-child care (Calkins, Burns, & Delbanco, 1986).

It is likely that some of the differential in quality health care between poor and nonpoor children is due to lack of health insurance by poor children. Individuals without health insurance tend to use the health care system less often than those with insurance (Aday, Fleming, & Anderson, 1984; Meyer & Lewin, 1986). Approximately 8 million American children have no health insurance; many children who do have insurance are covered for hospitalization only, and not for outpatient and preventive care (Weitz, 1982). Half of all black children and half of children living in female-headed households have no health insurance; the same is true for about a quarter of children in families with annual incomes of less than $5,000 (Select Panel for the Promotion of Child Health, 1981).

Despite the public's assumption that Medicaid fills this need for the poor, in fact the program covers only selected groups of the poor (Meyer & Lewin, 1986). Eligibility restrictions since 1981 have reduced the number of children who receive Medicaid benefits and virtually eliminated all whose families may be classified as "working poor" (Hughes, Johnson, Rosenbaum, Simon, & Butler, 1987). Newacheck and Halfon (1986) found that only about half of low-income children in the National Health Interview Survey were covered by Medicaid, and poor children without Medicaid coverage had substantially fewer physician visits than those with such coverage and in similar health.

A final point indicating the continued health needs of all children is that certain illnesses and conditions continue to cripple and handicap children for life, despite the fact that many of these conditions are now easily detected and treated using currently available therapies. In most cases these problems affect poor and minority children most frequently and most severely (Stine, 1982). Some are problems related to behavior or life-style, such as childhood suicide, accidents, and homicide. Most of these killers are believed to have strong preventive potential. The relatively new interest in such problems is due to the fact that many of the more pressing illnesses from the past that killed and maimed children have been conquered; thus, these behavior-related problems now account for a larger proportion of childhood deaths. In addition, with the epidemics and other childhood scourges no longer a priority, more resources may be directed at these other problems.

LONG-TERM EFFECTS OF POOR HEALTH

The consequences of poor health are serious for all children, but may be more damaging for disadvantaged children. For example, preschoolers in poor families spend many more days per year in bed because of illness and many more days in the hospital compared with children of more advantaged families (Kovar, 1982). In addition to being traumatic for the child and family, disability and hospital days deprive children of normal learning activity and also may involve costly treatment at public expense. Children with defective vision, hearing, and learning abilities or with developmental delays perform less adequately in school, reducing their capacity for learning and earning in the future (Goggin, 1987).

It has been estimated that nearly 60% of all children are incompletely immunized (House of Representatives, 1983), with minority children more likely than white children not to be immunized (Wallace, 1982). Children with incomplete immunizations against childhood diseases are at risk for the serious complications that arise from measles, mumps, pertussis, and other serious diseases including mental retardation.

One may well ask how a country as prosperous and as ostensibly "child centered" as the United States can tolerate continuing unnecessary suffering by children, especially in this time of modern medical "miracles." It is tempting to ascribe the deplorable situation solely and simply to politics. Indeed, politics may be the "bottom line" of health care, but in reality the complete answer may be somewhat more complex than it first appears. If social workers are to be effective in the provision of health services to children and in their ethical obligation to advocate for this constituency, it is imperative that they understand at least the basics of this complex situation.

DEFINITION OF PRIMARY CARE

Health care for young children (from 1 year of age to adolescence) encompasses an enormous range of types of care based on setting (such as a private pediatrician's office or a neighborhood health center), sector (private vs. public), and level of care.

Alpert (1982) states that the modern term *primary care* implies continuous responsibility by a single provider for a child's health, perhaps including referral to specialists, and integration and management of the timing of various examinations, tests, and immunizations. Primary care is usually also meant to imply an orientation that includes the family and community of the child, because both have a strong influence on children's health. Schlesinger (1985) describes primary care as "efforts to provide continuous care by concerned providers who have the knowledge and empathy to respond to physical and emotional concerns" (p. 305).

The term *comprehensive care* also is often used to refer to this function. Kaufman and Watkins (1981, pp. 4–5) define comprehensive care to include the following:

- Preventive health care including such services as health education and promotion, family planning, and well-child supervision
- Health maintenance, treatment, habilitation, and rehabilitation of patients with acute and chronic medical problems
- Continuous availability of medical care through 24-hour coverage, supervision of hospitalized patients, and patient follow-up
- Assurance of the delivery of essential services such as child and adolescent health and prenatal, obstetric care
- Response to local health needs through an appropriate mix of supplemental services such as mental health and treatment of drug and alcohol abuse

Hoekelman (1987) notes the controversy surrounding what some health experts consider to be excessive number of visits recommended for healthy children (generally about 20 between birth and 21 years of age). The purposes (and means) of visits according to Hoekelman include the prevention of disease (through immunizations and health education); the early detection and treatment of disease (through history taking, physical examination, and screening); and counseling and anticipatory guidance of parents regarding the psychosocial aspects of childrearing.

Categorical Programs

The United States is the only nation in the industrialized world that lacks a comprehensive health policy for children and families (Children's Defense Fund, 1987). Rather, a complex web of programs that ebbs and flows with the political and economic times covers (or does not cover, as the case may be) various categorical needs. To further complicate the situation, most programs are administered or operated jointly by various arms of the federal and state governments so that eligibility and benefits vary widely among the 50 states. Despite the complexity and the differences among states, however, a basic understanding of these programs is essential for social workers in the field. In the following discussion, several major programs are discussed including the major components, social work functions, and likely future course.

AFDC

Though AFDC is an income rather than a health program, it is an essential component of the MCH system, both because of its relationship to eligibility for Medicaid (described later), and because it provides at least a subsistence income for many children who otherwise would live in destitution.

The first "widows pension" in Illinois, enacted in 1909, grew out of concern for widows and other needy women who often were forced to have others care for their children because of poverty alone. At the National Conference on Care of Dependent Children in 1909, social workers in the child welfare movement sought to change the policy of removing children from their homes because of poverty alone. They proposed instead a system of assisting those who were "deserving." (Unfortunately, at this time "deserving" usually meant white widows only. Divorced and minority women usually were not eligible for such services, and never-married women were certainly not considered "deserving.") These mothers could remain at home with their children rather than working or placing their children elsewhere (Conference on the Care of Dependent Children, 1909). Additional support for the program followed the Children's Bureau's epidemiologic studies of increased infant mortality from spoiled cow's milk in families with employed mothers (Lathrop, 1919).

The modern AFDC program was authorized by Title IV of the Social Security Act. Against the wishes of social workers who participated in drafting the act, it was placed under the Federal Emergency Relief Administration as a welfare program, rather than under the Children's Bureau as a social program. So it has remained, despite occasional proposals to the contrary (e.g., Piliavin & Gross, 1977). The program provides a minimal subsistence income to the children of single parents, and in a few states to two-parent families in which one is unemployed or permanently disabled.

AFDC currently serves 3.7 million poor families (Children's Defense Fund, 1987), a substantial reduction from 1980. In 1979, AFDC reached 76% of all poor children, whereas in 1985 that proportion had shrunk to about 58% (Children's Defense Fund, 1987). Moreover, unlike other programs such as Social Security, AFDC is not indexed for inflation, so the actual purchasing power of AFDC declined about one third between 1970 and 1984 (Meyer & Lewin, 1986). All recipients of AFDC are entitled to

Medicaid, so that the loss of AFDC eligibility also results in the loss of Medicaid benefits.

Medicaid and Early, Periodic Screening, Diagnosis, and Treatment Program (EPSDT)

Medicaid is the single most important resource for the health of poor children. It was enacted as part of the War on Poverty in 1966 as Title XIX of the Social Security Act. Medicaid grew out of recognition that the poor had limited access to quality health care. It is a joint federal-state program that must be available to all recipients of AFDC and may be provided at state option to certain other medically needy groups.

Medicaid payments are made in the form of partial reimbursement to providers of care. Matters such as the exact amount of reimbursement, which services of those that are optional are covered, and who other than AFDC recipients are eligible vary widely among the states and from year to year as available resources fluctuate. For example, reimbursement is never 100% of the cost of the service and is often low enough to restrict access to private providers. In addition to AFDC recipients, some states cover nonrecipients of public assistance when high medical bills place them at risk, whereas others do not.

Medicaid is one of the most unpopular public programs in this country and an annual target for budgetary cuts (Children's Defense Fund, 1987). Much of the program's unpopularity may be due to its link with AFDC in the public mind. Yet most of the huge, annual, federal outlay for Medicaid is spent not on mothers and children, but on the needy elderly whose costs exceed those covered by Medicare. Only 13% of Medicaid vendor payments are made on behalf of mothers and children (Meyer & Lewin, 1986). Despite its unpopularity, evidence does indicate that Medicaid has been successful in increasing the availability of medical care to the vulnerable population of women and children (Davis & Schoen, 1979). It also appears that those most in need have accrued the greatest benefit from Medicaid; during the 15 years immediately preceding the enactment of Medicaid, the death rate for black infants dropped by only 5%; during the 15 years following the enactment of Medicaid that rate dropped more than 50% (Children's Defense Fund, 1987).

The Select Panel for the Promotion of Child Health (1979) noted the spotty coverage by Medicaid of social work services, particularly in the area of mental health, and has recommended that social work services provided in an organized health or mental health care setting be reimbursed consistently. Certainly, failure of the program to reimburse for social services results in reduced availability of such services, because the cost would have to be borne entirely by the provider agency.

One possible piece of good news for America's poor children is the Child Health Assurance Program, which was passed as part of the Deficit Reduction Act of 1984 (Public Law 98-369). This act requires states to begin phasing in Medicaid eligibility for all children less than 5 years of age who live in families with incomes below the respective state's AFDC eligibility standard. Other parts of the legislation will extend Medicaid to children who have not heretofore been eligible. The American Academy of Pediatrics estimated that as many as 217,000 children might become eligible for Medicaid coverage under this program. In addition, the Omnibus Budget Reconciliation Acts of 1985 and 1986 now extend Medicaid coverage to all children less than 5 years of age whose families have incomes below state AFDC eligibility levels, and permit such coverage for children whose family incomes fall between the state AFDC and the federal poverty levels.

The Early, Periodic Screening, Diagnosis and Treatment Program (EPSDT) was enacted as part of Medicaid in 1967 because despite the Medicaid program, many children continued to suffer and be handicapped from preventable or curable conditions (Foltz, 1982). Also, Medicaid operates on a crisis-oriented, curative basis, whereas the purpose of EPSDT is to provide screening and preventive care for all low-income children up to 21 years of age, and treatment and rehabilitation for those children found to have certain potentially handicapping conditions (Manela, Anderson, & Lauffer, 1977). (Table 5.1 is a selected list of conditions and screening procedures of the EPSDT.) States are required to draw from many existing health care agencies for implementation of EPSDT (Maternal and Child Health Block Grant programs, Neighborhood Health Centers, Head Start, school health programs, and others) and to inform potential clients of their eligibility for services.

The EPSDT program has an interesting history that is detailed in Foltz (1982) and in Goggin (1987). Although it was finally enacted as part of Medicaid and thus is in essence a "welfare" program, in its beginnings EPSDT was conceptualized as part of Title V, making it a health program. Although often touted as a failure, EPSDT may be seen primarily as a victim of inadequate federal commitment and sloppy state implementation, as evidenced by the fact that although the amendments were passed in 1967 Congress finally was forced to threaten penalties in 1975 if states did not complete implementation. Despite the problems, Goggin (1987) reports that EPSDT has screened about 2 million poor or near-poor children annually since 1976; about half have been found to have a potentially handicapping condition.

As conceptualized, EPSDT is truly a comprehensive care program from case finding through follow-up (Millar, 1976). Standards prescribe the screening evaluations to be performed for all children.

TABLE 5.1 Elements of Screening and Assessment in the Early, Periodic Screening, Diagnosis, and Treatment Program

General medical history
Physical examination
Immunization status
Dental disease
Vision problems
Growth assessment
Developmental assessment
Tuberculin sensitivity
Urinary tract infections
Anemia
Lead poisoning
Sickle cell anemia

Note. From *Child Health Information for Workers in the Medicaid Early Prevention Screening Diagnosis and Treatment Program* (pp. 2–3) by R. Manela and W. Hillebrand, 1977, Washington, DC: U.S. Department of Health, Education and Welfare, Health Care Financing Administration.

Moreover, coordination with other systems such as day care, juvenile justice, and child welfare is required. Although as implemented the program initially concentrated only on younger children, it was intended and designed to serve all children up to the age of majority. Indeed, coverage has been extended to older children in the last few years. Evaluations should detect not only physical problems (such as vision or hearing loss), but developmental delay and emotional problems as well. In addition, the program should track the child through treatment and rehabilitation.

Government guidelines (Manela et al., 1977) emphasize the importance of removing barriers to EPSDT through such procedures as centralizing all possible services in the community where clients live; keeping administrative procedures short and simple to avoid delays; providing transportation and convenient hours of operation; making facilities attractive and comfortable for clients; facilitating communication between providers and community leaders; and establishing and publicizing client grievance procedures. Federal law requires annual outreach efforts to inform AFDC recipients that they are entitled to EPSDT services. Once requested by clients, screening and follow-up services must be provided within 60 days.

Jackson (1980) asserts that social workers should be more involved in EPSDT if it is to be successful, especially in cases in which an excess of demands on family time, resources, and funds reduces the likelihood of follow-up for diagnosis and therapy. Indeed, one of the most commonly cited problems of EPSDT is that often even when problems are detected, neither referral for treatment nor follow-up occurs to be certain that the problem has been resolved (Margolis & Meisels, 1987; North, 1982). One reason for this "slippage" may be that the families of many EPSDT children are multiproblem families who cannot take responsibility for following through with treatment for the problems that are detected; the system itself must assume responsibility for these functions.

Social workers may be part of EPSDT through employment in various settings. Many foster children are AFDC eligible and thus are entitled to screening, so many child welfare workers have become familiar with the program. Social workers in schools, mental health clinics, hospitals, and other settings also have become involved with the program because EPSDT is mandated to work with many other health services.

EPSDT has been difficult to evaluate because of the complications of maintaining such large volumes of data; in general the data have been found to be incomplete and less reliable than desired (Irwin & Conroy-Hughes, 1982). Using a sophisticated research design that combined both a cross-sectional and longitudinal approach, and corrected for various threats to the validity of the data, Irwin and Conroy-Hughes concluded that EPSDT was responsible for 30% fewer abnormalities requiring treatment in a group of representative children.

Conversely, Margolis and Meisels (1987) found major barriers to the effectiveness of EPSDT for children with developmental disabilities. They sampled administrators of every EPSDT program in Michigan and found barriers such as insensitive and inappropriate screening procedures, lack of public awareness of the program, logistics that inhibited eligible children from obtaining services, and lack of training of EPSDT staff to work with developmentally delayed children. In addition, they found that a significant proportion of children who were found to have problems were either never referred for treatment, or never received needed services. Lack of access to providers was a major problem including lack of coverage by Medicaid for needed services.

Nutrition Programs

The provision of food to the poor may be the most recognized role of the federal government. Since the Great Depression, in-kind food assistance has been provided at different points by the government, perhaps owing in part to the need to provide some use for surplus farm products. Currently, several programs provide nutrition to the nation's poor mothers and children.

The most important of these programs is the Special Supplemental Food Program for Women, Infants, and Children. WIC was authorized in 1973 to provide certain nutritious food to pregnant and lactating women and small children. The program is administered by the U.S. Department of Agriculture. (Details on the WIC program may be found in Chapter 2.) Most evaluations of the WIC program have examined its impact on LBW and neonatal mortality, but the program is available for children up to 5 years of age. Unfortunately, although the Children's Defense Fund (1987) says WIC saves $3 for every $1 spent, the program reaches only 40.4% of the women and children who are eligible for it.

The Food Stamp program is the largest government food program; in 1984 it reached an estimated 21.6 million poor persons (Levitan, 1985). Food Stamps are coupons that recipients may redeem at participating stores for food and certain other items. All public assistance recipients and certain other low-income persons are eligible for Food Stamps. The cost to the recipient is determined by income on a sliding scale basis, with certain deductions allowed. The allotment of food stamps per person is based on a Department of Agriculture formula that assumes effective nutritional planning skills, storage facilities, equipment, and low-cost participating markets. Most of these resources are in short supply for the poor (Levitan, 1985).

Several other nutrition programs are specifically intended for low-income children including the School Lunch Program begun in 1946 and the School Breakfast Program begun in 1966, both of which provide meals to children in schools. Also available are the Special Milk Program and other food programs, which provide meals and snacks to children in various settings such as summer camps, day-care centers, and health clinics. Levitan (1985) estimates that about 24.6 million children receive some type of supplement from these programs in schools and day-care centers. The largest of these programs is the School Lunch Program, which provides a subsidized lunch to more than half of all school-aged children. The other programs serve substantially smaller numbers of children but are important sources of nourishment for many poor or near-poor children.

Federal support for child nutrition programs was substantially reduced during the Reagan administration. Levitan (1985) reported that, in the early 1980s, about 3 million children were dropped from the School Lunch Program and about 500,000 were dropped from summer food programs. Indeed, Levitan (1985) reports that for every two children who do receive school lunches one more child is in need but does not qualify. Some do not apply because they are required to stand in separate lines, sit at separate tables, or stigmatize themselves in other ways.

Maternal and Child Health Block Grant

The 1981 Omnibus Budget Reconciliation Act combined a number of Title V programs into one block grant program. (Many of the programs are still in existence, although they may not be known by the same names.) Included in the program was the Comprehensive Child and Youth Health Program (C & Y), which was enacted by a 1965 amendment to the Social Security Act. The projects were enacted because school health services had been inadequate for providing needed health services for children (Insley, 1981b). The purpose of these projects was not only to finance services, but to create resources for health care in areas that were inadequately served; to provide outreach; and to respond to specific local needs.

C & Y programs were intended to provide comprehensive, continuous health services including health promotion activities, case finding, preventive services, and aftercare. Medical, dental, nutritional, and mental health services were also provided for eligible children. Eligibility was generally based on low family income and geographic area of residence, although special circumstances may be considered in determining eligibility for services. Ideally these programs coordinated with MIC programs to ensure that no child was lost in the transition. (MIC, also now part of the Block Grant, served infants to 1 year of age.) Case finding was intended to occur in welfare offices and through the child welfare system (Nelson, 1968).

Wallace and Medina reported that 85 C & Y programs continued to function in all 50 states in 1983. Under the original plan, local providers would pick up the cost and administration of the program, and funds could be used to begin programs in other communities. The lack of other sources for funds limited this occurrence, however, and cuts in the reorganized MCH Block Grant no doubt further limited the abilities of communities to fund the services.

Social workers were involved early in the planning stages of the C & Y programs, and were mandated personnel for them (Seligman, 1982). Social workers performed two main functions in C & Y programs. First, they provided in-office counseling to families with medical or mental health problems. Second, through their knowledge of and relationship with other community agencies, social workers were helpful to clients in meeting basic needs that affected their health, such as housing, day care, and other needs.

For example, social workers in the Dallas C & Y Project perceived a need for a way to identify child neglect among their population of poor residents of West Dallas (Edgington, Hall, & Rosser, 1980). Consequently, they developed and tested an instrument that has proved to be highly useful in identifying various types of child neglect. Often the social workers administered the instrument in a home visit, permitting the assessment of home conditions and parental behavior in the home environment.

Many of the C & Y program's original goals have not met with complete success. Seligman (1982) reports that although budgetary restraints in the last 2 decades have not affected basic traditional pediatric services, they have tended to curtail mental health services, community outreach, health education programs, and special programs such as infant stimulation. Though evaluation is required of all programs, this function has perhaps been the most seriously affected by funding limitations.

Nevertheless, the C & Y projects have been successful in several significant ways detailed by Seligman (1982). For the first time, the collaboration between social service and medical personnel has emphasized the close connection between child health and social factors. This collaboration has been instrumental in providing avenues for intervention. Millions of American children have been screened for health problems, and about 500,000 are receiving quality health care services. The numbers of children receiving health supervision have steadily increased, whereas hospitalization rates have decreased. Nutrition case finding has improved, and many children with nutritional deficiencies have been identified, making WIC available to them. Insley (1981b) emphasized the success of the program in early case finding and continuity of care. Finally, the program has been demonstrated to be cost-effective.

Child Health and Family-Centered Practice

The family-centered approach to MCH that is discussed in chapter 1 is particularly relevant to the provision of primary health care to low-income children. In particular, assessment of the health care needs of the child must include an assessment of the family's social situation with particular emphasis on any factor (such as low income, mental retardation of the mother, or lack of transportation) that might limit access of the child to quality health care.

Significant factors that relate to family functioning as it affects child health in particular might include first the same sociodemographic factors that are assessed in the provision of prenatal care (see Chapter 2). In addition, the health status and use of health care by other family members, the growth of the child (even if it is within normal bounds), the child's school performance, and his or her appearance and behavior are important to assessment. It also is essential that the social worker who performs a family assessment be well versed in child development to assess any significant problems in this area. In many primary health care settings child psychologists participate on the MCH team and perform developmental testing using standardized instruments.

Several standardized instruments also may be helpful to the social worker in his or her assessment of families. Based on their examination of the human ecology and social support literature, Dunst and Leet (1987) took a "needs hierarchy" approach to the provision of health care services to young children. They hypothesized that households that lack adequate resources will be unable to pay adequate attention to their children's health care needs because of more elementary, pressing needs. Their 30-item Family Resource Scale showed reasonable reliability and validity and may be a promising approach to assessing which families may be too burdened by other needs to deal effectively with their children's health care needs. Affirmation of Dunst and Leet's hypothesis awaits further study.

The Home Observation for Measurement of the Environment Inventory (Caldwell & Bradley, 1978) has been widely used as a measure of the care given to children from birth to 6 years of age. The two different versions of this inventory (for birth to 3 years of age, and for preschoolers) include six and eight subscales, respectively, and must be administered by a professional in the home environment while observing the interacting mother and child. Administration requires approximately 1 hour. Despite some practical difficulties and the necessity of training for completely credible use, this measure has the advantage of thoroughness and a long history of use (Magura & Moses, 1986).

Finally, family-centered practice in the provision of health care services to young children often involves social work innovation and "going the additional mile." Barber (1987) reported on a project in Mississippi that involves a telephone line to assist low-income families who are having difficulty with the eligibility requirements of Medicaid, in addition to resources to provide medical care for indigent families when no other source can be located. This program and other such creative solutions to the problems of families present the best hope of fulfilling America's promise to all children of a healthy beginning.

6 Services for Children With Disabilities

The implications for the family of having a child with a handicap or disability are profound and long lasting. Moreover, for many of these families, the difficulties are exacerbated by the necessity of constant interaction with a social service system that is fragmented, often inadequate to their needs, and difficult to maneuver. Conflictual relationships with the professionals with whom they must interact further complicate parents' interactions with this system.

It is impossible to determine precisely how many children and families need special services because of disability or handicap. No central data collection agency or institution exists, and no precise definitions are available (Hayden & Beck, 1982). Some children suffer from disabilities or illnesses that are barely perceptible (often called "subclinical"), whereas others have severe problems that restrict their daily activities. Others suffer from several different handicapping conditions. Dane (1985) estimates that approximately 12% of school-aged children suffer from disabilities that qualify them for special education services.

Hayden and Beck (1982) categorized the major handicapping and risk conditions that may result in developmental disabilities as related to the period of onset: (a) prenatal onset—central nervous system abnormalities and syndromes; (b) perinatal onset—prematurity, infection, trauma, and hemolytic disease; and (c) unknown onset or combination—cerebral palsy; and (d) childhood onset owing to trauma, infection, or others—various disabilities. Such classifications may be used for purposes of planning, but Nash and Jauregry (1981) offer a more meaningful definition when they say "anything which will interfere with the developmental norms held for the infant or for the family" (p. 24).

A conservative estimate is that approximately 9,306 cases of prenatal-onset disabilities occur each year (Hayden & Beck, 1982). Central nervous system disorders include anencephaly, spina bifida, congenital hydrocephalus, and others. Approximately 6,606 of new syndrome-related handicaps occur each year, with Down syndrome responsible for more than half of these. Hayden and Beck (1982) report recent reductions of these conditions in the United States, probably related to genetic counseling, and prenatal diagnosis and abortion.

Several situations may cause problems in the perinatal period including hypoxemia, infection, and hemorrhage. Medical technology has improved the survival rates of infants who suffer such insults, but concern exists that this improvement in survival has also resulted in increased numbers of children with handicapping conditions (Hayden & Beck, 1982). The evidence does not seem to support these fears. Finally, cerebral palsy may occur either as a combination of prenatal and perinatal factors, such as maternal bleeding and LBW (Hayden & Beck, 1982). In other cases the origin of cerebral palsy may be unknown. Approximately 6,000 new cases of cerebral palsy occur each year.

This chapter uses examples of various types of childhood disabilities and handicapping conditions, but does not attempt to provide extensive information on each one. It would not be possible here to provide a thorough account of the vast amount of information needed by social workers in all settings that serve children with disabilities and their families. A good deal of independent research on each particular disease or condition is required, because it is likely that each childhood handicap is characterized by unique problems and family needs (Tavormina, Kasner, Slater, & Watt, 1976).

The family with a member who is disabled interacts with many systems including the health care system, the social service system, and the special educational system. In many cases it is difficult to distinguish whether particular services or programs should be classified as a special education program or an MCH health-related program. Because this book is concerned with the provision of MCH services, little emphasis will be placed specifically on educational services for children with handicaps, even though many social workers are employed in programs in this area. Social workers are most involved in the provision of MCH services in birth settings and in health-focused programs such as those funded by Title V. Other more educationally based services (such as early intervention and school services) are important to families of children with handicaps and so are summarized here; however, because they are not categorized as MCH services, they are not discussed in detail.

SPECIAL NEEDS OF THIS POPULATION

The effects of disability on children and their families vary according to the nature and severity of the handicap as well as the resources and coping abilities of the child and family (Meyer, 1986). In the following section, the needs of children with disabilities and their families are discussed. At every age in the life of the child with a handicap, a key role for the social worker in assisting the child lies in assisting the parents in their adjustment, for it is believed that the successful adjustment of the child lies in the parents' successful adjustment and reaction to the child (Darling & Darling, 1982; Ross, 1982b; Schild, 1981). J. Shapiro (1983) characterizes successful parental adjustment to include the imposing of only necessary and realistic restrictions on the child and the promotion of peer interaction, self-care, and school attendance. In some cases, parents may require considerable encouragement to avoid overprotection and restriction of their children with disabilities.

Early Effects of Diagnosis

The first crisis for most families of children with disabilities is the one created by the diagnosis. The diagnosis of disability is usually unexpected, particularly if it occurs at birth or shortly after birth; thus, the parents' first reaction is thus usually shock and disbelief (Murphy & Crocker, 1987). Conversely, Mori (1983) contends that the disability is even more difficult for parents to accept when the child is older and the disability is not obvious—for example, cases of mild or moderate retardation. In either case, some feel adjusting to having a child with a handicap or chronic illness is an ongoing process that may never be completed (Nash & Jauregry, 1981), and that one cannot describe this adjustment process by "stages" (Wikler, Wasow & Hatfield, 1981).

Others believe that the stages of adjustment for parents are somewhat predictable, although substantial variation exists among families. Theorists have compared the process of mourning a child's disability with mourning a death (e.g., Murphy & Crocker, 1987; Parks, 1977). The term *stages* is used here to describe that process, although it is recognized that the process is not as predictable as this term might imply, and indeed that parents may reexperience previous feelings as their children enter new developmental stages.

The early stages following diagnosis are marked by shock, anguish, disbelief, and hopelessness. Behavior may be severely psychologically disorganized (Parks, 1977), as the parents become frantic and unable to make decisions or plan for the future. Parks (1977) recommends that the social worker meet with the parents immediately following diagnosis; now it is not uncommon for social workers to be present when the information is given to the parents. The social worker should also ask about practical needs at this time, as the couple may require assistance with baby-sitting, using transportation, or notifying family and friends.

The diagnosis and consequent mourning that occur when parents learn that their children have a handicap may damage the bonding process that occurs at birth (Klaus & Kennell, 1982), especially if the disability is grossly apparent (Johnson, 1987). Therefore, the manner in which parents are told of their child's condition is important, because it may affect their perception of their child for many years to come. The two most important issues at this time are the parents' need for full information, and the manner in which the professional's attitude toward the child is communicated to the parents.

Parents are entitled to, and in need of, full information about their child's condition as soon as it is available (Darling & Darling, 1982; Nash & Jauregry, 1981). This will include the diagnosis (in terms they can understand), the prognosis if known, available treatments and services, and the child's potential abilities and skills. In the past, professionals have sometimes avoided full disclosure to parents, perhaps because they did not want to trouble or confuse them, or they did not wish to take the time, or they were defensive about being "the expert." Information is critical to the parents in that it increases their sense of control and self-esteem (Ross, 1982a), both necessary for their functioning as successful parents.

For the professional, the most troubling aspect of disclosure is striking a balance between realism and optimism. To be effective at this most painful of tasks, professionals must be able to sit and talk with parents honestly but optimistically, without platitudes that may foster unrealistic goals. At the same time, parents should be told of the child's positive attributes, his or her strengths, and the skills and abilities he or she may be able to master (Johnson, 1987). Striking this balance can be a difficult task, because it is not possible to predict a child's developmental outcomes based on medical condition or risk factors at birth.

The literature is replete with parental accounts of insensitivity, brisk-ness, instant advice to institutionalize and forget the child, and incredible bumbling by professionals when advising parents of their child's disability (e.g., Darling & Darling, 1982; Roberts, 1986). Most of these accounts concern physicians who are not trained in the techniques of imparting such information and may be expressing their own discomfort with dis-abilities as well as their profound sorrow and sympathy for the parents. Competent social workers should be present to support both parents and physicians during this difficult process. Guendelman (1981) advises physicians to consult with a competent social worker before talking with the family to find out about the family's special needs.

Parents often cannot absorb everything they need to know when first told of their child's condition (Johnson, 1987). Full understanding may require time, and social workers must show patience and compassion, perhaps repeating facts several times and requesting feedback to monitor the parents' understanding (Johnson, 1987).

It is not uncommon for parents to refuse to accept their child's diagnosis. This disbelief may take the form of "shopping" for another diagnosis, attempting to take the baby home from the hospital prematurely, or refusing to discuss the child's problem. Although denial is a normal part of the early response to trauma (Borg & Lasker, 1982), it can be destructive and may require aggressive intervention if it leads to delays in obtaining needed services for the child.

Some parents may express anger at physicians, each other, or even God, and may engage in "bargaining" following the denial stage. Because parents cannot accept their own anger they also may feel guilty about their anger as well as about their own imagined wrongdoings that led to the child's problem. Bargaining may take the form of prayer and self-sacrifice (in exchange for the child's recovery), or it may involve obtaining every possible service in the belief that something will cause the child to improve.

As parents begin to acknowledge their child's problem, most parents are able to accept their child's condition, although temporary depression and a lifelong sadness will probably be inevitable. Some parents attach new meaning to the disability (e.g., "It is God's will"), whereas others simply resign themselves. Grieving experts say that it is when the parents accept the child's problem that they can begin productive efforts to help the child reach his or her full potential. Most parents look toward the future with some dread (Moeller, 1986), however, especially as they contemplate the problems their children are likely to experience throughout life.

Olshansky (1962) and Wikler et al. (1981) have suggested that the simplistic process of "stages of grief" does not accurately portray the experiences of most parents of retarded children. Instead they have proposed that parents experience a "chronic sorrow" that is periodic and may be linked to certain developmental events. If parental grief is more chronic than the concept of stages would suggest, parents would require a continuum of services over time that should be linked to changing needs and coping abilities.

Whether handicapped or not, all children have the same basic needs and desires to grow and develop, learn, interact with their peers, and be part of a family while simultaneously becoming independent. Handicapped children have these same desires and needs as well as the same problems that other children have, but they have the additional challenges posed by their handicap or illness.

Depending on the degree of severity, handicap or chronic illness imposes some degree of limitation of certain activities for the child. Some children with disabilities or those with chronic illnesses may have vulnerable health in general if their condition predisposes them to frequent acute illnesses. This vulnerable health and their primary handicap or problem may lead to ongoing frequent contact with various health care professionals. Sometimes a great deal of time is lost to the child because of time spent in habilitation, health care, and hospitalization (Murphy & Crocker, 1987). Hospitalization in particular may be associated with separation from family, painful procedures, and exposure to unfamiliar and frightening people. All of these factors have disruptive and long-term effects on the development of children (Brill, Cohen, Fauvre, Klein, Clark, & Garcia, 1987; Gliedman & Roth, 1980), and deprive them of the normal learning and social activities that contribute to a happy childhood.

Preschool Years

Miller (1981) emphasizes an important point when she says that "social workers don't meet needs of pre-school children; parents do" (p. 69). The young child's needs center on the family, and social workers may be helpful to families who have children with disabilities by helping them to anticipate their child's needs and to prepare to meet those needs. The needs of the preschooler, as he begins to reach out and become part of a wider world, can only be understood fully within the context of the entire family's needs (Morris & West, 1981).

Several normal preschool needs are stressful to parents of preschoolers but require extra work of parents whose children have a handicap. For example, the young child's need for a safe environment in which he can explore requires eternal vigilance of parents; if the child is visually or hearing impaired, the parent must work even harder to be certain that the child is safe (Miller, 1981). Other issues include the preschooler's needs to socialize with other children (which is perhaps more difficult when the child has a problem), the child's developing body self-image, and self-esteem.

Morris and West (1981) emphasize that the needs of the family during the preschool years of the child with a handicap include the same needs as those of other families including the parents' needs to maintain and fulfill their marital relationship, the need to balance attention and resources among all the children in the family, and the need to pursue individual interests. Families including a child with a handicap may have a difficult time meeting this child's need while also meeting these other normal family needs.

The preschool years seem to be a time when social workers may have less contact with families of handicapped children than during infancy or later after the child enters school (Guendelman, 1981). Parents may be busy clarifying the diagnosis and becoming clear on their child's prognosis, or they may still be having difficulty accepting that their child has a problem. Moreover, if little contact with other children of similar age occurs, the child's handicap may easily be forgotten or denied.

School-Aged Child

Entering school is a milestone for children and their families, and it usually marks a period of accelerated learning and social involvement for the child. This time is a key one for families with handicapped children and may be considered a crisis period (Dindia, 1981). The evaluations and testing necessary for entering school are a reminder to the parents of the child's disability, and indeed the child may officially acquire the label of "mentally retarded" at this age (Dindia, 1981). If the child has marked deficits that are apparent in comparison with other "normal children," or if the child enters a special program with other handicapped children, the school environment may be stressful for the parents.

A common problem for school-aged children with handicaps or disabilities is isolation caused by limitations in normal activities and social opportunities, as well as by parental restriction. The child may suffer from a poor self-image that focuses on the handicap (Batshaw & Perret, 1986), especially if the condition causes any disfigurement, and thus may avoid interactions with peers. Peers may avoid the child who is different, and the child must suffer the special pain of not being invited to birthday parties or overnight parties (Dindia, 1981). Moreover, some parents deny their children the normal social interactions and independence that other children enjoy to protect them from possible rejection (Howard, 1982; Mori, 1983). Howard (1978) asserts that such parental behavior may result in these children developing into adults with passive, dependent personalities.

Some children with handicaps suffer from psychological and emotional problems as well. The Association for the Care of Children's Health (1983) estimates that psychiatric problems may be twice as common among this group as among the general population of children. They may be immature because of the excessive attention paid to them during their illness, or because parents are reluctant to discipline a sick child. In many cases the child has a poor self-image that focuses on the illness or handicap.

Adolescents

According to Hall (1981), "adolescents with handicapping conditions face the same problems as do all adolescents. However, due to personal limitations of their handicap (actual or perceived) and societal discrimination they must work against a double-negative public image problem: handicapped and adolescent" (p. 175). Placed within the context of the pressures of modern life, rapid growth and development, and a society that is not accepting of differences (and this is perhaps most apparent among teenagers), the adolescence of the handicapped child would seem to be particularly difficult. Dindia (1981) characterizes adolescence as a crisis period for the parents of handicapped children.

Indeed, adolescence is a period of increasing independence, as the child tests limits, takes risks, and rebels against the family. The adolescent who must be dependent because of an illness or handicap, who has limitations in self-care and mobility, or who has a poor self-image because of his condition, has great difficulty in achieving the important tasks of adolescence (Dindia, 1981). Indeed, because of the nature of their handicap, some adolescents will never live independent lives (Hall, 1981). In many cases the developmental task of selecting a career also is complicated by restrictions imposed by limitations in abilities.

The poor self-image that many children with disabilities have becomes particularly painful during adolescence, when it is normal for all children to feel self-conscious about appearance. Adolescents must come to grips with sexuality and any limitations in sexual behavior and reproductive capability that may exist as well as societal prejudice against sexuality in handicapped persons (Gliedman & Roth, 1980). Parents, too, must deal with their child's sexuality including their fears that he or she will be sexually exploited (Dindia, 1981). Often the normal social opportunities for learning and practicing appropriate sex role behaviors are limited for the handicapped adolescent (Dindia, 1981; Hall, 1981).

In some cases parents may overrestrict their handicapped adolescent because of their own fears or a wish to protect him from rejection. Unnecessary restrictions prevent the adolescent from learning the age-appropriate behaviors and from experiencing the kinds of interaction he needs to continue to grow and develop.

Family Strengths and Coping Resources

It is important not to view these families or their children solely from the perspective of their problems, however. Schilling, Gilchrist, and Schinke (1984) pointed out that such families may learn to adapt in positive ways through various coping strategies that can be quite effective. Indeed, the families of children with disabilities "possess far more strengths than needs and experience more success than failures" (Shelton et al., 1987, p. 27).

Bergman et al. (1979) advise: "It is helpful to view these families as normal families in a process of readjustment to a long-term and frequently unpredictable illness that will have an impact on every aspect of their lives" (p. 269). In practical terms, the social worker may operationalize this advice by assisting the family in identifying the child's strengths ("Johnny is very socially responsive"), and by avoiding labeling ("profound mental retardation") and professional jargon ("noncompliance") (Shelton et al., 1987).

It must be recognized, however, that families of children with disabilities often do suffer from an enormous amount of stress that results not just from their children's problems, but from the difficulties of obtaining the services they require and from the reactions of others in their environment. Moreover, they are subject to the same stresses of family life and childrearing that are experienced by all families. Although the evidence is not unequivocal, some studies have reported an increase in marital and family strain, and a decrease in marital satisfaction in families with children who have disabilities (Brimblecombe, 1984; Kazak, 1986). Fatigue and lack of privacy may damage their sexual relationship, and, in some cases, each partner may blame the other for the child's problems.

Concern has also existed about the effects on siblings of having a sister or brother with a disability. Murphy and Crocker (1987) categorize the various factors that might affect siblings negatively: (a) changes in the normal family schedule or living environment (e.g., having a ramp on the front porch); (b) competition for attention and resources from the parents; (c) misinformation about the causes or genetic implications of the sibling's condition; (d) surrogate parental responsibilities expected of the child; (e) obligations to achieve in order to "make up" for the sibling's disabilities; and (f) confusion about the source of the parents' grief or other emotional responses to the sibling's problems. Other factors may cause siblings of children with handicaps to feel "different" or to have problems, such as expectations that they totally accept and become involved in caring for the sibling, and disciplinary double standards.

Despite these potential problems and evidence that they do negatively affect some siblings, reviews of the literature by Batshaw and Perret (1986) and Kazak (1986) found that in general siblings of children with handicaps fare quite well. Social workers probably should assess parents' understanding of their other children's needs, however, and might want to encourage parents to remember those needs and to make special time for all their children.

Parks (1977) and Bergman et al. (1979) emphasize the importance of good family assessments including assessment of their strengths, limitations, supports, and other concerns. In particular, assessment may reveal that parents need to be reminded of the needs of their other children. For example, Koch-Hatten (1986) emphasized the importance of assessing the feelings and reactions of the siblings of young cancer victims to help parents recognize the needs of all their children.

The assessment may identify some families who may benefit from marriage or family counseling, especially around issues concerning their continued need to spend time with each other as a couple and a family. Family members may feel guilty if they want or need this time together, but they may require only support and encouragement to do so. In other cases the additional stresses of having a child with special needs have created or contributed to long-standing marital difficulties. Thus, families may be able to strengthen a major resource for themselves during this difficult time through counseling.

Family Needs and Challenges

Financial Hardship

Financial hardship can be a crushing burden for some families whose children have handicaps or chronic illness. Often this burden is because of the child's need for extraordinary medical care or services (Slater & Wikler, 1986). In addition, chronically ill children have greater health care needs than other children (Newacheck & McManus, 1988), and these needs usually extend throughout life. Anticipatory guidance may assist parents to plan realistically for these needs in advance.

Some of these extraordinary needs can be met by government programs or assistance, and about 75% of disabled children have some kind of private health insurance (Newacheck & McManus, 1988). Assistance is not likely to be available for every special need, however, and in any case it is often difficult to obtain. Childhood disabilities may further limit the family's income by restricting the family's employment mobility because of health insurance needs, or necessitating that the father hold two jobs or that the mother stay home to provide full-time child care rather than contributing to the family's income by working (Johnson, 1987).

The social worker's role in assisting the family to meet its financial needs begins with a thorough assessment of needs and resources and proceeds with an exploration of available programs and services, described in the following section. The social worker must not assume that the family is aware of available programs (few are), or that they understand the process for applying for services. In fact, some families will be reluctant to take advantage of available services because of shame or embarrassment, and will require encouragement and support in this area.

Child Care Needs

A second major problem for families may be due to the extraordinary child care needs they face. In cases in which the child's problems are severe, constant care and lack of leisure time may lead to permanent fatigue for the parents (Brimblecombe, 1984). The mother especially may feel continuing despair because of her added child care responsibilities (Healy et al., 1985a; Holroyd, 1974), perhaps especially if she has not been accustomed to full-time child care. Indeed, having a child with a handicap may force some families to divide child care responsibilities in new ways (Kazak, 1986).

Fathers of children with disabilities may experience stress differently from mothers, although Kazak's (1986) review of the effects of child handicaps on parents shows that research generally has neglected the effects of handicap on the father. Moeller (1986) described the sympathy and tenderness shown a mother when the diagnosis of Down Syndrome was given to her, even as the father was completely ignored. The great emotional stake that fathers have in their children and the long-term stress they suffer because of children with handicaps demand greater attention by both researchers and social workers.

Moeller (1986) suggests that separate services may be beneficial for fathers for several reasons. First, fathers are more likely to be employed full-time and may need services that are scheduled on weekends and during evening hours (Meyer, 1986). Perhaps because of these scheduling difficulties, professionals have been oriented toward the mother as the primary caretaker and have not worked to assist fathers to reach the same level of acceptance that mothers may reach by virtue of their more constant contact with those professionals (Morris & West, 1981). Second, men may express their feelings and concerns differently from women and may not benefit from group experiences that are designed primarily for women. Finally, fathers may experience unique stresses and problems that deserve exclusive attention. That attention may be diluted by the presence of mothers.

Depending on the nature and severity of the child's disability, the required treatment regimen may be time-consuming, physically fatiguing, and technically difficult. For example, the necessary home care of cystic fibrosis patients involves daily inhalation therapy and postural drainage, both of which are time-consuming and painful for the child. Moreover, a restricted diet and noxious dietary supplement are necessary, as is frequent medication (Oppenheimer & Rucker, 1980). Oppenheimer and Rucker (1980) found substantial variation in the quality of home care for children with cystic fibrosis that depended in part on the support and assistance available to the parents.

"Compliance" to a treatment regimen requires that parents have sufficient knowledge, skill, time, and commitment to carry through consistently. For some parents one or more of these elements are lacking, and failure to adhere to the recommended regimen may have serious long-term ramifications for the child. Social workers may be helpful to parents who are having difficulty with compliance in several ways. Both Schultz (1980) and Oppenheimer and Rucker (1980) emphasize first the importance of a thorough assessment to identify any barriers to compliance. Schultz's (1980) review of the compliance literature would suggest that poor family functioning, little social support, and low self-esteem may predispose parents to poor compliance with their child's medical regimen, especially when the regimen is complicated and likely to last a long time.

Social workers may be a major resource to the pediatrician when problems with meeting the treatment regime exist. Schultz (1980) suggests some negotiation in the design of the treatment regimen when possible as well as interventions designed specifically to deal with the preceding problems. Bergman, Lewiston, and West (1979) note that the social worker's knowledge of the family may help the pediatrician to design a treatment regimen that is consistent with the family's life-style. The social worker may function as an intermediary between the physician and the family in such cases.

Respite care is a resource that is often mentioned as an especially important one to families with special-needs children (Cacioppo & Andrews, 1979; Darling & Darling, 1982; Oppenheimer & Rucker, 1980). Slater and Wikler (1986) emphasized that families of children with developmental disabilities need leisure time just as other families do, and that vacations should be regarded as basic rights for these families.

Whether for an afternoon, evening, or 2 weeks in the summer, time away while the child receives competent care from a substitute in the home may provide relief from responsibilities, attention to normal marriage and family life, and the opportunity for "normal" enjoyable activities. Although evaluative studies have not been done to demonstrate the outcomes of respite care, it is believed to prevent unnecessary hospitalization, child abuse or neglect, or dysfunctional family life by restoring the parents' energy and coping abilities (Halpern, 1985).

Halpern (1985) compared 31 families with retarded children who used a respite service with 31 families who did not on several dimensions of the "social climate" of the families. (Some caution in interpretation of Halpern's results is necessary because of the small sample and the apparently large number of statistical tests performed. Some differences may have been due to chance.) She found that families that used the respite services tended to have children with more severe disabilities, had fewer family supports available to them, and felt that they were under more stress than families who did not use respite care. Users were more likely to be white and of higher social class than nonusers, so some barriers to the use of respite care by minority and lower income families may exist. Halpern emphasized the importance of outreach to families who are uninformed about the availability of services, those who are very young, and those whose disorganized and conflicted functioning may make it difficult for them to seek respite care.

Day care is another possible resource for parents, but competent day care is almost impossible to find for children with special needs (Kadushin & Martin, 1988). Chang and Teramoto (1987) surveyed private day-care centers and found that only 25 children with handicaps or disabilities were enrolled in 26 centers that had a total enrollment of 1590 children. In this nonrepresentative sample, centers that expressed no desire to enroll children with disabilities cited as their reasons lack of staff training and special equipment.

Social Isolation

Perhaps the most troublesome effect of having a child with a handicap is the isolation that many families endure (Brimblecombe, 1984; Kazak, 1986). Some families stop seeing their friends and extended family when they learn of their child's problem (Mori, 1983), and others feel uncomfortable with the reactions of others to their children. The resulting isolation places a family under considerable stress, which renders them less tolerant of and less able to cope successfully with daily problems. Consequently the family is placed at risk for several problems, including health and psychological problems (Slater & Wikler, 1986).

Many professionals regard parent support groups as the most important resource they can provide for parents of children with handicaps (Johnson, 1987; Murphy & Crocker, 1987; Schilling et al., 1984). Parents of other children with handicaps can provide information and support that professionals may not be able to offer. Several national and local organizations exist to provide emotional support. These organizations often provide practical assistance such as reciprocal child care arrangements as well.

A word of caution is in order regarding self-help groups, however. Some professionals emphasize that it may not be healthy for families to rely exclusively on such networks to meet their social needs (Dunst & Trivette, 1988). They suggest that self-help groups might weaken family commitment and willingness to provide support. Moreover, evaluations of self-help groups have not provided empirical support for their helpfulness to families (Kazak, 1986). Evaluative data would be helpful in documenting the specific effects of such groups, both positive and negative. Meanwhile, Slater and Wikler (1986) emphasize that families of children with disabilities require a "triad" of support including flexible nuclear family relationships, extended informal relationships, and formal social service supports.

Anticipatory guidance, defined as an essential preventive function of social work by Rapoport in 1961, may be helpful for parents in anticipating the predictable crises associated with developmental milestones (such as beginning school or entering puberty) or with the child's disability (such as having surgery or beginning physical rehabilitation). Some chronic illnesses such as cancer carry long-term implications even after remission has been achieved, and the family may benefit from both anticipatory guidance and the explicit possibility of later contact around major issues (Ross, 1982b). After parents have adjusted to and accepted their child's diagnosis, they may respond positively to the suggestion of a discussion of the future and long-term planning.

METHODS OF ASSESSMENT.   Despite recognition of the importance of assessing family needs, few models exist for such assessment (Bailey et al., 1986). This is true despite increased awareness of the importance of family functioning in child health and development in general, and more specifically broad consensus that the family is the chief resource of the handicapped child in his or her interaction with the health care system. Both Bailey et al. (1986) and Weiss and Jacobs (1988) recently reviewed several instruments that deal not with health specifically but with early educational intervention. Only a selection of those that appear to relate more directly to health are discussed here, but the reader is urged to refer to these sources for information about a broad array of instruments that may be relevant to specific programs and services.

The Questionnaire on Resources and Stress (Holroyd, 1974) was designed specifically to measure stress, coping, and adaptation in families with handicapped children. Although the original measure (it has been revised) has shown good validity, administration of this questionnaire presents some difficulties in that is is lengthy, requiring about 1 hour for administration.

The Impact-on-Family Scale (Stein & Riessman, 1980) measures four dimensions of the impact of chronic childhood illness on the family: financial, social-familial, personal strain, and mastery. The 24-item measure is administered by an interviewer, and thus requires a small amount of professional time and expense. Because the initial testing of the instrument involved only children with physical illnesses, additional testing is needed with other types of conditions. For example, the instrument may not be valid for chronic conditions such as developmental disabilities. Initial testing of the instrument did reveal acceptable reliability, however.

The Family Resource Scale (Dunst & Leet, 1987) appears to be an excellent instrument for identifying families who have inadequate financial and personal resources, and who therefore may not be able to meet their child's needs, whether handicapped or not. The simple 30-item (self-report) instrument has acceptable reliability and validity, and addresses the various types of personal and financial resources that are important to families with young children. Although it is simple, the fact that the instrument is completed by the respondent-client does mean that some subjects with limited education or reading ability might need assistance. To the author's knowledge, the measure has not been tested specifically on handicapped or chronically ill children, but it appears to be a promising measure for such uses.

Walker and Crocker (1988) review several other measures of family functioning that may be useful for the clinician's evaluation of family dysfunction. Although most of these measures do not pertain specifically to the handicapped or chronically ill child, they identify various types of problems that families may have including those related to the child's illness or handicap, and those that are not. Most of these instruments do not have sufficiently adequate psychometric properties to be useful for program evaluation, but they may be useful for providing indications to the social worker that the family has problems requiring further attention.

Services for Children and Their Families

An evaluation of services for chronically ill children requires a careful look at the system of health care. To the extent that the services are not coordinated, comprehensive, or continuous, added risk exists both for the child and for the healthy continuation of the family. The Select Panel for the Promotion of Child Health (1979) noted that a great burden is placed on such families when they must coordinate and manage their own cases within a maze of fragmented programs and services. Indeed, fragmentation and lack of coordination are mentioned in virtually every discussion of the child health care system.

It is incumbent on the social worker who has contact with chronically ill children and their families to be fully familiar with the availability and details of services and resources for the particular needs of such families. Because it is somewhat complicated to draw boundaries between MCH and special educational programs, for the sake of simplicity this discussion will consider MCH programs to revolve primarily around public health and medically oriented settings (e.g., the NICU or the follow-up clinic for high-risk infants). Services that are provided in more educationally oriented settings such as early intervention programs will be described in less detail and may be more properly considered school social work.

Children With Special Health Care Needs

Until passage of the Social Security Act in 1935, services to handicapped children consisted primarily only of institutional care, paid for either by the family or, in some cases, the public. Title V, Part 2 of the Social Security Act authorized Crippled Children's Services (CCS) through grants to the states in 1935:

> for the purpose of enabling each State to extend and improve (especially in rural areas and in areas suffering from severe economic distress) as far as practicable under the conditions in such State, services for locating crippled children, and providing medical, surgical, corrective and other services and care, and facilities for diagnosis, hospitalization and aftercare for children who are crippled or who are suffering from conditions which lead to crippling.

A formula including the number of children younger than 21 years of age and the per capita income in the state determined the federal contribution, and a portion had to be matched dollar-for-dollar by the state.

Rudolph and Borker (1987) document the history of CCS, noting that the need for services for handicapped children did not become apparent to the public as early as the general problems of MCH. Polio during the 1930s and blindness among children, caused by untreated ophthalmic neuropathy at birth, were of particular concern (Rudolph & Borker, 1987).

In 1981 CCS was combined with several other MCH programs under the authority of the Maternal and Child Health Block Grant and redesignated as the program for Children with Special Health Care Needs. About half of the states have renamed their programs (Ireys &

Eichler, 1988). Because the program has been known as CCS for many years, however, the following discussion uses that term.

As a block grant program, CCS programs are administered by the individual states under broad federal guidelines. All states must include preventive services aimed at early detection of handicapping conditions, but great variation exists among the states in their operation of the programs (Ireys & Eichler, 1988). In most states the CCS is administered by the state health department, but in some others the welfare department, a state university, or the department of education may administer the program. Diagnostic services must be provided for all children, but states may impose financial eligibility criteria for medical treatment.

The state CCS programs performed (and continue to perform under the block grant) many functions on behalf of children with handicaps including advocacy and drafting of legislation, the development and implementation of new services; the collection, analysis, and dissemination of data; and the oversight and coordination of prevention, treatment, and rehabilitation services for children with disabilities. The program also was responsible for administering the federal and matching state and local funds for the program, and the Supplemetal Security Income (SSI) program for children with disabilities (described later), which is also now part of the Maternal and Child Health Block Grant (Wallace & Medina, 1982). An important function of CCS was its standard-setting function, leading to a higher quality of health care for children with handicaps (Smith, 1981).

A recent survey of directors of CCS agencies revealed remarkable similarity among directors in their assessments of the importance of various professional activities (Ireys & Eichler, 1988). Directors ranked activities concerning patient care as most important, issues related to public health aspects as next important, those related to financing next, and issues related to relationships with other institutions next.

Some 125 established diagnostic categories now exist for CCS, in general covering conditions requiring care throughout childhood and adolescence, and conditions that are so severe that the cost of care is beyond the resources of the family (Wallace, 1987). When the program began, its emphasis was on certain "fixed deformity" conditions, such as birth defects and musculoskeletal disorders. As medical advances have led to more effective treatment for other conditions since 1935, they have been added to the list of those covered by CCS. In recent years CCS case loads have included fewer conditions associated with infections such as polio and more of those related to birth defects and neurological conditions (Wallace, 1987). Interest in mental retardation and improvements in the treatment of congenital heart disease in the 1950s led to the inclusion of these conditions in the list of CCS diagnoses (Nelson, 1983).

Great diversity exists in coverage of conditions by the states, however. An example is chronic otitis media, which can result in serious hearing loss if untreated, and which is covered by some states and not by others. Great diversity also exists in eligibility requirements, which are generally based on area of residence and income. Developmental disabilities were not recognized separately as an MCH problem deserving of prevention services until passage of legislation in 1963 (McDonald-Wikler, 1987). Much of the interest in mental retardation in the 1960s was due to the influence of President John F. Kennedy, who had a close family member with a developmental disability (Wallace, 1987).

Services for children with special health care needs are provided by the state's block grant program in conjunction with numerous other state agencies such as the Departments of Mental Health and Mental Retardation–Developmental Disabilities; and Public Welfare, Education, and the Rehabilitation Services Commission. Consultants also work with private councils and organizations such as the March of Dimes. Social workers form relationships with hospitals, physicians, school personnel, health departments, and other health care and social agencies to provide information and linkages that result in case finding and referral of children who require services.

Wallace (1982) reported that 57% of children in the CCS programs received case management services in 1982. Case management is a prime function of the CCS programs (Select Panel for the Promotion of Child Health, 1981), and is essential for such a multidisciplinary, multifaceted program. Case management services range from preparating an individualized service plan for each child to arranging the delivery of the various types of services and monitoring the child's condition to determine when changes in the service plan are required.

Stokes (1980) demonstrated the coordination function of the CCS when she described the Ohio Bureau of Crippled Children's Services, which (before the block grant) was separate from but related to that state's Bureau of Maternal and Child Health. (Two other related program areas were the Division of Dental Health, and the Division of Women, Infants and Children.) Each program area was made up of a multidisciplinary team including a social worker who was responsible for assuring that every Title V project addressed the social problems of client families. The Ohio Bureau of Crippled Children's Services also administered the SSI–Disabled Children's Program, which developed comprehensive service plans for all children 16 years of age and younger who received SSI benefits. Again, multidisciplinary teams including social workers operated in districts to coordinate and implement these plans.

Despite the popularity of the CCS, concerns have been expressed about various aspects. Despite the inclusion of more and more conditions in the list of "handicapping conditions" covered by the CCS, penetration is still only 30 to 40% of the handicapped/chronically ill child population (Nelson, 1983). Wallace (1987) suggested broadening the eligibility criteria, both diagnostic and financial, to serve all children who need services.

The Select Panel for the Promotion of Child Health (1979) feared that in some communities racial and ethnic prejudice may create barriers to care through discourteous and unfair treatment. Language also may constitute a barrier in some communities. Moreover, the diversity among the states in eligibility criteria, conditions covered, and services provided results in disparity among the states and localities. For example, the Select Panel for the Promotion of Child Health (1979) noted that in some states the CCS covers children with chronic otitis media, who may suffer serious permanent hearing loss, whereas in other states children with this disease are not eligible for services. It is interesting that one of the first activities undertaken by the Children's Bureau (by Edith Baker) after passage of Title V was a study of the barriers to access of the services provided by the CCS (Insley, 1981b).

Finally, many (Select Panel for the Promotion of Child Health, 1979; Wallace, 1987) have noted the problems of lack of coordination and fragmentation of services both within CCS, and between CCS and other services. If fragmentation and lack of coordination in the health care system is a problem for other families, the families of children with handicaps, who are dependent on the system for critical goods and services (sometimes on a daily basis), must suffer from the deficiencies of that system. No evidence exists that reorganization of these programs under the Maternal and Child Health Block Grant has reduced the fragmentation and lack of coordination.

Despite the noted flaws, however, the CCS has provided needed services to many children who could not have obtained those services elsewhere. The Association of State Health Officials Foundation reported in 1984 that 540,000 children received services from the program in 1982 for a rate of eight children per 1,000 less than 21 years of age. Most of these children lived in families whose incomes were at or below the federal poverty level (Wallace, 1987).

Supplemental Security Income—Disabled Children's Services

SSI-D is a means-tested cash income program for persons who are older than 65 years of age, blind, or disabled, which became part of the Social Security Act in 1972. It was extended to include other services to children younger than 16 years of age (SSI-D) in Title XVI in 1976 because of recognition that children with handicaps and disabilities have many needs beyond income and medical care. In 1981 it became part of the Maternal and Child Health Block Grant.

Once eligibility is established for a child with a handicap, the amount of that child's grant is determined by the income and SSI eligibility of the parent or guardian of the child. The child is also referred for appropriate rehabilitation services. The law requires an Individualized Service Plan for each child.

Social Services Block Grant (SSBG)

Under the Social Security Act, the SSBG provides funds to the states for the purpose of providing social services to low-income persons, with the nature of the services and categories of problems left largely to the discretion of the states. Although in theory the SSBG provides states with the opportunity of filling in many of the gaps of services to families of children with handicaps, in reality it has not been an effective means of doing so.

Hobbs, Perrin and Ireys (1985) detail the reasons for the failures of the SSBG in this regard. First, no real increase in funds has been available to SSBG since 1972. Second, despite considerable latitude to extend benefits above the poverty level, most states have elected to provide services only to very low-income families. Families at or just above the poverty level often cannot afford basic services such as respite care, homemaker services, and so forth, and continue to be unable to receive such services. Finally, the focus of SSBG has not been on families of children with handicaps and chronic illness; others, such as the elderly, have benefited most from the available services.

Early Intervention Programs

These programs are designed to provide early services to children (usually from birth to 3 years of age) who are at risk for developmental delay and other problems. The risk may be due to several specific diagnosed conditions or illnesses (such as cerebral palsy), or to certain risk factors (either medical such as LBW or socioeconomic). The programs grew originally from legislation passed by Congress in 1968, the Handicapped Children's Early Education Assistance Act (Public Law 90-583). Early intervention programs are not strictly categorical, for they may involve children with a wide range of problems or potential problems, and they may draw from many other categorical programs for funding.

Early intervention may begin at any time between birth and school age. It is generally agreed that the earlier intervention begins, the more successful it will be, and thus most programs concentrate on the period from birth to 3 years of age. These programs seek to provide services that will enrich the at-risk child's early development and learning. Such enrichment is generally provided through both direct stimulation and service to the at-risk child (e.g., groups and classes), and through support and education of the parents (e.g., instruction in developmental milestones and in stimulation of children) so that they will be prepared to provide the environment that is needed by the child.

It is generally believed that family support services may be the most important function of early intervention. Such services are difficult and expensive to deliver, however. For this reason and because many early intervention clients require such assistance, these services are often home based. Social workers often provide home visits to observe the child's behavior and activity in his or her own home (Phillips, 1982).

Phillips and her colleagues (Phillips, 1982; Phillips, Davidson, & Auerbach, 1980; Phillips et al., 1981) have reported on an early intervention program in New York that contains several elements including a therapeutic day-care center, a mother-child interaction group, and counseling services. The services are extended to infants and parents (generally single-parent mothers) whose poor environment and personal problems place the young children at risk of developmental delays. Social workers, child-care workers, teachers, psychiatrists, psychologists, and a public health nurse also provide home visits.

The program claims success, and indeed it appears to offer a valuable service to this depressed community and the deprived families who live there. Two criticisms might be offered, however. First, a pathology-oriented approach is evident from the description of services. (For example, the assumption is made that all clients require counseling for personal problems.) It seems possible that many clients' problems might derive simply from their social problems and might require services that do not include a psychotherapeutic approach. Second, as yet the authors have presented no empirical evaluation. Such an evaluation would be extremely valuable in documenting the program's success, and in evaluating the unique contribution of each separate component of the program.

Whether home or agency based, the bulk of evidence seems to suggest that early intervention services require the participation and involvement of parents to be successful (Darling & Darling, 1982). The programs described earlier include extensive maternal participation in the day-care center and interaction groups. Moreover, Philipp and Siefert (1979) found that mothers whose participation in early intervention services was strongly encouraged developed more favorable attitudes toward childrearing than mothers whose involvement was either discouraged or not encouraged. (Other parental measures and more direct outcomes on the children were not measured.)

Pertinent Legislation

Public Law 94-142

In attempting to help provide normal lives for special-needs children, social workers often assist the families with the special educational needs of those children. Because this often will involve referrals for special education, practitioners require a thorough understanding of pertinent legislation. Public Law 94-142, enacted in 1975, guarantees a free public education in the "least restrictive environment" to all handicapped children 3 to 21 years of age. The law covers children who are mentally retarded, hearing impaired, speech impaired, visually handicapped, seriously emotionally disturbed, orthopedically impaired, impaired in other health-related ways, or have specific learning or multiple other disabilities.

Under Public Law 94-142 the states are required to provide a broad range of services including school health services, speech therapy, psychological and counseling services, physical and occupational therapy, medical diagnostic or evaluation services, and parent counseling and training. Services should be coordinated using various other state programs, such as CCS and EPSDT. The law guarantees both the child and his or her parents due process rights including an impartial hearing for parents who disapprove of any matter regarding their child's education.

Public Law 94-142 requires that each student must be provided with a written individualized education plan (IEP) to guide service provision, with the plan to be developed jointly by parents, teachers, and other appropriate persons. In many cases the IEP and case management services are provided by a school social worker. Social work services are mandated for children who require such assistance to benefit from special education (Tabb, 1987). Examples of these social work services include assessment of special needs and referral to outside services, individual and group counseling for behavior problems that inhibit learning, and the provision of training for school personnel regarding a specific child's special needs or problems (Tabb, 1987).

Despite passage of Public Law 94-142 and its requirements for case finding and outreach, many children with disabilities still fail to receive needed services simply because those services do not exist in their geographic areas or are so fragmented that they are ineffective (Select Panel for the Promotion of Child Health, 1979). Nonetheless the panel evaluated this law as effective, noting that in 1979 approximately 75% of the nation's children with handicaps and disabilities were receiving a "free appropriate public education" (p. 72). The panel went further to say:

> The Panel believes that the major accomplishment of P.L. 94-142 has been the revolutionary change in attitude toward handicapped children. Undoubtedly, much work remains to be done before this attitudinal change is transformed into a comprehensive service system to meet all the needs of handicapped children. But at least in terms of educational opportunities, the framework is now in place to ensure that these children receive the individualized instruction and related services they require.

Public Law 99-457

Legislation enacted in 1987 (Public Law 99-457) extends the right of a free public education to infants and toddlers (from birth to 3 years of age) who are developmentally delayed (in cognitive, physical, or psychosocial development, language and speech development, or self-help skills), or who are diagnosed as having a condition that places them at risk for developmental delay. States are given wide latitude to construct their own definitions and criteria for the provision of services, but in general the legislation requires eligibility for children who are either experiencing developmental delay or who are diagnosed with conditions that are likely to lead to developmental delay. Services must be provided under public auspices at no cost to families, except when federal or state law mandates a schedule of sliding fees. The law requires that states place authority for organization and coordination of services under a lead state agency with a single line of authority to the state's governor. A 5-year plan enables states to implement the total program gradually.

Public Law 99-457 requires states to provide many of the same services provided to older children under Public Law 94-142, such as outreach and recruitment, comprehensive interdisciplinary assessment, medical services, social services, case management, and other services. In the past, one child (not the family) might have a separate treatment plan with each agency that was involved in providing services. Public Law 99-457 requires that each family have one Individualized Family Service Plan that is designed to coordinate all the community resources to meet the needs of the child and family as a unit.

Although Public Law 99-457 resembles Public Law 94-142 in many aspects, two differences stand out. First, this legislation marks a new commitment to families that heretofore has been lacking. Bishop (1988) notes that this legislation could be the most facilitating role for families ever written, and that much of the credit for the strong emphasis on families in the legislation belongs to social workers who helped shape the legislation and implementation. Second, the legislation includes a mandate for interdisciplinary work that recognizes that no single profession can meet the needs of these families. The recent Carolina Conference on Infant Personnel Preparation, held to determine policy and professional roles in the implementation of the legislation, demonstrated a commitment by social workers, nurses, physicians, special educators, and other members of the interdisciplinary team to real and meaningful involvement of the entire family.

The mission of the social work profession in implementing Public Law 99-457, as developed at the Carolina Conference on Infant Personnel Preparation is as follows: "To improve the quality of life for infants and toddlers and their families who are served by P.L. 99-457 through the provision of social work services." Some of the 14 specific social work roles included assuming primary responsibility for the assessment and provision of families' basic needs when appropriate; providing child protection services; linking families with community resources; and advocating for new services when needed resources do not exist (Carolina Conference on Infant Personnel Preparation, 1988).

Other Legislation

Other legislation with which social workers should be familiar includes the Developmental Disabilities Assistance and Bill of Rights Act of 1978 (Public Law 95-602), which supports planning and service activities and funds programs for certain persons with a severe chronic disability, and other programs specific to certain disabilities. These include programs such as the Comprehensive Hemophilia Diagnostic and Treatment Centers, which are part of Title XI of the Public Health Service Act. In particular, as social workers search for services for their clients, they should be aware that Section 504 of the Rehabilitation Act of 1973 (Public Law 93-112) prohibits federally funded programs from discriminating on the basis of handicap.

Partnership of Parents and Professionals

A special relationship exists between social workers and parents of children with disabilities. Yet in many ways, the professional relationship has not been an equal one. Often the social worker has a commodity that the family needs (knowledge and access to the services needed by the family). The social worker may be more educated or of a higher social class than the parent. The relationship often begins with the parents in a crisis state following discovery of their child's problems. All of these factors conspire to make the working relationship between parents and social workers a potentially difficult one.

At one time professionals were quick to offer advice at the time of diagnosis, such as, "He'll never be anything but a drain on you," and "you're young enough to have other children. Institutionalize him, and at least you can have a normal life." In the past parents often accepted such advice with resignation, even if it conflicted with their own values and desires. In recent years parents have become much less likely to be so passive, however. Shelton et al. (1987) trace major changes in the philosophy of care, from an institution- or agency-oriented focus, to a child-centered focus, to the recent family-centered focus.

Indeed, as a result of the recent consumer movement evident in many fields and with persons with disabilities in particular, many parents of special-needs children no longer accept unsolicited (or even solicited) advice, nor do they sit back and wait for professionals to provide what is needed; instead, they demand the services they want. As Healy et al. (1985) note, some parents have "broken the quiet-saint stereotype to articulate their need for services" (p. 34). In many cases, parents have been able to accomplish far more for their children than professionals could hope to accomplish. In addition, professionals are recognizing that it is in the child's best interest for parents to be actively involved in their care and treatment.

Working with families whose children have disabilities is often complicated by conflict. This conflict may be a normal outgrowth of several processes. First, although the goals of professionals and parents for the child are ostensibly the same, basic differences exist in several areas. As Healy et al. (1985) note, professionals have many children about whom they are concerned and for whom they are responsible. In addition, they are often constrained by bureaucratic requirements that exist solely for the benefit of the bureaucracy (Gliedman & Roth, 1980). These professionals often may forget that parents are singularly concerned with their own child, and his or her problems and development.

Moreover, professionals may forget that the child's handicap is but one part of the client families' lives. In addition to the time-consuming and often expensive requirements of the care of their handicapped child, they also must deal with the daily tasks and problems that involve other children, jobs, neighbors, and everything else. Often they must deal with these tasks in an environment that provides inadequate resources, stigma and social isolation, and little emotional support.

Darling and Darling (1982) state that negative attitudes by families toward physicians grow out of "physicians' avoidance of diagnosis, prognosis or treatment, incorrect diagnosis or prognosis, the depersonalization and red tape of hospital bureaucracy, and professionals' usurpation of the parents' right to make decisions about their own child" (p. 127). Moreover, medical staff is often insensitive to the problems and concerns of families (Darling & Darling, 1982). These authors state that parents often react to these situations by becoming more assertive.

For many years, the treatment and care of children with disabilities and handicaps has been marked by a professional dominance that belied the competence and abilities of parents and the special knowledge they possess about their own child (Gliedman & Roth, 1980). Parents are no longer willing to allow professionals to control all the information and make all the decisions about their children, however. First, parents are demanding more and complete information. The most powerful tool parents can possess is knowledge (Healy et al., 1985). Most already have the desire and the commitment to provide all that is available to their children, but in many cases they do not know where to start. The knowledge they require includes not only their child's diagnosis and prognosis, but an understanding of the uncertainties inherent in them. They also require the facts about available treatments and services, legislation and pending legislation that would affect them, and services to which they would be entitled if they did exist.

Second, parents are demanding a key role in decision making regarding their children. Legislation such as Public Laws 94-142 and 99-457 legally mandates the major decision-making role to the parents of children with disabilities, creating in some cases a natural adversarial situation (Dane, 1985). Although many professionals recognize the advantages of having parents who actively work with professionals toward common goals for the child, others are not so comfortable with these essential changes in roles.

Finally, parents are banding together and forming groups to support each other, exchange information, and advocate for their children (Dane, 1985; Shelton et al., 1987). Professionals can aid parents in obtaining this supportive resource by knowing and making parents aware of such resources when the diagnosis is made.

What then is the appropriate role for the professional who works with these special-needs families? The appropriate role will vary with the circumstances, strengths, and needs of the family. The appropriate role of the social worker may be as case manager, given the fragmented system within which parents must negotiate and maneuver and the difficulties some families face in dealing with this system. The training and skills of social workers prepare them to work within this system, but many parents will find this a difficult process. In particular, parents who are single, very young, have little education, or experience language or cultural barriers may rely on social workers to perform case management functions.

Conversely, many parents become proficient at managing their children's care, and some have suggested that their natural interest prepares parents to be the best case managers (Gliedman & Roth, 1980). Others (Burley, 1981) believe that the responsibility of case management constitutes an unreasonable and inappropriate burden on families. In some cases, the social worker may act as case manager initially and assist the parents in preparing to assume this role for themselves.

Whatever role is assumed and whatever tasks are performed, Darling and Darling (1982) emphasize respect of the parent's viewpoint, thorough explanations of all recommended treatments and procedures, parental involvement in decision making on all matters concerning the child, and absolute truthfulness in all cases. In addition, they make the point that may be lost all too often: Professionals should take the time to listen to parents.

Advocacy on behalf of families who have special needs is especially important considering the gross deficiency of resources and the crippling effects on families that result from the lack of such resources. Social workers have demonstrated their commitment (Dane, 1985) and abilities to assist such families in obtaining the resources they need.

Horejsi (1984) reported on a program in which six Michigan ventilator-dependent children were transferred from home to hospital in 1983. Professionals' judgments were that the reunited families were happier and calmer, and the children were healthier and developing more appropriately. The annual savings to third-party payers of more than $1 million a year was an added benefit, but such innovations still are not always possible. Such transfers are difficult to accomplish because institutions that depend on these funds for their livelihood and existence are understandably reluctant to relinquish them. For example, the home care of respirator children that would provide a more normal life for them and their families might also cause the closure of some institutions or portions of institutions that care for such children.

Another example of social work advocacy on behalf of children with disabilities and their families is provided by Cacioppo and Andrews's (1979) description of how social workers in one agency developed respite resources for parents of children with multiple handicaps when no such resources existed. The social workers in this special education program recruited and trained caregivers, who then provided care on a fee-for-service basis for the parents. Although the resource was useful only to middle-income families who could afford to pay for it, the authors noted that the agency's next goal was to develop resources for lower income families.

In the face of political and fiscal realities, the social worker's responsibility involves efforts to protect the rights of special-needs children and their families including the right to essential goods and services. In many cases, the most appropriate and effective means to these ends may be the "empowerment" of parents. Although this term may offend some because it connotes the notion of professions giving something to parents that they already possess by rights, it actually means making resources that exist more available and accessible to parents, and enabling them to obtain those resources for themselves.

Although effective advocacy involves several tasks for social workers, probably most important is working with parents to help them advocate effectively for their own children. Parents may be the most effective advocates for their children; indeed, in many recent cases, parents appealed directly to legislators, the president, and the press for what their children required and could not get through agency channels. Their appeals carried tremendous weight, as evidenced by the initiation of the "Katie Beckett" waivers created in 1982 to provide SSI and Medicaid eligibility for home care for certain children (Shelton et al., 1987). The waivers were named after the child who received the first waiver because of her parents' direct appeal to the president.

In fact, parental advocacy began in the 1940s with parents of children with cerebral palsy and mental retardation (Dane, 1985). Parents' continuing dissatisfaction with the lack of services led to greater activism and several class action lawsuits that have extended the rights of handicapped persons in general.

Direct appeals from social workers to policy makers also carry weight. A legislator must listen when a constituent expresses an opinion on a pending bill that would reduce the budget of a social agency. When the constituent is a social worker who says, "I work with developmentally at-risk children, and your bill would cause half of the children on my case load to go without adequate medical care," the legislator must recognize the authority of what he or she is hearing. Simple telephone calls and letter writing do not require the more sophisticated techniques learned in graduate school. Guides for effective advocacy are available from several sources including the Association for the Care of Children's Health (1983).

Dane (1985) noted that parent advocate groups have focused on several advocacy strategies including the provision of information and exerting political pressure to expand available resources. Because social workers generally are unable to maintain long-term relationships with families who have children with handicaps, she maintains that it may be more effective to engage in indirect advocacy, such as assisting parents to obtain the skills and resources they need to engage in advocacy for themselves.

Conversely, the demands of heavy workloads may make it difficult for social workers to stay abreast of the current legislative agenda. Social workers need assistance from their professional organizations and from their employers so that they know when to use their influence. They also need support for doing so. Support may take the form of the provision of agency resources for advocacy activities, and recognition of such activities when questions of promotions and raises occur. The acquisition and preservation of resources for children with handicaps and their families will require the commitment not only of parents, but of social workers and their supervisors and agencies.

7 Adolescent Sexuality and Pregnancy

Adolescent health care is a top priority in MCH because it provides the opportunity to intervene early in the reproductive cycle and thus to promote the health of two generations (Hall & Young, 1979). Whether through the prevention of adolescent pregnancy, the provision of services designed to ensure a healthy pregnancy in a teenager, or simply the delivery of services designed to maximize the health of adolescents, services provided during the adolescent years are considered "frontline" in the effort to improve the health of future, as well as current, generations.

In recent years adolescent health care has assumed new importance as teenagers have become increasingly sexually active and the predictable outcomes of pregnancy, abortion, and STDs have become apparent. Social workers have practiced for many years in various settings in the network of services offered to adolescents, but professional roles are changing and becoming more complex with the many changes in society's attitudes and behavior toward teenage sexuality. This chapter will concentrate primarily on those settings and roles that are part of the health care system, and will not deal with other settings such as adoption agencies which, although they are certainly crucial links in the system of services available for adolescents, are not primarily health oriented.

Until recently out-of-wedlock pregnancy was considered to be primarily a morality issue, even among social workers and researchers (Bolton, 1980). The key factor was not the age of the mother but her unmarried status. For example, a scholarly work in 1918 entitled *The Unmarried Mother: A Study of Five Hundred Cases* (Kammerer) conceptualizes unwed pregnancy as juvenile delinquency and includes chapters entitled "Bad Environment," "Bad Companions," and "Abnormal Sexualism." For the unmarried mother, options for handling the crisis of an unplanned pregnancy often were limited. Even into the 20th century infants were often forcibly removed from unmarried mothers (e.g., Barrett, 1910; Folks, 1911). Mudgett noted in 1935 that "the controversy between those who hold that mother and child should be kept together and those who believe it may be wiser to separate them is being settled on a case work basis" (p. 70). It is interesting that the guidelines discussed for when to separate mother and child failed to consider the wishes of the mother.

During the early part of the century, the proper social work role was to protect the out-of-wedlock child through assisting the mother-to-be in planning for the child and to attempt to help provide the illegitimate child with the same rights as those enjoyed by the legitimate child (Mudgett, 1935). Such a goal was critical because at the time illegitimate children were not afforded equal rights regarding such issues as inheritance. Mudgett (1935) and Lundberg (1939) also noted social work concern about the supervision of adoptions and prevention of independent adoptions in such cases. Other important social work services during this time included maternity and foster homes for unwed pregnant women.

Much of the social work profession's interest in the problem of illegitimacy also grew out of concern about the high rates of mortality among illegitimate infants, owing in part to separation of mothers and babies and subsequent artificial feeding, and from concern about the problems experienced by such children including secrecy, and feelings of insecurity and inferiority (Donahue, 1929).

Then in the 1950s and 1960s as social work's focus began to shift toward more internalized interpretations of problems and toward psychotherapy as the primary mode of practice (Chambers, 1963), unwed pregnancy became more a mark of psychopathology than of immorality, with the pregnancy itself seen primarily as a "symptom" of the real underlying pathology. For example, Millar (1955) said: "The caseworker should recognize that pregnancy for the unmarried woman is a symptom of underlying emotional difficulty" (p. 93). Bernstein (1965) also said: "The illicit pregnancy is seen as a quasi-purposeful effort on the part of the personality to deal with those emotional conflicts it has been unable to resolve through other psychological mechanisms" (p. 798).

In the 1950s the social work role expanded to include providing the unwed mother with knowledge of available resources and protecting her from making a hasty decision (Deuel, 1951). Nevertheless great concern still existed in the 1960s with helping the client get to the "real cause" of the problem to resolve her conflicts (Bernstein, 1965). Early planning and counseling with the adolescent about her relationship with her family and the baby's father were also described as important casework functions (Brown, 1960; Deuel, 1951). Brown (1960) noted the importance of an ongoing continuous relationship with one social worker who could assist in coordinating services among many agencies and professions. She also mentioned prevention of a second pregnancy as a casework goal.

The father was seldom involved in decision making for the baby during this time unless the parents chose to marry (and then the woman would probably not come to the attention of the social agency). This exclusion of the father was largely due to legal restrictions, however; early concern existed in the social work profession for the father's position. Establishing paternity was still a criminal or quasi-criminal procedure in the 1950s in most states, although unwed fathers were being asked increasingly to share in the care of their children (Deuel, 1951). Interestingly, the *Social Work Yearbook* did not deal individually with the unwed father until 1965 (Bernstein, 1965). That article noted that establishment of paternity conferred only obligations of support and no privileges to share in the care of the child.

Just as the pregnant adolescent was once considered to be pathological, the male adolescent was assumed for many years to have psychological problems, or at least to be different from his peers. Bolton (1980) found, however, that although the boy may not consider the consequences of his actions, no evidence exists of the exploitation often assumed to exist between the adolescent boy and his sexual partner. Pannor, Evans, and Massarik (1968) asserted that the "stereotype of the older male sophisticate seducing the young innocent is not valid" (p. 6). In Pannor et al.'s small sample, the adolescent fathers were close to the age of the adolescent mothers, 70% had high school educations, and most were not delinquent.

A discernible shift in thought about the nature of adolescent pregnancy occurred with the War on Poverty in the 1960s and was described by Furstenberg (1976). The trend of increasing sexual activity among young people that had intensified after World War II continued, but the trend of early marriage that also began with the war was reversed, and young people began to delay marriage; thus, the problem came to be defined not as unwed parenthood but as adolescent parenthood. (For example, Bernstein's 1965 article in the *Social Work Encyclopedia* made the first mention of the influence of the adolescent peer culture on unwed pregnancy.) In addition, the "baby boom" cohort began to reach adolescence during this time, resulting in many more teenagers and thus greater numbers available to become pregnant. The concern with poverty and dependency during the 1960s led to a view of adolescent pregnancy as a part of the "cycle of poverty," chiefly a social problem resulting in welfare dependency and great cost to the public.

During the 1960s amendments to the Social Security Act created programs that provided family planning and maternity services to teenagers as part of their overall focus. Federal efforts to prevent adolescent pregnancy specifically began in earnest in 1970 with the Family Planning and Services Act, which created the family planning clinics described in detail later. The *Social Work Yearbook* listed the services needed by unwed mothers including prenatal care (noting that adolescents often delayed seeking care), child welfare services, public assistance, and follow-up services that continued well beyond delivery. It was pointed out that some agencies served only those planning to relinquish their infants, and that blacks suffered great disadvantage regarding access to services (Bernstein, 1965).

With the 1970s came a growing concern in the social work profession specifically for adolescent pregnancy, but a continuing focus was on psychological causes. Navarre (1971) noted the increase in sexual behavior among young people and the need for early sex education in the public schools. She suggested group and individual therapy for adolescents who were "prone to acting-out, extreme dependency needs, or identity problems" (p. 649) to prevent pregnancy associated with psychological problems. In 1977 Schwartz noted that the term *illegitimate* was no longer acceptable and commented that unwed mothers were younger than ever before. Although she stated that no single etiology could account for adolescent pregnancy, she also commented on the "conscious or unconscious need for a baby" among many unwed mothers; described adolescent fathers as dropouts, drug and alcohol users, unemployed, or delinquent; and described their relationship as having little permanency or commitment.

Cain (1979) described the pregnancies of 40 adolescents as "symptomatic of other chronic problems" (p. 52), but Papademetriou (1971) defined adolescent pregnancy as a sign of family pathology only for middle-class families. Such approaches belie the extent of adolescent pregnancy (described later). Moreover, Bolton (1980) noted that "An overview of the studies which have sought to arrive at some genuinely unique differences in pathology between the pregnant adolescent and the adolescent who manages to escape pregnancy would suggest that only small differences exist" (p. 65).

Perhaps the 1990s will see a more useful approach that views adolescent pregnancy less in isolation (e.g., "What causes teenage pregnancy?") and more in the context of the full range of issues surrounding adolescent development: biologic development, sex education, the psychological consequences of premature sexual activity, contraception information and services, excess pregnancy risk for teens and specialized prenatal care for teenagers, the issue of abortion, special parenting problems, and educational and employment opportunities. In addition, although pregnancy is regarded as a primary crisis, adolescents require a full range of health care services that go far beyond the traditional limited approach and must include attention to other health issues.

ADOLESCENT SEXUAL ACTIVITY AND THE CAUSES OF ADOLESCENT PREGNANCY

More than 1 million teenage girls in the United States become pregnant each year. Although pregnancy occurs in all strata of American society, it is most common among minority and lower socioeconomic groups, and among teenagers who perform poorly in school (Phipps-Yonas, 1980).

Demographic data about adolescent fathers are scarce, with much being inferred from descriptions of adolescent mothers. Generally, though, adolescent fathers are similar in most respects to their female partners except that they are slightly older. One review of numerous studies (Kadushin & Martin, 1988) found unwed fathers to be of the same age, social class, and educational level as the single pregnant girl, and that they had known each other for some time before the conception.

It is certainly true that the statistics present an alarming picture, but it is not true that the problem is growing at an astounding rate. In fact, the birth rate among adolescent women 15 to 19 years of age is declining (Baldwin, 1981). The large number of teenagers in the population during the 1960s (owing to the "baby boom") is down, so fewer individuals are at risk for adolescent pregnancy (Dryfoos, 1982). Moreover, although black teens have the highest birth rates, those rates are decreasing (National Center for Health Statistics, 1984).

This is not to say that adolescent pregnancy is not a serious problem, just that the facts should not be distorted. Teenage pregnancy is a costly social problem. Burt (1986) estimated that in 1985 teenage pregnancy cost $16.65 billion for only three of the many programs involved: AFDC, food stamps, and Medicaid. Reis (1987) estimated the total cost of services to Illinois's teenage mothers and their children at all levels of government and in the private sector to be a total of $848 million in 5 years. Both authors note the existence of many hidden long-term costs that cannot be estimated but are no doubt significant.

Although adolescents have always been sexually active, more are sexually active and at younger ages today than ever before in history. In 1979, 50% of all teenaged girls reported having had sexual intercourse, up from 30% in 1971 (Zelnick and Kantner, 1980). Increases were apparent for both blacks and whites. In addition, adolescents are maturing earlier with each passing decade, placing them at risk of pregnancy earlier in their lives and for a longer period. (See Bolton [1980] for a review of the data on this point.)

Sexually active adolescent boys probably are even less informed and concerned about pregnancy than are their female partners, in part owing to a belief that family planning is a female responsibility (Freeman et al., 1980). Some of this abdication to female adolescents is due not to irresponsibility, but to the increased use and popularity of birth control pills since the 1960s; before that time, the use of condoms was the most common form of contraception (Scales & Beckstein, 1982). Sonenstein (1986) notes that the less serious consequences of an unintended pregnancy for the adolescent boy also may reduce their motivation to use contraception. Parents also may provide even less information to their sons than to their daughters, assuming that they will learn what they need to know from their peers.

Despite a lack of knowledge about sexuality and reproduction, however, sexual activity begins early for boys. Although Sonenstein's (1986) review of the research showed inconsistency among studies of sexual experience among male adolescents, it seems safe to conclude that a fair proportion of boys have experienced sexual intercourse by 15 years of age and most by 17 years of age. Finkel and Finkel's (1981) study of 421 urban adolescents found a mean age of 12.8 years for first sexual experience of boys. Zelnick and Shah's (1983) national survey showed mean ages of 15.9 years for white boys and 14.4 for black boys. Early initiation of sexual activity among both male and female adolescents is related not only to race but also to low income, lack of religiousness, having lower educational achievement goals, dating more or going steady, and earlier onset of puberty (Sonenstein, 1986).

It is possible that adolescent sexual behavior is decreasing, perhaps in response to the AIDS epidemic. Hofferth, Kahn, and Baldwin (1987) found a slight but statistically nonsignificant decrease in sexual activity among metropolitan whites in 1982 and a more significant 12-point decrease for black metropolitan teenagers. They interpreted their findings not as a decrease in sexual activity of teenagers, but as a slowing of the increase or a "leveling off."

Still the figures on the numbers of sexually active adolescents do not explain why so many adolescents get pregnant; other developed countries with equal or greater numbers of sexually active adolescents have much lower rates of pregnancy. In fact, American girls under 15 years of age are much more likely to get pregnant and give birth than their peers in other developed countries, despite similar levels of sexual activity (Jones et al., 1985).

The most likely reason for the excess in American teenage pregnancies appears to be contraceptive use. Researchers have reported a delay of several months between the initiation of sex by teenagers and the use of contraception (Zabin, Kantner, & Zelnick, 1979). Many only seek contraception then because of a pregnancy scare (Zabin & Clark, 1981). Zelnick and Kantner's (1980) survey of metropolitan women 15 to 19 years of age showed that in 1979, 36% of the blacks and 24% of the whites reported that they never used contraception during intercourse, whereas 31.2% of the blacks and 35% of the whites said they always used contraception. Others were classified as "sometimes users." Perhaps most distressing is that of the 40% of Zelnick and Kantner's (1974) sample who reported initiating contraception, 33% said they stopped using it even though they did not wish to become pregnant. Among those who are sexually active and who do not use contraception consistently, chance plays a role in who becomes pregnant.

Contraceptive use by adolescent boys is similar to that of adolescent girls. Zelnick and Shah's (1983) survey of young men 17 to 21 years of age indicated that only about 44.1% of men use contraception during first intercourse. Being older at first intercourse increases the probability of contraception. Black men were less likely to use contraception, especially at younger ages. In general the reasons that sexually active young men fail to use contraception are similar to the reasons given by young women.

Several explanations for adolescents' lack of use of contraception have been proposed. These include ignorance about reproduction and family planning, lack of access to family planning services, and failure to use available services because they are considered unacceptable. It is commonly thought that ignorance regarding sexuality, reproduction, and family planning might cause adolescents to fail to use contraception consistently, but this assumption assumes too simplistic a relationship between facts and behavior that is not well supported by the evidence. Chilman's (1983) review of studies of teens' knowledge about reproduction and contraception showed little, if any, relationship between knowledge and use of contraception.

A more important reason for their failure to use contraception may be teenagers' ambivalence about sex. Despite an impression of open and accepted sexuality, adolescents still feel guilty and uncomfortable about their sexual activity (Zakus & Wilday, 1987). The use of contraception requires an acknowledgment of sexual behavior and planning for sexual intercourse that many adolescents cannot face. Instead they allow themselves to be "carried away" by passion.

Others have explained the inconsistency between adolescents' knowledge and attitudes and their behavior with adolescent cognitive development. For example, adolescents tend not to plan ahead nor to connect behavior and its consequences (Gilchrist & Schinke, 1983). When they do understand the consequences, they tend not to personalize those consequences. For example, adolescents may have knowledge about how pregnancy is connected to unprotected intercourse but may not perceive that risk for themselves. Adolescent sexual behavior also is usually sporadic and spontaneous; effective contraception requires a high degree of planning and preparation that is not typical of adolescents. When weighed against the cost of contraception (in terms of inconvenience as well as monetary cost), teenagers may simply choose to believe that the risks do not apply to them.

The question of whether adolescents possess the appropriate skills to avoid pregnancy is no small issue. Gilchrist and Schinke's work, as well as that of others, emphasizes the cognitive and communication skills that are required to avoid pregnancy including the skills to refuse sex when it is not wanted. For example, Balassone (1988a) found that about a quarter of adolescents she questioned said that the frequency with which they had sexual intercourse was more than they desired, suggesting that they did not know how to avoid sex.

In addition, considerable skill is involved in the consistent and effective use of contraceptive methods. Adolescents would be expected to vary in their abilities to take birth control pills effectively, to use foam and condoms correctly, or to insert a diaphragm correctly.

Another important part of the effective use of contraception involves the abilities of teenagers to discuss contraception with their partners. Polit-O'Hara and Kahn's (1985) interviews of 83 adolescent couples showed good communication in general to be important to contraception. A discouraging finding, however, was that even among these stable couples, discussing birth control did not always lead to effective and consistent contraception. Teenagers may need specific instruction about how to discuss contraception with their partners.

In some cases it is likely that lack of access to family planning services affects adolescent pregnancy. Federal funding of family planning clinics has not increased in real dollars since 1973, and the 1981 Omnibus Budget Reconciliation Act reduced the total funding available for these services (Moore & Burt, 1982). Indeed, national data indicate that family planning services are available to only 31% of all teenaged women (Torres & Forrest, 1985). Teenagers living in rural areas or small towns may be at special disadvantage regarding access to services.

Even when services are available, however, several factors may make them unacceptable to teenagers. Clinics may only be open when adolescents are in school. Long waiting times (Chamie, Eismau, Forrest, Orr, & Torres, 1982); poor staff attitudes and behavior toward clients; and most important, lack of respect for confidentiality (Chamie et al., 1982) may influence teenagers not to take advantage of available family planning services. The latter factor is especially important in view of hereto-fore unsuccessful efforts to mandate parental notice when adolescents seek contraceptive services.

Torres, Forrest, and Eisman (1980) surveyed adolescent patients of family planning clinics and estimated that requiring parental notification or consent would result in 125,000 adolescent patients nationwide ceasing the use of contraception. Many report that confidentiality is important to teenagers, and that they would risk pregnancy by unprotected inter-course before revealing their sexual activity to their parents (Torres et al., 1980). Despite fears to the contrary, Moore and Burt (1982) point out that no evidence exists that confidentiality encourages teenage sexual activity.

Moreover, requiring parental notification might have little effect. Furstenberg, Herceg-Baron, Mann, & Shea (1982) found that many clinics already involve parents in their children's family planning in various ways including counseling, parent advisory groups, and discussion groups and training for parents. These authors found that agencies that encourage parental involvement had higher levels of actual participation of parents than those requiring notification. In fact, Furstenberg, Herceg-Baron, Shea, and Webb (1984) found that notification of mothers that their daughters were attending a family planning clinic did little to effect communication between them on this issue. They "hold out little hope for the effectiveness of efforts to mandate parental involvement" (p. 169) but suggest a flexible approach to encouraging unwilling parents to be-come involved.

STDs and AIDS

Even for sexually active teenagers who do not become pregnant, serious health risks exist. About 25% of reported cases of the total number of reported gonorrhea cases are teenagers 15 to 19 years of age, with the highest rates of infection in urban areas and among younger teens. The rate of gonorrhea among teenagers tripled between 1956 and 1975 (Chilman, 1983), in contrast to the rate for syphilis, which appears to be decreasing among sexually active adolescents (Bell & Hein, 1984). The incidence of *Chlamydia trachomatis* is not known precisely because re-porting is not required by law (Goodrich & Wiesner, 1982), but it ap-pears that adolescents have higher rates of this STD (Bell & Hein, 1984). The long-lasting effects of chlamydia may be serious including pelvic inflammatory disease and infertility (Bell & Hein, 1984).

STD is a particular problem among adolescents for most of the same reasons that pregnancy is a problem, but their anatomy and physiology may make adolescents (girls in particular) more susceptible to STDs than older people (Bell & Hein, 1984). Darrow (1979) attributed increasing cases of gonorrhea to "Proposition 3-P"—promiscuity, permissiveness and use of "the pill." That is, adolescents are more sexually active, increasingly unlikely to use condoms (which provide protection against STD), and are more likely to use birth control pills (which do not provide protection against STD). It is also possible that adolescents are even less informed about the risks and consequences of STD than they are about pregnancy because parents and school sex education classes may be reluctant to talk about STD, believing it is no longer a problem as it once was. Teenagers are at higher risk of the complications of STD because they are likely to fail to recognize or respond to the early symptoms of disease (Goodrich & Wiesner, 1982). Indeed, STD is often asymptomatic, especially in women (Cates, 1984b).

The consequences of STD may be serious for adolescents. At current rates, adolescents will constitute 5,000 cases of chronic pelvic pain, 1,600 cases of infertility, and 950 ectopic pregnancies annually; the infants of adolescent mothers will constitute 10,000 cases of chlamydial pneumonia (Bell & Hein, 1984).

As of September 19, 1988, 295 confirmed cases of adolescent AIDS existed (Centers of Disease Control, 1988). Adolescents may acquire AIDS through sexual contact, contaminated needle exposure during intravenous drug use, or infected blood during a blood transfusion. Little is known at the current time about the incidence of adolescent AIDS connected with the various modes of transmission, although research is currently under way.

Prevention of STD among sexually active adolescents should be a major priority of equal importance to the prevention of pregnancy. Pregnancy prevention programs offer the best opportunity for reaching adolescents, as these programs are already in existence and are most likely to reach the group at risk. The risk of STD and the effectiveness of condoms in preventing STD would suggest the importance of communicating clearly to teenagers the advantages and disadvantages of each type of birth control method. (See chapter 8 for a general discussion of STDs, and the social work role in treatment and prevention.)

Consequences of Adolescent Pregnancy

About 38% of adolescent pregnancies are terminated by induced abortions, and about 13% end in spontaneous abortions. Of the almost half who do give birth, 22% are still unmarried adolescents, 10% are teens who marry following conception, and 17% are teens who were married before conception (Alan Guttmacher Institute, 1981). Pregnant adolescents who choose to abort have higher educational aspirations for themselves (Chilman, 1979), are somewhat older, of higher social class, more independent, and come from more stable home environments than adolescents who do not choose to abort (Olson, 1980). In sum, the adolescent who chooses abortion is likely to be more psychologically mature than the adolescent who chooses to give birth (Zakus & Wilday, 1987). The consequences for those who do choose to give birth and to parent cover a broad range.

Health

The health risks to teenage adolescents (particularly very young adolescents) who become pregnant are serious and have been summarized by Sacker and Neuhoff (1982). They include spontaneous abortion and still-birth, and complications such as toxemia, pregnancy-induced hypertension, cephalopelvic disproportion, abruptio placenta, anemia, and urinary tract infections. Teenagers also are more likely to have LBW infants owing both to premature delivery and IUGR (Makinson, 1985; Sacker & Neuhoff, 1982).

Infants born to teenage mothers are more likely to die during the first year of life, owing in part to increased rates of LBW and prematurity (Makinson, 1985). Rates are higher both for neonatal mortality, which is correlated with LBW and prenatal factors, and for postneonatal mortality, which is more closely related to socioeconomic factors. For example, the infants of teenage mothers are more likely to die of SIDS, accidents, and gastrointestinal disease (Makinson, 1985).

It is generally agreed that most excess health risks to adolescents and their infants are due to the lower socioeconomic conditions faced by adolescent mothers (Makinson, 1985) and by behavioral factors such as poor nutrition, drug and alcohol use, smoking, and especially failure to seek good prenatal care (Baldwin & Cain, 1980). At least some small portion of the risk for very young teenagers (younger than 15 years of age, for example) may be due to physiological immaturity, but Makinson's (1985) extensive review of data from five developed countries provided little support for such an association.

Social Consequences

The future of the teenage parent is severely compromised. The mother (and often the father) is likely to suffer from reduced educational achievement (McCarthy & Radish, 1982) and poor future job and earning prospects (Card & Wise, 1978). It is important to point out, however, that poor academic achievement may contribute to pregnancy, just as pregnancy may limit achievement.

Marriage is less often chosen as a resolution to the problem of unwed pregnancy now than it was in past years. In 1950, about one half of the women who conceived outside marriage married thereafter; now about one third do so (Kadushin & Martin, 1988). Those who do marry face a reduced likelihood of a lasting and satisfying marriage, as divorce rates for teenage marriages are about twice the rate for marriages that occur later (Alan Guttmacher Institute, 1981). Bolton (1980) summarized the various reasons for the failures of such marriages including inadequate preparation for marriage and subsequent pregnancies that interfere with building the relationship. He emphasizes the role of extreme economic problems in destabilizing such marriages. Chilman (1983) also emphasizes that divorce rates are higher among the lower socioeconomic classes, among whom adolescent parents are overrepresented.

Other Consequences

Chilman (1983) discusses a result of adolescent sexuality that often is not discussed: the emotional consequences. Chilman asks important questions for which no empirical answers exist at this time but that should not be overlooked in favor of the justified concern for the consequences:

> Do such relationships inhibit further growth of adolescents as independent, competent young people who have worked out their own sense of selfhood? Do early sex involvements, which are necessarily egocentric and immature, prevent later partnerships of greater depth and maturity? Or do such relationships perhaps help in the gradual development of a more mature sexuality? (pp. 101–102)

Of special concern to many is the issue of subsequent pregnancies. A second pregnancy is likely for the adolescent mother, often within 12 months (Zelnick, 1980), especially if the adolescent parents marry. She also is likely to bear more children during her lifetime than women who delay their first pregnancy until a more mature age (Card & Wise, 1978). Balassone (1988a) reviewed several studies on repeat adolescent pregnancies, noting the deficiencies in each. She estimated that 17% of adolescent mothers become pregnant again within 1 year, and 38% within 2 years.

All of the negative consequences of adolescent pregnancies are exacerbated with subsequent pregnancies including the health risks (Scott, Field, & Robertson, 1981), the deficiencies in educational attainment (Furstenberg, 1976), and by implication other social disadvantages such as lowered income. Moreover, concern about higher order pregnancies among adolescents centers in part on the meaning of these pregnancies for prevention efforts. As Balassone (1988a) noted, "Obviously, the existence of substantial numbers of repeat pregnancies refutes the notion that access to birth control information and a desire to avoid prgnancy are sufficient to prevent adolescent pregnancies" (p. 2).

Parenting Deficits

Little is known about the quality of parenting by adolescents. The available literature suggests that adolescent parents may not be as effective as older parents, and that the parental behaviors of adolescents may not foster optimum cognitive and socioeconomic development in their children, especially given the considerable stress in the circumstances of most adolescent parents (Lamb & Elster, 1986). Conversely, the differences are not substantial, especially if one controls for socioeconomic variables. Chilman (1983) asserts that parental attitudes and perceptions of their infants are similar between adolescents and older parents, and cautions against expecting adolescents to be "bad parents," lest a self-fulfilling prophecy be created.

Adolescent fathers are often posited to be especially deficient in parenting skills, but little is really known about the quality of fathering by young men. Much of this lack of data probably is related to researchers' lack of interest in fatherhood in general, although evidence exists of a recent upsurge in research interest in fatherhood and its implications for the development of children (Lamb & Elster, 1986).

It is logical to assume that adolescents would not be as effective at parenting as older parents. Although it is deeply satisfying, parenting is an other-centered activity that involves considerable sacrifice, especially in the first few months; adolescence, conversely, is by definition self-centered (Bolton, 1980). In addition, adolescents are immature and often lack the skills and considerable knowledge necessary to good parenting. This combination of factors, in addition to the massive practical and economic problems faced by adolescent parents, makes teenage parenting extremely difficult and perhaps a risky venture.

The statistics bear out the difficulties. First, both neonatal and postneonatal morality are higher among the infants of adolescents (Stickle, 1982). Second, these infants suffer from excess morbidity during the first months of life (Makinson, 1985). These disadvantages to the infants of teenagers are probably due in large part to adolescents' lack of knowledge about the importance of primary care (also indicated by their own deficits in prenatal care), and about the meaning of childhood illnesses and symptoms, and the proper course of action. Third, several studies have shown that the children of teenaged parents suffer various kinds of deficits including intellectual, health, and social problems (Baldwin & Cain, 1980). Chilman (1983) asserts that the differences have been few and inconclusive, however.

Some evidence suggests that adolescent parents are more likely to engage in child abuse and neglect (Sacker & Neuhoff, 1982), or at least that their parenting skills are likely to be inadequate and result in parenting difficulties (Makinson, 1985). When the crisis of pregnancy itself is superimposed on the social problems adolescent parents often have, child maltreatment does not seem like an unlikely scenario (Bolton, 1980). The almost legendary assumption that adolescent parents are potential abusers is not substantiated by the evidence, however (Bolton & Belsky, 1986). Most of the parenting problems associated with adolescent parenting may be attributed to the social environment, especially the economic deprivation that is almost always present in a single-parent family. Bolton (1980) summarizes the bleak situation for some adolescent mothers:

> The child rearing demands upon this young mother are excessive, and her activities address the needs of others almost exclusively. There are few distractions from child care in her life, and a pervading sense of hopelessness confronts this mother. This is an environmental grip that may never be broken as a result of these and other demographic influences. (p. 153)

A serious problem with low-income mothers, and particularly with adolescents, is failure to obtain good primary health care for infants (Bierman & Street, 1982; Makinson, 1985). Smith, Spiers, and Freese (1987) reported on the TeenTot program, a comprehensive well-baby program for the infants of mothers 16 years of age and younger (mean age, 15 years). The interdisciplinary team (pediatrician, pediatric nurse practitioner, social worker, and nutritionist) provide group and individual counseling regarding child development, parenting skills, contraception, education, and financial management. Inconsistent appointment keeping by these mothers was not necessarily related to a lack of commitment, but with immaturity and a lack of resources. Smith et al.'s (1987) results suggest that adolescent mothers require aggressive, ongoing staff contact and encouragement to continue attendance.

Pregnancy Prevention

Despite agreement that adolescent pregnancy is a serious problem of national magnitude, it is clear that a national consensus has not developed on the most effective or appropriate means of prevention. This absence of agreement is due not only to differing values among different groups but also to a lack of data about the effectiveness of various prevention strategies. Abstinence may be the ideal method of preventing adolescent pregnancy, but does not appear to be a practical national strategy. The most commonly suggested alternatives include contraceptive services and sex education to adolescents. In addition to these alternatives, others have been suggested that concentrate not on sexual activity itself but providing incentives to the adolescent that would make pregnancy undesirable.

Enhanced Life Options

Some contend that the prevention of pregnancy should begin with the promotion of responsible behavior (sexual and otherwise) and self-respect among teens (e.g., Schinke, 1978). In an environment where adolescents are assured adequate life choices that make postponement of pregnancy a meaningful objective, and where adolescents possess the skills to refuse unprotected intercourse, pregnancy might be much rarer even among sexually active adolescents (Bolton, 1980).

The proponents of such an "enhanced life options" approach suggest that improved educational and vocational opportunities, exposure to successful role models, and an enriched daily environment would do more to prevent adolescent pregnancy that any other approach (Dryfoos, 1984). Despite the intuitive appeal of this approach, however, political realities make it unlikely that the public will be willing to expend the considerable funding that would be required to implement such an approach nationwide (Leland, 1987; Moore & Burt, 1982).

Sex Education

Most institutionalized sex education is not carried out in health care settings, but in schools or other community groups. Chilman reported in 1979 that about one third of all public schools offered sex education, but that figure is probably higher now. Contraception is not usually part of the typical sex education curriculum, however. In some programs, the purpose of school education programs may not be the prevention of pregnancy, but an increase in students' knowledge of reproduction. In any case, Furstenberg, Lincoln, and Menken (1981) confirm that most school-based sex education is not introduced until high school, when most adolescents have already initiated sexual activity, and that most programs do not communicate effectively about the risk of pregnancy and the means of preventing it.

Most non–school-based sex education is carried out by Planned Parenthood (Moore & Burt, 1982), which has yet to evaluate the impact of its programs. Furstenberg et al., (1981) maintain that other community groups (such as churches, voluntary organizations such as Scouts, and special interest groups) must take a more active role in sex education if it is to be .effective, and that parents must be part of such programs. Currently only about 7% of adolescent girls report receiving sex education in these community settings (Dawson, 1986).

Little is known about the effectiveness of sex education programs in preventing adolescent pregnancy or in bringing about other desired goals (Moore & Burt, 1982). Studies by Marsiglio and Mott (1986) using the National Longitudinal Survey of Work Experience of Youth and by Dawson (1986) using the National Survey of Family Growth both suggest that sex education courses have little influence on adolescents' sexual behavior or on their risk of becoming pregnant. Both note, however, that their studies cannot assess the quality or quantity of sex education, but only whether any was received. Moore and Burt (1982) summarize what is known about sex education:

> Curricula that help teenagers clarify their own values and goals, that explain the social and economic consequences of early parenthood, that develop decision-making skills so teens can evaluate their own behavior in means-end terms, that teach communication or assertiveness skills so teens can better explain and enforce their own values, seem likely to encourage a more considered and cautious approach among teenagers to the initiation of sexual activity. (pp. 78–79)

Clearly sex education is most effective when it is given at the local level combined with education of the parents of adolescents, who often know as little as their offspring (Moore & Burt, 1982).

Federal Programs

Since 1978 federal efforts to prevent adolescent pregnancy have been concentrated in the Office of Adolescent Pregnancy Prevention. The original purpose of the Office of Adolescent Pregnancy ostensibly was both the prevention of adolescent pregnancy, and the provision of support and services to adolescents who had already become pregnant. During the Reagan administration, this office's mission seemed to be rooted primarily in the promotion of chastity and parental rights to control adolescent access to contraceptive services and thus presumably limit their sexual activity. Other primary prevention efforts have been emphasized little (Gilchrist & Schinke, 1983).

Indeed, Burt and Sonenstein (1985) reviewed 21 programs funded under the Federal Office of Adolescent Pregnancy Prevention Programs and found that few included a primary prevention component; most focused on teenagers who were pregnant or who already had at least one child. A significant problem in efforts to prevent adolescent pregnancy is a lack of knowledge about the whole issue, especially knowledge about the role of adolescent boys in decision making about intercourse in general and contraception in particular. Research on the adolescent father in general is limited and has concentrated mostly on descriptions of the personalities of these young men, on their sexual knowledge and attitudes, and only recently on their actual sexual and contraceptive behavior.

In 1981 Congress passed the Adolescent Family Life Act, which required applicants for funding from the Office of Adolescent Pregnancy Prevention to work with religious organizations, and prohibited grants to agencies that provided abortions or made referrals to agencies that provided abortions. In fact, use of the word "abortion" was prohibited in programs receiving federal funds. The act was declared unconstitutional in 1987, partially because of its promotion of religion (Documents, 1987), but litigation continues.

The main source of federal services for adolescents has been provided through a system of family planning clinics (Orr & Brenner, 1981). Until 1981 funding for these clinics was mainly through four sources: Title X of the Public Health Service Act (the Family Planning Services and Population Research Act of 1970) and Titles V (Maternal and Child Health), XIX (Medicaid), and XX (Social Services) of the Social Security Act. In 1981 Titles V and XX were combined to become part of the new Maternal and Child Health and Social Service Block Grants. Funding for both the block grant and Title X, which continued as a separate program, was cut substantially with the reorganization. It is unlikely that these services will be expanded in the current political climate; federal funding of family planning has not increased in real dollars since 1973, and recent funding cutbacks are discernible at the local level (Moore & Burt, 1982).

Family planning clinics target specifically women (few services exist for men except for occasional free condom distribution) of low income, those with marginal incomes who cannot afford private care, and teenagers. The clinics provide not only medical examinations and contraceptive devices, but also other health services such as breast and pelvic examinations, Pap smears, STD testing, and blood pressure screening (Dryfoos, 1982). The provision of contraceptive devices (including birth control pills, intrauterine devices, and contraceptive foam) includes counseling and information about different methods and problems, as well as follow-up care.

Large-scale evaluations of federal efforts have generally shown that the family planning clinics have been successful in reducing overall pregnancy rates (see Moore & Burt's 1982 review of these evaluations). For example, Forrest, Hermalin, and Henshaw (1981) demonstrated that in the 1970s family planning clinics prevented an estimated 2.6 million unintended adolescent pregnancies including nearly 1 million unplanned births and 1.4 million abortions. They estimate that for every 10 teenagers enrolled in the clinics, 2.82 pregnancies were averted.

School-Based Clinics

Adolescent health clinics located in public schools are a recent innovation in adolescent health care, with more than 80 in operation or in the planning stages across the country (Cornell, 1987). Most such clinics are organized and at least partially funded by outside organizations and staffed by nurse-practitioners and social workers, with medical backup (Kenney, 1986). Kenney also notes that despite the fact that few school-based clinics actually provide contraception at the school, considerable community controversy often occurs about their operation.

The first school-based clinic, funded by federal MIC funds, was opened in a St. Paul, Minnesota, junior-senior high school in 1973 (Edwards, Steinman, Arnold, & Hakanson, 1980). Initially the clinic offered only prenatal and postpartum care, STD testing and treatment, pregnancy treatment, Pap smears and contraceptive information and counseling. When student response was minimal services were expanded to include "nonsexual services" including athletic, job, and college physical examinations; immunizations; and a weight-control program. This change resulted in increased student participation, perhaps because the change afforded anonymity to the sexually active teenager who used the clinic. The St. Paul program does not dispense contraceptive devices on campus but rather makes them available to students who request them at a nearby medical facility in the evenings.

Edwards et al. (1980) reported a 56% decrease in pregnancy rates in the school between 1973 and 1976 as well as high rates of continuation among contraceptive users. Although she did not present empirical data, Cornell (1987) listed the positive consequences of a school-based clinic in New Haven as improved attendance and school performance, higher graduation rates, and more involvement of parents. The staff of the New Haven program includes two social workers who work with students on issues concerning sexuality, peer and family relationships, and specific health problems both individually and in groups.

The success of school-based clinics probably lies in several areas. First, the easy access to service is an important variable for adolescents who are limited in their transportation resources and in the hours they can appear for service (Chilman, 1979). Second, although a major debate still exists regarding the importance and indeed the desirability of confidentiality of services for teenagers, the threat of parental notice reduces the proportion of teens willing to seek the services, if not the proportion who are sexually active. A school-based program offers clinic personnel the opportunity of maintaining confidentiality while still actively following up on program participants. For example, students who begin to use contraceptive devices or methods are contacted soon through the school to determine if they have any problems or concerns.

The multidisciplinary, multiservice nature of the St. Paul and similar clinics has been cited as a third positive factor (Zellman, 1982). In St. Paul, a social worker interviews each prospective client to discuss concerns such as her relationships with family and partner, and to work with these other parties if the girl so desires (Edwards et al., 1980). In an effort to encourage those girls who do become pregnant to continue their education, the clinic also has an on-site day-care center, an early education program for the children of enrolled students, and educational classes regarding prenatal care, parenting, family life, and human sexuality.

Debate continues about the appropriateness of the provision of family planning services in the public schools. Some educators maintain that this additional responsibility is a great burden on an already overburdened institution (Zellman, 1982). Yet it seems clear that the public school has a place in the prevention of adolescent pregnancy. The school setting has access to most adolescents and is the scene of a significant portion of their lives. Moreover, the school is where they see their friends and form many of their dating relationships. Although the school is important in the lives of adolescents and should play some role in preventing pregnancy, it is not clear what type of role the school should play, however. A good education that enhances the students' potential and opportunities for advancement could provide significant incentive to avoid pregnancy, for example. Whether the school should be the scene of more direct intervention in the form of sex education or even distribution of contraceptives is an issue that has not been settled.

Other Programs

Dryfoos and Heisler (1981) used the National Reporting System for Family Planning Services to identify 3,089 different agencies providing some type of contraceptive service to American adolescents in 1975. They identified 630 hospitals, 1,693 health departments, 172 Planned Parenthood affiliates, and 594 other agencies providing such services.

Social workers are involved in several different types of programs that attempt to go beyond the simple provision of contraceptive services. The work of Schinke and associates (Blythe, Gilchrist, & Schinke, 1981; Schinke, 1979; Schinke & Gilchrist, 1977; Schinke, Gilchrist, & Blythe,

1980) demonstrates that information about contraception is useful to adolescents only if they apply it to their personal decisions, and if they possess the appropriate skills to communicate with their sexual partners. Thus, in a well-developed program of research that emphasizes a developmental approach to adolescent pregnancy, they have proposed cognitive-behavioral group training for adolescents that involves four steps: (a) the provision of accurate information about sexuality, reproduction, and contraception; (b) the promotion of accurate perception, understanding, and retention of the information presented; (c) assistance in personalizing and using the information in decision making; and (d) implementation of the decision making in actual behavior. Techniques such as the use of modeling, role play, practice, reinforcement and feedback, and quizzes have been used to test the adolescents' understanding and retention of information and their skills in using the information.

Promising results with adolescent boys and girls (Blythe et al., 1981; Schinke et al., 1980) suggest that this approach may be effective in providing the knowledge and skills that should be correlated with the prevention of pregnancy. In addition, follow-up data on a small sample of 19 adolescents who received the training indicated greater commitment to postponing pregnancy as well as more consistent use of reliable birth control methods. Long-term follow-up of larger samples will be necessary to determine whether this promising intervention does actually reduce the occurrence of pregnancy among participants.

Another approach is illustrated by The Door: A Center of Alternatives in New York, which emphasizes the importance of the adolescent as a whole person (Armstrong, 1979). A group format is used to explore feelings, and to "practice" behavior such as talking about birth control with potential sex partners and saying "no" to pressure to have sex. The group setting appears to be ideal for the teaching and practicing of decision-making skills and probabilistic thinking (i.e., estimating the risk of pregnancy based on the number of incidents of unprotected intercourse) as well as enhancing the self-esteem of participants.

Programs for Adolescent Boys

Although data are not available to prove that prevention services for adolescent boys can have a significant positive impact, the accumulation of research suggests that young boys play a significant role in the decision to have intercourse and whether to contracept. (For a broader discussion of the role of boys in family planning, see Chapter 8.) Adolescent sexual activity may be the result of pressure by the young boy who must "score" to achieve peer recognition. In many cases, the young woman may put up little or no resistance even though she may not want to have sexual intercourse. Thus, roles for young men might address the issues of peer pressure, self-discipline (National Urban League, 1987), and respect for their partners' desires.

Moreover, many young men do not have the necessary information or skills to prevent pregnancy and will take advantage of services if they are offered in an acceptable way. Thus, it would seem that services for adolescent boys have at least the potential of positive outcomes. The available research, though limited, is promising, and interest is high in involving young men more fully in family planning.

Heightened concern by the federal government about adolescent pregnancy in the late 1970s resulted in little concern with the male adolescent other than "to include him in clinic rap sessions and to provide him with free condoms," however (Finkel & Finkel, 1981, p. 327). Not until action by the Office of Adolescent Pregnancy Prevention in 1978 did the federal government seem to recognize the male role in adolescent pregnancy in a significant way; a small amount of money was appropriated that year to create several new programs directed specifically at young men. Despite this new commitment, little success has been achieved because of continuing low levels of funding.

In addition, Sonenstein (1986) asserts that most of the funding was used to set up male clinics with male staffs that functioned parallel to female clinics, but most of these clinics failed because they were unable to attract clients. Scales and Beckstein (1982) assert that the level of funding for male-directed programs is simply too low, and that social workers and other professionals do not know enough about male sexuality and sexual decision making or how to provide effective sexual health care services for young men.

More recent efforts to involve male adolescents in contraceptive decision making include the National Urban League's (1987) Adolescent Male Responsibility Project. This program has as its motto "Don't make a baby if you can't be a father." The project is built on a philosophy that "is couched in an approach that instills pride by depicting historical ideals and perspectives that have shaped responsible black men of the past" (p. 11). This project, which sponsors several community programs throughout the country, emphasizes services for young black men that meet the specific concrete needs of that community, such as employment training and placement, continuing education, and skills training.

Although the National Urban League's project provides contraceptive information and devices (and a range of other health-related services), it also emphasizes more general services designed to promote self-sufficiency and success in young black men. In some locations peer and "mentor" counseling is provided on a range of topics from drug abuse to spiritual growth. Several locations emphasize the importance of positive role models for responsible sexual and other behavior. Some programs provide individual and group counseling, whereas others provide social activities such as field trips and recreation. One location holds workshops for single black mothers to prepare them to educate their sons about responsible male behavior.

Battle (1987) reports on "The Hub" in the south Bronx, which is designed to prevent adolescent pregnancy through comprehensive services to male and female adolescents including social activities, educational and exercise classes, tutoring, college and career counseling, and work experience programs. An additional component includes classes in family life and sex education. Battle reports that of 140 teenage participants, only two pregnancies have occurred in more than 3 years; however, it is not possible to evaluate effectiveness fully with such information.

Although it is difficult to say because data have been generally unavailable until recently, some researchers believe that young men are beginning to assume more responsibility for contraception (Vadies & Hale, 1977). Some change in contraceptive behavior may be due to the AIDS epidemic and increasingly open discussions about the use of condoms for protection against this disease.

Prenatal and Postpartum Services for Adolescents

Despite the demonstrated effectiveness of prenatal care in improving the outcomes of pregnancy (see chapter 2), and the excess risk of poor pregnancy outcome for teenagers, teenagers enter prenatal care later in their pregnancies and have fewer visits than women in the ideal childbearing years (20 to 24 years of age). Among women younger than 15 years of age, only 34.2% begin care in the first trimester; among those 15 to 19 years of age, the figure rises to 53% (Institute of Medicine, 1985). The importance of prenatal care takes on added significance in the face of evidence that most of the excess risks faced by pregnant adolescents can be mitigated with quality prenatal care (Sacker & Neuhoff, 1982). In addition, prenatal care may be an entry point for services designed to prevent subsequent pregnancies among this group.

The reasons teenagers delay seeking prenatal care include a lack of understanding of the importance of preventive care, especially in the absence of any obvious problems (Bolton, 1980). Many fear the physical examination, and others may have transportation problems (Cooper, 1982). Others attempt to deny the pregnancy or to hide it from their friends and family. Researchers have probed to discover why teenagers delay seeking prenatal care in an effort to determine what kinds of services might succeed in attracting them earlier. One approach is to offer prenatal care services in clinics or other settings that serve only teenagers.

Specialized Services

Although it is not clear whether adolescents benefit from specialized prenatal care, or whether their needs can be met by timely, competent prenatal care in a general setting, specialized care for adolescents is becoming increasingly popular (Klerman, Jekel, & Chilman, 1983). Adolescents face problems that may limit their access to care and that suggest the importance of specialized services. For example, it is desirable for pregnant adolescents who are still in school to remain in school, but many clinics have restricted hours that may not coincide with adolescents' available time. Furthermore, adolescents may not have transportation to reach the prenatal care clinics, especially in rural or dense urban areas with inadequate public transportation. Adolescents might be more likely to take advantage of services that deal with these special problems, perhaps through evening clinics and the provision of transportation.

Teenagers are more likely to cancel their medical appointments and less likely to follow medical advice than older women (Kadushin & Martin, 1988).

Moreover, several typical adolescent health habits present special challenges to the prenatal care professional that might be dealt with successfully in a setting especially for teenagers. For instance, adolescents are at high risk of nutritional deficiencies, suffering from a combination of ignorance, poverty, and junk food diets (Moore & Burt, 1982). Smoking is common among adolescent girls and has been linked closely to LBW, as have other dangerous substances such as alcohol and other drugs (Cooper, 1982).

The Institute of Medicine (1985) has recommended that the content of prenatal care be more individualized; a good diet and cessation of smoking might be emphasized strongly in services designed especially for adolescents. In addition, such services might provide education in infant care, parenting, and other areas that more mature women might be less likely to need.

Specialized programs tend to be sponsored by hospitals (Johnson, Walters, & McKenry, 1979). The Young Mothers Program of the Yale-New Haven Medical Center provides not only prenatal care, but education on nutrition, labor and delivery, and health care. Follow-up services continue for up to 2 years after birth. The authors briefly describe several other hospital-based programs and broadly call them "successful" in improving birth outcomes and other areas, but more empirical research is required to assess the particular components of services that are successful and to identify those clients who can benefit most from particular services.

Smith, Wait, Mumford, Nenney, and Hollins (1978) described a prenatal clinic for indigent adolescents 18 years of age and younger. Beginning in the second trimester, the multidisciplinary clinic provided weekly classes on nutrition, contraception, child development, labor preparation, and psychosocial aspects of pregnancy. The authors did not report whether a social worker was part of this team, and did not describe case management services or special attention to the material or personal needs of the clients, despite the fact that indigent subjects were targeted for the services. Nonetheless, compared with the control group (N = 100), the randomly selected participants in the experimental program (N = 99) had infants with significantly higher birthweights and Apgar scores, lower rates of cesarean sections and urinary tract infections, and higher likelihood of returning for their 4-week postpartum examination. Experimental mothers also had significantly more prenatal visits and fewer admissions for false labor.

Osofsky and Osofsky (1970) described the Young Mothers Educational Development Program in New York, an intensive multidisciplinary program for pregnant teenagers. The program consisted of schooling, medical care, social and psychological services, a nursery, and other services all located in a former school. Measures of receipt of prenatal care, anemia, pregnancy complications, prematurity, and infant mortality for 385 girls who had participated fully in the program showed that all were superior to the general population. In addition, participants appeared to make substantial gains in school completion, receipt of public assistance, and rate of subsequent unwanted pregnancies. The authors suggest that the improvements demonstrated were those located most closely in time to service provision; other measures may be more related to long-term poverty and poor diet that would require more comprehensive changes in the environments of low-income teenage mothers and their infants.

Several school-based programs (e.g., Johnson & Staples, 1979; McMurray, 1968; Stine & Kelley, 1970) have provided regular schooling, maternity and parenting education, nutritional education and supplementation, counseling, and other services to pregnant students. Pregnant adolescents often have attended special schools designed to promote completion of their education, owing in part to Title IX of the Educational Amendment Act of 1972 that recognizes the right of pregnant girls to have a public education. School-based programs generally have not provided on-site medical services, although referrals were often made. Such programs generally have been considered to be successful at keeping pregnant adolescents in school, perhaps in enhancing some pregnancy-related outcomes, and in reducing the number of subsequent pregnancies (Phipps-Yonas, 1980).

The Teenage Pregnancy and Parenting Project is an interagency program that provides coordinated services to deal with the particular problems of pregnant adolescents and teenaged parents in San Francisco (Barth, Claycomb, & Loomis, 1988). Both adolescent mothers and fathers receive health care, counseling, educational and vocational services, recreational services, and special educational classes such as family life education and parenting classes. The limited available evaluation data on this program suggests that it has been successful in encouraging adolescent fathers to be more involved in the pregnancy process. Paternal participation appears to result in small positive effects on birthweight as well.

Outreach and Recruitment

More aggressive outreach and public education may be required to recruit pregnant adolescent girls and especially their male partners into prenatal care and services. Effective recruitment of adolescents may need to be carried out in different locations and with various methods than is the case with other target groups.

A tendency exists to assume that the schools are the ideal place for recruitment; perhaps the school should be the starting place, but social workers should avoid concentrating exclusively on any single location such as the school. Many teenagers have already dropped out of school before becoming pregnant, and schools may have little personal involvement with students. This point is especially true for students with behavioral problems (Shoemaker, 1966).

Recruitment through the media (especially radio and television), laundromats, sports centers, and other places where teenagers congregate could be particularly effective with adolescents, although with adolescents "word of mouth" is probably the most effective recruitment method. Moore and Burt (1982) suggest that AFDC offices may prove to be productive settings for outreach efforts. Zilbergeld (1975) emphasizes the importance of "starting where the client is," both figuratively and literally when he suggests recruiting in liquor stores, barber shops, and grocery stores.

Recruitment of adolescent boys is a particularly difficult problem because adolescent boys are less likely to seek out any type of social service than are their female peers (Sander & Rosen, 1987). Some adolescent boys may be located when they accompany their pregnant girl friends to prenatal care appointments (Barth et al., 1988). The National Urban League (1987) Adolescent Male Responsibility Project uses a public information–community awareness approach to make potential clients aware of their services, and also supplies audio visual materials to high schools and other community groups that include adolescent boys. Varner (1984) encourages greater use of media in involving young men in family planning as well.

Barth et al. (1988) noted that the Teenage Pregnancy and Parenting Project sponsored a community basketball team as a means of outreach. They also pointed out the fact that unlike young women, young men often entered the program to obtain specific services, such as career counseling. They emphasized the importance of continued aggressive outreach in retaining male clients. Much more research is needed about the most effective means of reaching young male fathers.

Postpartum Care

Unfortunately, delivery and discharge from the hospital mark the end of services for many teen mothers and their infants (Schinke, 1978). As Furstenberg (1976) notes; "Most programs cease to offer services at the point that many of the gravest problems arise for the adolescent mother" (p. 224). One reason for this abandonment of the adolescent mother may be that fewer natural points exist for intervention following the birth of the baby. Nevertheless, the research about the long-term problems of adolescent parents demonstrates that this group continues to need services long after the traditional 6-week postpartum period.

The postpartum examination might be useful as a point of extending further services to the adolescent mother. Ordinarily, a postpartum examination is scheduled to occur when the infant is about 6 weeks of age to monitor the recovery of the mother as well as to initiate contraception if necessary and to stress the importance of well-baby care (Klerman et al., 1983). Many low-income patients do not appear for this examination, however, and adolescents may be particularly likely to disregard the need for follow-up.

Programs for Fathers

Social work service could benefit the young adolescent father, whether he marries or not, in several ways. For those who do not marry, the social worker might assist him in determining the extent of financial support he can realistically provide for his child (Kadushin & Martin, 1988). This assessment will also include issues such as whether he should remain in school or obtain employment, his long-term career goals, and his other obligations. The social worker can also be helpful with issues such as helping him define his relationship with his child and her mother, and deal with visitation decisions.

For those young men who do marry, similar problems require resolution. These young men may require advice and assistance in changing their goals and indeed their self-perceptions as they take on new obligations. Other important issues may include relationship difficulties with their parents and in-laws, confusion about relationships with unmarried friends, and problems adjusting to the conflicts between the duties of parenthood and marriage and the desires shared by all adolescents.

Parke, Power, and Fisher (1980) maintain that the most common myth about the adolescent father is that he seldom maintains contact with his child; their review of available studies indicates that substantial numbers of adolescent fathers do maintain frequent and long-lasting contact with their children. For example, Furstenberg (1976) found in the Baltimore study of more than 300 adolescent pregnancies that 63% of the fathers still maintained relationships with their children after 5 years. Many researchers and practitioners report that adolescent fathers are truly concerned about and interested in their children's well-being, but do not have the knowledge and resources to assume their responsibilities (Sander & Rosen, 1987).

Several new programs are taking innovative approaches to working with the adolescent father. "Parenting for Adolescent Fathers" is a program still in the planning stages that is sponsored by the Comprehensive School-Age Parenting Program in Boston (Battle, 1987). The program includes peer group support, educational training, career and life counseling, and a course that consists of 15 weekly sessions that include the topics of self-image, personal relationships, stress, male responsibility and parenting, child health and development, personal development, and so forth. Results are not yet available on this ambitious project.

The Teenage Pregnancy and Parenting Project in San Francisco makes available several services designed specifically to enhance young fathers' parenting skills (Barth et al., 1988). Father support groups discussed topics such as communication, child development, nutrition, and other topics. Evaluation of the effectiveness of this part of the program was not possible because of the small number of participants.

Practice Roles for Social Workers

Because the pathology-oriented model of the unwed adolescent and pregnancy has lost favor, the literature on adolescent pregnancy has provided little direction for the social worker in search of a "treatment modality." Some still see adolescent sexuality and pregnancy as pathological symptoms, and seek to treat the "underlying problems." Little empirical or theoretical support exists for such an approach, however, and generally little indication of what the observable outcomes of such an approach would be if it were successful. Moreover, no evidence is available that such an approach can be helpful with the serious day-to-day problems of the pregnant or parenting adolescent.

A diagnosis of pregnancy and the decision-making phase immediately following diagnosis may be classified as crises that warrant crisis intervention. A crisis intervention approach might be useful in assisting the client in dealing with the emotional shock of pregnancy, making a decision about resolution, and applying what is learned to improvement of overall coping skills (Kaminsky & Sheckter, 1979). Crisis intervention, however, is a short-term treatment model that provides little usefulness for ongoing work with the adolescent, whatever course she might choose. Moreover, it does not provide an adequate framework for intervention with adolescents who are not pregnant but who are sexually active, and with whom the social worker works regarding issues of contraception, responsibility, and so forth.

One practice model that is once again gaining increasing favor in social work in general is case management. Case management is a method of service delivery that is designed for clients with multiple complex problems and who must deal with numerous different providers in the health care and welfare systems (Rubin, 1987). The case manager assumes overall responsibility for linking the client with the appropriate resources and obtaining needed services.

Case management has been proposed by several authors (Bolton, 1980; Brindis, Barth, & Loomis, 1987; Burt & Sonenstein, 1985) as a useful model for working with the pregnant and parenting adolescent owing to the complex service needs of this group. For example, case management appears to be useful in the provision of prenatal care to adolescents (Bolton, 1980; Burt & Sonenstein, 1985). Burt and Sonenstein (1985) note that "someone must assume responsibility for monitoring individual cases, assessing clients' needs, and arranging for services to meet those needs" (p. 36). Bolton (1980) called the case manager role critical "because of the need for a variety of services as well as the need for an identified treatment provider to serve as the director of the casework services" (p. 183). Further development of the case management model is needed with adolescents, along with empirical evidence of usefulness.

Whatever model is used, some consensus exists in the literature about some essential tasks to be performed by the social worker, whether the adolescent's problem or goal concerns unprotected sexual intercourse, the possibility of pregnancy and consequent decision making, or ongoing work following abortion or delivery. These tasks center around assessment of the adolescent's needs, decision making about the resolution of unplanned pregnancy, provision of concrete resources and coordination of services, educational needs, emotional support, and follow-up services.

Assessment

Assessment is particularly critical with pregnant adolescents (Klerman et al., 1983). On many teams the social worker is responsible for obtaining the social and family history of the pregnant client (Cooper, 1982), which provides information regarding the degree of risk for poor outcome, as well as the social service needs of the client. In some clinics the social worker's assessment also may include some of the basic facts of the client's medical history including her use of alcohol, tobacco, and other drugs. The reader is referred to the discussion of assessment issues in Chapter 2. Many of the standard, high-risk, assessment tools automatically qualify a younger adolescent as high risk, based solely on her age (e.g., Hobel, Hyvarinen, Okada, & Oh, 1973).

Assessment, like screening for risk of poor pregnancy outcome, is an ongoing function (Kumabe et al., 1977). Service needs change as the adolescent's situation changes with the physiological changes of pregnancy, alterations in personal relationships, difficulties in school, and other factors. For example, ongoing assessment is critical as the time for delivery approaches and the adolescent should be preparing the nursery.

Decision Making

Assisting pregnant adolescents in decision making about the resolution of pregnancy is a well established role for social workers (Kadushin & Martin, 1987), but today more options than ever are available. For example, single parenthood is more acceptable now, despite the attendant problems. Despite recent changes, the 1973 Supreme Court decision *Roe v. Wade*, allows adolescents to abort their pregnancies. Finally, the increased demand for adoptable infants means that most communities provide resources for the pregnant adolescent who chooses to relinquish her child for adoption. The social worker's role in assisting the client in making a decision is a complex one. It should be noted that in some cases adolescents may be seeking someone to make the decisions for them; the social worker should avoid filling this role and instead should attempt to help clients mobilize their own decision-making skills (Klerman et al., 1983).

The decision about whether to abort often constitutes a serious crisis for the adolescent, her partner, and her family (Chesler & Davis, 1980). Significant barriers to the abortion option exist for some adolescents, the most important of which may be requirements of parental consent or notice (Moore & Burt, 1982). Others include the costs of abortion, which are no longer paid by Medicaid, and the lack of abortion facilities in some communities (Zakus & Wilday, 1987). Cultural, and in many cases religious, values may mitigate against an abortion decision by some teenagers. In many instances the family or the baby's father may exert pressure on the adolescent in one direction or the other (Chesler & Davis, 1980). The adolescent may know that she cannot be a good parent or may not wish to be a parent, but may fear the reactions of others if she chooses an abortion. The family also may fear the reactions of extended family or friends. Finally, teenagers are more likely to delay making a decision about abortion than older women (possibly because of conflict about abortion), and thus may face more difficult, risky, and painful procedures than if they had made an earlier decision (Zakus & Wilday, 1987).

The social worker who assists adolescent clients in their decision regarding abortion must attempt to provide full information to clients about the nature of the procedure and recovery from it, implications for future fertility, and the possible psychological effects (e.g., "anniversary" reactions) (Zakus & Wilday, 1987). Both Cain (1979) and Zakus and Wilday (1987) emphasize the importance of speed in decision making, as abortions that are delayed beyond the first trimester require more costly, painful, and risky procedures than those completed in the first trimester. The necessity of speedy decision making may place additional stress on the adolescent, but it cannot be avoided. (See chapter 8 for additional information on decisions regarding unwanted pregnancy.)

It is also important that all pregnant adolescents be fully informed of the option to relinquish their infants for adoption. Resnick (1984) cautions that social workers should not presume that clients are not interested in adoption or that further information might not be beneficial to them. He says, "Adolescents must be encouraged to explore the widest possible array of options for themselves, including implications for the present and future" (p. 8).

It is not clear how to inform clients of this option in the most effective way. Moore and Burt (1982) suggest that agencies offering pregnancy testing and maternity services post signs encouraging interested adolescents to inquire about adoption. The provision of information about relinquishment probably cannot be provided in one short interview, but probably should be delivered throughout the pregnancy by a counselor who has frequent contact with the pregnant adolescent through a structured program. Such programs are rare, but a prenatal care setting might be an ideal one for the ongoing social worker to provide such information in a supportive atmosphere.

Another important task is helping the adolescent decide whether to tell her parents about her pregnancy (Cain, 1979). In some cases a teenager must maintain secrecy for good reasons, and the social worker must respect that decision. Yet Klerman et al. (1983) note that parents are often unexpected resources for adolescents who find themselves in this position. Kadushin & Martin (1988) say:

> For most teenagers and many young adults, the family remains a central resource for meeting both material and emotional needs. Pregnant adolescents, like their nonpregnant counterparts, continue to turn to their families for support; families remain a significant resource even when they choose to marry. (pp. 490–491)

How to seek that support, and the type and extent of that support are usually complicated and difficult issues for adolescents.

Moreover, Chesler and Davis (1980) emphasize that pregnancy is a family crisis that should be resolved in a manner that is most advantageous or least destructive for the entire family, including the baby's father. Such a family approach would require involvement of the entire family and the baby's father in the decision-making process.

A more complicated issue is whether parents should be notified as a matter of course when their adolescent daughters seek abortions. Those who support a legal requirement of parental involvement point out the need for family communication on such a critical matter, the rights of parents to consent in medical matters, and the risks of abortion that mitigate against the ability of immature young people to make informed decisions. The similar issue of whether the male partner should be notified or consulted before abortion has only recently been raised.

Concrete Services

The provision of concrete services is the most important priority in working with the adolescent mother (Bolton, 1980) and is the issue of most importance to the young mother herself (Kadushin & Martin, 1988). Shoemaker (1966) decried social workers' reluctance to provide such services:

> Let us not underestimate the value of concrete services in their right. We in social work have tended to deprecate such services—monetary assistance, nursing services, educational help—perhaps out of our own lack of appreciation for the effects of physical deprivation. In social work we have often tended to view concrete service primarily as leverage to psychological helping; it may serve this purpose as well, but it has a place of importance of its own. (p. 106)

Effective provision of concrete services requires that the social worker be familiar with the services and eligibility requirements of outside agencies. Frequently used resources may include family planning services, parent-child centers, and adoption and abortion services; AFDC and Medicaid if the mother-to-be is low income; WIC continuing education programs in the school, and vocational training and placement (see Chapter 2). Other services may be needed in specific cases and may require knowledge of the mental health system, child protection agencies, self-help groups, and many other services. Moreover, coordination is required not only in dealing with resources outside the agency but also may be needed within the health setting itself. In a clinic setting it is easy for clients to become discouraged with the many stops and the time required to obtain many tests at each appointment; because clients are "on their own," they may leave before completing all of the necessary procedures. For example, most clinics provide classes in pregnancy, birth and delivery, and infant care; however, Burt and Sonenstein (1985) noted that among the 21 programs they studied, clients were often "lost" within the facility and failed to receive all of the on-site services. Periodic case reviews by the social worker should monitor the teenager's compliance with each step of the clinic protocol to be sure this does not occur. Bolton (1980) notes that the impulsivity of the typical adolescent may require that the case manager go far beyond the usual monitoring to provide frequent reminders and perhaps persuasion about keeping appointments consistently. The same might be true of follow-up appointments and refills of prescriptions for contraception.

The physical needs of the poor pregnant adolescent include all of the same needs experienced by the older, low-income women (see Chapter 2) but because of their immaturity these clients are more likely to have additional problems. First, adolescent mothers-to-be frequently may require help (either information or actual material assistance) in preparing for the baby including selecting and buying the layette, an infant seat, clothing and feeding supplies, furniture, and so forth. Long-range planning and follow-through are not typical of teenagers (Bierman & Street, 1982), and especially if the young mother-to-be attempts to deny her pregnancy, this may result in her failure to buy the equipment she needs in advance.

The social worker should be particularly alert to the possibility of lack of preparation for the infant in cases of immature first-time mothers who have few social supports or who live alone. Klerman et al. (1983) go further to flatly advise against a plan that includes the adolescent mother's living alone. In cases in which this cannot be prevented (and in other cases) the social worker or public health nurse may want to visit the home before the baby is discharged to be sure that it is adequate for an infant. For example, Cooper (1982) reported on the Rochester Adolescent Maternity Program, which has a social worker make frequent visits to the homes of pregnant teenagers to help them mobilize their resources to prepare for the baby's arrival.

Educational Services

The very young and isolated mother also usually requires education in several areas including the nutritional requirements of infants. The social worker may refer the adolescent client to a nutritionist or WIC worker, or if no referral is available may provide such information herself. Breast-feeding usually is not selected by adolescents (Martinez, 1984), so it is critical that the adolescent understand how to prepare and use infant formula, as improper preparation may seriously endanger the infant's health. The adolescent mother probably is qualified for WIC and Food Stamps, and the social worker should encourage the teenager to apply for and use the coupons. Either the social worker or a staff nutritionist also should instruct the mother in the timing and procedure for introducing solid foods, as it is common for adolescents to introduce them too early (Bierman & Street, 1982).

The social worker also probably should assume that the adolescent mother, even more than the older mother, requires education in infant care and parenting, and if educational services are not available within the agency, the social worker should have a close working relationship with such a program to facilitate referral. To the extent that she is pregnant for the first time, lives or will live alone, and has few social supports, it is a virtual certainty that the adolescent mother is unprepared for the enormous responsibilities of parenthood. Bolton (1980) reminds the social worker that the adolescent parent is often isolated from friends, parents, the baby's father. In such a situation the adolescent has no one from whom to seek advice and information when the infant is ill, will not sleep or eat, or simply when the new mother feels insecure. She may be especially unprepared to deal with discipline and her child's natural aggressive behavior (Bierman & Street, 1982).

Counseling and Support

As adolescent pregnancy is a crisis for all involved, counseling or support is often necessary for difficulties or relationship problems with parents (Young, Berkman, & Rehr, 1975) or the baby's father. In some cases questions may exist about where the mother and her baby will live or about division of responsibilities for child care (Young et al., 1975). Often conflicts occur about the future role of the father in the baby's life, visitation, or child support. The pregnant teenager also may be depressed, frightened, angry, or confused about her situation and future (Sacker & Neuhoff, 1982), and the social worker should invite the client to explore any of these feelings and possible solutions to her problems.

If the young client is considering abortion, the social worker also assists her in confronting her fears and feelings about the procedure in order to make an informed decision and reduce anxiety (Zakus & Wilday, 1987). The young adolescent boy may be especially ignorant of the actual abortion procedure and can only participate in the decision if he fully understands what would occur. Kaminsky and Sheckter (1979) emphasize the importance of the social worker's discussing future contraceptive plans at this time to reduce the likelihood of another unplanned pregnancy.

Although it is logical to assume that counseling might be effective in helping pregnant adolescents to deal with problems such as those described earlier, it is important to recognize that little empirical evidence exists to demonstrate positive outcomes associated with such counseling, or to suggest particularly effective modes of counseling. In fact, it may not be clear what outcomes are sought; the prevention of future pregnancies, enhancement of positive feelings about the pregnancy and parenting, and reduction of anxiety and depression in the adolescent parent all are possibilities. Further research is needed to establish the counseling needs of pregnant and parenting adolescents, and the most effective ways of meeting those needs.

Bolton (1980) recommends a group format for working with pregnant and parenting adolescents, noting that the focus of adolescents on their peers provides maximum opportunity for influencing many areas of the teenager's world. For example, the group may serve as an educational tool or as a forum for the expression and resolution of many fears and anxieties associated with pregnancy. Indeed Bolton's review of empirical support for groups with adolescents in general (not pregnant adolescents) does lend some promise to this approach as a part of the overall package of services for pregnant and parenting teenagers, but the social worker should be clear on the purpose of the group to evaluate its effectiveness for that particular purpose.

Follow-Up

The high rate of repeat pregnancies and discontinuation of contraception among adolescents, the likelihood of "anniversary reactions" and long-term effects of abortion or relinquishment, as well as the continuing problems experienced by many teenaged parents all suggest that some kind of mechanism for the provision of follow-up services for adolescents is essential.

Brindis et al. (1987) emphasize that adolescent clients are not likely to take advantage of services without follow-up. In these authors' report of the Teenage Pregnancy and Parenting Project, they emphasize that case managers made telephone or home visits to adolescent parent clients at least twice monthly, with clients considered to be at "high-risk" receiving more frequent visits. High-risk factors might include younger adolescents, adolescents with more children, those whose social or financial resources are especially deficient, or those with numerous health problems.

Despite the apparent advantages of long-term follow-up, the literature contains little guidance regarding appropriate schedules for service delivery, what types of services would be beneficial, or the desired duration of such follow-up. In addition, for such services to be cost-effective, it would be necessary to operationalize the expected outcomes and to identify which clients could benefit from specific types of follow-up services. Longitudinal research with adolescents is necessary to make these determinations.

8 Family Planning Services

The desire to limit family size is an age-old desire, and crude methods of birth control have existed for centuries. By 1865 in this country, physicians had publicly endorsed (and much of the public had accepted) several relatively effective means of contraception including withdrawal, spermicidal douches, the diaphragm or pessary, condoms, and periodic abstinence (Reed, 1984). A crude version of the rhythm method was also known. Indeed, the long-term decline in birth rates that began in the mid-19th century and extended to the 1930s demonstrated that some people knew about and were using contraception and abortion. Much of what was known about contraception was only widely available to the middle classes, however. In fact, physicians generally shared their knowledge only with married couples who desired to limit their family size to three or four children (Reed, 1984).

The lower classes and the very poor often accepted pregnancy as either fate or "God's will," whereas others made use of the "five dollar abortionist" (Reed, 1984). The other few available services were predicated on the assumption that women (mostly unmarried) who experienced unwanted pregnancies had "characterological disorders" and required casework services (Furie, 1966). These services generally consisted only of maternity homes (Balassone, 1983) and placement of "illegitimate" children in institutions or adoptive homes (Kadushin & Martin, 1988).

In this country the movement toward reproductive freedom was forced forward by Margaret Sanger's campaign (1914–1937), which grew from her concern for poor women and her feminist ideals (Reed, 1984). Although some ascribe the story to apocryphy, Sanger, who was a nurse, claimed that the event that sparked her great campaign was witnessing the death of a desperate poor woman from a self-induced abortion (Kennedy, 1970). Whatever the truth of this story, Margaret Sanger's great contribution was providing social justification for something that previously had been considered purely a personal or selfish matter (Reed, 1984).

Sanger's campaign was thwarted by the accomplishments of yet another great figure in American birth control history, Anthony Comstock. Comstock was a zealous dry-goods salesman who, with the help of backers obtained through his involvement in the Young Men's Christian Association, pushed a bill through the U.S. Congress in 1873 that built on previous legislation prohibiting the mailing of obscenity. By adding contraceptive material to the definition of obscenity, Comstock was able to prevent the dissemination of birth control methods and devices to physicians and others, beginning a new era of repression of birth control knowledge in the United States that would last for many years. Moreover, many states passed laws banning contraceptive material that were more formidable than the federal laws. The courts declined to review any of these laws until 1929 (Kennedy, 1970).

Sanger's campaign against the Comstock laws led her abroad to study European models of birth control, across the country on lecture tours, and sometimes to jail. She was also responsible in part at least for increasing public awareness of the effect of unrestrained fertility on the lower classes. Two events in the 1930s marked her triumph against the Comstock laws. First, in the mid-1930s conservative physicians began to recognize that birth control could not be purely a medical province, because physicians alone could not reach the millions of lower income families who needed birth control. The second event was *United States v. One Package*, the New York circuit court decision in 1936 that removed birth control from the definition of obscenity and allowed physicians to provide contraceptives for health purposes (Aries, 1987).

This decision permitted mailing and transporting information and devices that were necessary for widespread dissemination of birth control, and increasing medical acceptance and support provided the social recognition of the importance of birth control. The beginning of the Great Depression, the high fertility of unemployed Americans, and concern with high rates of maternal mortality also led many Americans to see birth control as a way of both reducing the relief rolls and improving health (Kennedy, 1970). Passage of the Social Security Act and nearly $4 million for MCH as part of Title V of that act thus presented the first opportunity for the wide dissemination of birth control services under public auspices.

That opportunity almost was lost. Social worker Katherine Lenroot, director of the Children's Bureau in the late 1930s, refused to allow the bureau to be associated with the birth control cause until a legal opinion forced her to relent and to allow a state plan that included birth control services. Her reluctance grew from fear of political reprisals against the bureau, and perhaps out of fear that effective birth control might weaken the Children's Bureau. Indeed, social workers whose major concerns were child welfare and MCH had long shied away from the issue of birth control out of fear that they would lose their tenuous public support (Aries, 1987; Kennedy, 1970).

Nevertheless social workers were keenly aware for many years of the consequences for their clients of unrestrained fertility. They could do little to obtain services for their clients unless some sensitive topics could be discussed in public, however. Thus Reed (1984) declares that social workers and physicians began the "repeal of the taboo against direct reference to sex" (p. 55). The goal of repression of sexual matters also tied in neatly with some social workers' goals of ending the exploitation of women that was inherent in prostitution and resulting venereal disease. Much of this interest had begun with Jane Addams and Lillian Wald, because many of these exploited women were immigrants (Reed, 1984).

Some individual social workers may have avoided involvement in the birth control movement for political reasons, but the profession did express support. Margaret Sanger was invited to speak at the 1916 meeting of the National Social Workers Congress in Indianapolis (Reed, 1984), and issues of the proceedings of the National Conference of Charities and Correction includes several presentations regarding birth control in the 1920s and 1930s.

Margaret Sanger had begun opening clinics even before this time (sometimes going to jail for doing so), but by the 1930s the clinics were no longer illegal and surreptitious enterprises. An interesting survey and description of 70 family planning clinics (in the United States and several European countries) was published in 1930 (Robinson, 1930). In addition to these 70 clinics, she included the names of 250 more, and noted the existence of many others who did not want to be listed.

Robinson's (1930) survey revealed that social workers were major purveyors of family planning services during this time. All 70 clinics in her survey were administered by physicians (except one run by a social worker and another run by a nurse), but most of the larger clinics employed at least one social worker. Some required patients to be referred by a physician or social worker, who had to certify that further births would be damaging to the health or finances of the woman. Indeed, some clinics offered services only to women who had medical reasons for wanting to curtail fertility. Family planning in the 1930s still was not seen as a service to which all families were entitled. Indeed, Robinson included a lengthy justification of birth control, asserting that "the use of contraceptives is right when practiced by married persons for adequate reasons" (p. xiv).

The clinics in the 1930s provided a surprising array of services including marriage counseling, some abortions (for health reasons only), home visits, and long-term follow-up. Social workers were deemed to be particularly needed to provide outreach through other social service agencies: "To cultivate the cooperation of 'the Charities' in sending the neediest cases, a high-priced social worker will be required" (Robinson, 1930, p. 119). Moreover, Robinson (1930) believed that at least one social worker should be an executive of the clinic: "She should be a trained medical social worker, whether or not she is a nurse as well" (p. 131).

With increasing numbers of clinics and greater public consumption of birth control knowledge, the previous decline in birth rates continued well in the 1930s and 1940s, at one point in the 1930s dropping below the rate needed to replace the population (Reed, 1984). Some observers of this trend grew concerned, especially because birth rates were declining with the greatest rapidity in the middle classes.

It is impossible to study the history of family planning without acknowledging the importance of the eugenics movement. Social workers and others who advocated family planning usually were motivated out of desire to help the poor and to guarantee that every child would be wanted. Nevertheless, they also believed that it was important that birth control be concentrated primarily in the lower classes, in hopes that their numbers would be reduced (e.g., Robinson, 1930). Several presentations at the National Conference of Charities and Correction (e.g., Berry, 1925; Jensen, 1927) supported the eugenics movement.

The major sponsor of family planning services for low-income families for many years was Planned Parenthood, which stepped in after the United States v. One Package court decision and began opening clinics throughout the country. Founded in 1939 as the Birth Control Federation of America by the merging of two other organizations, the organization changed its name to the Planned Parenthood Federation of America in 1942. The organization extended its influence to a national one during the 1940s, setting practice standards for clinics and winning increasing support from government officials (Reed, 1984).

World War II obscured government and perhaps public interest in birth control during the 1940s, but Planned Parenthood continued to operate clinics and offer services to clients. In 1943, 794 clinics were in operation in 28 states and the Virgin Islands (Planned Parenthood, 1943). Indeed, the war lent a certain urgency to the need for birth control for some women including those who hastily married men they did not know well and from whom they would be separated for years, women whose husbands were disabled by the war, and women who worked in war plants and could not obtain maternity leave or child care. Planned Parenthood (1943) quoted one case worker who believed that the war created a special need for birth control:

> My case load is the war in microcosm. I have families of soldiers, sailors, merchant seamen, war casualties, tax and ration problems, day care for children of women in war industry, shortage of doctors, increasing food costs and war neuroses. (p. 9)

Some, though not all, Planned Parenthood clinics employed social workers along with physicians and nurses in the 1940s. Services offered during this time included physical examinations, dissemination and renewal of supplies, advice regarding menopause, and sometimes marriage counseling. Clinics accepted and made referrals to and from family agencies, marriage counsel bureaus, ministers, and private physicians. Social workers were instructed in ways of encouraging acceptance of family planning, such as selecting the clients who were likely to be accepting, including the husband and family when possible, having thorough knowledge on the issue, and being positive in attitude. Follow-up was encouraged, as was working with physicians and medical social workers to promote wider use of birth control (Planned Parenthood, 1943).

It is difficult to find evidence of any social work involvement or interest in the birth control movement during the 1950s. None of the proceedings of the National Conference of Social Work during that decade contains articles on the topic. Few references exist to the subject in articles on other topics, with the exception of mentions of the birth rate. The same is true of the *Social Work Yearbook*, a volume published by the Russell Sage Foundation for many years. The *Social Work Yearbook*, a good indicator of the profession's interests and fields of practice, contained no articles on birth control in the 1950s and no mention of the subject in articles on MCH and Family Life Education.

The 1960s marked an upsurge in calls for accessible family planning services for all families in response to increasing worldwide birth rates after World War II (Reed, 1984) and to increasing welfare roles at home. Three events made a response to those calls possible: the approval of oral contraceptives in 1960, the availability of intrauterine devices beginning in 1964, and approval of the first federal money for family planning services in 1966 (Bradshaw, Wolfe, Wood, & Tyler, 1977). The U.S. Department of Health, Education and Welfare issued its first supportive policy statement on family planning that year, followed by amendments to the Economic Opportunity Act, and Titles IV-A, V (the Child Health Act), and XIX (Medicaid) of the Social Security Act, all providing funding for services. Not coincidentally, the increased availability of effective contraceptive devices and services occurred at a time when the feminist movement was coalescing and the war on poverty was being launched, calling attention to large families as one factor in poverty.

Social work was not widely involved in the family planning movement in the 1950s and early 1960s (Bean, Anderson, & Tatum, 1971). Professional concern began to develop within the profession in the 1960s as evidenced by the Adelphi University School of Social Work Institute in 1967 to "examine the implications of current knowledge for social work's role in the development, delivery, and utilization of family planning services" (Vigilante, 1968, p. 5). Few publications in the social work literature and few schools of social work provided instruction or field opportunities in the field (Meier, 1966).

It must be remembered that the process of professional involvement in a social cause requires time, however. The National Association of Social Workers made a public statement in favor of the availability of family planning services for all who desired them in 1967 (National Association of Social Workers, 1967). Other social work organizations, such as the Family Service Association of America and the Community Service Society of New York, also expressed support at about the same time (Gray, 1966). Following this expression of support, inculcation of family planning content into the social work curriculum required definition of what material should be included, how that material related to social work practice in general, and specific skills and tasks for social workers. Social work educators Haselkorn (1970) and Rapoport (1970) were actively struggling with questions of how the social work curriculum could incorporate material on family planning. The Council on Social Work Education also sought to determine the proper role of social work in the family planning movement (Kendall, 1970).

Still, active involvement by the profession in advocating for the development and wide dissemination of family planning services was somewhat slow to develop. Several reasons are possible for the profession's seeming reluctance to become more involved in this important issue. First, family planning (and sexuality in general) was a subject with which many individuals felt personally uncomfortable (Gray, 1966; Castor & Hudson, 1971; Rapoport, 1970). Social workers generally were not trained or knowledgeable in these areas (Bean et al., 1971), so they probably retained much of the discomfort and ambivalence of the general population (Castor & Hudson, 1971; Haselkorn, 1970; Meier, 1969).

Second, legislation prohibited the referral of public assistance clients to family planning services until the late 1960s. Even after amendments to the Social Security Act in 1967 mandated referrals and offering family planning services for all AFDC clients, social workers in public assistance agencies were reluctant to raise the subject of birth control with their clients because of fear of the appearance of coercion (Gray, 1966; Meier, 1969) or racism (Greenblatt, 1972; Rauch, 1970). Other social workers had contact with clients who feared that if they admitted their need for contraception, that information would lead to loss of their public assistance benefits. Indeed, some questioned whether federally financed family planning programs that were linked to public assistance programs could be free of coercion (Rauch, 1970).

Rauch's concerns were reasonable. Social workers had been active at one time in the eugenics and Malthusian population-control movements (see earlier discussion), and justification for family planning centered on antinatalist policies designed to limit population growth (Shlakman, 1968) or public assistance costs. Moreover, family planning services were being established mostly in urban ghettos. It was difficult to deny the connection.

In addition to these serious questions related to personal and professional values, some professionals did not perceive family planning as an appropriate function of social work practice for two reasons. First, this period was marked by great concern with the counseling function of social workers, and counseling often was seen as the defining feature of social work (Furie, 1966). The apparently less "psychologically complex" process of family planning counseling might have been seen as nonprofessional or paraprofessional in nature. Second, many regarded family planning as a medical matter largely in the domain of the medical profession (Rapoport, 1970). Indeed, the two major new methods at the time, birth control pills and the intrauterine device, required close medical supervision.

Yet pressing reasons existed to justify social work involvement in family planning. The connection between poverty and large family size was clear; research indicated that lack of access to effective birth control resulted in many undesired births to poorly educated and low-income families (Meier, 1966). Gray (1966) and Rainwater (1970) emphasized that poor families actually desired fewer children than more affluent families did. Gray (1966) provided a cogent argument for commitment to the availability of family planning services for poor families:

> In their day-to-day contact with deprived families, the need to limit family size becomes obvious to social workers. It is made evident by the poor health of mothers and children, the substandard living conditions that produce overcrowding and poor sanitation; by distraught parents attempting to make ends meet on limited income; and by child abuse, behavior problems and delinquency, marital conflicts, educational problems and school dropouts, illegitimacy, and precipitous teen-age marriage. (p. 491)

SOCIAL WORK AND FAMILY PLANNING

The beginning of social work involvement in the family planning movement in the late 1960s centered first on advocating for wider access to
services and then developing practice methods. Meier (1969) identified
social work constituencies who did not have access to family planning
including rural and small-town residents, persons in custodial care, psychologically immobilized clients, and new arrivals to urban ghettos.
Meier urged social workers to work to reduce the barriers to service
including lack of transportation, communication problems, a history of
problems with contraception, lack of orientation to prevention, and emotional or intellectual obstacles. She also included obstacles related to
daily or extraordinary crises, and obstacles related to the agencies themselves. Most of the barriers to family planning were the same barriers
faced by poor families in getting quality general medical care (Shlakman,
1968).

Because of the aforementioned legislation requiring referrals of public assistance clients, the development of social work roles in the direct
provision of family planning services began with roles appropriate to
practice in public assistance settings. For example, because of findings
that social workers were infrequently referring clients to family planning
services, Castor and Hudson (1971) surveyed social workers in San Francisco about their attitudes toward family planning. They found that social
workers thought referring was appropriate but often failed to do so because of lack of information and confidence about the subject.

In response to social workers' discomfort, Planned Parenthood published a guide for in-service training of public welfare workers in 1970
(Manisoff, 1970). The purpose of the guide was to provide a rationale for
involvement in the issue, to promote family planning as a preventive
health measure, and to educate the workers about all aspects of reproduction and the various contraceptive methods. The training also included information about community family planning resources and how
to do referrals and follow-up, and methods of enabling families to use
family planning effectively.

Indeed, the appropriate means and time to refer clients for family
planning services were matters of great concern to social workers. Bradshaw et al. (1977) discussed methods of dealing with "resistant" clients,
those who were ambivalent about contraception because of religion or
fear, and issues related to confidentiality and follow-up. Manisoff (1970)
identified the social worker's responsibilities as offering information
(stressing the optional nature of the discussion), protecting the client's

freedom of choice as guaranteed in the Constitution ("A couple has little freedom of choice to determine the number of their children or their spacing if no one is willing or able to spend time in discussing modern family planning with the mother and providing her with efficient, safe and acceptable contraception" [p. 69]), and counseling. Positive attitude and respect for the client's wishes were stressed.

Burnstein (1968) began to clarify social workers' role in family planning agencies by declaring that social workers should "neither recommend methods of contraception nor preempt the role of religious advisers" (p. 137). A reading of the literature of the late 1960s and 1970s demonstrates that recommendations about particular contraceptive methods has never been seen as a social work function. Conversely, education and clarification of misconceptions about contraception (and specific methods) has been fairly uniformly held to be an appropriate social work task (Bradshaw et al., 1977; Christopher, 1980; Greenblatt, 1972; Sung, 1978). Education has included providing basic facts about reproduction and contraception as well as correcting any false information clients may have about contraception.

Another educational function advocated for social workers was discussion of several issues regarding life-style that are relevant to the client's selection of a contraceptive method. These included the cost of the method and the level of cooperation of the male partner(s), whether the method requires daily action (e.g., oral contraceptives), or only when coitus occurs (e.g., the diaphragm). Hatcher et al. (1986) provided two tools for use with clients who are unsure about the appropriate contraceptive methods. The Personal Life Plan is a list of 23 questions about personal, education, and occupational goals and plans that are relevant to the selection of a method. The Self-Assessment Questionnaire is made up of 18 questions that measure clients' comfort with a specific method.

If social workers are to be educators, they must be familiar with basic sexuality and reproduction as well as the common methods of contraception. It is wise to consult a recent reference such as *Contraceptive Technology* (Hatcher et al., 1986). Christopher (1980) noted the importance of using terminology that the client can understand, without attempting to use language that may be embarrassing or uncomfortable to both worker and client.

Burnstein (1968) ascribed a second major function to social workers when she declared that they should help people recognize how contraception could help them prevent family problems and promote their health. In this regard, social workers have discussed clients' personal problems and concerns with emphasis on how additional children would complicate their lives and problems (Sung, 1978). Clarification of clients' life goals may alleviate fears and misconceptions about contraception and enable clients to use the medical services of a family planning clinic more effectively (Sung, 1978).

Bradshaw et al. (1977) addressed the issue of practice techniques when they illustrated the application of four social work practice models to family planning counseling: a problem-solving model, task-centered casework, crisis intervention, and an adaption of the problem-oriented record used in many medical settings. Their case materials illustrate how family planning counseling can deal not only with contraceptive needs, but with broader issues of concern to clients. For instance, they provide examples of:

- How the side effects of contraceptives (such as depression from the pill) can cause or exacerbate family and personal problems
- How difficulties with contraceptives can actually be hiding sexual dissatisfaction or insecurity
- How family planning can assist a client to assume more responsibility and control over her life
- How discussion of family planning in the context of counseling can contribute to improved marital communication

Finally, several facilitative tasks have been claimed for social work. These include practical assistance such as providing transportation, providing follow-ups to referrals, providing payment for medical services, and conducting outreach (Greenblatt, 1972), as well as procuring general types of resources and making referrals for services that might facilitate clients' use of family planning services (Sung, 1978).

Several techniques for accomplishing the various social work functions have been suggested in the literature. Burnstein (1968) recommended anticipatory guidance, logical discussion, education, and support. Like others since that time (e.g., Christopher, 1980), she recommended that social workers initiate discussions about family planning rather than waiting for clients to do so. Greenblatt (1972) included other, broader methods for social workers in family planning including advocacy for policy change at the agency and community level, analysis of policy, and research.

A review of the social work literature since the beginning of the 1980s demonstrates that family planning is no longer a high priority for direct practice in professional (M.S.W.-level) social work. Few articles in the social work literature concern practice issues or clients' needs in family planning. The most recent volume of the *Social Work Encyclopedia* (Minahan, 1987) contains few references to the subject, with some specific exceptions to be discussed subsequently. Several reasons exist for this reduction of social work interest in family planning.

First, it appears again that many of the services offered in family planning agencies may fall outside what is considered to be professional social work. Torres (1979) reported that social workers were employed by 40% of all metropolitan and 20% of all nonmetropolitan family planning agencies, but she did not specify whether the social workers were graduate-level professionals. The commonest methods of contraception in use now (oral contraceptives overwhelmingly and the diaphragm) must be prescribed or fitted, respectively, by a physician; nurses or technicians provide much of the instruction about side effects and proper use (Rainwater, 1970). Joffe's (1986) detailed study of family planning workers in one large urban clinic is illustrative of this issue. She found that most of these workers (who were all paraprofessionals) considered the bulk of family planning work to be dull and routine. Little counseling is involved, in part because time spent in counseling does not produce revenue.

In addition to such professional concerns, however, social workers and many others may no longer feel that access to services is a problem and thus may not perceive the necessity of advocacy. Unfortunately, this perception is mistaken, as the following section demonstrates.

Current Services and Needs

Federal family planning services are funded primarily through Medicaid and Title X of the Public Health Service Act (each of which accounts for approximately one third of all public expenditures), and two block grants: Maternal and Child Health Block Grant, and Social Services (Title XX). The two block grants each account for approximately 16% of public expenditures. State governments also finance approximately 16% of the total (Gold & Macias, 1987).

In 1983 nearly 5 million women received contraceptive services from family planning clinics in this country (Torres & Forrest, 1987). Approximately 83% of these women had low incomes (incomes less than 150% of the poverty index). Of the 2,462 agencies delivering family planning services from more than 5,000 sites in 1983, approximately 56% were under the auspices of public health departments, 13% were Planned Parenthood clinics, approximately 7% were sponsored by hospitals, and 23% accounted for other agencies. Approximately 76% of all counties had family planning clinics, down slightly from 1975 (Torres & Forrest, 1987).

Family Planning and the Poor

The importance of family planning to lower income and minority women relates to the connection between planned pregnancies and health; infant and maternal mortality are reduced to the extent that pregnancies occur during ideal childbearing years (Morris, Udry, & Chase, 1975) and that women have fewer pregnancies spaced further apart (Siegel, 1971). Unfortunately, despite what appear to be widely available services, 18% of low-income women at risk of pregnancy were not using a contraceptive method in 1982 compared with only 10% of higher income women (Bachrach, 1984). Jones, Forrest, Henshaw, Silverman, and Torres's (1988) comparison of this country with other nations showed that the high rates of both unintended pregnancy and abortion in this country (relative to rates in other industrialized countries) are directly related to relatively low rates of use of the most highly effective contraceptive methods (i.e., the pill, intrauterine device, and sterilization).

The reasons for the relatively high rate of non-use of contraception by poor women are complicated and relate to both issues of access and attitude. Regarding access, nearly one fourth of the counties in the United States do not have public family planning clinics (Gold & Macias, 1986). Moreover, counties that lack clinics tend to be nonmetropolitan counties; women who reside there may lack transportation and other resources (child care, time off from work, etc.) to travel to facilities in other counties.

The lack of family planning clinics is due in part to the fact that federal funding of family planning services has declined significantly in recent years. The fiscal year 1982 budget changed the funding mechanisms for family planning services, cutting Title X of the Public Health Service Act by 22%, combining Title V and Title XX programs into block grants (and reducing their funding by 24% and 22%, respectively), and cutting the federal Medicaid match by about 3% (Orr, 1983). Indeed, Federal funding for family planning services for fiscal year 1985 was less than funding for fiscal year 1980 (in constant 1980 dollars) (Gold & Macias, 1986). State governments are not able to replace these funds, and low-income families often are unable to afford services from private physicians.

Even when communities do have clinics, low-income women may not seek contraceptive services because of issues such as perceived cost, inconvenience, and issues related to quality of care (Silverman, Torres, & Forrest, 1987). Cost can be a significant deterrent to low-income women to obtaining contraceptives. For example, a year's worth of birth control pills currently costs about $156, in addition to office visit charges. Initial outlays for other methods such as intrauterine devices or sterilization are even greater (Forrest, 1988). Although most family planning clinics offer contraceptives at no charge, some charge fees based on income.

Access to family planning also may be limited because of lack of knowledge about where to go. Twenty-seven percent of the women in the Silverman et al. (1987) sample who had never visited a family planning provider did not know where they could go for services. A telephone survey in New Orleans, conducted before the opening of the first Planned Parenthood clinic in Louisiana in 1984, found that 51% of the respondents had never heard of Planned Parenthood, and another one fourth were mistaken about the nature of services provided by the organization (Bertrand, Proffitt, & Bartlett, 1987).

In many cases in which family planning resources are available and known to potential users, they may be unacceptable to low-income women. Many low-income women have negative attitudes about contraception including fears related to side effects and damage to their health (Silverman et al., 1987). In addition, many expect family planning clinics to provide lower quality care and would prefer a private physician if they could afford one (Silverman et al., 1987).

Moreover, the American system differs from that of other countries in that family planning is not imbedded within the general health care system such as in general medical clinics or family practices. Most family planning in the United States is provided by specialists, who are expensive and unknown to many women, or by family planning clinics that a woman would not visit for other reasons. In other countries, it is common for family planning to be dispensed at well-baby clinics and by family physicians, so that outreach is facilitated and women are familiar with the personnel and the facility when the need arises.

Services for Men

Lack of access in general is not the only problem on the current family planning scene. Despite recent nominal federal interest in services for men (especially adolescents), most family planning programs are designed for and used by women (Swanson & Forrest, 1984). (For a discussion specific to adolescent boys, see Chapter 7.) Previous efforts to involve men in family planning services have failed, owing largely to lack of attention to specific male roles and needs. Yet evidence exists that men want and can use family planning information and assistance (Rappaport, 1981).

Moreover, Kaufman (1975) makes the essential and undeniable point about why male involvement in family planning is important:

Men are involved in family planning whether we recognize that fact or not. They are using, or not using, contraception, interfering or supporting their partner's use of contraception and fathering, or not having children, with or without formal family planning programs. (p. 5)

In addition to this compelling argument, Kaufman (1975) also notes several positive outcomes of male involvement in the family planning process. First, male involvement contributes to reduction of sex role stereotypes in general in society, providing broader alternatives for both men and women. Second, it promotes better communication between partners, both about sex and presumably in other areas. Third, male involvement increases men's level of knowledge about contraception and sexuality in general. Finally, participation of men in family planning might encourage better sexual relations between them. As a bonus, Kaufman (1975) suggests that taking greater responsibility for family planning might encourage men to assume greater parental responsibility as well.

Broad consensus exists that the lack of male involvement in family planning is largely due to their not being offered services that are acceptable to them. Stereotypes about men are a large part of this professional neglect (Kaufman, 1975). Major stereotypes include the beliefs that men are irresponsible about sex, both within marriage and outside of marriage; and that they are not interested in family planning. In addition, male involvement may be taken to mean only male methods of contraception, such as condoms or withdrawal. Zilbergeld (1975) makes the important point that the two issues of the type of method and the extent of male participation are separate issues.

Rappaport (1981) focused on rigid male sex roles and the relationship of those roles to men's reluctance to use family planning services. Specifically, he discussed the general reluctance of men to seek assistance, and the reluctance of men to discuss sex except in terms of boasting. The Men's Support Center of Oakland, California, has adopted new strategies in providing services to men. The center provides counseling to men whose partners are seeking abortion, individual counseling regarding sexuality and contraception to adolescent boys, male infertility counseling, and educational groups for young men in public schools. The strategy advocated by Rappaport (1981) focuses on reducing barriers to male participation in family planning by presenting information in a nonthreatening, educational atmosphere that does not require "asking for help." Rigid sex roles are discussed and questioned, but not challenged in a provocative manner that might provoke defensiveness. Although Rappaport (1981) provides anecdotal evidence of positive outcomes, he provides no empirical data.

Other authors have noted the importance of not linking family planning services for men with an open admission of ignorance, because such open admissions contradict society's expectation that men, even very young ones, should be sexually sophisticated and experienced (Semler, 1975; Zilbergeld, 1975). Although some social workers may feel uncomfortable about seeming to reinforce stereotypes with which they do not agree, Zilbergeld emphasizes the social work axiom of "starting where the client is."

Both Zilbergeld (1975) and Robinson (1975) emphasize the importance of targeting issues that are important to the population being served. For example, Zilbergeld suggests using male concern with sexual performance, rather than the issue of "sexual responsibility," and conducting outreach efforts in the locations where potential clients are, such as liquor stores or record shops.

Other strategies suggested by Bradshaw et al. (1977) are the use of male social workers and services provided within groups. These authors note that men may have trouble discussing such issues on a one-to-one basis, especially with the female workers that are found in most agencies. They suggest that counseling should emphasize the supportive role of the man, rather than the man as the one responsible for contraception. Semler (1975) also stresses the importance of the visibility of men in family planning agencies, not only in professional positions but also in clerical and support positions.

Currently insufficient information remains to offer appropriate widespread family services to men, despite recognition that the male role in family planning is an important one (Varner, 1984) and despite recognition for 2 decades that the research and services are insufficient. Future research must address male attitudes and beliefs about family planning, how they may be induced to participate in family planning decisions and implementation, what kinds of services they prefer, and what services are most effective with men.

Comprehensive Versus Specialized Services

Should family planning services be offered as part of general health care, or should they be provided under separate auspices? Concern for comprehensive MCH care was prevalent in the 1960s, and it was believed that family planning services should be offered as part of a comprehensive continuum of MCH services. Comprehensiveness of care was seen as one way of reaching and following low-income women and children who had tended to remain outside the health care system. Moreover, integration of family planning with the existing health care system long has been favored by the medical profession and by federal authorities because such integration is likely to reduce unnecessary fragmentation or duplication (Aries, 1987).

Some comprehensive programs have appeared to be quite successful. Sung's (1978) family planning program was imbedded in a comprehensive program so that "each time a worker provides . . . a service, he or she has an opportunity to introduce family planning" (p. 160). Social workers provided outreach to women who came in for maternity care or to obtain pediatric care for their children, bringing in many new family planning clients. Likewise, Crump's (1974) program was offered within an MIC prenatal care clinic for high-risk maternity patients. The program also took patients who were referred before or after abortion, and prenatal and postpartum patients from the city's Department of Health. Finally, case finding on obstetric wards also was used to locate potential family planning clients. Discussions about family planning began early in the course of pregnancy and centered around the patient's obstetric history, whether the current pregnancy was planned or unplanned, how the partner was involved in pregnancy planning, and the couple's intentions regarding ultimate family size.

A comprehensive approach has appeal because of its promise for reaching many more potential clients. Social workers and other professionals might offer family planning services as part of comprehensive care at numerous points in the health care and social service delivery system, including prenatal and postpartum clinics, abortion services, pediatric clinics, child welfare agencies, STD treatment facilities, and services to families with children who have disabilities (Wallace, 1970).

The issue of providing family planning as a part of comprehensive care is not one without controversy, however. Three issues are pertinent to the controversy. First, concern still exists that offering such services only to the poor (which would occur because most clients of public health care facilities are poor) suggests a motive of reducing the numbers of the poor and minorities and thus cutting the costs of public assistance. Second, many believe that services should be kept simple and easy to obtain, given the practical problems of low-income clients (Rainwater, 1970). To the extent that other services require additional paper work, delays, and complications, clients may be reluctant to use them. Finally, the categorical nature of federal health care programs makes coordination and comprehensive care most difficult to achieve (Aries, 1987). It is this final point that is likely to guarantee continuation of the fragmented, categorical approach to health care for the poor in general and family planning in particular.

Sterilization Services

One third of all American women who use a method of contraception rely on either male or female sterilization (Bachrach, 1984). For couples who want no more children, sterilization is a safe and effective method. Concerns lie in the fact that sterilization must be regarded as permanent. Therein lies the continued importance of social work in the provision of sterilization services, because couples may not be certain that they want no more children.

The two major methods of sterilization are tubal ligation (performed on the woman) and vasectomy (performed on the man). Both can usually be performed on an outpatient basis now, and both are extremely safe and effective. Social workers should consult Hatcher et al. (1986) or another reference for detailed information about sterilization procedures.

Legislation did not address the issue of sterilization until the emergence of the eugenics movement in the 1920s. At that time, legislation took the form of requiring compulsory sterilization for some persons, such as the mentally retarded and public dependents (Pilpel, 1971). (Some states retained compulsory sterilization laws well into the 1970s.) At that time few legal restrictions existed for voluntary sterilization, although "as a practical matter . . . it is often not available—especially to the poor" (Pilpel, 1971, p. 193). Moreover, fearing law suits, many hospitals and physicians erected practical barriers to voluntary sterilization. For example, many physicians applied the "Rule of 120" to requests for sterilization. This policy required that a woman's age multiplied by the number of children she had must equal 120 before sterilization could be performed (Bradshaw et al., 1977). Thus a 30-year-old woman had to have four children before she could be sterilized, a 20-year-old had to have six, and so forth.

Compulsory sterilization laws and the Civil Rights movement of the 1960s heightened concerns about coercion. Now patients who request sterilization that is financed by Medicaid are required by federal law to comply with certain regulations designed to guarantee informed consent. Sterilization patients must be 21 years of age or older and mentally competent, and must wait a minimum of 30 days following their signing a consent form for the procedure (Hatcher et al., 1986). Specific states may have additional regulations, and most private physicians attach their own requirements. For example, physicians often require the spouse's consent, a minimum age or number of children, a waiting period, or that the patient be an established patient.

Current Services

Less than a quarter of family planning clinics offer sterilization services, although most refer to other providers for sterilization services (Forrest, 1988). Almost all tubal ligations and vasectomies are performed by private physicians, most of whom are specialists (Forrest & Henshaw, 1983).

Medicaid is the largest public funding source for sterilization services, accounting for 84% of all public expenditures (Gold & Macias, 1986). Other sources are the other federal programs (the Maternal and Child Health Block Grant, the Social Services Block Grant, and Title X of the Public Health Service Act) and state revenues. Because many private physicians do not accept Medicaid (owing to low rates of reimbursement, large amounts of paperwork, and long waiting times for reimbursement), it can be difficult for low-income women to obtain sterilization services (Forrest, 1988).

Sterilization Counseling

Many hospitals and clinics that offer sterilization as a method of contraception offer sterilization counseling as a recommended or required service of applicants. Sterilization counseling, much of which is provided by social workers, has three purposes: (a) to conform with informed consent regulations; (b) to reduce the likelihood of regret following sterilization; and (c) to promote the choice of a reliable family planning method, whether permanent or temporary (Kohn, 1985–86). Social workers appear to be more involved in services for women considering tubal ligation (Goodman & Hiestand, 1982; Kohn, 1985–86; Shapiro-Steinberg & Neamatalla, 1979) than for men considering vasectomy (Hafemann & Chilman, 1974; Smith, 1981), perhaps because men most often seek sterilization directly from a private physician.

Although substantial progress has occurred in recent years in surgery for reversal, sterilization procedures are considered to be permanent. Yet substantial numbers of men and women who are sterilized later request reversal or indicate regret (Gomel, 1978). Counseling before surgery is designed to assess the applicant's reasons for requesting sterilization, and any life circumstances that may affect the desirability of permanent sterilization. In addition, counseling should include full information about the procedure itself and about alternative methods of birth control, and an exploration of any ambivalence or anxiety the client may have about sterilization (Goodman & Hiestand, 1982; Kohn, 1985–86; Smith, 1981). The promotion of a reliable method of birth control, whether temporary or permanent, also is accomplished in part by the provision of information and clarifying clients' misconceptions about sterilization (Bradshaw et al., 1977).

Research has identified several risk factors for later regret among those requesting sterilization. These include for women being younger than 30 years of age, being single, having a history of emotional or psychiatric problems, or being in an unstable relationship or recently separated or divorced (Kohn, 1985–86). The risk factors for later problems (including promiscuity and various types of emotional dysfunction) for men include ambivalence or lack of understanding of the permanence of the surgery by self or partner; the state of being single, young, or childless; sexual or relationship problems between the partners; expectations that the vasectomy will correct other unrelated problems; rigid ideas concerning sex roles; or mental or emotional problems that might compromise informed consent (Smith, 1981). Barron and Richardson (1978), Hafemann and Childman (1974), and Smith (1981) all emphasize the importance of cultural and ethnic factors in assessing the advisability of sterilization.

Shapiro-Steinberg and Neamatalla (1979), Kohn (1985–86), Barron and Richardson (1978), and Goodman and Hiestand (1982) all discussed various approaches to sterilization counseling. Shapiro-Steinberg and Neamatalla (1979) described a group counseling program that included a social worker and a family planning counselor. Some individuals were referred for individual counseling when it was thought to be necessary.

Kohn's (1985–86) model encompasses the major aspects described by all of these authors and will therefore be described in some detail. Kohn (1985–86) described the process of sterilization counseling as beginning with an explanation of the sterilization procedure and alternative methods of birth control, followed by a discussion of the candidate's medical and psychosocial history and functioning as they relate to the sterilization request. This information provides relaxed subject matter with which to begin the discussion and supplies information regarding high-risk factors that may be pertinent for counseling.

Discussions about the client's reasons for seeking sterilization proceed with issues regarding the candidate's obstetric and contraceptive history, family functioning, and any current problems that might be related to the request (for example, parenting or marital problems). Low-risk candidates often express satisfaction with their current family size, career satisfaction, long consideration of sterilization, or medical risks associated with pregnancy. With candidates judged to be at low risk, the social worker reviews information about the procedure, elicits questions, and discusses the mutuality of the decision.

High-risk candidates often report marital problems or dissatisfaction with their general lives. Some do not understand other appropriate birth control options. In cases in which the social worker believes the candidate to be in a state of crisis because of marital or other problems, the social worker attempts to convince the client to delay the sterilization while using an effective method of temporary birth control (Kohn, 1985–86). In cases in which the couple is not in agreement about sterilization, couples are advised that the law does not require the husband's consent, but couples' counseling is suggested owing to the implications for the relationship. Some clients are referred for psychiatric or medical consultation. Women with histories of mental retardation, psychiatric problems, or psychiatric hospitalizations are also referred for additional assessment.

Kohn (1985–86) performed an retrospective analysis on 148 case records of clients who received sterilization counseling in 1983. Her findings showed that approximately one third of women younger than 30 years of age either were ambivalent about sterilization, requested sterilization when they were under emotional stress, or appeared during life changes that might predict later regret (e.g., divorce proceedings). Moreover, these women were younger, had fewer children, and were more often single or having marital problems than the older women. Her methodologically limited study indicated that of the 72 "high-risk" women who received counseling, 60% pursued their plan for sterilization, 26% changed their minds, and 14% did not complete counseling so outcomes were unknown. Kohn's (1985–86) results, in combination with these other reports and the potential seriousness of regret of sterilization, suggest that social workers have an important role to play in reducing the numbers of sterilization candidates who later regret the procedure.

Abortion

Abortion is the expulsion of the fetus from a woman's body before it is viable—usually before 20 or 28 weeks of gestation (Chilman, 1987). Abortion may be spontaneous (often called "miscarriage") or induced. (This section discusses induced abortion, whereas spontaneous abortion is discussed in Chapter 4.)

Abortion has been widely practiced throughout history, with the use of various herbs, roots, and medications being most prominent (Hatcher et al., 1986). Early abortion (before quickening or the first movement of the fetus) was not illegal in the United States until individual states began passing legislation against it in the 1820s (Francomme, 1986). Indeed, early abortion was legal in most states and widely practiced through the beginning of the 20th century. Although most abortions were practiced by untrained lay persons (including several questionable persons) until the late 1800s, legislation restricting advertising of birth control devices and services (the famous Comstock laws) led to the practice of more abortions by physicians.

Abortion was controversial well into the 1930s, despite the fact that estimates at the time were that up to 2 million illegal abortions were performed annually in the United States (Francomme, 1986). The incidence decreased during and following World War II, owing in part to the absence of so many men, and perhaps in part to the increasing availability and effectiveness of contraceptive methods, such as foam and the diaphragm. In the late 1950s and 1960s, increasing openness about illegal abortion occured, however, and support grew for legalization.

Early Social Work Involvement

Social workers have been actively involved in efforts to legalize and extend the availability of abortion services since the 1970s (e.g., Cohen & Perry, 1981; Freeman, 1976; Johnson, 1978). Advocacy for abortion has been more or less inextricably linked with advocacy for family planning because of a general disposition toward freedom of choice and recognition that (a) even the best contraceptive methods fail, and (b) some women who do not desire pregnancy will not use contraception effectively. Social workers also expressed concern about the many women they saw who obtained illegal abortions and developed complications related to incompetence or aseptic conditions (Addelson, 1971).

As early as 1971, the social work profession noted that abortion was becoming more widely available (as New York and other states liberalized their abortion laws) and that the profession must deal with the issue (Rapoport & Potts, 1971). Abortion was recognized as a stressful life event requiring psychological support, if not a crisis in all cases (e.g., Dauber, Zalar, & Goldstein, 1972). Rapoport and Potts (1971) also dealt extensively with the negative effects on clients of hostile or negative attitudes of abortion staff.

The legalization of abortion with the 1973 Supreme Court decision Roe v. Wade marked a major change in social work's involvement in abortion. Since Roe v. Wade advocacy efforts among social workers have centered largely on public funding of abortion, which was discontinued in 1976 by the Hyde Amendment and subsequently confirmed by the Supreme Court. Justification for concern on this issue has centered around the same issues that justify social work interest in family planning: the improvement of MCH and the right of women to control their own reproduction. Concerns for the rights of poor women to equal protection against unwanted pregnancies and to equal health care have motivated those who support Medicaid funding for abortion. In addition, the profession's involvement in abortion has grown in part from involvement of many social workers in the women's movement. Fertility control and feminism have been inextricably linked since Margaret Sanger's campaign early in this century (Muller, 1974). Yet proponents of abortion do not work solely from political motivation. Abortion has also had a significant effect on women's health.

Although many would question abortion as a means of preventing infant mortality (and that controversy is discussed in chapter 9 of this book), studies have shown that legal abortion is associated with lower infant mortality rates (e.g., Grossman & Jacobowitz, 1981). That reduction in mortality is largely because abortion averts births disproportionately in high-risk populations (minorities and the poor) and categories (high parity women, for example). In this country, the availability of Medicaid funds for abortions for poor, high-risk women lowered birth rates among those groups; however, with the discontinuation of Medicaid funding for abortions in 1980, some of that effect may have been mitigated.

Social workers were actively providing direct services related to abortion before *Roe v. Wade*. Smith (1972), Ullmann (1972), Young, et al. (1973), and Addelson (1973) described abortion recipients, their emotional and psychological needs, and the services being provided. In general the women were in their early to mid-20s, unmarried (although a substantial number were married), and representative of all racial and most religious groups. Women were distressed, ambivalent, or fearful about abortion and interested in receiving counseling by the social workers, but Smith's (1972) and Addelson's (1973) follow-ups revealed no regrets after the procedure.

Each of the three preceding studies indicated that services to women seeking or considering abortion included information and education about abortion and future contraception, with two (Ullmann, 1972; Young et al., 1973) providing this service within a group format. Addelson (1973) noted a team approach of social worker, nurses, and physicians. All emphasized the emotional difficulties associated with obtaining abortion and indicated that they provided counseling. Only Smith (1972) specifically mentioned offering the women other options, such as relinquishment for adoption.

The legalization of abortion in 1973 changed the nature of abortion services and the social work role in the provision of abortion services. First, the "social reform" fervor was gone for social workers. Second, abortion became more routinized to some extent (Joffe, 1986), probably reducing the emotional trauma for some women. Finally, the sheer numbers of abortions performed and the numbers of women who obtain repeat abortions began to make some social workers uncomfortable with their role in abortion (Kaminsky & Sheckter, 1979).

Three sources of conflict and strain for abortion workers are the larger social and political climate surrounding abortion (which in more recent years has included constant demonstrations outside clinics, harassment of staff and patients, and clinic bombings); personal moral dilemmas regarding abortion; and the behavior and perceived attitudes of clients (Joffe, 1978, 1979). In particular, workers are distressed by abortion recipients who seem cavalier about abortion and those who obtain repeated abortions (Peachey, 1982).

Current Services

Abortion in the 1980s is safer than childbirth (Tyrer & Wilson, 1982). The most common early method of abortion is the suction or vacuum curettage method, whereby a plastic tube or cannula attached to a pump suctions the fetal tissue out through the vagina. A sharp curettage then may be used to confirm complete evacuation of the uterus (Hatcher et al., 1986). Second-trimester abortions are more dangerous and unpleasant, often requiring a short hospital stay. The most common method is injection of the uterus with prostagladins or saline, which causes fetal death, and then administration of hormones that lead to labor and delivery. Thus, the woman must endure much the same process as if she experienced a live birth (Christopher, 1980). The social worker should be thoroughly familiar with the procedures used in various types of abortion (Shapiro, 1980), and should consult Hatcher et al. (1986) or another good reference for this purpose.

The most recent estimates are that approximately 1.59 million abortions were performed in the United States in 1985, of which the overwhelming majority (90%) were done in the first trimester (Henshaw, Forrest, & Van Vort, 1987). The recipients of abortion are mostly white and unmarried, have low religiosity, and have high educational and occupational aspirations (Chilman, 1987). Abortion recipients are likely to have high self-esteem and favorable attitudes about contraception and abortion. They also perceive little help or support from partner and family regarding the unplanned pregnancy (Chilman, 1987).

Faria, Barrett, and Goodman (1985) studied a nonrandom sample of 517 women seeking abortions from two outpatient abortion clinics and one family planning agency. Their findings indicated that abortion recipients tend to be single (59%), in their early 20s, white (81%), and Protestant (53%). In this sample, 25% had had previous abortions, and 51% had been using no birth control during the 6 months before conception.

Abortion services are provided outside the mainstream of the American health care system, with most (60% in 1985) provided in freestanding clinics established for that purpose. Thirteen percent were performed in hospitals (down significantly from previous years), and 23% and 4% respectively, were performed in other types of clinics and private physicians' offices (Henshaw et al., 1987).

The average cost of an abortion in mid-1986 (performed at 10 weeks of gestation, out of hospital, and with local anesthesia) was $213. Later abortions and those performed in hospitals or with general anesthesia were more expensive. Most women who obtain abortions must pay for them with cash in advance (Henshaw & Wallisch, 1984). Low-income women have two main sources of help in paying for abortion: providers who reduce their fees or provide services free of charge, and public funding, mostly through states because Medicaid has been unavailable for this purpose since 1980. Only 14 states and the District of Columbia provided abortion assistance in 1985; their funds covered 22% of the abortions in those states (Henshaw et al., 1987).

Abortion Counseling

In some facilities all clients have been required to see a social worker as part of the procedure (Smith, 1972), although some agencies do this in a group format (Ullmann, 1972; Young et al., 1973). In other settings, only clients who are perceived by other staff to be at risk of problems or in need of help for some other reason may be referred to a social worker (Asher, 1972).

A broad, growth-oriented approach to abortion counseling was offered by Potts (1971) "to resolve an already existing crisis . . . [and] to avert a crisis, to help the client mobilize inner strengths and outer resources, and to help her move in the direction of increased self-understanding and autonomy of choice and action" (p. 267). Faria et al. (1985) described the ultimate aim of abortion counseling more narrowly as "to help her make the best decision in light of her particular circumstances" (p. 86). Likewise, Peachey (1982) emphasizes the narrow purpose of providing abortion recipients the services they request, even when the social worker would prefer to engage in counseling toward broader goals.

L. Shapiro (1980) described the purposes of early social work intervention with women who request abortions as helping clients verbalize their feelings regarding pregnancy and their circumstances, examining alternatives for dealing with the pregnancy, providing information about abortion and dealing with emotional responses to that information, helping clients use available resources, and providing emotional support in dealing with the crisis.

One may break the process of abortion counseling down into specific components based on when services are delivered: counseling before the decision to abort, counseling following the decision and before and during the procedure, and postabortion counseling.

Decision Making

The abortion counselor has three main tasks as she assists the woman in decision making (Christopher, 1980). First, she confirms that the woman understands all the alternatives available to her including relinquishment for adoption and parenting. (See Chapter 7 for a discussion of this issue.) A problem-solving approach does not assume that abortion is a client's only alternative but helps each individual to determine the best alternative for her. Second, the counselor explains the abortion procedure itself in detail. Finally, the counselor assists the client in articulating her feelings about the pregnancy, abortion, and the other alternatives available to her.

The client who requests an abortion cannot make an informed decision until she is fully informed about the alternatives for a problem pregnancy including relinquishment for adoption and parenthood. The purpose of this part of counseling is not to convince the client of the rightness of one particular alternative but to determine which alternative is best for her (Bradshaw et al., 1977). Potts (1971) notes that

> in helping a woman decide what to do about an unwanted pregnancy the social worker is truly dealing with a matter that will have life-long consequences for her client. For this reason the social worker must be scrupulous in letting the decision rest with her client and must avoid imposing her own values and preferences. (p. 269)

As a way of exploring the alternatives to abortion, Potts (1971) suggests first asking a client to articulate her understanding of her options. For example, does she understand what it means to relinquish a child for adoption? Does she know of resources in her community to do so? Would she know how to reach them? A similar approach can be taken to resources available for parenting (public assistance benefits, educational and vocational resources, housing, child care etc.) and abortion itself.

To address the client's options fully, the social worker's assessment should focus on the circumstances surrounding the conception, the woman's financial and occupational situation, and the supportive relationships available to her (Christopher, 1980). Some alternatives that may seem feasible are not available to some clients because of their life circumstances.

The second aspect of decision making is explaining the various methods of abortion (given the client's medical condition), and the risks and consequences of each. The detailed explanation of abortion should include the possible effects on fertility (e.g., the effects of multiple abortions) as well as the possibility of emotional reactions. The purpose of this explanation is not to sway the client against abortion; risks should be explained in relationship to the risks of the other alternatives available to the woman. For example, although the abortion procedure involves a certain amount of risk, the medical risks of childbirth are greater than those for abortion (Cates, 1984a).

The third aspect of decision making involves an exploration of the client's feelings about abortion. The social worker may open discussion of this issue by asking the client explicitly why she is seeking an abortion. The client's answers may lead to discussion of important issues. Perhaps some of the most significant factors that must be examined are the client's feelings and convictions about abortion itself. The client who has strong religious convictions against abortion but who feels that "no other way" exists for her may experience crippling guilt for years (Potts, 1971). It is particularly important to discuss all the client's options in such cases.

Some clients may become pregnant as a way of coping with poor self-esteem, conflicts about their sexuality, or immature relationships with men. In addition to clarifying the best action for the client to take with this pregnancy, discussion of these issues may enable the client to learn and mature from the experience (Shapiro, 1980).

In other cases clients' answers may reveal significant ambivalence (e.g., "I know it's murder, but there's nothing else I can do"), misunderstanding of other alternatives (e.g., "My girlfriend said you have to pay a lot of money to have your baby adopted"), or pressure from others to abort against the client's will (e.g., "My mother said if I don't I'm on my own").

The issue of pressure from others is an important one. Women who abort under pressure, and despite significant ambivalence or strong negative feelings about abortion, are at risk of emotional problems later (Zakus & Wilday, 1987). The feelings of family and partner are important to the client's life and circumstances and must be considered, but others' feelings must be weighed against the client's own cultural, religious, and personal background and her feelings about abortion. As Potts (1971) states:

> Relevant others can assume important roles with respect to a problem pregnancy. They may constitute a tremendous source of support, both emotional and financial. On the other hand, they may represent a source of coercion or opposition. Sometimes a client's indecision is simply the paralysis of being caught between conflicting pressures from significant other people. (p. 272)

An important issue in decision making concerns the role of the male partner. With some exceptions, little indication exists that most abortion counseling services include men in their services (Christopher, 1980). One reason for neglect of men is that many women seeking abortion indicate little involvement or support from their partners (Faria et al., 1985). The law currently does not require consent of the partner for a woman to obtain an abortion, but some men are beginning to assert that they should have such a right of consent. Christopher (1980) maintains that inclusion of the male partner in abortion counseling can be a beneficial experience for all involved.

An overriding issue in the decision-making phase of abortion counseling is the stress imposed by the element of time (Smith, 1972). Abortions obtained early in pregnancy (during the first trimester) are easier and safer, and generally can be performed under local anesthesia in an outpatient setting (Christopher, 1980). Second-trimester abortions, which are not legal in all states and not performed in all agencies and hospitals that provide abortions, involve a hospital stay and considerably more pain and expense.

It is desirable for women who obtain abortions to do so as early as possible. Yet many women do not confirm pregnancy and seek abortion counseling until well into the first trimester. For those who are undecided or ambivalent, the time issue may complicate the decision-making process considerably. Appearing late for services may indicate ambivalence about abortion, ignorance about where to get help, denial of the pregnancy, or extreme guilt and shame (Christopher, 1980). Persistent indecision may indicate that the woman really does not want the abortion but is unable to say so. "Here it is helpful to point out gently that 'not to decide is to decide' " (Potts, 1977, p. 275). Bradshaw et al. (1977) also note that abortion counseling must be direct and follow specific objectives because of the limited time factor.

Indeed, the decision-making phase of counseling requires compassion combined with directness. Although it is the social worker's responsibility to assist the woman to make her own choices, the time constraints require that she "stick to the task at hand," rather than spend a great deal of time dealing with tangential issues.

Preparation for the Procedure

When a client has decided to proceed with abortion, the social worker must prepare her for the actual procedure and help her resolve her doubts and fears. Having knowledge about the procedure will reduce the client's anxiety and enable her to cope with it more effectively (Shapiro, 1980). The social worker must have extensive knowledge of the medical procedure, and should explain it clearly and truthfully to the client (Bradshaw et al., 1977; Christopher, 1980). For example, the client should be prepared for how long it will take, how much pain is involved, how many people will be in the room, and any side effects she may experience during the procedure and afterward. Smith (1972) states that "if abortion is discussed in careful detail as a medical procedure, without disgust or shame, the woman can cope more effectively with the experience" (p. 67).

Ambivalence, fears, and anxiety are not uncommon feelings for recipients of abortion (Ullmann, 1972). Guilt is a fairly typical emotion, and it is not uncommon to experience grief following abortion that is similar to grief following other types of infant death (Hager, 1987). The social worker should discuss and explore these feelings, eliciting them if necessary from the client who does not volunteer them. If feelings are not adequately explored, some women may experience tragic regret later (Smith, 1972). It is part of "practice wisdom" that if these feelings are not properly expressed and resolved, a subsequent pregnancy may occur as the client attempts to expiate her guilt, although evidence does not exist to support this belief.

Potts (1971) emphasized the importance of preparing the woman for any regret or guilt she may feel after the abortion, assuring her that such feelings are normal, and offering further services at that time if the woman so desires. Preparation for the procedure also should include information regarding what the woman should and should not do regarding douching and personal hygiene, resumption of sexual relations, her follow-up gynecologic examination, and initiation of the selected method of contraception (Bradshaw et al., 1977).

Postabortion Counseling

Chilman (1987) estimated that negative consequences occurred for about 25% of women who obtain abortions, but few data exist on long-term effects or effects on male partners and other family members. Negative effects appear to be associated with previous emotional problems, religious convictions prohibiting abortion, pressure from others to abort, lack of support from partner and family, and strong ambivalence. The sociodemographic correlates of negative effects include low SES, low education, and low educational and occupational aspirations.

Even for clients who do not suffer long-term or serious negative effects, follow-up counseling appears to be an important facet of abortion counseling (Bradshaw et al., 1977; Christopher, 1980). Follow-up services can be offered in the context of the follow-up gynecologic examination (Addelson, 1973). Smith (1972) offered follow-up services by telephone approximately 1 week after the abortion. Services also can be offered through a mail-back questionnaire (Potts, 1971).

At least two important reasons exist for follow-up services. First, depression is common following abortion, owing in part to the sudden changes in hormones associated with the termination of pregnancy (Potts, 1971). Follow-up can assure the woman that this depression is normal. Assessment also can be helpful in determining whether the woman's depression is more serious and further services may be required.

Second, an important purpose of follow-up is a discussion of contraceptive methods and plans, to prevent another pregnancy. Young et al. (1973) and Bradshaw et al. (1977) advocated beginning these discussions even before the abortion. Dauber et al.'s (1972) study demonstrated that contraceptive counseling that is part of the entire process of abortion counseling (from before the procedure through follow-up) can be effective in this regard. They found that 9 out of 10 women who received counseling (including contraceptive counseling) from a paraprofessional abortion counselor accepted and were using contraception 2 weeks after their abortions, whereas only 6 out of 10 who did not receive counseling were using contraception. Haselkorn, (1971), Bradshaw et al. (1977), Shapiro (1980), and Christopher (1980) provide some excellent case material on abortion counseling.

STDs

Despite the availability of effective methods of treatment, STDs remain a serious problem in the 1980s. Together, more than 979,000 cases of gonorrhea and syphilis in the United States occurred in 1985, and approximately 23,000 cases of the other types of STD (Centers for Disease Control, 1987). In recent years concern about STD has grown to include several new conditions including genital warts, herpes, and AIDS (discussed later) (Hatcher et al., 1987).

The consequences of STD are serious and long lasting including ectopic pregnancy, impaired fertility, long-term menstrual irregularity and pelvic pain, blindness, and even death. When STD is acquired during pregnancy (congenital syphilis), infection of the fetus is possible and often results in fetal demise or serious malformation. In some cases STD may be linked to future excess risk of carcinoma of the cervix or neurological or cardiovascular damage. Goodrich and Wiesner (1982) estimated the cost of STD at about $1 billion annually, not including most of the long-term effects of complications that are generally unknown.

Despite some pressing reasons for doing so, professionals of all disciplines whose concern is STD and those whose concern is unplanned pregnancy have done little to combine their efforts (Cates, 1984b). Cates (1984b) has enumerated some of the commonalities between these two social problems (STD and unplanned pregnancy) that would support more combined efforts. First, sexual contact is necessary for both to occur. Second, the consequences of both conditions fall disproportionately on women. Third, the groups at risk for both outcomes are remarkably similar: young, nonwhite, and poor. Fourth, many of the same methods can be successful in preventing STD and pregnancy. Finally, use of the various prevention methods can be effective in promoting other long-term positive consequences (e.g., good general health and continuation of education).

Several factors also mitigate against combined efforts to prevent STD and unplanned pregnancy, however. Perhaps most significant is the different research and professional approaches taken to the two problems. Different professional backgrounds, research approaches, and even organizational affiliations have led to a lack of contact between these two groups (Cates, 1984b). Thus, family planning services tend to occur in agencies and settings devoted entirely to family planning, and STD services tend to be confined to public health departments or specialty clinics. In some cases common facilities may be used, but absolutely no overlap in clinic hours and personnel occurs.

The separation of services to prevent STD and pregnancy is cumbersome, illogical, and possibly detrimental to the group at risk of both. For example, outreach, case finding, and preventive education could be enhanced if services were combined or some relationship between the two types of services could be developed.

The Social Work Role

STDs generally have not been defined as a social work problem. Curtiss's (1986) review of social work literature from 1977 to 1987 revealed fewer than 25 articles on the subject of STD (most related to AIDS), and little practice knowledge is related to the prevention or treatment of STD and its psychosocial correlates.

Despite the difficulties of doing so, social workers in the South Carolina Department of Health and Environmental Control became involved in 1984 in a 5-year plan to address the problems of STD (Curtiss, 1986). As part of the project, a pilot program was initiated to deliver preconceptional education and counseling to women at risk of STD. Female patients of family planning clinics were assessed, and those with a history of STD were referred to a social worker. Advocacy and brokerage were also used to attempt to reduce the stigma attached to STD and to support the inclusion of information on STD in sex education programs in the public schools.

Several factors suggest that social work should be more concerned with STD and active in its prevention and treatment. First, social work traditionally has been concerned with the problems of disadvantaged groups, and STD affects women, minorities, and the poor disproportionately (Cates, 1984b; Curtiss, 1986). In particular, STD is both more difficult to diagnose and more damaging when left untreated for women (Curtiss, 1986). Second, in addition to its serious medical consequences, STD has profound psychosocial consequences that fall into the social work domain and are not handled by any other profession (Carlton & Mayes, 1982). In particular, STD patients may suffer anxiety, depression, and loss of self-esteem. Finally, the AIDS epidemic is of such magnitude that a large-scale approach may be required to slow its growth, and in particular to protect the health of women and children. AIDS has resulted in a new focus of social work concern on STD (Curtiss, 1986).

AIDS in Children

When the AIDS diagnosis was first recognized in the early 1980s it could not have been predicted that the disease would become an epidemic, nor that it would become a major MCH issue. As of September 19, 1988, however, 1,171 pediatric cases of AIDS in children younger than 13 years of age and 295 adolescents have been definitely diagnosed with AIDS (Centers for Disease Control, 1988). Many experts predict that this count will turn out to be a gross underestimate of the actual number of infected children. Moreover, unless major prevention efforts are successful, continued use of intravenous drugs by women of childbearing age will result in some 10,000 AIDS cases in children by 1991. Virtually all will die (Hutchins, 1987).

AIDS is a MCH problem because its mode of transmission places fetuses at great risk of infection from several routes through the pregnant mother. First, the pregnant woman may infect herself and thus her fetus through use of an infected needle for intravenous drug use, or through sexual relations with an intravenous drug user or other infected partner. Seventy-eight percent of cases in children younger than 13 years of age were infected this way (Centers for Disease Control, 1988). Second, approximately 13% of the pediatric cases apparently were infected with AIDS through infected blood before the beginning of national blood screening procedures in 1985 (Centers for Disease Control, 1988). Finally, approximately 6% of the pediatric cases were due to homosexual or drug activity (Centers for Disease Control, 1988). At this time no known cases exist of children being infected with AIDS through casual contact with infected persons.

The health care needs of children with AIDS cannot even be detailed at this time because too little is known. They are likely to be long-term and expensive, however, because the breakdown of the body's natural immune system leads to numerous infections until one of these infections causes death. Even the common cold can be fatal to children with AIDS. Death usually occurs within 2 to 3 years of diagnosis of infection.

The social services needs of children with AIDS are now being recognized, although as yet the available resources are grossly inadequate to meet the need (Kaplan, 1987), especially in large metropolitan areas. Social workers should be at the forefront in the development of AIDS-related social services (Combs-Orme, 1987). The services in the domain of the social work profession include foster and adoptive home resources for AIDS-infected children, and in-home supportive services that would enable families with AIDS-infected members to stay together as long as possible.

Families whose children are infected with AIDS face extreme social isolation because of public fear as well as their own. Some may be uncertain how to care for their children properly to avoid infection of themselves and their other children. Parents of AIDS-infected children also must confront their fears and feelings surrounding the eventual and probably inevitable death of their child. Such families require a great deal of support, education, and practical day-to-day assistance.

Many infants who are infected in utero with AIDS also will require out-of-home placement at some time in their lives because their parents are either infected themselves and will die, or because the parents are judged to be inadequate, neglectful, or unfit parents (e.g., drug addicts or prostitutes). In any case an infected parent will find it difficult to provide the intensive care required by a child with AIDS. The need for foster care or adoptive placement of AIDS children is becoming a crisis for child welfare personnel, as it is extremely difficult to find families who are willing and able to care for these children (Anderson, 1984).

Social workers must go beyond being involved in treatment and services to those infected with AIDS to become committed to the prevention of the disease, but pediatric AIDS will not be stopped or controlled until the AIDS epidemic itself is slowed. The overwhelming number of children who acquire AIDS do so through their parents; thus prevention of pediatric AIDS will lie in reducing high-risk adult behavior, especially that of women.

As a first step, women of childbearing age must be warned of the risk factors for AIDS, and those at risk must be tested. This is especially true of women in groups known to be at risk of the disease: substance abusers, women with multiple sex partners, and women who have sex partners in high-risk groups (Pies, 1987). Current preventive efforts are grossly inadequate in reaching this group, but they might be developed by social workers using family planning agencies, abortion clinics, and prenatal care facilities, both private and public. As is the case with other STDs, those at risk of unplanned pregnancy are also often at risk of AIDS, and coordinated efforts may be necessary to inform clients of the risks and to help them avoid those risks.

Social workers have made a commitment to advocacy and the provision of services for patients with AIDS. It is now required that they work with other professions in innovative ways to commit themselves to the prevention of this disease.

9

Ethics and Personal Values in the Practice of Maternal and Child Health Social Work

A 30-year-old prostitute is pregnant with her fourth child. Two children were removed from her custody by the state for neglect, and one died of untreated medical illness when he was two years old. She misses most of her prenatal care appointments, and she refuses her clinic social worker's suggestions that she should be tested for AIDS. Despite the fact that she is beginning her 11th week of pregnancy, she says she not decided whether or not to have an abortion.

Lydia is a social worker in a secular agency that provides adoption services to pregnant adolescents, and her friend Adelle is a social worker in an abortion clinic. Both are concerned about the ethical implications of their agencies' policies; Lydia's prohibits telling clients about abortion, whereas Adelle's discourages discussions about adoption. Both wonder if they are practicing ethical social work if they do not disclose all the options for unplanned pregnancy with their clients.

It is impossible to practice in any area of social work without confronting issues that involve ethical conflict. Conflicts may occur between clients' and practitioners' values, or between social workers' values and agency policy, and between professional duties and individual social workers' personal values. Seldom can these conflicts be resolved easily.

The field of MCH, by its very nature, presents some potentially complex ethical issues because it involves the most sensitive aspects of clients' personal and family lives: choices about sexual behavior, childbirth, and childrearing. Moreover, the profession has had little time to develop its ethics in many of these areas, which have surfaced only recently as advances in technology and medical science have opened up new realms of decision making that previously did not exist.

ETHICS AS A PROFESSIONAL CONCERN

This chapter will explore the issue of ethics and personal values in MCH using both a philosophical and practical approach. The chapter begins with a discussion of professional codes of ethics and the purposes they serve. More detailed information is presented about the Code of Ethics of the National Association of Social Workers. A discussion of the various philosophical frameworks on which ethics may be based then follows. Finally, some ethical difficulties encountered in MCH social work practice are illustrated using three contemporary areas of ethical controversy.

Codes of Ethics

Every profession develops codes of ethics that are designed to provide guidance and direction to the practitioner's behavior. Ethics are a defining feature of professions (A. Johnson, 1955) that provide assurance to the public of the trustworthiness of the profession. Each of the professions assumes considerable authority over clients in important aspects of their lives, so such assurance is a necessity. A profession's code of ethics is developed based on values that are generally shared to a large degree by the members of a profession (lest they enter some other profession more in consonance with their values). The code of ethics also serves a protective function by setting standards that are used to evaluate and expose individuals within the profession who are unscrupulous.

The medical profession has grappled with ethical issues since the time of Hippocrates and continues to do so. The Hippocratic Oath, long held as the guiding force of medical ethics, does not provide absolute guidance for all dilemmas, and indeed today's physician faces many ambiguities in the application of modern medicine. Many of the questions and problems discussed in this chapter are shared by the medical and nursing professions (Arras & Hunt, 1983; Benjamin & Curtis, 1986).

The social work profession's code of ethics was first enacted by the American Association of Social Workers in 1947 after much discussion and debate (Johnson, 1955). The current version was revised in 1979 and published by the National Association of Social Workers in 1980 (National Association of Social Workers, 1980). Like any professional code of ethics, it is a broad collection of general principles, which is continually being refined and developed. The principles of the code cover social workers' responsibilities toward clients, colleagues, employers, the profession, and society as well as issues surrounding the social worker's "conduct and comportment." Although a perusal of the major social work journals and practice texts reveals that ethical issues in general are of concern to social workers, less attention is paid to the issue than is merited, given its importance. Little guidance is offered in relation to the specific issues encountered by the social worker in the practice of MCH in particular.

The National Association of Perinatal Social Workers (1985), which represents practicing social workers in the area of MCH, also has a code of ethics (NAPSW, no date). It is similar to the National Association of Social Workers' (NASW) (1980) code in many respects (e.g., in its categories of personal conduct and responsibilities to clients, colleagues, employers, the profession and society), but goes somewhat further to specify explicitly its focus on the family as the client and its emphasis on the social worker as part of the "service delivery team."

Philosophies of Ethics

The volumes that have been written on ethics need not be reviewed here, but some consideration of ethical philosophies is necessary to place social work's code of ethics within a philosophical framework. A code of ethics cannot serve as its own justification but must be embedded in some larger moral framework. This is because a code must necessarily be simplistic, and it is not possible to cover every situation that may arise. A larger framework encourages extension of the basic principles to new situations, and may facilitate resolution of uncertainties and conflicts.

Reamer's (1979, 1980, 1982, 1983b) work provides a useful summary of ethical frameworks as they are applied to the social work profession. He draws a classical distinction among various ethical frameworks—that is, between those that are based on cognitive reasoning versus those that are based on noncognitive reasoning. Cognitive theorists, by Reamer's account, maintain that it is possible to determine for a particular situation whether a specific ethical principle is true or false using facts and deductive reasoning; noncognitivists counter that one may only hold an opinion or preference for an ethical principle and that "proof" is not possible.

Within the cognitive school of thought, some discuss how one may divine which principles are true. Some maintain that truth can be determined using science or empirical data, whereas others counter that truth can be determined only by intuition. Most of the work by social work ethicists seems to be based on the premise that reasoning must be invoked in ethical decision making (the cognitivist school).

Several social work ethicists, including Reamer (1979) and Rhodes (1986) seem to rely on Gewirth's (1978) principle of generic consistency for a "rights-based" approach to reasoning about which ethical principles are "true." That is, assuming that freedom and well-being are rights of all persons, reason dictates the necessity that all persons act to promote not only their own freedom and well-being but that of others as well.

Normative applications of Gewirth's principle to social work may be classified as either "direct" (applications regarding interpersonal actions of particular individuals) or "indirect" (social rules that govern the activities of groups of individuals or institutions) (Reamer, 1979). Direct applications are covered under the social worker's responsibilities of personal conduct in Part I of the Code of Ethics of the National Association of Social Workers. For example, these standards prohibit lying, breaking promises, and so forth.

Indirect applications justify social rules (Reamer, 1979) including the voluntary nature of associations (e.g., one's freedom to join the National Association of Social Workers) and the necessity of such associations having rules and penalties for breaking those rules. Further, indirect applications also justify free discussion and criticism of those rules. Finally, the indirect applications call for equal opportunity for all individuals to pursue the desirable goods and advantages of life.

Ethical decisions may be justified in one of two broad ways (Reamer, 1980). The deontologist's approach emphasizes obligation or inherent duties, which may be prescriptive (e.g., the social worker should treat clients with courtesy) or proscriptive (e.g., a social worker should not misrepresent her qualifications). A deontologist would not misrepresent her qualifications to a client because she has a duty to be honest. Conversely, a teleologist's approach derives guidance not from obligations or duties, but is based on the consequences of behavior. A teleologist would not misrepresent her qualifications because to do so would harm the profession and corrupt the client's ability to select the best service available.

The most widely known teleological approach to ethics is utilitarianism. Utilitarian ethics are not simply "situational ethics," which connotes reacting to each circumstance without previously derived guidelines. Rather, when faced with an ethical dilemma, the utilitarian would select the alternative that would result in either the "greatest good" (the positive utilitarian) or the "minimum harm" (the negative utilitarian). A great deal has been written about the difficulties of implementing utilitarian ethics including how to quantify "good" and "bad," whether one should provide the greatest amount of happiness for a small number of people or some happiness for a large number of people, and so forth. Perhaps most troubling for some is the implication that utilitarianism would not preclude the sacrifice of a minority for the greater good of the majority. In practice then, utilitarianism alone (which perhaps is the most often cited approach to resolving ethical dilemmas discussed in the social work literature) is not entirely adequate.

Rhodes (1986) proposes two other related frameworks with a slightly different focus. First she places social work ethics in a Kantian framework, which is based on deontology. Kantians seek an explanation of morality in rational thought, but the Kantian framework bases ethical behavior squarely on the principles behind an action (rather than its consequences), and especially emphasizes respect for the dignity of the individual. Thus, before acting, the Kantian would ask, "If everyone did what I propose, what kind of world would it be?" Within this framework, altruism is a primary duty quite apart from any consequences it might have, and the needs of the individual take precedence over those of the group.

Second, Rhodes (1986) proposes a framework that is similar to deontology and that is perhaps the simplest of the various frameworks presented here: a "virtue-based" framework. Such a framework emphasizes not rules or consequences of behavior, but rather certain moral qualities that are viewed as inherently desirable (kindness, generosity, honesty) or undesirable (mean-spiritedness, deviousness, selfishness). Behavioral choices are made based purely on what is consistent with essential virtues.

Social work ethics probably have evolved from a combination of all of the preceding frameworks. Widespread consensus exists among social workers on certain professional obligations (deontology), such as the proscription against charging unreasonable fees. Conversely, certain broad principles, such as the importance of keeping client communications confidential, can be violated ethically under certain circumstances, such as to protect the client's life (a utilitarian approach). A Kantian approach is evident from the positive view social workers have of altruism, and social workers do hold certain virtues (such as honesty and kindness) in esteem, regardless of circumstances. Different social workers place different emphases on the various frameworks, however, and different situations may even call for resolution using different frameworks.

The challenge to social workers, as well as to these various ethical philosophies, is how to resolve ambiguous situations that do not seem to be specifically covered by the code of ethics. A well-known example of this type of situation is when a client tells his social worker that he plans to rob a bank; the two primary obligations to keep the client's communication confidential and to promote the general welfare of society are in direct contradiction to each other.

Reamer (1982) has attempted to define the "primary" duties of social workers when such conflicts occur by proposing the application of "lexical ordering." Lexical ordering consists of an ordered set of rules by which one may select which obligations take priority when primary obligations conflict. For example, when duties conflict, protection of the conditions essential to life (e.g., food or safety) takes precedence over protection against the harm resulting from lying, breaking a confidence, or protecting against the loss of less essential items such as recreation or excess wealth. The protection of life also takes precedence over the protection of freedom, and an individual's right to freedom overrides that individual's right to basic well-being. The obligation to obey laws and rules to which one has willingly agreed is more important than the right to break those rules or laws.

It is unlikely that most practicing social workers can engage in the kind of reasoning that Reamer's and others' work suggests when faced with dilemmas in daily practice. Few social workers are fully familiar with the various complex ethical frameworks and their applications, and often they must make decisions and take action in a time span that does not allow philosophical debate. Such reasoning is extremely useful to the profession, though, because it provides a background for professional sensitivity to the complexity of ethical obligations. That complexity is belied by the simple language of the code and reminds us that a true dilemma seldom will be resolved by turning to the appropriate page of the Code of Ethics of the National Association of Social Workers. Moreover, the solutions to most of our problems will not always seem completely "right."

The remainder of this chapter will illustrate the complexity of dilemmas faced by social workers in the field of MCH by examining four conflictual practice areas: (a) adolescent sexuality; (b) resolution of unplanned or unwanted pregnancy; (c) treatment of extremely ill infants that is withheld or discontinued and (d) professional responsibilities to engage in advocacy and social reform on behalf of clients. This list is not an exhaustive one of all possible ethical dilemmas faced by the MCH social worker, but these examples offer a representative picture of the situations that are encountered in practice.

ADOLESCENT SEXUALITY

A 17-year-old drug user has had two abortions. She rejects offers of contraceptive services, claiming contraception is too much trouble, "and besides I can always have another abortion."

A 16-year-old boy admits that he lied when he told his 14-year-old girl friend that he is sterile because of mumps. "Real men take their chances," he says, and forbids the social worker to tell his girl friend the truth.

Adolescent sexuality provides a cogent example of the source of a common ethical dilemma faced by social workers in MCH practice: a conflict between the duty to promote clients' self-determination, and the duty to promote the best interests of clients. The promotion of self-determination of clients is a guiding principle of social work practice that is mandated by the Code of Ethics of the National Association of Social Workers (1980): "The social worker should make every effort to foster maximum self-determination on the part of clients" (Part II, G, p. 5). Support for this principle as a "basic duty" can be derived from several sources: consensus among social workers, public support, utilitarianism (assuming that persons usually will act in their own interests), rights-based theories, a Kantian respect for the individual, and virtue-based theories. It is hard to find a social worker who is opposed in principle to self-determination.

Likewise, it is also a primary duty of the social worker to promote the best interests of the client (Code of Ethics of the National Association of Social Workers, Part II, F), and in fact promotion of clients' best interests constitutes the basis of social work practice. Yet it is not uncommon for a conflict to occur between the obligations of the promotion of self-determination and that of the promotion of clients' best interests. For example, to protect the client's best interests (e.g., to prevent pregnancy or STD in a sexually active 13-year-old), should a social worker violate the rule of self-determination by attempting to persuade the client to obtain protection in which she is not interested? Should a social worker even broach the subject with the very young client that she may be too young to understand the meaning of sexual intimacy and might do better to wait until she is older? In the broader context, when the social worker has access to information that clearly indicates that the client's behavior may be harmful to him or her, how far should the social worker go in efforts to "persuade" the client to change her behavior?

Paternalism

A precedent exists for violation of the client's right to self-determination. Most agree that in certain cases it is ethical to interfere in clients' lives—for example, when a client is temporarily deranged or is unable to act rationally, when clients do not have all the information they need to make a decision (Reamer, 1983a), or when the client may harm others. The principle of "paternalism" is invoked, that is interfering in someone's right to self-determination for her "own good." Paternalism can take three forms: deceiving, withholding information, or interfering physically.

These three forms of paternalism have not been explored in detail in the social work literature.

But paternalism must be differentiated from interference based solely on the social worker's preferences. Reamer's (1983a) explication of the assumptions behind paternalistic interference are important: first, that the action truly is for the client's good; second, that we are qualified to judge what is in the client's interests; and third, that protection of the client justifies the interference. If one or more assumptions are not met, the social worker may be engaging in "pseudopaternalism"—that is, interfering with the client's right to self-determination for reasons other than the client's best interests.

An example is in order. A social worker in a school-based clinic for adolescents might be placed in the uncomfortable position of attempting to "convince" a young client who is not interested that she has a need for services, whether those services consist of contraceptive services, or of information and advice about sexuality, contraception, AIDS, or personal relationships. Is the social worker justified by paternalism in such interference? This question is controversial.

Timms (1983) has operationalized the social work value of self-determination of clients to proscribe any type of persuasion (because the authoritative or powerful position of the social worker may constitute coercion), but not all social work ethicists reject persuasion so summarily (e.g., Lewis, 1984). Moreover, Wells and Masch (1986) caution that it is not always clear what is in the best interests of clients, and that what professionals and society believe to be in individuals' best interests changes over time, as is seen in the reduction in preference for institutionalizing developmentally delayed children. Finally, Reamer's three types of paternalism (deceiving, withholding information, and interfering physically) do not seem to include persuading.

Given these difficulties, it is uncertain how the social worker can meet her obligation to promote the client's best interest in an appropriate manner and still encourage the client's right to self-determination. A partial answer to this dilemma may lie in the social worker's obligation of full disclosure to the client of the available services and of the related rights, risks, opportunities, and obligations (National Association of Social Workers, 1980):

6. The social worker should provide clients with accurate and complete information regarding the extent and nature of the services available to them.
7. The social worker should apprise clients of their risks, rights, opportunities, and obligations associated with social service to them. (Part II, F, 5)

Fulfillment of this obligation would seem to entail a thorough discussion of each of the various means of contraception as well as extensive discussion of the risks associated with unprotected intercourse. (Such an interpretation is made from a specific value stance.) It is a generally recognized fact that an individual cannot give informed consent for a procedure if she is not fully informed of the alternatives (Reamer, 1987b). At least two different interpretations could grow from these standards.

Interpretation 1

These standards indicate that the social worker must present all viable options to a client, whether or not the social worker is comfortable with each of those options. Priority is given to self-determination. Few social workers feel comfortable with the idea of young adolescents being sexually active, and sexual activity does carry certain well documented risks for younger adolescents. Nevertheless, adolescents are independent clients in most agencies, and in any case the social worker is unlikely to be able to control their behavior. Whether to risk pregnancy is the client's decision, and we can only hope to help her avoid becoming pregnant.

Interpretation 2

This approach emphasizes paternalism. Ethical standards cannot be applied to children as they are applied to adults, and the profession has yet to decide how to apply them to children and adolescents. In any case, adolescents are not cognitively capable of judging the merits of the various options associated with family planning, and initiating such a discussion has at least the potential of harming the young client. The social worker who bypasses the interests of the family to present options such as abortion and contraception to the young adolescent is behaving irresponsibly.

Regardless of the interpretation one assumes, it would seem in this instance that good ethics demands competence in the order of an extraordinary ability to communicate with the adolescent in a knowledgeable and respectful manner that maximizes the client's likelihood of deciding to take advantage of services. Although it will not be entirely satisfactory in a personal sense for the social worker (and social workers may not even agree that the code of ethics requires full disclosure in all cases—for example, with children), ultimately this situation requires the professional to work to help the client develop her own problem-solving, decision-making, and communication skills. The unmotivated adolescent client (whether because of lack of knowledge or lack of concern) will not use services consistently and effectively anyway (see Chapter 7).

In some cases, however, the social worker's conflict may be more fundamental. For example, a social worker may observe that a very young, naïve female client is being sexually exploited or is engaging in behavior that she is likely to regret later. Initiating a discussion of the advisability of sex in such cases may seem qualitatively different to some social workers than discussing contraception because it may seem more intrusive or personal. Indeed, this is a more complex dilemma, for the social worker must probe her own motives; does she genuinely believe that sexual involvement will result in real harm to the client, or is she expressing a moral preference that is best left to the client to decide? The age of the client is a factor in her ability to make reasonable choices (DiBlasio, 1988; Reamer, 1985) as well as in the consequences of sexual behavior.

Johnson and Shore (1982) make a case for discussing directly with clients the context and consequences of their sexual choices, suggesting that at times it may be appropriate to confirm with young clients whether or not they feel comfortable engaging in sexual intercourse. Evidence in chapter 7 would suggest that adolescents often do not feel morally comfortable about having sex, even when they do so. When social workers avoid discussion of the moral components of clients' problems (perhaps because they think it is not appropriate to do so because it would seem judgmental), they may deprive clients of opportunities to clarify their own values and to deal with the issue that is disturbing them. Conversely, Rhodes (1986) cautions that in the course of such discussions, social workers easily can use their own moral views to coerce their clients in subtle ways.

Resorting to the philosophical frameworks in an earlier section of this chapter may result in different answers. "Rights-based" and Kantian frameworks place priority on the client's dignity and her right to self-determination. "Virtue-based" frameworks might emphasize the importance of being honest with the client, or of being helpful to her in the long run. Lexical ordering might suggest that the client's right to self-determination should take precedence over her right to basic well-being.

Before the social worker can consider issues regarding the "client's best interests," however it is necessary to determine whether the young adolescent is the client, and whether he or she is competent and fully informed. Moreover, because the entire family is seen as the client by the National Association of Perinatal Social Workers (1985) and some other organizations and social agencies, the issue becomes more complicated. The dilemma may extend beyond paternalism, which seems to imply a single client, to the needs of other individuals who may be considered either third parties or part of the "client system."

Identification of Client

Increasingly in health care settings, the client is considered to be not only the individual but the family as well (Ross, 1982a). A family focus is derived from growing knowledge that health and illness have serious consequences for the family, and also are strongly influenced by the family. Yet using this broader definition of "client," it may be difficult to apply the "primacy of the client's interests" principle. Adolescent sexuality is a perfect example of this dilemma, for it brings home the uncomfortable point that sexual intercourse today is not a private act (if indeed it ever was). The young girl or boy who engages in unprotected intercourse is not making a private decision, but one that may have profound consequences for himself or herself, the sexual partner(s), a possible child, and at least two families. Society itself has a stake in sexual behavior, because it may bear the cost of long-term support of a child that may result, or of health care costs associated with STDs. How can the social worker consider the best interests of the client when "the client" involves numerous parties with different and conflicting "best interests"?

A completely satisfactory resolution of conflicting loyalties will rarely be possible, but the wise social worker might take two steps. First, it is advisable to encourage the early involvement of all interested parties in planning and decision making, to the extent possible without violating confidentiality. The social worker can only advise, however. The social work ethic of confidentiality of communications (Code of Ethics of the National Association of Social Workers, 1980, pp. 5–6, Part II, H, 1: "The social worker should share with others confidences revealed by clients, without their consent, only for compelling professional reasons") prohibits sharing information about clients without their permission except under highly specific situations.

The profession has yet to deal effectively with the question of whether this standard is to be applied equally to children and adults, and professional discussion is needed on this issue. The Supreme Court ruled in 1976 that adolescents are entitled to make their own decisions regarding sex-related health care. (See Chilman, 1987, and Zimring, 1982, for a discussion of this issue.) Nonetheless some confusion remains because of the court's reference to "mature minors" in one decision and a failure to define that term. Efforts are being made to require parental consent or notification for contraceptive services or abortion for adolescents, and states vary considerably in the extent to which parental notice or consent is required (Reamer, 1987b). Litigation continues on this issue. (See Chapter 7 for further discussion of the issue of parental consent.)

The social worker should remember, however, that the adolescent's developmental level limits her judgment. Sexual activity, the possibility of pregnancy or AIDS, and the implications of parenthood all have different meanings at various stages of adolescence (Young, 1987). The early adolescent (11 to 14 years of age) is unlikely to comprehend the issues and long-term consequences of her decisions fully. In the extreme, the actions that would be ethical with a 17-year-old client are probably different from those that would be ethical with an 11-year-old, but it is impossible to draw an arbitrary boundary on age that clarifies the social worker's responsibilities.

In addition to including all interested parties as soon as possible, the social worker should be sure that her assessment provides detailed information about the client's needs and resources in the area of social supports. If a client is very young and experiencing a crisis related to decision making and sexuality, she requires as much involvement and support of family, sexual partner, and friends as she will permit.

In the final analysis, in cases in which the adolescent rejects involvement of the family or sexual partner, the social worker might want to work toward such involvement over several visits as trust develops, with the knowledge that the decision ultimately and realistically rests with the client. If the client elects not to involve significant others, at least the relationship with the social worker may provide needed support. Rhodes (1986) also suggests that social workers honestly inform clients of their biases in such cases. Recognizing that such honesty might drive the young client away (and that this approach results from the author's own ethical position), the social worker might say:

> It is your decision whether to talk with your parents about contraception, and because you are my client I will respect that decision. I should tell you, though, that I believe a 13-year-old is usually too young to make such an important decision without talking to her parents, and I think your boyfriend also should have some responsibility in this matter. I won't badger you about this, but I may bring it up occasionally in the next few weeks as we talk. I do assure you, though, that I will not call them or talk to them about this without your permission.

UNPLANNED PREGNANCY RESOLUTION

Fourteen-year-old Lisa and 15-year-old Peter have decided to marry keep the baby she is carrying. Peter will stay in school and support them on a part-time job at a fast food restaurant, and Lisa will stay home with the baby. Both families have said they will disown the couple if they go through with their plan, but they refuse to discuss other options or the difficulties they are likely to encounter. They are fixated on how wonderful it will be to live together and to have a "sweet little baby" to cuddle.

A married woman in her late 30s gives birth in a public hospital. She and her disabled husband and five children barely get by financially, but she attends night school and hopes to finish high school and go on to college. She expresses interest in relinquishing her baby for adoption, but no hospital staff member will encourage her in this idea. They all tell her she will "regret it forever" and encourage her to think about it for a while.

No controversial social issue arouses more emotion and real moral outrage than the issue of unplanned pregnancy resolution. It is important to remember that as individuals, social workers have strong personal feelings on all sides of these issues. No "social work position" on abortion exists (Reamer, 1985), despite a disposition toward freedom of choice generally espoused by social workers. Social workers come to the profession with different religious and moral convictions as well as different life experiences.

Historically the profession has not been neutral on these issues, but rather has favored different solutions at different times (see Chapter 7). Only recently have the wishes of the client begun to be a major factor in the "intervention of choice" with the single unwed mother, for example. One reason that unplanned pregnancy presents such a dilemma is that often none of the available alternatives (abortion, relinquishment for adoption, or parenting with or without marriage) is completely satisfying.

Indeed, many social workers feel uncomfortable not only with abortion (Joffe, 1978) but also with relinquishment for adoption. Some may equate relinquishment with desertion or abandonment, whereas others assume that adopted children will suffer poor outcomes. During some periods of its history the social work profession has not supported adoption as a desirable option for the unplanned pregnancy, and even today social workers frequently fail to present the option of relinquishment to their pregnant clients (See Chapter 7). Other social workers also may be uncomfortable when a pregnant adolescent decides to raise her infant. In many cases it will be painfully apparent to the social worker that the individual is simply not capable of being a parent at this time in her life (e.g., Joffe, 1979) and that outside supports in the form of family and public resources are insufficient to provide an adequate home for the child. In such cases, the social worker may question whether the decision to parent can be made with mature thought about the consequences.

Self-determination of the client is a key issue in this dilemma. Many of the same issues from the previous section on sexuality hold: best interests of the client; the client's inability to know what is in her best interests (paternalism); and also concern for others in the situation including the baby, the baby's father, the families involved. Moreover, promotion of the client's right to self-determination may be complicated by the fact that the woman does not know what she wants. It is not unusual for a pregnant woman to attempt to get the social worker to decide how to resolve her problem for her.

Unwanted pregnancy presents two common sources of conflict for the MCH social worker. The obligation to inform the client fully of all options and services may conflict with the agency's policies, or that obligation may conflict with the individual social worker's own personal morals. The substance of each of these dilemmas is different, but each calls for application of similar principles.

Full Disclosure Versus Agency Policy

As discussed earlier, the social worker is obligated by professional ethics to explain all of the legal alternatives to the pregnant client, despite personal misgivings about any particular alternative. This ethic is based on the premise that clients cannot make reasonable choices about how to proceed with services if they are not fully informed about all available services and the relative merits of each for themselves. All of the viable ethical frameworks discussed earlier in this chapter would support adult clients' absolute right to be made aware of all the legal solutions to their problems. Yet many agencies are dedicated to one particular alternative to unwanted pregnancy (such as abortion clinics or religiously affiliated adoption agencies), and may discourage or prohibit discussion of other alternatives. For example, federally funded agencies are prohibited under current guidelines to use the word "abortion."

Johnson and Shore (1982) provide the following example. A social work student expressed discomfort because the Catholic agency in which she worked prohibited the provision of any information to clients regarding abortion. It is not unusual for religiously affiliated agencies to deny clients access to information about pregnancy termination, considering the stance of many religions against abortion.

The same is true of information about adoption by agencies that provide abortions, who may believe that providing such information might upset or confuse women who come to them seeking abortions. Phipps-Yonas (1980) reviewed available data to conclude that currently only about 5% to 15% of infants born to teenagers are adopted compared with 90% in the 1960s. Failure to provide information about adoption may be a significant factor in this drop in adoption, as clients cannot be presumed to be fully informed of the various services in their community.

Even on a broader level, adoption is seldom treated as a viable alternative. Pierce (1987) criticized the report on adolescent pregnancy of the distinguished National Academy of Sciences, noting that although adoption is mentioned as an option in this important report, it is presented as a "last resort." These negative attitudes persist despite the Adolescent Family Life Act of 1986, which states:

> The program promotes adoption as a positive alternative for pregnant adolescents who are unwilling or unable to care for their child. Adoption is a means of providing permanent families for such children who become legally free for adoption. The program requires both prevention and care projects to provide information about adoption and to establish formal linkages with adoption agencies and residential maternity homes. (Pierce, 1987, p. 3)

Ethically sensitive social workers may be troubled to find that their agencies do not encourage, or even permit, full disclosure to clients. Johnson and Shore (1982) stress the National Association of Social Workers' ethic of adhering to agency policy in such cases, while trying to effect change from within (Code of Ethics of the National Association of Social Workers, 1980, p. 7, Part IV, L: "The social worker should adhere to commitments made to the employing organization").

An inherent assumption guiding the principle that social workers adhere to agency policy is that agency and social worker share the same goal: the best interests of their clients. If social workers did not make such assumptions about their agencies, it would be impossible for them to function, and it would be impossible for agencies to function without rules and regulations. Yet well-meaning professionals may differ on what they believe to be in the best interests of clients, so this issue does not resolve such a dilemma.

Moreover, what if the social worker feels that in general the agency protects clients' best interests, but that in a particular instance this is not the case?

> Clayton is a social worker at a religious agency in a small farm community. He is working with a 12-year-old client who is pregnant as a result of incest. The client and her 26-year-old mother refuse to consider adoption, and in any case a history of medical problems exists in the family that might make the infant hard to place. Yet Clayton is hesitant about the client's plan to raise her child. The client's mother is neglectful, mildly retarded, and abuses drugs and alcohol frequently. She clearly did not protect the client from her brother. Moreover, although the brother has left the home, he is known to return periodically. Clayton thinks that given the unwholesomeness of the home and the fact that adoption is being rejected, he should discuss abortion with the client and her mother. Yet his agency strictly forbids discussion of this option, and he is not personally comfortable with

abortion. Referral to agencies that are more favorable toward abortion is not strictly prohibited, but the nearest such agency is 70 miles away, and the family has limited transportation.

In such situations, social workers may feel compelled to disobey agency regulations for the "greater good" of clients. Rhodes (1986), however, notes: "If you refuse outright to implement . . . policy, you risk losing your job without affecting [sic] any change." (p. 152). She suggests other alternatives to the extremes of adherence or refusal, such as organizing other social workers against the policy, organizing clients, going to the professional organization, and focusing public attention on the policy. Realistically, the social worker who takes such action is still in danger of being fired.

Full Disclosure Versus Personal Morals

Perhaps a more common ethical problem is that many social workers feel uncomfortable themselves with one or more of the available alternatives, and may consider not discussing all the options with their clients. Such withholding of information is often justified on the grounds of its being in the client's best interests ("paternalism," Reamer, 1983a), but the social worker must be careful that the action is not actually based on personal motives.

> Jessica is a social worker in an agency that counsels women with unplanned pregnancies. Her client is a married woman with three children who has become pregnant despite contraception. She does not want any more children, and her husband is adamant that he will leave if she does not have an abortion. She has delayed her decision too long to have an abortion, however, so she is considering relinquishing the child for adoption. Jessica feels that this family could accommodate another baby and that relinquishing would be irresponsible. It is difficult for her to advise her client about relinquishment.

Pressure on pregnant clients to select the currently favored option is not new to social work. It is interesting that in 1960 Bernstein cautioned against pressuring unwed mothers to relinquish their infants:

> Technically we may claim that our underlying point of view does not influence us and that each girl is allowed to make her own decision regarding her baby. And technically this is probably correct in most cases. But the subtle communication of our essential attitude cannot be denied. (p. 28)

In 1965, the same author stated in the *Social Work Yearbook* that adoption "is now generally considered the plan of choice for the white, healthy illegitimate baby" (p. 800). The wishes of the mother were not mentioned.

Social workers' personal preferences or ignorance about adoption clearly can influence them to withhold information from their clients and thus limit their options. For example, Cain (1979) described her experiences with 40 pregnant adolescents and stated that "in the girls' minds, adoption is seldom a realistic alternative" (p. 53). Mech's (1985) interviews with 131 counselors in various settings showed that workers in health-oriented settings were the least likely to view adoption as a good alternative. Finally, Bolton's (1980) review of the issue of relinquishment points to "negative effects [of relinquishment for adoption] which are often worse than the problems of the moment that she may be facing in child rearing or marital relationships" (p. 137) without documenting his assertions. In fact, a good deal of evidence exists to the contrary of Bolton's assertions.

The emotionalism associated with unwed pregnancy and the variety of not altogether satisfying alternatives make it difficult for social workers to be objective in presenting the options, which vary in desirability and acceptability with the times. The issue of relinquishment certainly touches on some sensitive issues including feelings about child abandonment and responsibility. As a human and perhaps a parent, the social worker may have deep feelings about these issues.

Yet social workers are ethically obligated to be fully aware of the alternatives available to their clients, and the facts about each of those alternatives. For example, when social workers do not advise pregnant clients of the available resources for adoption and the empirical evidence of many happy outcomes (as well as the possibility of some ongoing unhappiness and "anniversary reactions"), they are violating the Code of Ethics (National Association of Social Workers, 1980, p. 9) requirement to base practice on current recognized knowledge:

1. The social worker should base practice upon recognized knowledge relevant to social work.

2. The social worker should critically examine, and keep current with emerging knowledge relevant to social work. (Part V, O, 1-2)

Ethical Frameworks

Application of the prominent ethical frameworks does not resolve either dilemma (conflicts between full disclosure and agency policy or between full disclosure and personal morals), but it may assist the social worker in clarifying the issues. The deontologist's position, which is based on inherent duties or obligations, would seem to dictate following agency policy in either case, because accepting a position in an agency involves implicit acceptance of the agency's policies. The social worker is obligated to be fully informed of agency policies and practices before accepting employment (Wells & Masch, 1986), and should be particularly alert to specific questions regarding policies he or she might find objectionable. If an agency's policy seems to conflict with the best interests of clients in general, professional obligations would mitigate against the social worker's accepting a position in that agency in the first place (Part II, F, 4 of the Code of Ethics [National Association of Social Workers, 1980, p. 4] states: "The social worker should avoid relationships or commitments that conflict with the interests of clients").

The teleologist would consider the consequences of his actions. This approach, for example, would require Clayton and Jessica to look at the consequences of their actions for these families (and the unborn infants)—that is, what might occur (to the client and other parties) if they tell the client of all the available options versus what might occur if they do not. It is important to emphasize here that the consequences under consideration for the utilitarian approach are *not* the consequences of the client's actions (whether they abort or relinquish), but the consequences of the social worker's actions (disclosing or not disclosing all the options). In the former case a social worker might feel that she is responsible for something of which she disapproves, whereas in the latter case it is the client who is responsible for the resolution of the pregnancy. Social workers must acknowledge that it is the client's right and responsibility to decide what to do with their lives, and the social worker's obligation to provide information and professional guidance.

As part of consideration of the consequences the teleological social worker also must consider at least two consequences to himself. First, if Clayton violates agency policy because he believes that in this particular instance it is required of him if he is to meet his professional ethical obligations, the consequences may include his own reprimand or dismissal. At least in principle, most social workers would place their client's best interests above their own situation, but resolving this situation might require comparing the seriousness of the various outcomes (e.g., "lexical ordering"). Fortunately, few dilemmas require this degree of sacrifice from the social worker.

Second, a social worker who violates her own conscience may suffer personal recrimination. This dilemma is best dealt with before it occurs; a social worker should not accept employment in an agency whose policy is contrary to the worker's personal morals, because then dilemmas are certain to arise that might lead the social worker either to violate agency policy or to violate his own convictions. The following scenario is an example of such a situation:

John is a new M.S.W. graduate who is also a devout fundamentalist Christian. He sought a job at an agency that counsels pregnant adolescents about adoption. In keeping with their interpretation of the code of ethics, agency social workers inform their clients not only of adoption services but also of abortion through other agencies, and of available resources to help them if they wish to parent their babies. John understands the importance of fully informing clients of their options, but he is so morally opposed to abortion that his conscience would not allow him to have even a small part in a client's obtaining one. If this agency also worked with other parties to adoption (for example, with adoptive couples), perhaps he could work solely with them and thus avoid the dilemma, but because they do not, John seeks employment at another agency.

It seems then that both deontology and teleology would lead the social worker in the same direction. First, she should be fully informed about the obligations imposed upon her by employment in the agency, and about the various resources and alternatives available to the clients of that agency. Second, she should not accept employment in an agency that she believes would require her to act unethically or in a manner that is morally repugnant to her. Finally, in certain instances it may be necessary to engage in lexical ordering and to suffer negative personal consequences in order to act ethically.

Of course in the final analysis any code of ethics must be enforced by each professional on an individual basis, but this particular dilemma may be most problematic for social workers. Some individuals feel so strongly in favor of some issues such as abortion or adoption that they enter the profession with the mission of promoting their views. Social workers might do well to question their motivations in such cases, for they may portend serious ethical difficulties that will defy satisfactory resolution.

WITHHOLDING OR WITHDRAWING TREATMENT

Two months ago, Joshua was born at 24 weeks of gestation weighing just 1 lb. Since then he has been on a respirator and has been fed through a tube, barely holding his weight. He has had several brain hemorrhages, and the physicians say severe brain damage is almost certain. They ask the parents (who tried for more than 4 years for this pregnancy and probably will be unable to conceive again) for permission to turn off the respirator because they see little chance for improvement, and the treatment itself involves discomfort for Joshua. The parents refuse their consent and request permission to move their son to an NICU in another state, where they say "miracles are being accomplished."

A premature baby girl with Down syndrome is born with multiple defects, but most are correctable with the surgery. Her prognosis is unknown with surgery, but she will probably die without it. The parents have refused surgery because it must be done without anesthesia because of the baby's immature respiratory system, and they do not want her to suffer pain. Moreover, they are in their 40s, have five other children, and they fear they cannot care for a retarded child. "Even if we leave her everything we have, who will care for her after we die?" they ask.

The issue of allowing ill or deformed infants to die without extraordinary treatment is one that generates great controversy (e.g., Lyon, 1985). Again the fundamental conflict is between the social worker's own moral standards and her duty to the client, who in this case is represented by the parents (Code of Ethics of the National Association of Social Workers, 1980, Part II, G, 2, p. 5: "When another individual has been legally authorized to act in behalf of a client, the social worker should deal with that person always with the client's best interest in mind").

Withholding or withdrawing medical treatment from an infant in the NICU may be one of the most painful decisions a parent or professional can make. It is also a relatively recent phenomenon, as it was not until medical technology made survival possible for many tiny and premature infants that the choice of when to use such technology emerged. Increases in options inevitably carry with them an increased need for a values framework within which to make such choices (Abramson & Black, 1985). For example, in 1950 an infant born weighing approximately 2 lb had only about a 2% chance of survival with standard treatment; now about 60% of such infants who are treated in major perinatal centers survive (Poland & Russell, 1987).

Yet "life-and-death" choices are not new to social work. The issue of euthanasia for the dying and especially the elderly remains a matter of deep personal concern to many social workers (Abramson & Black, 1985; Holmes, 1980). The situation is similar in the NICU where infants' lives may be extremely fragile and many of the treatments are extensive, invasive, and painful to the infants, and emotionally distressing and expensive for the families (see chapter 3.) An essential difference is that the infant cannot speak for himself and has had no opportunity to do so in the past; his fate rests entirely with the family and medical team. The infant also has had no opportunity to live the "rich, full life" that comforts many families as they decide to terminate life supports for their elderly relatives.

The role of the social worker in this situation does not include independent decision making. (Even physicians are less likely than they once were to make such decisions independently.) In most cases, the social worker's involvement is in the capacity of providing information or support to families as they face such decisions, and of advocating for families when their decisions conflict with the wishes of the medical staff. Other social workers consult only with medical and nursing staffs around the staff's emotional distress with such issues (e.g., from chapter 3).

In some cases social workers serve on institutional ethical review committees that are charged with the responsibility of either making decisions regarding when to withdraw treatment or of reviewing such decisions after the fact (Annas, 1984). These committees, which have evolved during the last few years in response to increasingly difficult ethical questions, are found in most large American hospitals (Furlong, 1986). They usually include representation by all the major health professions including social workers (e.g., Furlong, 1986), and serve purposes of education and policy formation in addition to review of specific cases (Reamer, 1987a).

In one way, this dilemma is like that described in the previous section. Some social workers have deep religious or personal convictions that may render them unable to be associated with decisions to withhold or discontinue life-saving treatment, either on a policy level or with individual cases. In such a case they should seek a position with which they feel more comfortable. More often, as in most ethical dilemmas, the social worker will feel uncomfortable with the necessity of making such decisions and ambivalent about whatever the decision is. Rarely will the situation occur when the decision that is made will feel "right" and there are no regrets. Such certainty is not desirable in the face of subjective judgments with such far-reaching consequences (Gelman, 1986).

The difficulties for social workers in supporting family decisions and advocating for families' interests may operate whatever the decision is regarding treatment. That is, parents may elect to subject themselves and their hopelessly ill infants to procedures of which we as individuals disapprove because of the pain or discomfort for the infant. In other cases, parents may prohibit treatment under circumstances when we as individuals would pursue treatment vigorously. In either case the social worker's responsibility is the same: to be sure the family is fully informed of the facts and that they are emotionally capable of making the decision at the current time, and then to support the family's right to make the decision that they feel is best.

Family Decision Making

It is not always clear that the family is capable of making such an enormous decision in a reasonable way. (That is, the clients may not be capable of making a decision in their best interests.) Specifically, two situations exist when the social worker may feel that the parents are not acting in the child's best interests. First, many experts have noted that it is typical for families of very ill infants to experience shock and disbelief about their infant's condition. This natural response may result in mental confusion and disorganization, rendering them unable to plan or make rational decisions (see Chapter 3). In all but the most pressing emergencies, patience would seem to be advised, and no hasty decisions should be made until the family is capable. In such cases the social worker may have to act as advocate for the family if pressure exists to move ahead before the family is truly able to make a decision.

Second, in some cases parents' behavior may be judged to be abusive or neglectful; in such cases the courts may intervene. The social worker would not make this decision alone, but would discuss and consult with other NICU staff. The social worker might be in the position of making a protective services report, however, because social workers are mandated reporters of child abuse and neglect (Kadushin & Martin, 1988).

One source of discomfort for some social workers is the issue of discontinuing treatment based on economic justifications alone. One frequently hears that the high cost of NICU for hopelessly ill infants, or for infants who will suffer permanent disability, is unjustified, given the calls for reducing the enormous public burden incurred. Yet these arguments are often addressed with equally pressing arguments for distributive justice. Such infants are often minority and poor, and they might not have been born prematurely and requiring such care if their mothers had had access to better prenatal care, nutrition, and other resources during and before pregnancy. Indeed, the questions of discontinuing treatment do not seem to arise as often when families can pay for services. Questions regarding equitable allocation of health care resources must be answered on a different level than the case-by-case approach presented here, and the social work profession has yet to deal with such issues (Reamer, 1985). Nevertheless, the implications of this issue should not be forgotten in daily practice. (See the following section on advocacy and social reform.)

Application of the Ethical Frameworks

Application of the ethical frameworks to the dilemma of withholding or stopping treatment for a severely ill infant is difficult, because both major frameworks require the identification of a primary client. For example, the deontologist's approach emphasizes one's duties to the client. The neonatologist easily identifies the infant as her client, but the social worker's client is the family as a whole. The teleological or utilitarian approach would assess the consequences to determine the proper course of action. Yet it is usually impossible to assess how much "good" or "bad" results from the various alternatives in this situation, and for whom.

Indeed, if one can judge or quantify the consequences of withholding treatment, the situation probably is not a dilemma at all. "If the infant is surely going to die in spite of all efforts to resuscitate, then the discomfort incurred by those efforts may not be justified. If the infant might survive after a resuscitation, but is surely going to survive with no apparent brain function, then that too may lead one to question the effort" (Poland & Russell, 1987, p. 258). In such a case, the obligation may be to make the experience of the infant's death as enhancing for family functioning as possible, through measures described in chapter 3.

Both frameworks would seem to require the social worker and physician to work together with the family to make the necessary decisions. That is, because decisions are not imposed on the family but are made with them, one may look at both one's obligations and the consequences of behavior and draw the same conclusions. For the social worker, this means presenting all the information to the family, assisting them with the practical problems and emotional stress of the situation, and then supporting them in their decision. Competent practice is ethical practice.

A final note on this issue concerns the personal stress that is experienced by social workers in the NICU. Social workers who are continually involved in such decisions are likely to experience considerable distress and anxiety. Individual social workers must recognize their own limits and deal with them properly (perhaps through use of peer consultation or supervision), so it does not interfere with professional performance.

ADVOCACY AND SOCIAL REFORM RESPONSIBILITIES

Greg is an M.S.W. in the High-Risk Follow-up Clinic of a large metropolitan hospital. In his work with low-income families he constantly encounters families who do not adhere to the recommended schedule of follow-up appointments for their high-risk infants because they do not have transportation to the clinic and other services. The medical staff criticizes families and treats them with contempt because they do not "comply with medical advice," but Greg understands the practical difficulties such families face.

One public hospital in a large midwestern city has seen a constant rise in the incidence of LBW in the last 5 years. During that time, a tightening of AFDC regulations has removed many low-income women from eligibility for Medicaid, and there has been a corresponding reduction in the proportion of low-income, high-risk women who seek prenatal care early in their pregnancies. Social workers in the hospital believe they can trace the increase in the number of LBW babies directly to this reduced access to preventive medical care, and their supervisor suggests that they contact their state legislators to suggest that the state enact some of the more liberal Medicaid policies that are permitted by the federal government.

A common thread running through each of the chapters of this book has been the responsibility social workers bear to engage in advocacy on behalf of their clients. Each of the major ethical frameworks described in this chapter requires social workers to work for social reform. The deontologist's position would hold that such action is an inherent duty of the social worker, whereas the teleolgist would emphasize that advocacy on behalf of many clients can result in much more good than more limited action on behalf of individual clients.

Both the National Association of Social Workers and the National Association of Perinatal Social Work Codes of Ethics require that social workers engage in advocacy on behalf of their clients. The Code of Ethics of the National Associaiton of Social Workers states that the social worker should promote the "general welfare of society" (Part VI, P, p. 9), and further specifies that this should be done through advocating appropriate policy and legislation, and by informing the public about clients' problems and what can be done about those problems. The Code further exhorts social workers to "act to ensure that all persons have access to the resources, services, and opportunities which they require" (Part VI, P, 2) and to "act to expand choice and opportunity for all persons, with special regard for disadvantaged or oppressed groups and persons" (Part VI, P, 3).

The code of the National Association of Perinatal Social Workers is similar, but further specifies that the social worker's public activities should "foster the integrity of the family unit and the good of parents and their infants" (Part VI, C) and that social workers should "encourage consumer participation in shaping policies which impact upon families" (Part VI, D).

Advocacy may entail both case advocacy (working to obtain rights and services for individual clients) and class advocacy (working to obtain those rights and services for a group of individuals) (Weinrich, 1987). Social workers are probably more accustomed to working for individual clients than they are to working for client groups, but current funding realities demonstrate that class advocacy will be increasingly important as essential programs face continued cuts. It is both inefficient and irresponsible to help clients "work around" the fact that certain basic services are unavailable to them, rather than working to obtain those services for them and for others with similar problems. Yet today few social workers appear to be aware of the meaning of their professional obligations to advocate for their clients, much less to engage in meaningful activity in that direction.

An example is in order. Recent concern about the alarming increase of homeless persons in this country has resulted in many individual compassionate social workers volunteering their free time to serve on "soup lines" or in shelters. Such efforts are laudable, and prove that social workers' concern goes way beyond "putting in their 40 hours." Unfortunately, voluntarism is not adequate to deal with a problem as massive as homelessness. The problem, which involves many women and children (Bassuk et al., 1986), will require profound changes in policy, and apparently will not occur in the absence of fundamental political changes. Perhaps social workers' most valuable contribution to alleviation of this tragic situation will lie in interpretation to the public of the real nature of the problem, and in agitation for changes in policy on behalf of a client group with little power to advocate for themselves. Providing one-to-one service is an important affirmation of concern and can provide social workers with credibility on this issue, but it is insufficient.

Reasons for Neglect of Advocacy

Why are social workers not advocating for change? First, many scholars believe that social workers have abandoned social issues as a priority, preferring to concentrate on individual services that carry more prestige (Brilliant, 1986; Reamer, 1985). Despite action by some individual social workers and important work by certain organizations (such as the Children's Defense Fund), the commitment that resulted in creation of the Children's Bureau, the end of child labor, and the passage of Sheppard-Towner is no longer evident. Moreover, no other profession has "picked up the slack" to serve as the advocates for poor and disadvantaged mothers and children, social work's original constituency.

Second, the educational process does not promote advocacy and social reform. It has been noted that such specialized skills are not taught in graduate schools of social work (Morris, 1978), especially to students who select the "direct practice" or "clinical" track in schools whose curricula are so divided. Such a division sends a clear message that social reform is not a "core activity" of social work, and leaves social workers who are interested in pursuing a social reform agenda unsure of how to pursue that agenda.

Finally, large case loads and administrative responsibilities that are common in the bureaucracies within which social workers usually practice do not encourage social workers to engage in class advocacy (Rhodes, 1986). Agencies may see such action as too political (perhaps even involving action against funding agents), or as requiring too much time that could be spent on reimbursable direct-contact time. Off-duty political action even may be prohibited by some organizations, such as some government agencies.

Despite the problems, social workers may be effective advocates in several capacities. Administrators and program planners have access to data that may illustrate the needs of mothers and children and that may be used to influence policy (Watkins, 1979). This method was used so successfully by social workers in the Children's Bureau in the Progressive Era. Kumabe et al. (1977) emphasize the role of such information in advocacy when they note:

> Daily practice gives social workers a strategic position from which to observe the gaps in community health and social welfare services, to identify those trends in social conditions which suggest the need for new, improved or expanded services and to enable other members of the team to be continuously aware of such trends so that an organized effort can be brought to planning and funding the agency. (p. 20)

In addition to organized efforts such as those above and those that are supported by professional organizations, all social workers may exercise their rights as individuals to call and write their Congressional representatives regarding pending legislation and pressing social problems. Awareness of representatives' voting records on pertinent legislation is also useful as social workers vote in local, state, and national elections. Information on individual voting records is available from the National Association of Social Workers and the American Public Health Association.

Rhodes (1986) maintains that it is not possible to maintain an ethical stance apart from the social and political realities in which one practices. Julia Lathrop might agree. What she said nearly 70 years ago remains fundamentally true today: "But finally, and fundamentally, [what is needed is] a general recognition throughout the country that a decent income . . . [is] the strongest safeguard against a high infant mortality rate" (Lathrop, 1919, p. 274).

This chapter illustrates some potential ethical dilemmas faced by MCH social workers in their daily practice. These are not always extraordinary dilemmas; most social workers confront such dilemmas frequently. Nor do these examples constitute an exhaustive description, although the ones discussed earlier may be representative. Others may include issues of informed consent, new types of reproductive technology (e.g., surrogate parenting), and the rights of fathers to participate in decisions about abortion and relinquishment.

As changes occur in medical technology, health care delivery, the political climate, and cultural values, new dilemmas will arise. No ready answers will be available to "plug in" to make the necessary decisions easy. The profession and individual social workers will have to apply professional values, their own ethical standards, and what has been learned up to now to face these new challenges. That is the nature of ethics; new situations call for new applications.

Herein lies one of the responsibilities of the profession. As technology has evolved, new dilemmas such as those described in this chapter have arisen. Social work, like the other helping professions, is bound to meet the challenges of these new dilemmas with guidelines for ethical practice. Developing new guidelines requires open discussion, argumentation, and acceptance of divergent viewpoints. Several issues currently await such discussion, including the broad and far-reaching issue of how to resolve family-centered practice with the individual rights of family members.

Goldstein (1987) makes a disturbing point when he asserts that a fundamental misunderstanding of professional responsibility has led social workers to attempt to avoid moral issues altogether in practice and that this avoidance may operate to the detriment of social workers and clients alike. Indeed, he contends that many of the problems with which clients come to social workers are essentially moral dilemmas: e.g., the pregnant woman who asks "should I have an abortion?" and the parents of the NICU baby asking "should we continue treatment or turn off the respirator?" Many social workers are also uncomfortable with these issues, so they attempt to avoid the entire issue of morality or ethics. In some cases they may even recast an ethical issue as a matter of pathology (Rhodes, 1986) (e.g., "The parents refuse to turn off the respirator because they have inadequate personalities"). In the final analysis, avoidance does not work:

> Finally, we cannot escape these ethical questions. We must focus on them if we want to act well towards others and act with personal integrity. As professionals, we have power over clients' lives and our moral choices can radically affect them, for good or ill. If we avoid the issues, we run the risk of acting in muddled or damaging ways, blindly assuming that we are 'helping others' when we may not be. (Rhodes, 1986, p. 9)

In recognition of the often difficult process of resolving ethical problems using a document such as a written code, Levy (1976) emphasizes the importance of each social worker's going beyond the philosophies and restrictions of professional ethics to develop a personal sense of ethics that would guide behavior in ambiguous situations. Rhodes (1986) concurs and takes the argument further, suggesting that the profession must acknowledge the diversity of ethical views that exist. "Each social worker must determine her own position—the sort of social worker she will be" (p. 19). This position is in opposition to the oft-repeated maxim that personal values should play no part in social work practice—that is, behavior should be guided by professional values with personal values kept at bay to avoid "imposing" them on clients.

It is necessary for the profession to operate from a common value base, and social workers rightly should try to avoid imposing their personal values on clients. They also should not allow ambiguity to influence them to avoid confronting their own convictions, however; nor should they deny clients the opportunity to discuss the moral dilemmas that trouble them. Many of the moral and ethical problems social workers encounter in their practice are due to social workers' lack of clarity about their own values, and their failure to confront complex ethical dilemmas directly and responsibly. Individuals cannot lay aside the convictions that grow from their deep religious and moral standards, in favor of the behavioral standards of others. Rhodes (1986) reminds us: "Moral responsibility is not transferable from one person to another, and it goes beyond instrumentality to consideration of one's obligations to act for the overall good of others and society—the very concerns promoted by social work ideals" (p. 136).

Conclusion

It may appear that social workers can do little more to improve the health of mothers and infants. After all, great strides have been made, beginning with the great reforms of the Progressive Era, the Social Security Act, the War on Poverty, and even those of recent times. In terms of infant mortality alone, rates have gone from approximately 124 per 1,000 in 1910 (Duke, 1915) to approximately 10.4 (provisional data) in 1986 (Wegman, 1987). Indeed, many of the prominent causes of death in 1910 seem strange today, because improvements in sanitation and public hygiene have caused them to be nearly forgotten. Infants no longer die in large numbers of diarrhea and contagious disease. Many major diseases that once ravaged children such as polio, rheumatic fever, and rickets are virtually unknown now.

Infant mortality is not the only indicator that has improved dramatically. Maternal mortality has declined significantly; in 1913, childbirth killed more women 15 to 44 years of age than any other disease except tuberculosis (Meigs, 1917). Now it is a rare occurrence in this country for a woman to die in childbirth. Very tiny premature infants—some weighing barely a pound—once died almost inevitably, but now often survive, frequently with no handicaps. Extensive rehabilitation and support services are now available for children with handicaps; they now can look forward to lives that are much fuller than was the case at one time.

If social workers think we are no longer needed, however, we are mistaken. Black infants remain twice as likely to die before their first birthdays as white infants (Wegman, 1987). Children from low-income families are still less healthy, but have less access to quality medical care, than children from more advantaged families (Miller, 1985). Poor women remain twice as likely as more advantaged women to give birth without prenatal care (Institute of Medicine, 1985) and minority mothers are 3 to 4 times as likely to die in childbirth as white women (Children's Defense

Fund, 1988). More than half of all black infants are now born to unmarried and very young mothers, whose rates of complications and LBW far exceed the average. Our rate of LBW is a shameful one relative to the rest of the world, and indeed the United States infant mortality rate is only the 16th best in the world (Miller, 1985). Finally, it has been estimated that nearly half of the perinatal deaths in this country are preventable (Goldenberg & Koski, 1984). All of these facts derive not from lack of medical technology, an area in which this nation rightfully can claim to be number one in the world, but from social factors that remain of central concern to social workers.

Poverty, poor housing and nutrition, teenage and unmarried pregnancy, and lack of access to adequate health care continue to kill and handicap American children unnecessarily (Miller, 1985; Starfield, 1985). Indeed, the Children's Defense Fund (1987) estimates that poverty kills 10,000 children every year in the United States.

In general, we remain as a profession committed to fighting these social problems. Certainly on an individual basis, many social workers are involved in social work practice that confronts these factors daily. Many social workers are in prenatal clinics, in NICUs, and many other settings, working with pregnant adolescents to improve the health of low-income families. Others perform important administrative tasks, planning and implementing new services and working for equal access to quality care. Some are at the federal level in influential positions, such as Juanita Evans and Virginia Insley before her. These influential professionals have contributed in numerous ways to the improvement of maternal and child health in this country. Others at the state level, such as Gardenia Ruff, Ernestine Player, and Judy Barber, are responsible for tremendous programmatic innovations in their states that directly affect mothers and children everyday.

Still, however, social work as a profession has failed to define and clarify its methods, to act with unity and conviction toward social reform, to perform the high-quality research that is necessary, and to fully assert its leadership in the MCH field (Combs-Orme, 1988). In particular, much work remains to be done to demonstrate the profession's effectiveness along with other major professions in MCH.

Lambert exhorted the profession to define its role in MCH in 1968 so that effectiveness could be assessed, but much still remains to be done. Much of the work being done is untested and has not been submitted for scrutiny by the scientific community. The written literature that exists remains scattered and located where it may not be readily accessible to many social work practitioners and students, such as in conference proceedings (which although often excellent, are often difficult to obtain) and in the literature of other professions. The credibility of the social work profession, and of MCH social work in particular, can only be enhanced by rigorous empirical research and publication in the leading professional journals.

The 1980s have presented a special challenge to the social work profession in the wake of extensive cuts to social programs since 1981. The reorganization of many Title V and other programs (e.g., lead-based paint poison prevention, SIDS prevention, hemophilia, genetic disease, and adolescent pregnancy programs) into block grants under the 1981 Omnibus Reconciliation Act may portend further cuts and growing competition among vital services for the limited dollars available. Social programs were targets of budget cuts with every budget proposed by the Reagan administration, and programs that directly affect poor families have been diminished by millions of dollars during this decade. These developments have led to necessary but extremely difficult choices regarding which vital programs to trim.

Some positive developments have occurred, however. Several changes to the Medicaid program contained in the Consolidated Omnibus Reconciliation Act (Public Law 99-272) and the Sixth Omnibus Budget Reconciliation Act (Public Law 99-509) have broadened eligibility criteria and extended coverage to more pregnant women and children, and proposed legislation is before the new Congress to further extend coverage. Through new regulations and the child health assurance program, the federal government has relaxed legal requirements so that states may now extend the Medically Needy Medicaid program to more children of the "working poor" and other groups previously not covered (Meyer & Lewin, 1986). It is too soon to know to what extent states will take advantage of these opportunities, but reason exists for hope. As this book goes to press, the Bush administration is preparing its first budget, and it is impossible to say how poor families will fare.

Future Possibilities

Potential for Change

It is not likely that the next century will hold the dramatic changes and improvement in children's health that have been seen in the previous century, but the potential exists for important improvements.

As public health and other improvements have reduced the risk of death owing to disease, the health care system has increasingly turned its attention to other significant threats to the health of American children. For example, policy changes could significantly reduce injuries—one of the three leading causes of death for children 1 to 4 years of age (injuries, congenital anomalies, and malignancies). Automobile injuries are the largest single component of these fatal injuries; car restraints have the potential of saving 90% of children who die in automobile crashes (Margolis, 1983). Burns are the second largest injury category; action requiring smoke detectors and reducing settings on hot water heaters in all homes could reduce these numbers greatly.

Little reason exists to believe that these changes will occur in the absence of public action. Public sentiment against social legislation requiring seat belts, gun control, and other safety measure suggests a long battle. Miller (1985) pessimistically notes:

> The initiatives that are most effective in improving children's health have to do with food and nutrition, reproductive behavior, and improved sanitation. Even more dramatic improvement might come from injury prevention and improved safety in home, at job sites, and on highways. Most require publicly sponsored service or a degree of regulation strongly resisted by some people. (p. 25)

Social workers have not assumed leadership in the move to reduce childhood injuries, but it is clear that this problem falls within their purview. Will the profession be active in convincing the public of the importance of policy changes to protect children from this needless cause of death?

Mortality does not even tell the whole story. Morbidity is generally believed to be 1.5 to 3 times the rate of infant and child mortality (Margolis, 1983). Automobile injuries contribute to disability, at a ratio of about 5.7 disabled to one killed. Other morbidity is more hidden from public view; nutritional deficits probably limit many children's potential to an unknown degree.

Ominous Trends

Other trends whose effects are difficult to estimate at this time may vitiate any improvements in child health that could come from significant policy changes. As of September of 1988, AIDS has already stricken 1171 children younger than 13 years of age (Centers for Disease Control, 1988), and the predictions concerning its growth in the next few years are frightening. In addition to provision for their medical needs, social workers are involved in the heart-breaking and growing need to place many of these children in loving environments to live out their allotted time. Indeed, AIDS could prove to be the most significant and tragic part of the child health story in the coming decade.

Although homelessness has been recognized as a serious national problem for several years, its implications for MCH are only beginning to be documented. One study demonstrated that 80% of homeless families were headed by women, and half of the children had significant health or developmental problems (Bassuk et al., 1986). Another study demonstrated not only that about half of homeless children had acute or chronic health problems, but that they were 4 times as likely as American children in general to be in "fair" or "poor health" (Miller & Lin, 1988).

Homelessness is not the exclusive problem of alcoholics and the mentally ill. The effects of homelessness on children are serious and inextricably tied to the well-being of the entire family.

Barber (1989a) urges social workers to advocate for homeless children by telling their stories. She recommends case management as a tool for helping such families move through an incredibly complex bureaucracy to obtain needed health care services as well as the other basic services they need. Barber reminds us that "Without full employment, adequate family income, decent housing, good nutrition, well-funded public education, and affirmative action in all areas of our national life, we cannot assure good health" (pp. 11–12).

Demographic trends that suggest a shrinking child population for a time may mean that fewer children will vie for the available resources in the coming few years. At the same time single parent households are likely to continue to grow as a proportion of families, however, and probably will remain at great economic disadvantage. The economy is likely to continue as the greatest influence on children's health, and it is always dangerous to predict the course of the economy. Recent history demonstrates that children are the first to suffer from an economic downturn and are the least powerful in demanding their share of what is available (Hopps, 1986).

The basic structure of medical care also appears to be changing. Health maintenance organizations (HMOs), prepaid medical plans, are becoming more common (Hoekelman, 1987) and many states are experimenting with providing Medicaid services through HMOs. HMOs are likely to change health care for children, but it is unclear to what extent they will meet the needs of low-income children. It is impossible to say whether social workers and social services will be part of HMOs in coming years.

It is dangerous to make predictions about changes in policy and services. Many children's advocates (e.g., Children's Defense Fund, 1987) predict further cuts in social programs, AFDC, and Medicaid, decreasing immunization rates among poor children, and further weakening public commitment to health care for low-income children. Already most poor children are outside the primary health care system (Hoekelman, 1987), and further reductions in services could result in a 180-degree turn in the century-old improvement in child mortality and morbidity.

Professional Issues

The future of the social work profession also will affect our role in providing the full range of health care services to children. First, accountability and our failure to provide evidence of our usefulness in this arena constitute a critical challenge for the 1990s and beyond. Indications are that the public is becoming increasingly unwilling to pay for services to the poor unless cost-effectiveness can be demonstrated. How can effectiveness be demonstrated? What part will "quality-of-life" issues play in demonstrating that these services are worthwhile?

The scientific approach taken by the Children's Bureau toward the health of mothers and babies that has been so successful in this century must be attributed in large part to the great leadership and vision of its first director, social worker Julia Lathrop, and its subsequent early directors. From the beginning the Children's Bureau was committed to using the scientific method to benefit children, as is shown by the approach to a series of conferences the bureau sponsored about children:

> Actuated by the faith that the scientific method is the most useful of the tools possessed by the modern world, the organizers of the conferences brought together men and women whose sole purpose was to apply to the service of the American child what has been proved to the incontestably true. Nothing doctrinaire nor anything unsupported by the burden of scientific data now available was admitted. (Children's Bureau, 1919, p. 12)

Demonstrating the effectiveness and the value of social work in MCH in the 1990s will be a difficult enterprise, given limited methodologies, interest and abilities of social workers in the area of research, and support for evaluation. Some beginning effort must be made, however. These are times that demand accountability, and if we do not test ourselves and our services, we will find that we are no longer needed.

Perhaps an even more fundamental question for social work in the 1990s is whether social workers will want to be part of the child health care system. Diminishing interest in the public sector and increasing interest in for-profit social work does not bode well for this traditional constituency of the social work profession, which usually does not bring generous third-party payment. Advocacy is often cited as a social work function, but it is little evident in day-to-day social work practice. Goggin (1987) has defined the problem for America's poor children:

> Health policy in the United States has relegated children to the status of second-class citizen. They have not received their fair share of the federal health dollar. Nor are American children as healthy as their counterparts in many other countries with a similar standard of living. (p. 3)

These dismal facts surely must stand as a challenge for the social work profession in the 1990s and beyond.

References

Abbott, G. (1915). The midwife in Chicago. *American Journal of Sociology, 20,* 684–699.

Abbott, G. (1941). *From relief to Social Security.* Chicago: University of Chicago Press.

Abramson, A., & Black, R. B. (1985). Extending the boundaries of life: Implications for practice. *Health and Social Work, 10,* 165–173.

Aday, L. A., Fleming, G. V., & Andersen, R. (1984). *Access to medical care in the U.S.: Who has it and who doesn't.* Chicago: Pluribus Press.

Addelson, F. (1973). Induced abortion: Source of guilt or growth? *American Journal of Orthopsychiatry, 43,* 815–823.

Allison, P. (1979). Social work research in perinatology. In I. S. Zemzars & R. A. Ritvo (Eds.), *Perinatology: The Role of Social Work in Practice, Research and Professional Education* (pp. 128–132). Based on proceedings of a national conference jointly sponsored by the Department of Health, Education and Welfare and Case Western University. Cleveland, OH: Case Western Reserve University.

Alpert, J. J. (1982). Primary health care for children and youth. In H. M. Wallace, E. M. Gold, & A. C. Oglesby (Eds.), *Maternal and child health practices: Problems, resources, and methods of delivery.* (2nd ed.). (pp. 382–395). New York: John Wiley & Sons.

American College of Obstetricians and Gynecologists and American Academy of Pediatrics. (1983). *Guidelines for perinatal care.* Washington, DC: American College of Obstetricians and Gynecologists and American Academy of Pediatrics.

American Nurses' Association. (1987). *Access to prenatal care: Key to preventing low birthweight.* Report of consensus conferences. Kansas City, MI: American Nurses' Association.

Anderson, G. R. (1984). Children and AIDS: Implications for child welfare. *Child Welfare, 63,* 62–73.

Anderson, V. (1981). Family network systems and the Latino adolescent. In L. Riehman & B. Reichert (Eds.), *Social Work Practice: Meeting the Life Cycle Needs of Children and Youth with Handicapping Conditions* (pp. 193–197). Based on the proceedings of the 19th annual multi-regional workshop for Maternal Child Health/Crippled Children Services Social Workers in Regions VII, VIII, IX & X. San Diego, CA: San Diego State University.

Annas, G. J. (1984). Ethics committees in neonatal care: Substantive protection or procedural diversion? *American Journal of Public Health, 74,* 843–845.

Appel, Y. H. (1981). Issues in the evaluation of direct practice. In J. Rauch (Ed.), *Applied social work research in maternal and child health: Instrument for change* (pp. 95–101). Based on proceedings of a conference sponsored by the Philadelphia Regional Pediatric Pulmonary Disease Program.

Aral, S. O., & Cates, W. (1983). The increasing concern with infertility: Why now? *Journal of the American Medical Association, 250,* 2327–2331.

Aries, N. (1987). Fragmentation and reproductive freedom: Federally subsidized family planning services, 1960–80. *American Journal of Public Health, 77,* 1465–1471.

Armstrong, B. (1979). Family planning services/Veneral disease prevention and treatment. In W. T. Hall & C. L. Young (Eds.), *Proceedings: Health and social needs of the adolescent: Professional responsibilities* (pp. 29–35). Pittsburgh: University of Pittsburgh.

Arras, J., & Hunt, R. (1983). Ethical theory in the medical context. In J. Arras & R. Hunt (Eds.), *Ethical issues in modern medicine* (pp. 1–33). Palo Alto, CA: Mayfield Publishing.

Asher, J. D. (1972). Abortion counseling. *American Journal of Public Health, 62,* 686–688.

Association for the Care of Children's Health (1983). *Guidelines for developing community networks: Support for families of children with chronic illnesses or handicapping conditions.* Washington, DC: Association for the Care of Children's Health.

Bachrach, C. A. (1984). Contraceptive practice among American women, 1973–1982. *Family Planning Perspectives, 16,* 253–259.

Bailey, D. B., Simeonsson, R. J., Winton, P. J., Huntington, G. S., Comfort, M., Isbell, P., O'Donnell, K. J., & Helm, J. M. (1986). Family-focused intervention: A functional model for planning, implementing, and evaluating individualized family services in early intervention. *Journal of the Division for Early Childhood, 10,* 156–171.

Bakketeig, L. S., Hoffman, H. J., & Oakley, A. R. T. (1984). Perinatal mortality. In M. B. Bracken (Ed.), *Perinatal Epidemiology* (pp. 99–151). New York: Oxford University Press.

Balassone, M. L. (1983). *The history of social workers and teenage pregnancy.* Unpublished manuscript, School of Social Work, University of Washington, Seattle.

Balassone, M. L. (1988). Multiple pregnancies among adolescents: Incidence and correlates. *Health and Social Work, 13,* 266–276.

Balassone, M. L. (1988b). Predicting consistent contraceptive use among adolescents. *Proceedings of the 4th National Symposium on Doctoral Research and Social Work Practice*. Ohio State University: Columbus, Ohio.

Baldwin, W. (1981). Adolescent pregnancy and childbearing: An overview. *Seminars in Perinatology*, 5(1), 1–8.

Baldwin, W., & Cain, V. S. (1980). The children of teenage parents. *Family Planning Perspectives*, 12, 834–843.

Barber, J. (1987). *Postneonatal death impact*. Speech to the Southern Health Association, Nashville, Tennessee.

Barber, J. (1988). *Making the difference: Advocacy initiatives for mothers and babies*. Paper presented at the Biregional Public Health Social Work Conference for Public Health Social Workers, Regions 4 and 6: "Empowering Families for Better Health." University of South Carolina, South Carolina.

Barber, J. (1989a). *Going upstream with the homeless*. Unpublished manuscript. Jackson, Mississippi: Mississippi State Department of Health.

Barnard, K. E., & Sumner, G. A. (1981). The health of women with fertility-related needs. In L. V. Klerman (Ed.), *Research Priorities in Maternal and Child Health* (pp. 49–102). Report of a conference sponsored by Brandeis University and the United States Department of Health and Human Services. Boston: Brandeis University.

Barnett, H. L., & Hunter, J. C. (1983). *Sudden Infant Death Syndrome: An evaluation and assessment of the state of the science*. Bethesda, MD: National Institute of Child Health and Human Development.

Barrett, K. (1910). The unmarried mother and her child. *Proceedings of the Annual Meeting of the National Conference of Charities and Correction*, 37, 96–100.

Barron, E., & Richardson, J. A. (1978). Counseling women for tubal sterilization. *Health and Social Work*, 3(1), 48–58.

Barth, R. P., Claycomb, M., & Loomis, A. (1988). Services to adolescent fathers. *Health and Social Work*, 13, 277–287.

Bartlett, H. M. (1954). Perspectives in public health social work. *Children*, 1(1), 21–25.

Bass, M., Kravath, R. E., & Glass, L. (1986). Death-scene investigation in sudden infant death. *New England Journal of Medicine*, 315, 100–105.

Bassuk, E. L., Rubin, L., & Lauriat, A. S. (1986). Characteristics of sheltered homeless families. *American Journal of Public Health*, 76, 1097–1101.

Batshaw, M. L., & Perret, Y. M. (1986). *Children with handicaps* (2nd ed.). Baltimore: Paul H. Brookes Publishing

Batterman, R. (1985). A comprehensive approach to treating infertility. *Health and Social Work*, 10, 46–54.

Battle, S. F. (1987). Unmarried adolescent fathers. In D. H. Rodman & A. Murphy (Eds.), *Adolescent Issues: Pregnancy-Parenting-Health* (DHHS Grant No. MCJ-009060–3) (pp. 49–55). Proceedings of a course sponsored by the University Affiliated Training Program, Shriver Center, Waltham,

Massachusetts and the Department of Health and Human Services.

Bazzoli, G. J. (1986). Health care for the indigent: Overview of critical issues. *Health Services Research, 21,* 353–393.

Bean, L. L., Anderson, R. K., & Tatum, H. J. (1971). *Population and family planning manpower and training.* New York: The Population Council.

Beardslee, W. R., & DeMaso, D. R. (1982). Staff groups in a pediatric hospital: Content and coping. *American Journal of Orthopsychiatry, 52,* 712–718.

Beckwith, B. (1979). *The Sudden Infant Death Syndrome* (DHEW Publication No. (HSA) 79–5251). Rockville, MD: United States Department of Health, Education and Welfare.

Behrman, S. J., & Patton, G. W. (1988). Evaluation of infertility in the 1980s. In S. J. Behrman, R. W. Kistner, & G. W. Patton (Eds.), *Progress in infertility* (3rd ed.) (pp. 1–22). Boston: Little, Brown and Company.

Bell, T. A., & Hein, K. (1984). Adolescents and sexually transmitted diseases. In K. K. Holmes, P. Mardh, P. F. Sparling, & P. J. Wiesner (Eds.), *Sexually transmitted diseases.* New York: McGraw-Hill.

Benfield, D. G., Leib, S. A., & Reuter, J. (1976). Grief response of parents after referral of the critically ill newborn to a regional center. *New England Journal of Medicine, 294,* 975–978.

Benford, M. S., & Stokes, D. J. (1988). Potentual use of computerized information network for planning social work programs. In E. L. Watkins & L. R. Melnick (Eds.), *Implementing solutions to problems of infant mortality and morbidity* (DHHS Grant No. MCJ009056–03-0) (pp. 61–66). Based on proceedings of a biregional conference sponsored by the University of North Carolina at Chapel Hill.

Benjamin, M., & Curtis, J. (1986). *Ethics in nursing* (2nd ed.). New York: Oxford University Press.

Bergman, A. S., Lewiston, N. J., & West, A. M. (1979). Social work practice and chronic pediatric illness. *Social Work in Health Care, 4,* 265–274.

Bergman, B., & Weissman, L. A. (1983). Applied social work research. In R. S. Miller & H. Rehr (Eds.), *Social Work Issues in Health Care* (pp. 221–251). Englewood Cliffs, NJ: Prentice-Hall.

Bernstein, R. (1960). Are we still stereotyping the unmarried mother? *Social Work, 5,* 22–28.

Bernstein, R. (1965). Unmarried parents. In H. L. Lurie (Ed.), *Encyclopedia of social work* (15th ed.) (pp. 797–801). New York: National Association of Social Workers.

Bernstein, R., & Cyr, F. E. (1957). A study of interviews with husbands in a prenatal and child health program. *Social Casework, 38,* 473–480.

Bernstein, R., & Sauber, M. (1960). *Deterrents to early prenatal care and social services among women pregnant out-of-wedlock.* Albany, NY: New York State Department of Social Welfare.

Berry, C. S. (1925). The case for the mentally retarded. *Proceedings of the annual meeting of the National Association of Social Work, 52,* 440–444.

Bertrand, J. J., Proffitt, B. J., & Bartlett, T. L. (1987). Marketing family planning services in New Orleans. *Public Health Reports, 102*, 420–426.

Bibring, G. L., & Valenstein, A. F. (1976). Psychological aspects of pregnancy. *Clinical Obstetrics and Gynecology, 19*, 357–371.

Biering-Sorensen, F., Jorgensen, T., & Hilden, J. (1979). Sudden infant death in Copenhagen 1956–1971. *Acta Paediatrica Scandinavia, 68*, 1–9.

Bierman, B. R., & Street, R. (1982). Adolescent girls as mothers: Problems in parenting. In I. R. Stuart & C. F. Wells (Eds.), *Pregnancy in adolescence: Needs, problems, and management* (pp. 407–426). New York: Van Nostrand Reinhold.

Binkin, N. J., Williams, R. L., Hogue, C. J. R., & Chen, P. M. (1985). Reducing black neonatal mortality: Will improvement in birth weight be enough? *Journal of the American Medical Association, 253*, 372–375.

Bishop, K. K. (1988). The role of the Federal Office of Maternal and Child Health in Public Law 99–457. Comments at the Carolina Conference on Infant Personnel Preparation. A consensus conference on the implementation of Public Law 99–457 sponsored by the University of North Carolina, August 18–21, Washington, DC.

Blau, A., Welkowitz, J., & Cohen, J. (1964). Maternal attitude to pregnancy instrument. *Archives of General Psychiatry, 10*, 324–331.

Blythe, B. J., Gilchrist, L. D., & Schinke, S. P. (1981). Pregnancy-prevention groups for adolescents. *Social Work, 26*, 503–504.

Bolton, F. G. (1980). *The pregnant adolescent.* Beverly Hills: Sage Publications.

Bolton, F. G., & Belsky, J. (1986). The adolescent father and child maltreatment. In A. B. Elster & M. E. Lamb (Eds.), *Adolescent fatherhood* (pp. 123–140). Hillsdale, NJ: Lawrence Erlbaum Associates.

Borg, S., & Lasker, J. (1981). *When pregnancy fails.* Boston: Beacon Press.

Bradshaw, B. R., Wolfe, W. M., Wood, T. J., & Tyler, L. S. (1977). *Counseling on family planning and human sexuality.* New York: Family Service Association of America.

Breslin, R. L. (1974). Delivery of social work service in newborn special care unit. In R. L. Breslin (Ed.), *Selected papers based on the Proceedings of the First National Workshop on the Delivery of Hospital Social Work Services in Obstetrics/Gynecology and Services to the Newborn* (pp. 77–88) (DHEW Publication No. HSA 77–5026). Rockville, MD: U. S. Department of Health, Education, and Welfare.

Brewster, D. (1979). *You can breastfeed your baby . . . Even in special circumstances.* Emmaus, PA: Rodale Press.

Brill, N., Cohen, S., Fauvre, M., Klein, N., Clark, S., & Garcia, L. (1987). Caring for chronically ill children: An innovative approach for care. *Children's Health Care, 16*, 105–113.

Brilliant, E. L. (1986). Social work leadership: A missing ingredient? *Social Work, 31*, 325–331.

Brimblecombe, F. S. W. (1984). The needs of parents of young handicapped children living at home. In N. R. Butler & B. D. Corner (Eds.), *Stress and disability in childhood: The longterm problems* (pp. 78–86). Bristol: Wright.

Brindis, C., Barth, R. P., & Loomis, A. B. (1987). Continuous counseling: Case management with teenage parents. *Social Casework, 68*, 164–172.

Brooks, J. G. (1987). Facts about apnea and other apparent life-threatening events. McLean, Virginia: National Sudden Infant Death Syndrome Clearinghouse.

Brown, F. G. (1960). Adoption: Services for unmarried mothers. In R. H. Kurtz (Ed.), *Social work yearbook* (14th ed.) (pp. 85–90). New York: National Association of Social Workers.

Bullough, B. (1972). Poverty, ethnic identity, and preventive health care. *Journal of Health and Social Behavior, 13*, 347–359.

Burley, M. M. (1981). A parent's perspective: You are right, I have no credentials, but. . . . In J. A. Browne, A. B. Kirlin, & S. Watt (Eds.), *Rehabilitation services and the social work role: Challenge for change* (pp. 129–133). Baltimore: Williams & Wilkins.

Burnstein, M. J. (1968). Social work practice toward enhancing competence in family planning. In F. Haselkorn (Ed.), *Family planning: The role of social work* (pp. 136–143). Perspectives in Social Work, Vol. II, No. 1. New York: Adelphi University School of Social Work Publication.

Burt, M. R. (1986). Estimating the public costs of teenage childbearing. *Family Planning Perspectives, 18*, 221–226.

Burt, M. R., & Sonenstein, F. L. (1985). Planning programs for pregnant teenagers. *Public Welfare, 43*(2), 28–36.

Butler, R. (1985). Social work strategies where there are unusual barriers to maternity care. In E. L. Watkins & A. E. Johnson (Eds.), *Removing cultural and ethnic barriers to health care* (DHEW Grant No. 001049–01-0) (pp. 211–223). Based on proceedings of a national conference sponsored by the University of North Carolina at Chapel Hill.

Cacioppo, B., & Andrews, S. (1979). Respite care for parents of handicapped children: A pilot project. *Social Work in Health Care, 5*, 97–101.

Cain, L. P. (1979). Social worker's role in teenage abortions. *Social Work, 24*, 52–56.

Caldwell, B. M., & Bradley, R. H. (1978). *Home Observation for Measurement of the Environment.* Little Rock, Arkansas: University of Arkansas.

Calkins, D. R., Burns, L. A., & Delbanco, T. L. (1986). Ambulatory care and the poor: Tracking the impact of changes in Federal policy. *Journal of General Internal Medicine, 1*, 109–115.

Caplan, G., Mason, E. A., & Kaplan, D. M. (1965). Four studies of crisis in parents of prematures. *Community Mental Health Journal, 1*, 149–161.

Card, J. J., & Wise, L. L. (1978). Teenage mothers and teenage fathers: The impact of early childbearing on the parents' personal and professional lives. *Family Planning Perspectives, 10*, 199–205.

Carlton, T. O., & Mayes, S. M. (1982). Gonorrhea: Not a "second-class" disease. *Health and Social Work, 7*, 301–313.

Carolina Conference on Infant Personnal Development. (1988). A consensus conference on the implementation of Public Law 99–457 sponsored by the University of North Carolina, August 18–21, Washington, DC.

Castor, J., & Hudson, P. S. (1971). Social work attitudes toward referral to Planned Parenthood. *Social Service Review, 45,* 302–309.

Cates, W. (1984a). Induced abortion. In M. B. Bracken (Ed.), *Perinatal Epidemiology* (pp. 301–324). New York: Oxford.

Cates, W. (1984b). Sexually Transmitted Diseases and family planning: Strange or natural bedfellows? *The Journal of Reproductive Medicine, 29,* 317–322.

Centers for Disease Control (1987). *Morbidity and Mortality Weekly Report 35* (Suppl.).

Centers for Disease Control (September 19, 1988). *AIDS Weekly Surveillance Report.*

Chabot, A. (1971). Improved infant mortality rates in a population served by a comprehensive neighborhood health program. *Pediatrics, 47,* 989–994.

Chambers, C. A. (1963). Social service and social reform: A historical essay. *Social Service Review, 37,* 76–90.

Chamie, M., Eismau, S., Forrest, J. D., Orr, M. T., & Torres, A. (1982). Factors affecting adolescents' use of Family Planning Clinics. *Family Planning Perspectives, 14,* 126–139.

Chang, A., & Teramoto, R. (1987). Children with special needs in private day care centers. *Child & Youth Care Quarterly, 16,* 60–67.

Cheetham, J. (1977). *Unwanted pregnancy and counselling.* London: Routledge & Kegan Paul.

Chesborough, S. (1987). Models of prenatal psychosocial self-assessment. In E. L. Watkins & L. R. Melnick (Eds.), *Implementing solutions to problems of infant mortality and morbidity* (DHHS Contract No. MCJ009056–03-0) (pp. 16–28). Based on proceedings of a biregional conference sponsored by the University of North Carolina at Chapel Hill.

Chesler, J. S., & Davis, S. A. (1980). Problem pregnancy and abortion counseling with teenagers. *Social Casework, 61,* 173–179.

Children's Bureau (1919). *Standards of child welfare: A report of the Children's Bureau Conferences, May and June, 1919.* Washington, DC: United States Department of Labor, Children's Bureau. Conference Series No. 1, Bureau Publication No. 60.

Children's Defense Fund (1987). *A children's defense budget—FY 1988: An analysis of our nation's investment in children.* Washington, DC: Children's Defense Fund.

Children's Defense Fund (1988). *A children's defense budget—FY 1989: An analysis of our nation's investment in children.* Washington, DC: Children's Defense Fund.

Chilman, C. S. (1979). Teenage pregnancy: A research review. *Social Work, 24,* 492–498.

Chilman, C. S. (1983). *Adolescent sexuality in a changing American society: Social and psychological perspectives for the human services professions* (2nd ed.). New York: John Wiley & Sons.

Chilman, C. S. (1987). Abortion. In A. Minahan (Ed.), *Encyclopedia of Social Work* (18th ed.) (Vol. 1) (pp. 1–7). Silver Spring, MD: National Association of Social Workers.

Christopher, E. (1980). *Sexuality and birth control in social and community work*. London: Temple Smith.

Clark, J. I. A. (1968). The use of knowledge about families as a basis for program planning. In W. T. Hall & H. B. Monahan (Eds.), *Proceedings of the Tri-Regional Workshop on Planning and Implementing Social Work Programs in Community Health Services for Mothers and Children* (pp. 19–29). Pittsburgh: University of Pittsburgh.

Cleary, P. D. (1988). Social support: Conceptualization and measurement. In H. B. Weiss & F. H. Jacobs (Eds.), *Evaluating Family Programs* (pp. 195–216). New York: Aldine De Gruyter.

Clyman, R. I., Green, C., Mikkelsen, C., Rowe, J., & Ataide, L. (1979). Do parents utilize physician follow-up after the death of their newborn? *Pediatrics, 64,* 665–667.

Cochrane, R., & Robertson, A. (1973). The Life Events Inventory: A measure of the relative severity of psychosocial stressors. *Journal of Psychosomatic Research, 17,* 135–139.

Cohen, M., & Perry, J. (1981). Abortion demand: Policy and implementation. *Health and Social Work, 6*(1), 65–72.

Collins, J. (1974). Social work service in comprehensive maternity care. In R. L. Breslin (Ed.), *Selected Papers Based on Proceedings of the First National Workshop on the Delivery of Hospital Social Work Services in Obstetrics/ Gynecology and Services to the Newborn* (pp. 57–66) (DHEW Publication No. HSA 77–5026). Rockville, MD: U.S. Department of Health, Education, and Welfare.

Combs-Orme, T. (1987). Infant mortality: Priority for social work. *Social Work, 32,* 507–511.

Combs-Orme, T. (1988). Infant mortality and social work: Legacy of success. *Social Service Review, 62,* 83–102.

Combs-Orme, T., Fishbein, J., & Summerville, C. (1987). Early discharge of very-low-birth-weight infants. *New England Journal of Medicine, 316,* 629.

Combs-Orme, T., Fishbein, J., Summerville, C., & Evans, M. (1988). Rehospitalization of NICU survivors: A two-year followup. *American Journal of Diseases in Children, 142,* 1109–1113.

Combs-Orme, T., Reis, J., & Ward, L. (1985). Effectiveness of home visits by Public Health Nurses and Maternal and Child Health: An empirical review. *Public Health Reports, 100,* 490–499.

Conference on the Care of Dependent Children (1909). Proceedings of a conference held in Washington, DC, January 25–26, 1909. Senate documents, Vol. 13, 60th Congress, 2nd session. Washington, DC: Government Printing Office.

Cooper, E. (1982). Prenatal care for the pregnant adolescent. In I. R. Stuart & C. F. Wells (Eds.), *Pregnancy in adolescence: Needs, problems, and management* (pp. 66–79). New York: Van Nostrand Reinhold.

Corcoran, K., & Fischer, J. (1987). *Measures for clinical practice: A sourcebook*. New York: The Free Press.

Corman, H., & Grossman, M. (1985). Determinants of neonatal mortality rates in the United States: A reduced form model. *Journal of Health Economics, 4,* 213–236.

Cornell, P. (1987). School-based clinics: The New Haven experience. In D. H. Rodman & A. Murphy (Eds.), *Adolescent issues: Pregnancy-parenting-health* (DHHS Grant No. MCJ-009060–3) (pp. 43–47). Proceedings of a course sponsored by the University Affiliated Training Program, Shriver Center, Waltham, Massachusetts.

Coulton, C. J. (1979). Education for research on social work in perinatology: Single subject design. In I. S. Zemzars & R. A. Ritvo (Eds.), *Perinatology: The role of social work in practice, research and professional education* (pp. 109–119). Based on proceedings of a national conference jointly sponsored by the Department of Health, Education and Welfare and Case Western University. Cleveland, OH: Case Western Reserve University.

Cowell, C. (1985). Nutrition, psychosocial and medical aspects: Risk factors for the pregnant woman. In D. H. Rodman & A. Murphy (Eds.), *Perinatal care in the 80s: Social work strategies for prevention and intervention* (DHHS Grant No. MCJ-009060–01-0) (pp. 113–119). Based on proceedings of a course sponsored by the University Affiliated Training Program, Eunice Kennedy Shriver Center, Waltham, Massachusetts, and the Department of Health and Human Resources.

Cowin, R. (1968). Perspectives from public health social work. In W. T. Hall & H. B. Monahan (Eds.), *Proceedings of the Tri-Regional Workshop on Planning and Implementing Social Work Programs in Community Health Services for Mothers and Children* (pp. 94–100). Pittsburgh: University of Pittsburgh.

Cranshaw, L. (1978). The Sudden Infant Death Syndrome: A psychophysiological consideration. *Smith College Studies in Social Work, 48,* 132–170.

Creasy, R. K., Gummer, B. A., & Liggins, G. C. (1980). System for predicting spontaneous preterm birth. *Obstetrics and Gynecology, 55,* 692–695.

Crnic, K. A., Ragozin, A. S., Greenberg, M. T., Robinson, N. M., & Basham, R. B. (1983). Social interaction and developmental competence of preterm and full-term infants during the first year of life. *Child Development, 54,* 1199–1210.

Cropley, C., & Bloom, R. S. (1975). An interaction guide for a neonatal special care unit. *Pediatrics, 55,* 287–290.

Crump, E. (1974). Delivery of social work service in a family planning program. In R. L. Breslin (Ed.), *Selected papers based on the Proceedings of the First National Workshop on the Delivery of Hospital Social Work Services in Obstetrics/Gynecology and Services to the Newborn* (pp. 102–106) (DHEW Publication No. HSA 77–5026). Rockville, MD: U. S. Department of Health, Education, and Welfare.

Curtiss, C. R. (1986). *Sexually transmitted diseases, women and social work.* Unpublished paper presented at the National Association of Social Work National Conference on Women's Issues, Atlanta, Georgia.

Cyr, F. E., & Wattenberg, S. H. (1957). Social work in a preventive program of Maternal and Child Health. *Social Work, 2,* 32–39.

Dane, E. (1985). Professional and lay advocacy in the education of handicapped children. *Social Work, 30,* 505–510.

Daniels, K. R. (1986). New birth technologies: A social work approach to researching the psychosocial factors. *Social Work in Health Care, 11*(4), 49–60.

Daniels, P., & Weingarten, K. (1979). A new look at the medical risks in late childbearing. *Women & Health, 4,* 5–36.

Darling, R. B., & Darling, J. (1982). *Children who are different: Meeting the challenges of birth defects in society.* St. Louis: C.V. Mosby.

Darrow, W. W. (1979). Adolescents and veneral diseases. In R. C. Jackson, J. Morton, & M. Sierra-Franco (Eds.), *Social factors in prevention* (pp. 85–92). Berkeley: Public Health Social Work Program, School of Public Health, University of California.

Dauber, B., Zalar, M., & Goldstein, P. J. (1972). Abortion counseling and behavioral change. *Family Planning Perspectives, 4*(2), 23–27.

David, R. J. (1980). The quality and completeness of birthweight and gestational age data in computerized birth files. *American Journal of Public Health, 70,* 964–973.

Davis, K., Gold, M., & Makuc, D. (1981). Access to health care for the poor: Does the gap remain? *Annual Review of Public Health, 2,* 159–182.

Davis, K., & Schoen, C. (1979). *Health and the war on poverty: A ten-year appraisal.* Washington, DC: The Brookings Institution.

Dawson, D. A. (1986). The effects of sex education on adolescent behavior. *Family Planning Perspectives, 18,* 162–170.

Delgado, M. (1981). Social work research and program development: Implications for maternal and child health. In J. Rauch (Ed.), *Applied social work research in maternal and child health: Instrument for change* (pp. 39–50). Based on proceedings of a conference sponsored by the Philadelphia Regional Pediatric Pulmonary Disease Program.

Deuel, E. W. (1951). Child welfare. In M. B. Hodges, Ed., *Social work yearbook* (11th ed.) (pp. 88–101). New York: American Association of Social Workers.

DiBlasio, F. A. (1989). Adolescent sexuality: Promoting the search for hidden values. *Child Welfare, 68,* 331–337.

Dillard, R. G., Auerbach, K. G. & Showalter, A. H. (1980). A parents' program in the intensive care nursery: Its relationship to maternal attitudes and expectations. *Social Work in Health Care, 5,* 245–251.

Dindia, G. (1981). Handicapped children as a family stressor. In L. Riehman & B. Reichert (Eds.), *Social Work Practice: Meeting the Life Cycle Needs of Children & Youth with Handicapping Conditions* (pp. 199–206). Based on the proceedings of the 19th annual multi-regional workshop for Maternal Child Health/Crippled Children Services Social Workers in Regions VII, VIII, IX & X. San Diego, CA: San Diego State University.

Documents. (1987). Adolescent Family Life Act of 1981 found unconstitutional. *Family Planning Perspectives, 19,* 134–136.

Donahue, A. M. (1929). Children born out of wedlock. *Social work yearbook* (pp.

73–75). New York: National Association of Social Workers.

Dott, C. P., & Dott, A. B. (1985). Promoting family health in the perinatal period. In *Perinatal Health Care: Responding to Community Needs in an Era of High Technology* [Summary]. Proceedings of the Ninth National Conference on Perinatal Social Work, New Orleans.

Dryfoos, J. G. (1982). The epidemiology of adolescent pregnancy: Incidence, outcomes, and interventions. In I. R. Stuart & C. F. Wells (Eds.), *Pregnancy in adolescence: Needs, problems, and management* (pp. 27–47). New York: Van Nostrand Reinhold.

Dryfoos, J. G. (1984). A new strategy for preventing unintended teenage childbearing. *Family Planning Perspectives, 16,* 193–195.

Dryfoos, J. G., & Heisler, T. (1981). Contraceptive services for adolescents: An overview. In F. F. Furstenberg, R. Lincoln, & J. Menken (Eds.), *Teenage Sexuality, Pregnancy, and Childbearing* (pp. 394–408). Philadelphia: University of Pennsylvania Press.

Duke, E. (1915). *Infant mortality: Results of a field study in Johnstown, Pa., based on births in one calendar year.* Washington, DC: United States Department of Labor, Children's Bureau. Infant Mortality Series No. 3.

Dunst, C. J., & Leet, H. E. (1987). Measuring the adequacy of resources in households with young children. *Child: Care, Health and Development, 13,* 111–125.

Dunst, C. J., & Trivette (1988). Toward experimental evaluation of the Family, Infant and Preschool Program. In H. B. Weiss & F. H. Jacobs (Eds.), *Evaluating Family Programs* (pp. 315–346). New York: Aldine De Gruyter.

Dutton, D. B. (1985). Socioeconomic status and children's health. *Medical Care, 23,* 142–156.

Dwyer, J. (1974). Nutrition in comprehensive maternity care-Part 1. In R. L. Breslin (Ed.), *Selected papers based on Proceedings of the First National Workshop on the Delivery of Hospital Social Work Services in Obstetrics/ Gynecology and Services to the Newborn* (pp. 29–49) (DHEW Publication No. HSA 77–5026). Rockville, MD: U.S. Department of Health, Education and Welfare.

Edgington, A., Hall, M. J., & Ross, R. S. (1980). Neglectful families: Measurement of change resulting from social work intervention. In E. L. Watkins (Ed.), *Social work in a state-based system of child health care* (DHHS Grant No. MCT-009002–01-0) (pp. 111–124). Based on the proceedings of the 1980 tri-regional workshop for social workers in Maternal and Child Health services. Sponsored by the University of North Carolina at Chapel Hill and the Department of Health and Human Services.

Edwards, L. E., Steinman, M. E., Arnold, K. A., & Hakanson, E. Y. (1980). Adolescent pregnancy prevention services in high school clinics. *Family Planning Perspectives, 12,* 6–7, 11–14.

Emery, C. (1985). Responding to maternal needs in era of high technology [Summary]. In *Perinatal Health Care: Responding to Community Needs in An Era of High Technology.* Proceedings of the Ninth National Conference on Perinatal Social Work, New Orleans.

Ershoff, D. H., Aaronson, N. K., Danaher, B. G., & Wasserman, F. W. (1983). Behavioral, health, and cost outcomes of an HMO-based prenatal health education program. *Public Health Reports, 98,* 536–547.

Everett, M. (1980). Group work in the prenatal clinic. *Health and Social Work, 5*(1), 71–74.

Ewy, D. H., & Ewy, R. F. (1984). *Death of a dream.* New York: E. P. Dutton.

Fairley, A. L. (1979). Essentials of social work practice in perinatology. In I. S. Zemzars & R. A. Ritvo (Eds.), *Perinatology: The Role of Social Work in Practice, Research and Professional Education* (pp. 38–43). Based on proceedings of a national conference jointly sponsored by the Department of Health, Education and Welfare and Case Western University. Cleveland, OH: Case Western Reserve University.

Faria, G., Barrett, E., & Goodman, L. M. (1985). Women and abortion: Attitudes, social networks, decision-making. *Social Work in Health Care, 11*(1), 85–99.

Finkel, M. L., & Finkel, D. J. (1981). Sexual and contraceptive knowledge, attitudes and behavior of male adolescents. In F. F. Furstenberg, R. Lincoln, & J. Menken (Eds.), *Teenage Sexuality, Pregnancy, and Childbearing* (pp. 327–335). Philadelphia: University of Pennsylvania Press.

Folks, H. (1911). The rate of progress (Presidential Address). *Proceedings of the Annual Meeting of the National Conference on Charities and Correction, 38,* 1–8.

Foltz, A. (1982). *An ounce of prevention: Child health politics under Medicaid.* Cambridge, MA: The MIT Press.

Forrest, J. D. (1988). The delivery of family planning services in the United States. *Family Planning Perspectives, 20,* 880–95, 898.

Forrest, J. D., & Henshaw, S. K. (1983). What U. S. women think and do about contraception. *Family Planning Perspectives, 15,* 157–166.

Forrest, J. D., Hermalin, A. I., & Henshaw, S. K. (1981). The impact of Family Planning programs on adolescent pregnancy. *Family Planning Perspectives, 13,* 109–116.

Francomme, C. (1986). *Abortion practice in Britain and the United States.* London: Allen & Unwin.

Freeman, E. W. (1976). Abortion: Beyond rhetoric to access. *Social Work, 21,* 483–487.

Freeman, E. W., Rickels, K., Huggins, G. R., Mudd, E. H., Garcia, C.-R., & Dickens, H. O. (1980). Adolescent contraceptive usage: Comparisons of male and female attitudes and information. *American Journal of Public Health, 70,* 790–797.

Friedlander, S., & Shaw, E. (1975). Psychogenic factors in sudden infant death: Some dynamic speculations. *Clinical Social Work Journal, 3,* 237–253.

Furie, S. (1966). Birth control and the lower-class unmarried mother. *Social Work, 11,* 42–49.

Furlong, R. M. (1986). The social worker's role on the institutional ethics committee. *Social Work in Health Care, 11*(4), 93–100.

Furstenberg, F. F. (1976). *Unplanned parenthood: The social consequences of teenage childbearing.* New York: The Free Press.

Furstenberg, F. F., Herceg-Baron, R., Mann, D., & Shea, J. (1982). Parental involvement: Selling family planning clinics short. *Family Planning Perspectives, 14,* 140–144.

Furstenberg, F. F., Herceg-Baron, R., Shea, J., & Webb, D. (1984). Family communication and teenagers' contraceptive use. *Family Planning Perspectives, 16,* 163–170.

Furstenberg, F. F., Lincoln, R. & Menken, J. A. (Eds.). (1981). *Teenage sexuality, pregnancy, and childbearing.* Philadelphia: University of Pennsylvania Press.

Gallivan, L. P., & Saunders, J. (1982). Prenatal information series for women at risk. *Health and Social Work, 7,* 134–139.

Gelman, S. R. (1986). Life vs. death: The value of ethical uncertainty. *Health and Social Work, 11,* 118–125.

George, G. (1979). The role of social work in perinatal clinics. In I. S. Zemzars & R. A. Ritvo (Eds.), *Perinatology: The Role of Social Work in Practice, Research and Professional Education* (pp. 29–37). Based on proceedings of a national conference jointly sponsored by the Department of Health, Education and Welfare and Case Western University. Cleveland, OH: Case Western Reserve University.

George, J., & Ahmann, E. (1986). Community resources for the family of the high risk infant. In E. Ahmann (Ed.), *Home care for the high risk infant: A holistic guide to using technology* (pp. 307–320). Rockville, MD: Aspen Publications.

Gewirth, A. (1978). *Reason and morality.* Chicago: University of Chicago Press.

Gilchrist, L. D., & Schinke, S. P. (1983). Teenage pregnancy and public policy. *Social Service Review, 57,* 307–322.

Gilson, G. J. (1976). Care of the family who has lost a newborn. *Postgraduate Medicine, 60,* 67–70.

Gitterman, A., Black, R. B., & Stein, F. (1985). Public health social work in maternal and child health: A forward plan. Report of the Working Conference of the Public Health Social Work Advisory Committee for the Bureau of Health Care Delivery and Assistance. Sponsored by Columbia University School of Social Work, June 23–June 26, 1985.

Gliedman, J., & Roth, W. (1980). *The unexpected minority: Handicapped children in America.* New York: Harcourt Brace Jovanovich.

Gluck, L. (1974). Perspectives in perinatology, present and future. In R. L. Breslin (Ed.), *Selected papers based on Proceedings of the First National Workshop on the Delivery of Hospital Social Work Services in Obstetrics/ Gynecology and Services to the Newborn* (pp. 67–76). (DHEW Publication No. HSA 77–5026). Rockville, MD: U.S. Department of Health, Education and Welfare.

Goggin, M. L. (1987). *Policy design and the politics of implementation: The case of child health care in the American states.* Knoxville: The University of Tennessee Press.

Golan, N. (1987). Crisis intervention. In A. Minahan (Ed.), *Encyclopedia of*

Social Work (18th ed.) (Vol. 1) (pp. 360–372). Silver Spring, MD: National Association of Social Workers.

Gold, E. M. (1982). The high-risk pregnancy. In H. M. Wallace, E. M. Gold, & A. C. Oglesby (Eds.), *Maternal and child health practices. Problems, resources, and methods of delivery* (2nd ed.) (pp. 240–248). New York: John Wiley & Sons.

Gold, R. B., & Kenney, A. M. (1985). Paying for maternity care. *Family Planning Perspectives, 17,* 103–111.

Gold, R. B., & Macias, J. (1986). Public funding of contraceptive, sterilization and abortion services, 1985. *Family Planning Perspectives, 18,* 259–264.

Goldenberg, R. L., & Koski, J. F. (1984). *The Improved Pregnancy Outcome Project: An analysis of the impact of a federal program on infant mortality.* Birmingham, Alabama: The Division of Maternal-Fetal Medicine, Department of Obstetrics and Gynecology, the University of Alabama in Birmingham.

Goldstein, H. (1987). The neglected moral link in social work practice. *Social Work, 32,* 181–186.

Gomel, V. (1978). Profile of women requesting reversal of sterilization. *Fertility and Sterility, 30,* 39–41.

Goodman, J. R., & Hiestand, E. E. (1982). Permanent decision making: Counseling women for sterilization. *Social Casework, 63,* 73–81.

Goodrich, J. T., & Wiesner, P. J. (1982). Sexually Transmitted Diseases in adolescents. In H. M. Wallace, E. M. Gold, & A. C. Oglesby (Eds.), *Maternal and child health practices. Problems, resources, and methods of delivery* (2nd ed.) (pp. 702–722). New York: John Wiley & Sons.

Gortmaker, S. L. (1979). The effects of prenatal care upon the health of the newborn. *American Journal of Public Health,39,* 653–660.

Gould, J. B. (1987). The risk approach: Concepts and applications. In J. Morton, M. L. Balassone, & S. Guendelman (Eds.), *Preventing Low Birthweight and Infant Mortality: Programmatic Issues for Social Workers* (pp. 89–94). Based on proceedings of the 1986 Public Health Social Work Institute, sponsored by the University of California, Berkeley.

Gray, N. T. (1966). Family planning and social welfare's responsibility. *Social Casework, 47,* 487–493.

Greenberg, M., & Morris, N. (1974). Engrossment: The newborn's impact upon the father. *American Journal of Orthopsychiatry, 44,* 520–531.

Greenblatt, B. (1972). Family planning goals and social work roles. *Family Planning Perspectives, 4*(1), 54–59.

Greenfeld, D. (1986). Birth technology and infertility: What impact for perinatal social work? *NAPSW Forum, 6*(2), 1, 3–5.

Greenfeld, D., Diamond, M. P., Breslin, R. L., & DeCherney, A. (1986). Infertility and the new reproductive technology: A role for social work. *Social Work in Health Care, 12*(2), 71–81.

Grossman, M., & Jacobowitz, S. (1981). Variations in infant mortality rates among counties in the United States: The roles of public policies and programs. *Demography, 18,* 695–713.

Guendelman, S. R. (1981). Socialization and the development of a self-concept in the pre-school child. In L. Riehman & B. Reichert (Eds.), *Social Work Practice: Meeting the Life Cycle Needs of Children & Youth with Handicapping Conditions* (pp. 79–85). Based on the proceedings of the 19th annual multi-regional workshop for Maternal Child Health/Crippled Children Services Social Workers in Regions VII, VIII, IX & X. San Diego, CA: San Diego State University.

Guendelman, S. (1987). Screening for psychosocial risk. In C. J. Morton, M. L. Balassone, & S. R. Guendelman (Eds.), *Preventing Low Birthweight and Infant Mortality: Programmic Issues for Public Health Social Workers* (pp. 85–88). Based on proceedings of the 1986 Public Health Social Work Institute. Berkeley: University of California.

The Alan Guttmacher Institute (1981). *Teenage pregnancy: The problem that hasn't gone away.* New York: Author.

The Alan Guttmacher Institute (1987). *Blessed events and the bottom line: Financing maternity care in the United States.* New York: Author.

Gyulay, J. (1976). SIDS: Emergency room care for families. *Issues in Comprehensive Pediatric Nursing, 1,* 35–47.

Hack, M., DeMonterice, D., Merkatz, I. R., Jones, P., & Fanaroff, A. A. (1981). Rehospitalization of the very low birthweight infant. *American Journal of Diseases of Children, 135,* 263–266.

Hafeman, S. F., & Chilman, C. S. (1974). Implications of vasectomy for social work practice. *Social Casework, 55,* 343–351.

Hager, A. (1987). Early pregnancy loss: Miscarriage and ectopic pregnancy. In J. R. Woods & J. L. Esposito (Eds.), *Pregnancy loss: Medical therapeutics and practical considerations* (pp. 23–50). Baltimore: Williams & Wilkins.

Haggerty, J. T. (1980). Life stress, illness and social supports. *Developmental Medical Child Neurology, 22,* 391–400.

Hall, B. L. (1979). Coordination of social work services in perinatal care. In I. S. Zemzars & R. A. Ritvo (Eds.), *Perinatology: The Role of Social Work in Practice, Research and Professional Education* (pp. 47–49). Based on proceedings of a national conference jointly sponsored by the Department of Health, Education and Welfare and Case Western University. Cleveland, OH: Case Western Reserve University.

Hall, J. (1981). Adolescence: Life cycle needs of adolescents with handicapping conditions. In L. Riehman & B. Reichert (Eds.), *Social Work Practice: Meeting the Life Cycle Needs of Children & Youth with Handicapping Conditions* (pp. 175–186). Based on the proceedings of the 19th annual multi-regional workshop for Maternal Child Health/Crippled Children Services Social Workers in Regions VII, VIII, IX & X. San Diego, CA: San Diego State University.

Hall, W. T., & Young, C. L. (1979). Introduction. In W. T. Hall & C. L. Young (Eds.), *Proceedings: Health and Social Needs of the Adolescent: Professional Responsibilities* (pp. 1–2). Pittsburgh: University of Pittsburgh.

Halpern, P. L. (1985). Respite care and family functioning in families with retarded children. *Health and Social Work, 10,* 138–150.

Hancock, E. (1976). Crisis intervention in a newborn nursery intensive care unit. *Social Work in Health Care, 1,* 421–432.

Hare, E. K. (1985). Staff reflections on caring for drug addicted pregnant women. In D. H. Rodman & A. Murphy (Eds.), *Perinatal Care in the 80s: Social Work Strategies for Prevention and Intervention* (DHHS Grant No. MCJ-009060–01-0) (pp. 59–63). Based on proceedings of a course sponsored by the University Affiliated Training Program, Eunice Kennedy Shriver Center, Waltham, Massachusetts, and the Department of Health and Human Resources.

Harris, L. J., Keeler, E., & Michnich, M. E. (1977). *Algorithms for health planners: Vol. 2, Infant mortality.* Santa Monica, CA: Rand Corporation.

Hartman, A. (1981). The family: A central focus for practice. *Social Work, 26,* 7–13.

Haselkorn, F. (1966). Introduction and overview. In F. Haselkorn (Ed.), *Mothers-At-Risk: The Role of Social Work in Prevention of Morbidity in Infants of Socially Disadvantaged Mothers* (pp. 9–14). Based on an institute sponsored by Adelphi University and the United Cerebral Palsy Associations, Inc. New York: Adelphi University School of Social Work Publications.

Haselkorn, F. (1970). Family planning: Implications for social work education. *Journal of Education for Social Work, 6*(2), 13–19.

Haselkorn, F. (Ed.). (1971). *Family planning: A source book and case material for social work education.* New York: Council on Social Work Education.

Hatcher, R. A., Guest, F., Stewart, F., Stewart, G. K., Trussell, J., Cerel, S., & Cates, W. (1986). *Contraceptive technology 1986–87* (13th rev. ed.). New York: Irvington Publishers.

Hawkins, D. G. (1980). Enigma in swaddling clothes: Sudden Infant Death Syndome. *Health and Social Work, 5,* 21–27.

Hayden, A. H., & Beck, G. R. (1982). The epidemiology of high-risk and handicapped infants. In C. T. Ramey & P. L. Trohanis (Eds.), *Finding and educating high-risk and handicapped infants* (pp. 19–51). Baltimore: University Park Press.

Healy, A., Keesee, P. D., & Smith, B. S. (1985). *Early services for children with special needs: Transactions for family support.* Iowa City, IA: Division of Developmental Disabilities, University Hospital School.

Henshaw, S. K., Forrest, J. D., & Van Vort, J. (1987). Abortion services in the United States, 1984 and 1985. *Family Planning Perspectives, 19,* 63–70.

Henshaw, S. K., & Wallisch, L. S. (1984). The Medicaid cutoff and abortion services for the poor. *Family Planning Perspectives, 16,* 170–180.

Hobel, C. J., Hyvarinen, M. A., Okada, D. M., & Oh, W. (1973). Prenatal and intrapartum high-risk screening I. Prediction of the high-risk neonate. *American Journal of Obstetrics and Gynecology, 117,* 1–9.

Hobbs, N., Perrin, J. M., & Ireys, H. T. (1985). *Chronically ill children and their families.* San Francisco: Jossey-Bass.

Hoekelman, R. A. (1987). Child health supervision. In R. A. Hoekelman, S. Blatman, S., Friedman, S. B., Nelson, N. M., & Seidel, H. M. (Eds.), *Primary pediatric care* (pp. 28–33). St. Louis: C.V. Mosby.

Hofferth, S. L., Kahn, J. R., & Baldwin, W. (1987). Premarital sexual activity among U.S. teenage women over the past three decades. *Family Planning Perspectives, 19*(2), 46–53.

Holmes, K. A. (1980). Euthanasia: A social work perspective. *Health and Social Work, 4,* 5–12.

Holmes, T. H., & Rahe, R. H. (1967). The social readjustment rating scale. *Journal of Psychosomatic Research, 11,* 213–219.

Holroyd, J. (1974). The questionnaire on resources and stress: An instrument to measure family response to a handicapped family member. *Journal of Community Psychology, 2,* 92–94.

Hoppenbrouwers, T., & Hodgman, J. E. (1983). Sudden Infant Death Syndrome (SIDS). *Public Health Reviews, 11,* 363–390.

Hopps, J. G. (1986). Editorial: Compromise budget or compromised children. *Social Work, 31,* 163–164.

Horejsi, G. A. (1984). Specialized home care for children. *Health and Social Work, 9,* 241–242.

House of Representatives (1983). *U.S. Children and their families: Current conditions and recent trends.* New York: Foundation for Child Development (reprinted).

Howard, J. (1978). The influence of children's developmental dysfunctions on marital quality and family interaction: A life-span perspective. In R. M. Lerner & G. B. Spanier (Eds.), *Child influences on marital and family interaction: A life-span perspective* (pp. 275–298). New York: Academic Press.

Howard, J. (1982). A service delivery system for handicapped children, from birth to three, and their families. In L. A. Bond & J. M. Joffe (Eds.), *Facilitating infant and early childhood development* (pp. 503–512). Published for the Vermont Conference on the Primary Prevention of Psychopathology. Hanover: University Press of New England.

Hughes, D. (1985). Strategies and organization for advocacy. In E. L. Watkins & L. R. Melnick (Eds.), *Infant mortality, morbidity, and childhood handicapping conditions: Psychosocial factors* (DHHS Grant No. MCJ009056–01-0) (pp. 121–129). Based on proceedings of a biregional conference sponsored by The University of North Carolina at Chapel Hill.

Hughes, D., Johnson, K., Rosenbaum, S., Simon, J., & Butler, E. (1987). *The health of American's children. Maternal and Child Health data book.* Washington, DC: Children's Defense Fund.

Hunt, P. T. (1985). Brief overview of the Maternal and Child Health system, Oklahoma area Indian Health Service. In E. L. Watkins & L. R. Melnick (Eds.), *Infant Mortality, Morbidity, and Childhood Handicapping Conditions: Psychosocial Factors* (DHHS Grant No. MCJ009056–01-0) (pp. 69–72). Based on proceedings of a biregional conference sponsored by The University of North Carolina at Chapel Hill.

Hurt, H. (1984). Continuing care of the high-risk infant. *Clinics in Perinatology, 11*(1), 3–17.

Hutchins, V. L. (1987). Federal initiative: Perinatal and pediatric AIDS. In E. L.

Watkins & L. R. Melnick (Eds.), *Implementing Solutions to Problems of Infant Mortality and Morbidity* (DHHS Contract No. MCJ009056–03-0) (pp. 103–111). Proceedings of a biregional maternal and child health conference, New Orleans.

Ichord, R. (1986a). Developmental issues in care of the high risk infant. In E. Ahmann (Ed.), *Home care for the high risk infant: A holistic guide to using technology* (pp. 281–292). Rockville, MD: Aspen Publications.

Ichord, R. (1986b). Profile of the high risk infant. In E. Ahmann (Ed.), *Home Care for the High Risk Infant: A Holistic Guide to Using Technology* (pp. 1–11). Rockville, MD: Aspen Publications.

Ilse, S. (1982). *Empty arms: Coping after miscarriage, stillbirth and infant death.* Long Lake, MN: Wintergreen Press.

Ilse, S. & Burns, L. H. (1985). *Miscarriage: A shattered dream.* Long Lake, MN: Wintergreen Press.

Insley, V. (1966). Some implications of recent legislation for social work. In F. Haselkorn (Ed.), *Mothers-At-Risk: The Role of Social Work in Prevention of Morbidity in Infants of Socially Disadvantaged Mothers* (pp. 48–59). Based on an institute sponsored by Adelphi University and the United Cerebral Palsy Associations. New York: Adelphi University School of Social Work Publications.

Insley, V. (1971). Health services: Maternal and child health. In R. Morris (Ed.), *Encyclopedia of social work* (16th ed.) (pp. 552–560). Washington, DC: National Association of Social Workers.

Insley, V. (1980). Some observations on social work in health programs for families, mothers, and children. In E. L. Watkins (Ed.), *Social Work in a State-Based System of Child Health Care* (DHHS Grant No. MCT-009002–01-0) (pp. 23–29). Based on the proceedings of the 1980 tri-regional workshop for social workers in Maternal and Child Health services. Sponsored by the University of North Carolina at Chapel Hill and the Department of Health and Human Services.

Insley, V. (1981a). Research in maternal and child health: Historical perspectives. In J. Rauch (Ed.), *Applied social work research in maternal and child health: Instrument for change* (pp. 1–10). Based on proceedings of a conference sponsored by the Philadelphia Regional Pediatric Pulmonary Disease Program.

Insley, V. (1981b). Social work practice in service delivery to children with handicapping conditions: Historical overview, current and future needs. In L. Riehman & B. Reichert (Eds.), *Social Work Practice: Meeting the Life Cycle Needs of Children & Youth with Handicapping Conditions* (pp. 15–22). Based on the proceedings of the 19th annual multi-regional workshop for Maternal Child Health/Crippled Children Services Social Workers in Regions VII, VIII, IX & X. San Diego, CA: San Diego State University.

Institute of Medicine (1985). *Preventing low birthweight.* Washington, DC: National Academy Press.

Ireys, H. T., & Eichler, R. J. (1988). Program priorities of Crippled Children's agencies: A survey. *Public Health Reports, 103,* 77–83.

Irwin, P. H., & Conroy-Hughes, R. (1982). EPSDT impact on health status: Estimates based on secondary analysis of administratively generated data. *Medical Care*, *20*, 216–234.

Jackson, R. C. (1980). Developing networks in a state-based system of health care for families. In E. L. Watkins (Ed.), *Social Work in a State-Based System of Child Health Care* (DHHS Grant No. MCT-009002-01-0) (pp. 12–22). Based on the proceedings of the 1980 tri-regional workshop for social workers in Maternal and Child Health services. Sponsored by the University of North Carolina at Chapel Hill and the Department of Health and Human Services.

Jacobson, H. N. (1982). Nutrition and pregnancy. In H. M. Wallace, E. M. Gold, & A. C. Oglesby, (Eds.), *Maternal and Child Health Practices. Problems, Resources, and Methods of Delivery* (2nd ed.) (pp. 302–313). New York: John Wiley & Sons.

Jensen, H. (1927). Is social work contributing to racial degeneration? Proceedings of the National Conference of Social Work (pp. 16–35), 55th annual session, Memphis, Tennessee.

Joffe, C. (1978). What abortion counselors want from their clients. *Social Problems*, *25*, 112–121.

Joffe, C. (1979). Abortion work: Strains, coping strategies, policy implications. *Social Work*, *24*, 485–490.

Joffe, C. (1986). *The regulation of sexuality*. Philadelphia: Temple University Press.

Johnson, A. (1955). Educating professional social workers for ethical practice. *Social Service Review*, *29*, 125–136.

Johnson, B. S. (1978). Abortion: Yesterday, today, and tomorrow. *Health and Social Work*, *3*(1), 3–7.

Johnson, C., Walters, L. H., & McKenry, P. (1979). Trends in services for pregnant adolescents. *Health and Social Work*, *4*(3), 26–47.

Johnson, D. (1974). Nutrition in comprehensive maternity care–Part 2. In R. L. Breslin (Ed.), *Selected Papers Based on the Proceedings of the First National Workshop on the Delivery of Hospital Social Work Services in Obstetrics/Gynecology and Services to the Newborn* (DHEW Publication No. HSA 77-5026) (pp. 50–56). Rockville, MD: U.S. Department of Health, Education and Welfare.

Johnson, H. C. (1987). Human development: Biological perspective. In A. Minahan (Ed.), *Encyclopedia of social work* (18th ed.) (Vol. 1) (pp. 835–850). Silver Spring, MD: National Association of Social Workers.

Johnson, J. D., & Shore, D. A. (1982). Teaching human sexuality and social work values. *Health and Social Work*, *7*, 41–49.

Johnson, L. B., & Staples, R. E. (1979). Family planning and the young minority male: A pilot project. *The Family Coordinator*, *28*, 535–543.

Johnson, M. P., & Hufbauer, K. (1982). Sudden Infant Death Syndrome as a medical research problem since 1945. *Social Problems*, *30*, 65–81.

Robert Wood Johnson Foundation (1987). Four-year effort cuts infant deaths in isolated rural counties by medical school–public health linkages. Special report, No. 2.

Jones, H. W. (1988). In Vitro Fertilization. In S. J. Behrman, R. W. Kistner, & G. W. Patton (Eds.), *Progress in infertility* (3rd ed.) (pp. 543–561). Boston: Little, Brown and Company.

Jones, E. F., Forrest, J. D., Goldman, N., Henshaw, S. K., Lincoln, R., Rosoff, J. I., Westoff, C. F., & Wulf, D. (1985). Teenage pregnancy in developed countries: Determinants and policy implications. *Family Planning Perspectives, 17,* 53–63.

Jones, E. F., Forrest, J. D., Henshaw, S. K., Silverman, J., & Torres, A. (1988). Unintended pregnancy, contraceptive practice and family planning services in developed countries. *Family Planning Perspectives, 20,* 53–67.

Joyce, K., Diffenbacher, G., Greene, J., & Sorokin, Y. (1983) Internal and external barriers to obtaining prenatal care. *Social Work in Health Care, 9,* 89–96.

Kadushin, A., & Martin, J. A. (1988). *Child welfare services* (4th ed.). New York: Macmillan Publishing.

Kaltreider, D. F., & Kohl, S. (1980). Epidemiology of preterm delivery. *Clinical Obstetrics and Gynecology, 23*(1), 17–31.

Kammerer, P. G. (1918). *The unmarried mother: A study of five hundred cases* (Publication No. 58). Reprinted Montclair, NJ: Patterson Smith Reprint Series in Criminology, Law Enforcement, and Social Problems, 1969.

Kaminsky, B. A., & Sheckter, L. A. (1979). Abortion counseling in a general hospital. *Health and Social Work, 4*(2), 92–103.

Kaplan, D. M., & Mason, E. A. (1960). Maternal reactions to premature birth viewed as an acute emotional disorder. *American Journal of Orthopsychiatry, 30,* 539–547.

Kaplan, M. (1987). Children and AIDS: Psychosocial issues. In C. J. Morton, M. L. Balassone, & S. R. Guendelman (Eds.), *Preventing Low Birthweight and Infant Mortality: Programmic Issues for Public Health Social Workers* (pp. 215–217). Based on proceedings of the 1986 Public Health Social Work Institute. Berkeley: University of California.

Kaufman, H. (1975). Everything we've always known about men without ever asking. In S. Plopper, S. Varner, & E. Wagman (Eds.), *The male role in family planning* (pp. 5–11). Conference proceedings from two workshops sponsored by the Office Family Planning, California Department of Health, Planned Parenthood of Alameda-San Francisco, and Planned Parenthood Association of Sacramento.

Kaufman, M., & Watkins, E. L. (1981). *Promoting comprehensive integrated health care with emphasis on nutrition care and social work services.* Based on a national workshop on nutrition and social work in primary care services sponsored by the Department of Health and Human Services and the University of North Carolina.

Kay, J. (1987). Pregnancy loss and the grief process. In J. R. Woods & J. L. Esposito (Eds.), *Pregnancy loss: Medical therapeutics and practical consider-*

ations (pp. 5–20). Baltimore: Williams & Wilkins.

Kazak, A. E. (1986). Families with physically handicapped children: Social ecology and family systems. *Family Process, 25,* 265–281.

Kendall, K. A. (Ed.). (1970). *Population dynamics and family planning: A new responsibility for social work education.* Proceedings of an International Conference on Social Work Education, Population, and Family Planning. New York: Council on Social Work Education.

Kennedy, D. M. (1970). *Birth control in America: The career of Margaret Sanger.* New Haven: Yale University Press.

Kennell, J. H., Slyter, H., & Klaus, M. H. (1970). The mourning response of parents to the death of a newborn infant. *New England Journal of Medicine, 283,* 344–349.

Kennell, J. H., & Trause, M. A. (1978). Helping parents cope with perinatal death. *Contemporary Ob/Gyn, 12,* 53–68.

Kenney, A. M. (1986). School-based clinics: A national conference. *Family Planning Perspectives, 18,* 44–46.

Kerson, T. S. (1982). Public health services. In T. S. Kerson (Ed.), *Social Work in Health Settings* (pp. 181–183). New York: Longman Press.

King, J. F. (1987). Dilemmas in the treatment of preterm labour and delivery. In J. Bonnar (Ed.), *Recent advances in obstetrics and gynaecology* (Vol. 15). Edinburgh: Churchill Livingstone.

Kirkley-Best, E., & Kellner, K. R. (1982). The forgotten grief: A review of the psychology of stillbirth. *American Journal of Orthopsychiatry, 52,* 420–429.

Klaus, M. H., & Fanaroff, A. A. (1979). *Care of the high-risk neonate* (2nd ed.). Philadelphia: W.B. Saunders.

Klaus, M. H., & Kennell, J. H. (1976). Maternal–infant bonding. St. Louis: C.V. Mosby.

Kleinman, J. C. (1976). Infant mortality. *Statistical Notes for Health Planners,* Number 2, National Center for Health Statistics.

Klerman, L. V., Jekel, J. F., & Chilman, C. S. (1983). The service needs of pregnant and parenting adolescents. In C. S. Chilman, *Adolescent Sexuality in a Changing American Society: Social and Psychological Perspectives for the Human Services Professions* (2nd ed.). New York: John Wiley & Sons.

Knapp, R. J., & Peppers, L. G. (1979). Doctor-patient relationships in fetal/infant death encounters. *Journal of Medical Education, 54,* 775–780.

Koch-Hatten, A. (1986). Siblings' experience of pediatric cancer: Interviews with children. *Health and Social Work, 11,* 107–117.

Kohlstaat, B. (1975). Quality assurance "model": Social services to families of infants cared for in Neonatal Intensive Care Units. In W. T. Hall & G. C. St. Denis (Eds.), *Proceedings: Quality Assurance in Social Services in Health Programs for Mothers and Children* (DHEW Contract No. HSA-105–74-83) (pp. 19–22). Proceedings of a conference sponsored by the University of Pittsburgh and the Department of Health, Education and Welfare.

Kohn, I. (1985–86). Counseling women who request sterilization: Psychodynamic issues and interventions. *Social Work in Health Care, 11(2),* 35–60.

Kornblum, H., & Marshall, R. E. (1981). A clinical social worker's function as consultant in the Neonatal Intensive Care Unit. *Social Work in Health Care*, 7(1), 57–64.

Kotch, J. B., & Cohen, S. R. (1985–86). SIDS counselors' reports of own and parents' reactions to reviewing the autopsy report. *Omega*, *16*, 129–139.

Kotch, J. B., & Whiteman, D. (1982). Effect of a WIC program on children's clinic activity in a local health department. *Medical Care*, *20*, 691–698.

Kotelchuck, M. (1984). Infant mortality vital statistics data: New uses for an old measure. In D. K. Walker & J. B. Richmond (Eds.), *Monitoring Child Health in the United States: Selected Issues and Policies* (pp. 105–122). Cambridge, MA: Harvard University Press.

Kovar, M. G. (1982). Health status of U.S. children and use of medical care. *Public Health Reports*, *97*, 3–15.

Kovar, M. G., & Meny, D. J. (1981). A statistical profile. Select Panel for the Promotion of Child Health (1979). *Better health for our children: A national strategy. Volume 3. Analysis and recommendations for selected Federal programs*. Washington, DC: The U.S. Department of Health and Human Services. DHHS (PHS) Publication No. 79–55071.

Krauss, M. W. (1988). Measures of stress and coping in families. In H. B. Weiss & F. H. Jacobs (Eds.), *Evaluating Family Programs* (pp. 177–194). New York: Aldine De Gruyter.

Kübler-Ross, E. (1969). *On death and dying*. New York: Macmillan.

Kugler, K. E., & Hansson, R. O. (1988). Relational competence and social support among parents at risk of child abuse. *Family Relations*, *37*, 328–332.

Kumabe, K., Nishida, C., O'Hara, D., & Woodruff, C. (1977). *A handbook for social work education and practice in community health settings*. Honolulu: University of Hawaii School of Social Work.

Lamb, M. E., & Elster, A. B. (1986). Parental behavior of adolescent mothers and fathers. In A. B. Elster & M. E. Lamb (Eds.), *Adolescent fatherhood* (pp. 89–106). Hillsdale, NJ: Lawrence Erlbaum Associates.

Lambert, C. (1968). Recording and reporting for program evaluation. In W. T. Hall & H. B. Monahan (Eds.), *Proceedings of the Tri-Regional Workshop on Planning and Implementing Social Work Programs in Community Health Services for Mothers and Children* (pp. 121–132). Pittsburgh: University of Pittsburgh.

Lang, P. A., & Oppenheimer, J. R. (1968). The influence of social work when parents are faced with the fatal illness of a child. *Social Casework*, *69*, 161–166.

Langone, J. (September 19, 1988). Crack comes to the nursery. *Time*, *132*, p. 85.

Lathrop, J. (1919). Income and infant mortality. *American Journal of Public Health*, *9*, 270–274.

Leland, M. (1987). The role of Congress. *Family Planning Perspectives*, *19*(3), 121–122.

Lesser, A. J. (1966). High-risk mothers and infants: Problems and prospects for prevention. In F. Haselkorn (Ed.), *Mothers-At-Risk: The Role of Social Work in Prevention of Morbidity in Infants of Socially Disadvantaged Mothers* (pp. 15–25). Based on an institute sponsored by Adelphi University and the

United Cerebral Palsy Associations, Inc. New York: Adelphi University School of Social Work Publications.

Levey-Mickens, G. (1987). Program planning and proposal writing. In E. L. Watkins & L. R. Melnick (Eds.), *Implementing Solutions to Problems of Infant Mortality and Morbidity* (DHHS Contract No. MCJ009056–03-0) (pp. 52–60). Proceedings of a Bi-Regional Conference, New Orleans.

Levitan, S. A. (1985). *Programs in aid of the poor* (5th ed.). Baltimore: Johns Hopkins University Press.

Levy, C. S. (1976). Personal versus professional values: The practitioner's dilemmas. *Clinical Social Work Journal, 4*, 110–120.

Lewis, E. (1979). Mourning by the family after a stillbirth or neonatal death. *Archives of Disease in Childhood, 54*, 303–306.

Lewis, H. (1984). Ethical assessment. *Social Casework, 65*, 203–211.

Lilienfeld, A. M., & Lilienfeld, D. L. (1980). *Foundations of epidemiology* (2nd ed.) New York: Oxford University Press.

Lowman, J. (1979). Grief intervention and Sudden Infant Death Syndrome. *American Journal of Community Psychology, 7*, 665–677.

Lundberg, E. O. (1939). Child welfare services. In R. H. Kurtz, Ed., *Social Work Yearbook* (5th ed.) (pp. 63–76). New York: Russell Sage Foundation.

Lyon, J. (1985). *Playing God in the nursery.* New York: W.W. Norton & Company.

Mack, S. (Mod.). (1985). Initiating change through political action [Summary]. In *Perinatal Health Care: Responding to Community Needs in An Era of High Technology.* Proceedings of the Ninth National Conference on Perinatal Social Work, New Orleans.

Magura, S., & Moses, B. S. (1986). *Outcome measures for child welfare services: Theory and applications.* Washington, DC: Child Welfare League of America.

Mahan, C. K., Krueger, J. C., & Schreiner, R. L. (1982). The family and neonatal intensive care. *Social Work in Health Care, 7*(4), 67–78.

Mahan, C. K., & Schreiner, R. L. (1981). Management of perinatal death: Role of the social worker in the newborn ICU. *Social Work in Health Care, 6*(3), 69–76.

Mahan, C. K., Schreiner, R. L., & Green, M. (1983). Bibliotherapy: A tool to help parents mourn their infant's death. *Health and Social Work, 8*, 126–132.

Mahlstedt, P. P. (1985). The psychological component of infertility. *Fertility and Sterility, 43*, 335–346.

Makinson, C. (1985). The health consequences of teenage fertility. *Family Planning Perspectives, 17*(3), 132–139.

Mandell, F., McAnulty, E., & Reece, R. M. (1980). Observations of paternal response to sudden unanticipated infant death. *Pediatrics, 65*, 221–225.

Manela, R., Anderson, R., & Lauffer, A. (1977). *Delivering EPSDT services. Outreach and follow-up in Medicaid's program of Early Prevention Screening Diagnosis and Treatment.* Washington, DC: United States Department of Health, Education and Welfare, Health Care Financing Administration.

Manela, R., & Hillebrand, W. (1977). *Child health information for workers in the Medicaid Early Prevention Screening Diagnosis and Treatment Program.* Washington, DC: United States Department of Health, Education and Welfare, Health Care Financing Administration.

Manisoff, M. T. (Ed.). (1970). *Family planning training for social service.* New York: Planned Parenthood–World Population.

Mantell, J. E. (1984). Social work and public health. In R. J. Estes (Ed.), *Health Care and the Social Services: Social Work Practice in Health Care.* St. Louis: Warren H. Green, Inc., 207–259.

Margolis, L. H. (1983). The effects of the status quo in child health programs: A look at children in 1990. In R. Haskins (Ed.), *Child Health Policy in An Age of Fiscal Austerity: Critiques of the Select Panel Report* (pp. 120–131). Norwood, NJ: Ablex Publishing.

Margolis, L. H., & Meisels, S. J. (1987). Barriers to the effectiveness of EPSDT for children with moderate and severe developmental disabilities. *American Journal of Orthopsychiatry, 57,* 424–430.

Marsiglio, W., & Mott, F. L. (1986). The impact of sex education on sexual activity, contraceptive use and premarital pregnancy among American teenagers. *Family Planning Perspectives, 18,* 151–170.

Martinez, G. A. (1984). Trends in breastfeeding in the United States. In *Report of the Surgeon General's Workshop on Breastfeeding and Human Lactation,* U.S. Department of Health and Human Services (pp. 18–22). (DHHS Publication Number No. HRS-D-MC 84-2).

Martinez, R. A. (1985). Ethnic and cultural factors associated with high-risk maternity outcomes: A Hispanic (Mexican-American) perspective. In E. L. Watkins & L. R. Melnick (Eds.), *Infant Mortality, Morbidity, and Childhood Handicapping Conditions: Psychosocial Factors* (DHHS Grant No. MCJ009056-01-0) (pp. 50–60). Proceedings of a biregional conference sponsored by The University of North Carolina at Chapel Hill.

Mathis, O. (1980). Enabling immigrants to obtain early preventive care. In E. L. Watkins (Ed.), *Social Work in a State-Based System of Child Health Care* (DHHS Grant No. MCT-009002-01-0) (pp. 125–131). Based on the proceedings of the 1980 tri-regional workshop for social workers in Maternal and Child Health services. Sponsored by the University of North Carolina at Chapel Hill and the Department of Health and Human Services.

Matthews, A. (1987). Social worker: Hospital advocate for the immediate and extended family. In J. R. Woods & J. L. Esposito (Eds.), *Pregnancy loss: Medical therapeutics and practical considerations* (pp. 144–152). Baltimore: Williams & Wilkins.

May, H. J., & Breme, F. J. (1982–83). SIDS Family Adjustment Scale: A method of assessing family adjustment to Sudden Infant Death Syndrome. *Omega, 13,* 59–74.

McCarthy, J., & Radish, E. S. (1982). Education and childbearing among teenagers. *Family Planning Perspectives, 14,* 154–155.

McCormick, M. (1985). The contribution of low birth weight to infant mortality and childhood morbidity. *New England Journal of Medicine, 312,* 82–90.

McDonald-Wikler, L. (1987). Disabilities: Developmental. In A. Minahan (Ed.), *Encyclopedia of social work* (18th ed.) (Vol. 1) (pp. 422–434). Silver Spring, MD: National Association of Social Workers.

McMurray, G. L. (1968). Project Teen Aid: A community action approach to services for pregnant unmarried teen-agers. *American Journal of Public Health, 58,* 1848–1853.

Mech, E. (1985). *Orientations of pregnancy counselors toward adoption.* Washington, DC: National Committee for Adoption.

Meigs, G. (1917). Maternal mortality from all conditions connected with childbirth in the United States and certain other countries. Washington, DC: United States Department of Labor, Children's Bureau. Miscellaneous Series No. 6, Publication No. 19.

Meier, G. (1966). Research and action programs in human fertility control: A review of the literature. *Social Work, 11,* 40–55.

Meier, G. (1969). Implementing the objectives of family planning programs. *Social Casework, 50,* 195–203.

Menning, B. (1977). *Infertility: A guide for the childless couple.* Englewood Cliffs, NJ: Prentice-Hall.

Meyer, D. J. (1986). Fathers of handicapped children. In R. B. Fewell & P. F. Vadas (Eds.), *Families of handicapped children: Needs and supports across the life span* (pp. 35–73). Austin, TX: Pro-ed.

Meyer, J. A., & Lewin, M. E. (1986). Poverty and social welfare: An agenda for change. *Inquiry, 23,* 122–133.

Millar, H. E. C. (1976). Early and Period Screening, Diagnosis, and Treatment. *Proceedings of the 1976 tri-regional workshop on Maternal and Child Health Services* (pp. 35–41). Conference sponsored by the University of Texas, Austin, Texas.

Millar, M. W. (1955). Casework services for the unmarried mother. *Casework Papers from the National Conference of Social Work* (pp. 91–100). New York: Family Service Association of America.

Miller, C. A. (1985). Infant mortality in the U.S. *Scientific American, 253,* 31–37.

Miller, D. S., & Lin, E. H. B. (1988). Children in sheltered homeless families: Reported health status and use of health services. *Pediatrics, 81,* 668–673.

Miller, N. B. (1981). Meeting the needs of the pre-school handicapped child. In L. Riehman & B. Reichert (Eds.), *Social Work Practice: Meeting the Life Cycle Needs of Children & Youth with Handicapping Conditions* (pp. 69–78). Based on the proceedings of the 19th annual multi-regional workshop for Maternal Child Health/Crippled Children Services Social Workers in Regions VII, VIII, IX & X. San Diego, California: San Diego State University.

Miller, R. S. (1986). Case to cause: Public health concepts associated with infant mortality and morbidity. In E. L. Watkins & L. R. Melnick (Eds.), *Interventive Strategies in Infant Mortality, Morbidity, and Childhood Handicapping Conditions* (DHHS Grant No. MCJ009056–02-0) (pp. 1–10). Based on proceedings of a bi-regional conference sponsored by The University of North Carolina at Chapel Hill.

Minahan, A. (Ed.). (1987). *Encyclopedia of social work* (18th ed.). Silver Spring, MD: National Association of Social Workers.

Minde, K. K. (1984). The impact of prematurity on the later behavior of children and on their families. *Clinics in Perinatology, 11*(1), 227–244.

Minton, C. (1983). Uses of photographs in perinatal social work. *Health and Social Work, 8,* 123–125.

Moeller, C. T. M. (1986). The effect of professionals on the family of a handicapped child. In R. R. Fewell & P. F. Vadas (Eds.), *Families of handicapped children: Needs and supports across the life span* (pp. 149–166). Austin, Texas: Pro-ed.

Moore, K. A., & Burt, M. R. (1982). *Private crisis, Public cost: Policy perspectives on teenage childbearing.* Washington, DC: The Urban Institute Press.

Mori, A. A. (1983). *Families of children with special needs.* Rockville, Maryland: Aspen Systems.

Moroney, R. M. (1987). Strategies for change: Theories for program planning and implementation. In E. L. Watkins & L. R. Melnick (Eds.), *Implementing Solutions to Problems of Infant Mortality and Morbidity* (DHHS Contract No. MCJ009056–03-0) (pp. 1–11). Based on proceedings of a biregional conference, New Orleans.

Morris, E., & West, M. P. (1981). The handicapped preschool child's family: Assessment issues. In L. Riehman & B. Reichert (Eds.), *Social Work Practice: Meeting the Life Cycle Needs of Children & Youth with Handicapping Conditions* (pp. 105–120). Based on the proceedings of the 19th annual multi-regional workshop for Maternal Child Health/Crippled Children Services Social Workers in Regions VII, VIII, IX & X. San Diego, CA: San Diego State University.

Morris, N. M., Udry, J. R., & Chase, C. L. (1975). Shifting age-parity distribution of birth and the decrease in infant mortality. *American Journal of Public Health, 65,* 359–362.

Morris, R. (1978). Social work function in a caring society: Abstract value, professional preference, and the real world. *Journal of Education for Social Work, 14,* 82–89.

Mudgett, M. D. (1935). Children of unmarried parents. In F. S. Hall, Ed., *Social Work Yearbook* (pp. 68–71). New York: Russell Sage Foundation.

Muller, C. F. (1974). Feminism, society and fertility control. *Family Planning Perspectives, 6,* 68–72.

Murphy, A., & Crocker, A. C. (1987). Impact of handicapping conditions on the child and family. In H. M. Wallace, R. F. Biehl, A. C. Oglesby & L. T. Taft (Eds.), *Handicapped children and youth: A comprehensive community and clinical approach* (pp. 26–41). New York: Human Sciences Press.

Nash, K., & Jauregry, B. (1981). Laying the perinatal groundwork for life cycle adaptation: An emphasis on preventive services for handicapping conditions. In L. Riehman & B. Reichert (Eds.), *Social Work Practice: Meeting the Life Cycle Needs of Children & Youth with Handicapping Conditions* (pp. 23–36). Based on the proceedings of the 19th annual multi-regional workshop for Maternal Child Health/Crippled Children Services Social Workers in

Regions VII, VIII, IX & X. San Diego, CA: San Diego State University.

National Association of Perinatal Social Workers. (1985). Code of Ethics. Committee Reports—Membership Committee. *NAPSW Forum*, 6(3), 4.

National Association of Social Workers. (1967). *Goals of public policy*. New York: National Association of Social Workers.

National Association of Social Workers. (1980). *Code of Ethics of the National Association of Social Workers*. Silver Spring, MD: National Association of Social Workers.

National Association of Social Workers. (1981). *Standards for social work in health care settings*. Washington, DC: National Association of Social Workers.

National Center for Health Statistics. (1984). *Trends in teenage childbearing, United States 1970–1981* (Publication Number (PHS) 84–1919). Rockville, MD: National Center for Health Statistics.

National Institute of Mental Health. (1979). *Talking to children about death* (DHHS Publication No. [ADM] 79–838). Rockville, MD: National Institute of Mental Health.

National Urban League. (1987). *Adolescent male responsibility pregnancy prevention and parenting program: A program development guide*. New York: National Urban League.

Navarre, E. L. (1971). Illegitimacy. In R. Morris, Ed., *Encyclopedia of social work* (16th ed.) (pp. 646–653). Washington, DC: National Association of Social Workers.

Needleman, S. K. (1987). Infertility and in vitro fertilization: The social worker's role. *Health and Social Work*, 12, 135–143.

Nelson, R. P. (1983). Are we aggravating chronic conditions in children? In W. T. Hall, G. C. St. Denis, & C. L. Young (Eds.), *The Family: A Critical Factor in Prevention* (DHHS Grant No. MCJ-00014–25) (pp. 66–73). Based on proceedings of a workshop sponsored by the University of Pittsburgh and the Department of Health and Human Services.

Nelson, S. A. (1968). Coordination of M & I and C & Y projects. In W. T. Hall & H. B. Monahan (Eds.), *Proceedings of the Tri-Regional Workshop on Planning and Implementing Social Work Programs in Community Health Services for Mothers and Children* (pp. 110–120). Pittsburgh: University of Pittsburgh.

Nersesian, W. S., Petit, M. R., Shaper, R., Lemieux, D., & Naor, E. (1985). Childhood death and poverty: A study of all childhood deaths in Maine, 1976 to 1980. *Pediatrics*, 75, 41–50.

Nesbitt, R. E., & Aubry, R. H. (1969). High-risk obstetrics II. Value of semiobjective grading system in identifying the vulnerable group. *American Journal of Obstetrics and Gynecology*, 103, 972–985.

Newacheck, P. W., & Halfon, N. (1986). Access to ambulatory care services for economically disadvantaged children. *Pediatrics*, 78, 813–819.

Newacheck, P. W., & McManus, M. A. (1988). Financing health care for disabled children. *Pediatrics*, 81, 385–394.

Newcomb, G. C. (1979). The Intensive Care Nursery: Practice issues for social workers. In I. S. Zemzars & R. A. Ritvo (Eds.), *Perinatology: The Role of Social Work in Practice, Research and Professional Education* (pp. 44–46). Based on proceedings of a national conference jointly sponsored by the Department of Health, Education and Welfare and Case Western University. Cleveland, OH: Case Western Reserve University.

Newton, R. W., Webster, P. A. C., Binu, P. S., Maskrey, N., & Phillips, A. B. (1979). Psychosocial stress in pregnancy and its relation to the onset of premature labor. *British Medical Journal, 10,* 411–413.

Noble, D. N., & Hamilton, A. K. (1981). Families under stress: Perinatal social work. *Health and Social Work, 6*(1), 28–35.

Norris, F. D., & Williams, R. L. (1984). Perinatal outcomes among Medicaid recipients in California. *American Journal of Public Health, 74,* 1112–1117.

North, A. F. (1982). Early and Periodic Screening, Diagnosis, and Treatment: EPSDT. In H. M. Wallace, E. M. Gold, & A. C. Oglesby, (Eds.). *Maternal and Child Health Practices. Problems, Resources, and Methods of Delivery* (2nd ed.) (pp. 577–582). New York: John Wiley & Sons.

Northen, H. (1987). Assessment in direct practice. In A. Minahan (Ed.), *Encyclopedia of social work* (18th ed.) (Vol. 1) (pp. 171–183). Silver Spring, MD: National Association of Social Workers.

Nuckolls, K. B., Cassel, J., & Kaplan, B. H. (1971). Psychosocial assets, life crisis, and the prognosis of pregnancy. *American Journal of Epidemiology, 95,* 431–441.

Okazaki, G. (1981). Selected social work concepts and their application in social work practice with ethnic minorities. In L. Riehman & B. Reichert (Eds.), *Social Work Practice: Meeting the Life Cycle Needs of Children & Youth with Handicapping Conditions* (pp. 99–120). Based on the proceedings of the 19th annual multi-regional workshop for Maternal Child Health/Crippled Children Services Social Workers in Regions VII, VIII, IX & X. San Diego, CA: San Diego State University.

Olds, D. L., Henderson, C. R., Tatelbaum, R., & Chamberlin, R. (1986). Improving the delivery of prenatal care and outcomes of pregnancy: A randomized trial of nurse home visitation. *Pediatrics, 77,* 16–28.

Olshansky, S. (1962). Chronic sorrow: A response to having a mentally defective child. *Social Casework, 43,* 190–192.

Olson, L. (1980). Social and psychological correlates of pregnancy resolution among adolescent women: A review. *American Journal of Orthopsychiatry, 50,* 432–445.

Oppenheimer, J. R., & Rucker, R. W. (1980). The efffect of parental relationships on the management of cystic fibrosis and guidelines for social work intervention. *Social Work in Health Care, 5*(4), 409–419.

Orme, J. G., & Hamilton, M. A. (1987). Measuring parental knowledge of normative child development. *Social Service Review, 61,* 655–669.

Orr, M. T. (1983). Impact on state management of family planning funds. *Family Planning Perspectives, 15,* 176–188, 191.

Orr, M. T., & Brenner, L. (1981). Medicaid funding of family planning services. *Family Planning Perspectives, 13,* 280–287.

Orr, S. T., Miller, C. A., & James, S. A. (1984). Differences in use of health services by children according to race. *Medical Care, 22,* 848–853.

Osofsky, H. J., & Osofsky, J. D. (1970). Adolescents as mothers: Results of a program for low-income pregnant teenagers with some emphasis upon infants' development. *American Journal of Orthopsychiatry, 40,* 825–834.

Ouellette, E. (1985). The Fetal Alcohol Syndrome. In D. H. Rodman & A. Murphy (Eds.), *Perinatal Care in the 80s: Social Work Strategies for Prevention and Intervention* (DHHS Grant No. MCJ-009060–01-0) (pp. 43–58). Based on proceedings of a course sponsored by the University Affiliated Training Program, Eunice Kennedy Shriver Center, Waltham, Massachusetts, and the Department of Health and Human Resources.

Palmer, C. E. & Noble, D. N. (1986). Premature death: Dilemmas of infant mortality. *Social Casework, 67,* 332–339.

Pannor, R., Evans, B. W., & Massarik, F. (1968). *The unmarried father: Findings and implications for practice. Casework aids for reaching and working with unmarried fathers.* New York: The National Council on Illegitimacy.

Papademetriou, M. (1971). Use of a group technique with unwed mothers and their families. *Social Work, 16,* 85–90.

Parke, R. D., Power, T. G., Fisher, T. (1980). The adolescent father's impact on the mother and child. *Journal of Social Issues, 36,* 88–106.

Parks, R. M. (1977). Parental reactions to the birth of a handicapped child. *Health and Social Work, 2,* 51–66.

Peachey, H. (1982). An unsuccessful contraceptor: Family planning agency. In T. S. Kerson (Ed.), *Social work in health settings* (pp. 202–215). New York: Longman Press.

Peoples, M. D., & Siegel, E. (1983). Measuring the impact of programs for mothers and infants on prenatal care and low birth weight: The value of refined analyses. *Medical Care, 21,* 586–608.

Peppers, L. G., & Knapp, R. J. (1980). Maternal reactions to involuntary fetal/infant death. *Psychiatry, 43,* 155–157.

Peterson, D. R. (1984). Sudden infant death syndrome. In M. B. Bracken (Ed.), *Perinatal Epidemiology* (pp. 339–354). New York: Oxford.

Philipp, C. (1984). The relationship between social support and parental adjustment to low-birthweight infants. *Social Work, 29,* 547–550.

Philipp, C., & Siefert, K. (1979). A study of maternal participation in preschool programs for handicapped children and their families. *Social Work in Health Care, 5,* 165–175.

Phillips, N. K. (1982). Intervention with high-risk infants and toddlers. *Social Casework, 63,* 586–592.

Phillips, N. K., Davidson, M., & Auerbach, A. B. (1980). Discussion groups for mothers of high-risk infants and toddlers: An early intervention approach to treatment. *Child Care Quarterly, 9,* 206–208.

Phillips, N. K., Gorman, K. H., & Bodenheimer, M. (1981). High-risk infants and mothers in groups. *Social Work, 26,* 157–161.

Phipps-Yonas, S. (1980). Teenage pregnancy and motherhood: A review of the literature. *American Journal of Orthopsychiatry, 50,* 403–431.

Pierce, W. (1987). The adoption alternative. *Family Planning Perspectives, 19,* 125.

Pies, C. (1987). Women, children and AIDS: Concerns and recommendations. In C. J. Morton, M. L. Balassone, & S. R. Guendelman (Eds.), *Preventing Low Birthweight and Infant Mortality: Programmic Issues for Public Health Social Workers* (pp. 219–226). Based on proceedings of the 1986 Public Health Social Work Institute. Berkeley: University of California.

Piliavin, I., & Gross, A. E. (1977). The effects of separation of services and income maintenance on AFDC recipients. *Social Service Review, 51,* 389–406.

Pilpel, H. (1971). The law, social welfare, and family planning. In F. Haselkorn (Ed.), *Family planning: A source book and case material for social work education* (pp. 190–196). New York: Council on Social Work Education.

Planned Parenthood Federation of America. (1943). *The case worker and family planning.* New York: Planned Parenthood Federation of America.

Player, E. (1979). Commentary on Dr. Watkins' paper. In I. S. Zemzars & R. A. Ritvo (Eds.), *Perinatology: The Role of Social Work in Practice, Research and Professional Education* (pp. 22–28). Based on proceedings of a national conference jointly sponsored by the Department of Health, Education and Welfare and Case Western University. Cleveland, OH: Case Western Reserve University.

Player, E., & Oviatt, B. (1976). Public health social work in South Carolina. In *Proceedings of the 1976 Tri-Regional Workshop on Maternal and Child Health Services* (pp. 14–29). Based on a conference sponsored by the University of Texas and the Department of Health, Education and Welfare.

Poland, R. L., & Russell, B. A. (1987). The limits of viability: Ethical considerations. *Seminars in Perinatology, 11,* 257–261.

Polit-O'Hara, D., & Kahn, J. R. (1985). Communication and contraceptive practices in adolescent couples. *Adolescence, 20,* 33–43.

Potts, L. (1971). Counseling women with unwanted pregnancies. In F. Haselkorn (Ed.), *Family planning: A source book and case material for social work education* (pp. 267–282). New York: Council on Social Work Education.

Pratt, M. W. (1982). The demography of maternal and child health. In H. M. Wallace, E. M. Gold, & A. C. Oglesby, (Eds.), *Maternal and child health practices: Problems, resources, and methods of delivery* (2nd ed.) (pp. 75–109). New York: John Wiley & Sons.

Price, M., Carter, B. D., Shelton, T. L., & Bendell, R. D. (1985). Maternal perceptions of Sudden Infant Death Syndrome. *Children's Health Care, 14,* 22–31.

Pritchard, J. A., MacDonald, P.C., & Gant, N. F. (1985). *Williams pediatrics* (17th ed.). Norwalk, Conn.: Appleton-Century-Crofts.

Rainwater, L. (1970). Family planning in the United States. In J. F. Gorman (Ed.), *The Social Worker and Family Planning* (pp. 5–12). Based on the proceedings of the 1969 Annual Institute for Public Health Social Workers. Rockville, MD: United States Department of Health, Education, and Welfare. DHEW Publication No. (HSA) 77–5204.

Rando, T. A. (1985). Bereaved parents: Particular difficulties, unique factors, and treatment issues. *Social Work, 30,* 19–23.

Rapoport, L. (1961). The concept of prevention in social work. *Social Work, 6,* 3–12.

Rapoport, L. (1970). Education and training of social workers for roles and functions in family planning. *Journal of Education for Social Work, 6*(2), 27–38.

Rapoport, L., & Potts, L. (1971). Abortion of unwanted pregnancy as a potential life crisis. In F. Haselkorn (Ed.), *Family planning: A source book and case material for social work education* (pp. 249–266). New York: Council on Social Work Education.

Rappaport, B. M. (1981). Helping men ask for help. *Family Planning Perspectives, 39*(2), 22–27.

Rappaport, C. (1981). Helping parents when their newborn infants die: Social work implications. *Social Work in Health Care, 6*(3), 57–67.

Rauch, J. B. (1970). Federal family planning programs: Choice or coercion? *Social Work, 15,* 68–75.

Raymond, F. B. (1985). Implications for social work intervention in biopsychosocial factors associated with infant mortality and morbidity. In E. L. Watkins & L. R. Melnick (Eds.), *Infant Mortality, Morbidity, and Childhood Handicapping Conditions: Psychosocial Factors (DHHS Grant No. MCJ009056–01-0) (pp. 6–12). Based on proceedings of a bi-regional conference sponsored by The University of North Carolina at Chapel Hill.*

Reamer, F. G. (1979). Fundamental ethical issues in social work: An essay review. *Social Service Review, 53,* 229–243.

Reamer, F. G. (1980). Ethical content in social work. *Social Casework, 61,* 531–540.

Reamer, F. G. (1982). Conflicts of professional duty in social work. *Social Casework, 63,* 579–585.

Reamer, F. G. (1983a). The concept of paternalism in social work. *Social Service Review, 57,* 254–271.

Reamer, F. G. (1983b). Ethical dilemmas in social work practice. *Social Work, 28,* 31–35.

Reamer, F. G. (1985). The emergence of bioethics in social work. *Health and Social Work, 10,* 271–281.

Reamer, F. G. (1987a). Ethics committees in social work. *Social Work, 32,* 188–192.

Reamer, F. G. (1987b). Informed consent in social work. *Social Work, 32,* 425–429.

Reed, J. (1984). *The birth control movement and American society. From private vice to public virtue.* Princeton, NJ: Princeton University Press.

Rehr, H., Berkman, B., & Rosenberg, G. (1980). Screening for high social risk: Principles and problems. *Social Work, 25,* 403–406.

Reichert, K. (1980). Essentials of social work practice in public health programs. In E. L. Watkins (Ed.), *Social Work in a State-Based System of Child Health Care* (DHHS Grant No. MCT-009002–01-0) (pp. 30–51). Based on the proceedings of the 1980 Tri-Regional Workshop for Social Workers in

Maternal and Child Health Services sponsored by the University of North Carolina at Chapel Hill and the Department of Health and Human Services.

Reis, J. (1987). Teenage pregnancy and parenthood in Illinois: Estimated 1979–1983 costs. *Journal of Adolescent Health Care, 8,* 177–187.

Renne, D. (1977). "There's always adoption": The infertility problem. *Child Welfare, 56,* 465–470.

Resnick, M. D. (1984). Studying adolescent mothers' decision making about adoption and parenting. *Social Work, 29,* 5–10.

Rhodes, M. L. (1986). *Ethical dilemmas in social work practice.* Boston: Routledge & Kegan Paul.

Rice, E. P. (1959). Social work in public health. *Social Work, 4,* 82–88.

Rivara, F. P. (1985). Traumatic deaths of children in the United States: Currently available prevention strategies. *Pediatrics, 75,* 456–462.

Roberts, M. (1986). Three mothers: Life-span experiences. In R. R. Fewell & P. F. Vadas (Eds.), *Families of Handicapped Children: Needs and Supports Across the Life Span* (pp. 193–220). Austin, TX: Pro-ed.

Robinson, C. H. (1930). *Seventy birth control clinics.* Baltimore: Williams & Wilkins.

Robinson, J. (1975). Panel presentation: How can we involve men in family planning education and outreach programs? In S. Plopper, S. Varner, & E. Wagman (Eds.), *The male role in family planning* (pp. 40–44). Conference proceedings from two workshops sponsored by the Office Family Planning, California Department of Health, Planned Parenthood of Alameda-San Francisco, and Planned Parenthood Association of Sacramento.

Robson, K. S. (1967). The role of eye to eye contact in maternal-infant attachment. *Journal of Child Psychiatry, 8,* 13–25.

Roghmann, K. J. (1985). Intervention strategies for children: A research agenda. *Health Services Research, 19,* 887–943.

Rosenbaum, S. (1987). Medicaid eligibility for pregnant women: Reforms contained in the Sixth Omnibus Budget Reconciliation Act (SOBRA). Unpublished manuscript. Washington, DC: Children's Defense Fund.

Ross, G., Lipper, E. G., & Auld, P. A. M. (1985). Consistency and change in the development of premature infants weighing less than 1,501 grams at birth. *Pediatrics, 76,* 885–891.

Ross, J. W. (1982a). Ethical conflicts in medical social work: Pediatric cancer care as a prototype. *Health and Social Work, 7,* 95–102.

Ross, J. W. (1982b). The role of the social worker with long term survivors of childhood cancer and their families. *Social Work in Health Care, 7*(4), 1–13.

Rowe, J., Thomas, C., & Combs-Orme, T. (1988). Social services for low income Neonatal Intensive Care infants and their families. Unpublished manuscript.

Royer, T. D., & Barth, R. P. (1984). Improving the outcome of pregnancy. *Social Work, 29,* 470–475.

Rubin, A. (1987). Case management. In A. Minahan (Ed.), *Encyclopedia of Social Work* (18th ed.) (Vol. 1) (pp. 212–222). Silver Spring, MD: National Association of Social Workers.

Rubin, S. S. (1984–85). Maternal attachment and child death: On adjustment, relationship, and resolution. *Omega, 15,* 347–352.

Rudolph, C. S. (1985). Comprehensive health planning in perinatal care: Macro/ micro approach. In D. H. Rodman & A. Murphy (Eds.), *Perinatal Care in the 80s: Social Work Strategies for Prevention and Intervention* (DHHS Contract No. 009060–01-0) (pp. 1–20). Based on proceedings of a course sponsored by the University Affiliated Training Program, Eunice Kennedy Shriver Center, Waltham, Massachusetts, and the Department of Health and Human Resources.

Rudolph, C. S., & Borker, S. R. (1987). *Regionaliation: Issues in intensive care for high risk newborns and their families.* New York: Praeger.

Rudolph, C. S., & Porter, K. L. (1986). Social services utilization by families of infants discharged from a Neonatal Intensive Care Unit. *Journal of Social Service Research, 9*(4), 1–20.

Ruff, G. B. (1985). Social work program efforts in reducing infant mortality and morbidity. In E. L. Watkins & L. R. Melnick (Eds.), *Infant Mortality, Morbidity, and Childhood Handicapping Conditions: Psychosocial Factors* (DHHS Grant No. MCJ009056–01-0) (pp. 13–18). Based on proceedings of a bi-regional conference sponsored by The University of North Carolina at Chapel Hill.

Rush, D. (1982). Is WIC worthwhile? *American Journal of Public Health, 72,* 1101–1103.

Sacker, I. M., & Neuhoff, S. D. (1982). Medical and psychosocial risk factors in the pregnant adolescent. In I. R. Stuart & C. F. Wells (Eds.), *Pregnancy in adolescence: Needs, problems, and management* (pp. 107–139). New York: Van Nostrand Reinhold.

Sameroff, A. J., & Chandler, M. J. (1975). Reproductive risk and the continuum of caretaking casualty. *Review of Child Development Research, 4,* 187–244.

Sander, J. H., & Rosen, J. L. (1987). Teenage fathers: Working with the neglected partner in adolescent childbearing. *Family Planning Perspectives, 19*(3), 107–110.

Sarason, I. G., Levine, H. M., Basham, R. B., & Sarason, B. R. (1983). Assessing social support: The Social Support Questionnaire. *Journal of Personality and Social Psychology, 44,* 127–139.

Scales, P., & Beckstein, D. (1982). From macho to mutuality: Helping young men make effective decisions about sex, contraception, and pregnancy. In I. R. Stuart & C. F. Wells (Eds.) *Pregnancy in adolescence: Needs, problems, and management* (pp. 264–289). New York: Van Nostrand Reinhold.

Schild, S. (1981). The effects of handicap on the young child: Implications for interventions. In L. Riehman & B. Reichert (Eds.), *Social Work Practice: Meeting the Life Cycle Needs of Children & Youth with Handicapping Conditions* (pp. 165–169). Based on the proceedings of the 19th annual multi-regional workshop for Maternal Child Health/Crippled Children Services Social Workers in Regions VII, VIII, IX & X. San Diego, California: San Diego State University.

Schild, S., & Black, R. B. (1984). *Social work and genetics: A guide for practice.* New York: Haworth Press.

Schiff, H. (1977). *The bereaved parent.* New York: Crown Publishers.

Schilling, R. F., Gilchrist, L. D., & Schinke, S. P. (1984). Coping and social support in families of developmentally disabled children. *Family Relations, 33,* 47–54.

Schinke, S. P. (1978). Teenage pregnancy: The need for multiple casework services. *Social Casework, 59,* 406–410.

Schinke, S. P. (1979). Research on adolescent health: Social work implications. In W. T. Hall & C. L. Young (Eds.), *Proceedings: Health and Social Needs of the Adolescent: Professional Responsibilities* (pp. 63–68). Pittsburgh: University of Pittsburgh.

Schinke, S. P., & Gilchrist, L. D. (1977). Adolescent pregnancy: An interpersonal skill training approach to prevention. *Social Work in Health Care, 3,* 159–167.

Schinke, S. P., Gilchrist, L. D., & Blythe, B. J. (1980). Role of communication in the prevention of teenage pregnancy. *Health and Social Work, 5*(3), 54–59.

Schlesinger, E. G. (1985). *Health care social work practice: Concepts and strategies.* St. Louis: Times Mirror/Mosby.

Schmidt, W. W. (1982). Teen mother-well baby clinic: Maternal and child health. In T. S. Kerson (Ed.), *Social work in health settings* (pp. 184–201). New York: Longman Press.

Schoysman-Deboeck, A., Van Roosendaal, E., & Schoysman, R. (1988). Artificial Insemination: AID. In S. J. Behrman, R. W. Kistner, & G. W. Patton (Eds.), *Progress in infertility* (3rd ed.) (pp. 713–736). Boston: Little, Brown and Company.

Schreiner, R. L., Gresham, E. L., & Green, M. (1979). Physician's responsibility to parents after death of an infant. *American Journal of Diseases in Children, 133,* 723–726.

Schultz, S. K. (1980). Compliance with therapeutic regimens in pediatrics: A review of implications for social work practice. *Social Work in Health Care, 5,* 267–278.

Schwartz, B. A. (1977). Unwed parents. In J. B. Turner, Ed., *Encyclopedia of Social Work* (17th ed.) (pp. 1564–1566). Washington, DC: National Association of Social Workers.

Schwarz, J. E. (1983). *America's hidden success. A reassessment of twenty years of public policy.* New York: W. W. Norton & Company.

Scott, K. G., Field, T., & Robertson, E. (1981). *Teenage parents and their offspring.* New York: Grune & Stratton.

Searight, H. R., & Handal, P. J. (1986). Premature birth and its later effects: Towards preventive intervention. *Journal of Primary Prevention, 7,* 3–16.

Select Panel for the Promotion of Child Health (1981). *Better health for our children: A national strategy. Volume 2. Analysis and recommendations for selected Federal programs.* Washington, D.C.: The U.S. Department of Health and Human Services. DHHS (PHS) Publication No. 79–55071.

Seligman, F. (1982). Children and Youth Projects. In H. M. Wallace, E. M. Gold, & A. C. Oglesby, (Eds.), *Maternal and Child Health Practices. Problems, Resources, and Methods of Delivery* (2nd ed.) (pp. 511–530). New York: John Wiley & Sons.

Selmar, C. (1987). Development of a prenatal psychosocial tool. In C. J. Morton, M. L. Balassone, & S. R. Guendelman (Eds.), *Preventing Low Birthweight and Infant Mortality: Programmic Issues for Public Health Social Workers* (pp. 95–101). Based on proceedings of the 1986 Public Health Social Work Institute. Berkeley: University of California.

Semler, B. (1975). Panel presentation: How can we involve men in family planning education and outreach programs? In S. Plopper, S. Varner, & E. Wagman (Eds.), *The male role in family planning* (pp. 45–49). Conference proceedings from two workshops sponsored by the Office Family Planning, California Department of Health, Planned Parenthood of Alameda-San Francisco, and Planned Parenthood Association of Sacramento.

Shapiro, C. H. (1982). The impact of infertility on the marital relationship. *Social Casework, 63,* 387–393.

Shapiro, C. H. (1986). Is pregnancy after infertility a dubious joy? *Social Casework, 67,* 306–313.

Shapiro, J. (1983). Family reactions and coping strategies in response to the physically ill or handicapped child: A review. *Social Science and Medicine, 17,* 913–931.

Shapiro, L. (1980). Pregnancy termination. In *Social work in maternal and child health: A casebook* (pp. 101–124). Columbia University School of Social Work and St. Luke's-Roosevelt Hospital Center, Department of Social Work, Roosevelt Division.

Shapiro-Steinberg, L., & Neamatalla, G. S. (1979). Counseling for women requesting sterilization: A comprehensive program designed to insure informed consent. *Social Work In Health Care, 5,* 151–163.

Shelton, T. L., Jeppson, E. S., & Johnson, B. H. (1987). *Family-centered care for children with special health care needs.* 2nd ed. Washington, DC: Association for the Care of Children's Health.

Sheridan, M. S., & Johnson, D. R. (1976). Social work services in a high-risk nursery. *Health and Social Work, 1*(2), 86–103.

Shlakman, V. (1966). Unmarried parenthood: An approach to social policy. *Social Casework, 47,* 494–501.

Shlakman, V. (1968). Social work's role in family planning: Social policy issues. In F. Haselkorn (Ed.), *Family planning: The role of social work* (pp. 69–89). Perspectives in Social Work, Vol. II, No. 1. New York: Adelphi University School of Social Work Publication.

Shoemaker, L. P. (1966). Adaptation of traditional methods in services to individuals in families and groups. In F. Haselkorn (Ed.), *Mothers-At-Risk: The Role of Social Work in Prevention of Morbidity in Infants of Socially Disadvantaged Mothers* (pp. 103–115). Based on an institute sponsored by Adelphi University and the United Cerebral Palsy Associations. New York: Adelphi University School of Social Work Publications.

Siefert, K. (1983). An exemplar of primary prevention in social work: The Sheppard-Towner Act of 1921. *Social Work in Health Care, 9*(1), 87–103.

Siefert, K., Thompson, T., ten Bensel, R. W. T., & Hunt, C. (1982). Perinatal stress: A study of factors linked to the risk of parenting problems. *Health and Social Work, 7,* 107–121.

Siegel, E. (1971). The biological effects of family planning–Preventive pediatrics: The potential of family planning. Reprinted in F. Haselkorn (Ed.), *Family planning: A source book and case material for social work education* (pp. 5–13). New York: Council on Social Work Education.

Siegel, R. (1982). A family-centered program of neonatal intensive care. *Health and Social Work*, 7, 50–58.

Silverman, J., Torres, A., & Forrest, J. D. (1987). Barriers to contraceptive services. *Family Planning Perspectives*, 19, 94–102.

Simos, B. G. (1987). Loss and bereavement. In A. Minahan (Ed.), *Encyclopedia of social work* (18th ed.) (Vol. 2) (pp. 72–81). Silver Spring, MD: National Association of Social Workers.

Sinai, N., & Anderson, O. W. (1948). *EMIC (Emergency Maternity and Infant Care)*. Ann Arbor, Michigan: School of Public Health, University of Michigan.

Slater, M. A., & Wikler, L. (1986). 'Normalized' family resources for families with a developmentally disabled child. *Social Work*, 31, 385–390.

Smilkstein, G. (1978). The Family APGAR: A proposal for a family function test and its use by physicians. *The Journal of Family Practice*, 6, 1231–1239.

Smilkstein, G., Ashworth, C., & Montano, D. (1982). Validity and reliability of the Family APGAR as a test of family function. *The Journal of Family Practice*, 15, 303–311.

Smilkstein, G., Helsper-Lucas, A., Ashworth, C., Montano, M., & Pagel, M. (1984). Prediction of pregnancy complications: An application of the biopsychosocial model. *Social Science and Medicine*, 18, 315–321.

Smith, A. V. (1986). Parent outreach in a neonatal intensive care nursery. *Social Work*, 31, 69–71.

Smith, E. M. (1972). Counseling for women who seek abortion. *Social Work*, 17, 62–68.

Smith, E. S. (1981). Crippled Children's Services: Overview. In L. Riehman & B. Reichert (Eds.), *Social Work Practice: Meeting the Life Cycle Needs of Children & Youth with Handicapping Conditions* (pp. 9–14). Based on the proceedings of the 19th annual multi-regional workshop for Maternal Child Health/Crippled Children Services Social Workers in Regions VII, VIII, IX & X. San Diego, California: San Diego State University.

Smith, H. Y. (1981). Vasectomy counseling and clinical social work. *Health and Social Work*, 6(3), 64–70.

Smith, J. C., Hughes, J. M., Pekow, P. S., & Rochat, R. W. (1984). An assessment of the incidence of maternal mortality in the United States. *American Journal of Public Health*, 74, 780–783.

Smith, K. E., Spiers, M. V., & Freese, M. P. (1987). Adolescent mothers' successful participation in a well-baby care program. *Journal of Adolescent Health Care*, 8, 193–197.

Smith, P. B., Wait, R. B., Mumford, D. M., Nenney, S. W., & Hollins, B. T. (1978). The medical impact of an antepartum program for pregnant adolescents: A statistical analysis. *Public Health Briefs*, 68(2), 169–172.

Sonenstein, F. L. (1986). Risking paternity: Sex and contraception among adolescent males. In A. B. Elster & M. E. Lamb (Eds.), *Adolescent Fatherhood* (pp. 35–54). Hillsdale, NJ: Lawrence Erlbaum Associates.

Sosin, M., & Caulum, S. (1983). Advocacy: A conceptualization for social work practice. *Social Work, 28,* 12–17.

Sosnowitz, B. G. (1984). Managing parents on Neonatal Intensive Care Units. *Social Problems, 31,* 390–402.

Starfield, B. (1982). Family income, ill health, and medical care of U.S. children. *Journal of Public Health Policy, 3,* 244–259.

Starfield, B. (1985). Postneonatal mortality. *Annual Reviews in Public Health, 6,* 21–40.

Starfield, B., & Budetti, P. P. (1985). Child health status and risk factors. *Health Services Research, 19,* 817–886.

Stein, R. E. K., & Riessman, C. K. (1980). The development of an Impact-on-Family Scale: Preliminary findings. *Medical Care, 58,* 465–472.

Stevens, J. W. (1979). Crisis intervention: Anticipatory functioning related to family-infant separation. In I. S. Zemzars & R. A. Ritvo (Eds.), *Perinatology: The Role of Social Work in Practice, Research and Professional Education* (pp. 50–58). Based on proceedings of a national conference jointly sponsored by the Department of Health, Education and Welfare and Case Western University. Cleveland, OH: Case Western Reserve University.

Stickle, G. (1982). Pregnancy in adolescents. In H. M. Wallace, E. M. Gold, & A. C. Oglesby, (Eds.), *Maternal and child health practices: Problems, resources, and methods of delivery* (2nd ed.) (pp. 356–366). New York: John Wiley & Sons.

Stine, O. C. (1982). The measurement of morbidity in epidemiology and the evaluation of health services. In H. M. Wallace, E. M. Gold, & A. C. Oglesby, (Eds.), *Maternal and child health practices. Problems, resources, and methods of delivery* (2nd ed.) (pp. 369–381). New York: John Wiley & Sons.

Stine, O. C. & Kelley, E. B. (1970). Evaluation of a school for young mothers. *Pediatrics, 46,* 581–586.

Stokes, D. J. (1980). Development of services for children with handicapping conditions. In E. L. Watkins (Ed.), *Social Work in a State-Based System of Child Health Care* (DHHS Grant No. MCT-009002–01-0) (pp. 89–96). Based on the proceedings of the 1980 tri-regional workshop for social workers in Maternal and Child Health services. Sponsored by the University of North Carolina at Chapel Hill and the Department of Health and Human Services.

Stringham, J. G., Riley, J. H., & Ross, A. (1982). Silent birth: Mourning a stillborn baby. *Social Work, 27,* 322–326.

Sung, Kyu-Taik (1978). Family planning services for indigent women and girls. *Health and Social Work, 3,* 152–172.

Swanson, J. M., & Forrest, K. (1987). Men's reproductive health services in family planning settings: A pilot study. *American Journal of Public Health, 77,* 1462–1463.

Szybist, C. M. (1988). Sudden Infant Death Syndrome revisited. *Developmental and Behavioral Pediatrics, 9,* 33–37.

Tabb, S. M. (1987). Social work services in schools. In M. M. Esterson & L. F.

Bluth (Eds.), *Related Services for Handicapped Children* (pp. 113–120). Boston: Little, Brown and Company.

Tadmor, C. S. (1986). A crisis intervention model for a population of mothers who encounter neonatal death. *Journal of Primary Prevention, 7,* 17–26.

Tavormina, J. B., Kasner, L. S., Slater, P. M., & Watt, S. L. (1976). Chronically ill children: A psychologically and emotionally deviant population. *Journal of Abnormal Child Psychology, 4,* 99–110.

Timms, N. (1983). *Social work values: An enquiry.* London: Routledge & Kegan Paul.

Toedter, L. J., Lasker, J. N., & Alhadeff, J. M. (1988). The Perinatal Grief Scale: Development and validation. *American Journal of Orthopsychiatry, 58,* 435–449.

Torres, A. (1979). Rural and urban family planning services in the United States. *Family Planning Perspectives, 11,* 109–114.

Torres, A., & Forrest, J. D. (1985). Family planning clinic services in the United States, 1983. *Family Planning Perspectives, 17,* 30–35.

Torres, A., & Forrest, J. D. (1987). Family planning clinic services in U.S. counties, 1983. *Family Planning Perspectives, 2,* 54–58.

Torres, A., Forrest, J. D., & Eisman, S. (1980). Telling parents: Clinic policies and adolescents' use of family planning and abortion services. *Family Planning Perspectives, 12,* 284–292.

Towbin, L. (1985). Ethnic and cultural factors associated with high-risk maternity outcomes in Southeast Asian refugees. In E. L. Watkins & L. R. Melnick (Eds.), *Infant Mortality, Morbidity, and Childhood Handicapping Conditions: Psychosocial Factors* (DHHS Contract No. MCJ0090506–01-0) (pp. 61–68). Based on proceedings of a biregional conference sponsored by The University of North Carolina at Chapel Hill.

Troyer, R. (1987). Funeral director. In J. R. Woods & J. L. Esposito (Eds.), *Pregnancy loss: Medical therapeutics and practical considerations* (pp. 153–166). Baltimore: Williams & Wilkins.

Tyrer, L. B., & Wilson, R. A. (1982). Fertility regulation. In H. M. Wallace, E. M. Gold, & A. C. Oglesby, (Eds.), *Maternal and child health practices: Problems, resources, and methods of delivery* (2nd ed.) (pp. 249–267). New York: John Wiley & Sons.

Ullmann, A. (1972). Social work service to abortion patients. *Social Casework, 53,* 481–487.

U.S. Department of Health, Education and Welfare (1953). Medical social services for children in the maternal and child health and crippled children's programs. Washington, DC: Social Service Administration, Children's Bureau.

U.S. Department of Health, Education and Welfare (1975). *The Maternity and Infant Care projects. Reducing risks for mothers and babies.* Rockville, MD: U.S. Department of Health, Education and Welfare.

U.S. Department of Health, Education and Welfare (1979). *Healthy people. The Surgeon General's report on health promotion and disease prevention.* DHEW Publication No. 79–55071.

U.S. Department of Health and Human Services (1982). Reproductive impairments among married couples: United States. Data from the National Survey of Family Growth, Series 23, No. 11, DHHS Publication No. (PHS) 83–1987.

Vadies, E., & Hale, D. (1977). Attitudes of adolescent males toward abortion, contraception, and sexuality. *Social Work in Health Care*, 3(2), 169–174.

Valadian, I. (1982). Physical growth and development. In H. M. Wallace, E. M. Gold, & A. C. Oglesby, (Eds.), *Maternal and child health practices: Problems, resources, and methods of delivery* (2nd ed.) (pp. 396–416). New York: John Wiley & Sons.

Valentine, D. (1986). Psychological impact of infertility: Identifying issues and needs. *Social Work in Health Care*, 11(4), 61–69.

van Dyck, P. C. (1982). Identification and care of high-risk infants and children. In H. M. Wallace, E. M. Gold, & A. C. Oglesby, (Eds.). *Maternal and child health practices: Problems, resources, and methods of delivery* (2nd ed.) (pp. 455–474). New York: John Wiley & Sons.

Van Gheluwe, B., & Barber, J. K. (1986). Legislative advocacy in action. *Social Work*, 31, 393–395.

Varner, S. (1984). The male role in family planning. Paper presented at the annual National Health Conference of the National Association of Social Workers, Washington, DC.

Videka-Sherman, L. (1982). Coping with the death of a child: A study over time. *American Journal of Orthopsychiatry*, 52, 688–698.

Vigilante, J. L. (1968). Forward. In F. Haselkorn (Ed.), *Family planning: The role of social work* (pp. 5–6). Perspectives in Social Work (Vol. 2, No. 1.). New York: Adelphi University School of Social Work Publication.

Waldron, J. A., & Asayama, V. H. (1985). Stress, adaption and coping in a maternal-fetal intensive care unit. *Social Work in Health Care*, 10(3), 75–89.

Walker, D. K., & Crocker, R. W. (1988). Measuring family systems outcomes. In H. B. Weiss & F. H. Jacobs (Eds.), *Evaluating Family Programs* (pp. 153–176). New York: Aldine De Gruyter.

Wallace, H. M. (1970). Family planning: One part of comprehensive maternal and child health care. In J. F. Gorman (Ed.), *The Social Worker and Family Planning* (pp. 13–19). Based on the proceedings of the 1969 Annual Institute for Public Health Social Workers. Rockville, Maryland: United States Department of Health, Education, and Welfare. DHEW Publication No. (HSA) 77–5204.

Wallace, H. M. (1982). Application of the concept of high risk to the health care of mothers, children, and families. In H. M. Wallace, E. M. Gold, & A. C. Oglesby, (Eds.), *Maternal and Child Health Practices: Problems, Resources, and Methods of Delivery.* (2nd ed.) (pp. 110–115). New York: John Wiley & Sons.

Wallace, H. M. (1987). Organization and provisions of major public programs for handicapped children and youth and their families. In H. M. Wallace, R. F. Biehl, A. C. Oglesby & L. T. Taft (Eds.), *Handicapped children and youth: A comprehensive community and clinical approach* (pp. 50–70). New York: Human Sciences Press.

Wallace, H. M., & Medina, A. S. (1982). The organization of and legislative base for health services for mothers and children. In H. M. Wallace, E. M. Gold, & A. C. Oglesby, (Eds.), *Maternal and Child Health Practices: Problems, Resources, and Methods of Delivery* (2nd ed.) (pp. 50–74). New York: John Wiley & Sons.

Watkins, E. L. (1973). Conceptual framework for evaluation of social service programs. In *Evaluation of social work services in community health and medical care programs* (DHEW Publication No. (HSA) 78–5205) (pp. 13–36). Based on proceedings of the 1973 Annual Institute for Public Health Social Workers.

Watkins, E. L. (1979). Social work in regional perinatal programs. In I. S. Zemzars & R. A. Ritvo (Eds.), *Perinatology: The Role of Social Work in Practice, Research and Professional Education* (pp. 4–21). Based on proceedings of a national conference jointly sponsored by the Department of Health, Education and Welfare and Case Western University. Cleveland, OH: Case Western Reserve University.

Watkins, E. L. (1980). Program planning activities performed by social workers in regional perinatal programs. *High Hopes, 1*(1), 3–5.

Watkins, E. L. (1981). The use of research to build the knowledge base of social work practice in maternal and child health. In J. Rauch (Ed.), *Applied social work research in maternal and child health: Instrument for change* (pp. 11–27). Based on proceedings of a conference sponsored by the Philadelphia Regional Pediatric Pulmonary Disease Program.

Watkins, E. L. (1985). The conceptual base for public health social work. In A. Gitterman, R. B. Black, & F. Stein (Eds.), *Public Health Social Work in Maternal and Child Health: A Forward Plan* (pp. 17–33). Report of the working conference of the Public Health Social Work Advisory Committee for the Bureau of Health Care Delivery and Assistance sponsored by Columbia University.

Watkins, E. L., & Player, E. C. (1981). Maternal and child health care. *Health and Social Work, 6*(4), 44S–53S.

Wegman, M. E. (1987). Annual summary of vital statistics—1986. *Pediatrics, 80,* 817–827.

Weinberg, N. (1985). The health care social worker's role in facilitating grief work: An empirical study. *Social Work in Health Care, 10,* 107–117.

Weinrich, E. (1987). Advocacy. In H. M. Wallace, R. F. Biehl, A. C. Oglesby & L. T. Taft (Eds.), *Handicapped Children and Youth. A Comprehensive Community and Clinical Approach* (pp. 81–87). New York: Human Sciences Press.

Weinstock, N. (1986). The family of the high risk infant. In E. Ahmann (Ed.), *Home care for the high risk infant* (pp. 293–301). Rockville, MD: Aspen Publications.

Weiss, H. B. (1988). Family support and education programs: Working through ecological theories of human development. In H. B. Weiss & F. H. Jacobs (Eds.), *Evaluating Family Programs* (pp. 3–36). New York: Aldine De Gruyter.

Weiss, H. B., & Jacobs, F. H. (1988). Family support and education programs—challenges and opportunities. In H. B. Weiss & F. H. Jacobs (Eds.), *Evalu-*

ating Family Programs (pp. xix–xxix). New York: Aldine De Gruyter.

Weitz, J. (1982). Perspectives on improvement of health care of school age children—A panel. In J. C. Swart, J. B. Igoe & J. Gephart (Eds.), *Health of School-Age Children: Expectations for the Future* (pp. 7–10). Proceedings of a national conference sponsored by the University of Colorado School of Nursing and the Department of Health and Human Services.

Wells, C. C., & Masch, M. K. (1986). *Social work ethics day to day: Guidelines for professional practice.* New York: Longman.

West, M. (1914). Infant care (pamphlet). Washington, DC: Department of Labor, Children's Bureau. Care of Children Series No. 2.

West, M. (1915). Prenatal care (pamphlet). Washington, DC: Department of Labor, Children's Bureau. Care of Children Series No. 1.

White, R. B. (1981). Evaluating program consultation effectiveness. In J. Rauch (Ed.), *Applied social work research in maternal and child health: Instrument for change* (pp. 105–111). Based on proceedings of a conference sponsored by the Philadelphia Regional Pediatric Pulmonary Disease Program.

White, R. B. (1985). Environmental factors impinging on families at risk. In G. C. St. Denis & C. L. Young, (Eds.), *Families At Risk: A Public Health Social Work Perspective* (DHHS Grant No. MCJ-00014–27) (pp. 55–67). Based on a workshop sponsored by the University of Pittsburgh and the Department of Health and Human Services. Pittsburgh: University of Pittsburgh.

Wikler, L., Wasow, M., & Hatfield, E. (1981). Seeking strengths in families of developmentally disabled children. *Social Work, 51,* 313–315.

Williams, R. A., & Nikolaisen, S. M. (1982). Sudden Infant Death Syndrome: Parents' perceptions and responses to the loss of their infant. *Research in Nursing and Health, 5,* 55–61.

Wilson, R. W., & White, E. L. (1977). Changes in morbidity, disability and utilization differentials between the poor and the nonpoor: Data from the Health Interview Survey: 1964 and 1973. *Medical Care, 15,* 636–646.

Winslow, C. E. A. (1923). *The evolution and significance of the modern public health campaign.* New Haven: Yale University Press.

Wolff, J. R., Nielson, P. E., & Schiller, P. (1970). The emotional reaction to a stillbirth. *American Journal of Obstetrics and Gynecology, 108,* 73–76.

Woods, J. R. (1987). Stillbirth. In J. R. Woods & J. L. Esposito (Eds.), *Pregnancy loss: Medical therapeutics and practical considerations* (pp. 51–74). Baltimore: Williams & Wilkins.

World Health Organization (1975). *Manual of the international statistical classification of diseases, injuries, and causes of death.* Vol. 1, 9th revision. Geneva: World Health Organization.

Wortis, H., Cutler, R., Rue, R., & Freedman, A. M. (1964). Development of lower-class premature children born in and out of wedlock. *Social Work, 9*(4), 42–49.

Wortman, C. B. (1982). Research on childbirth settings: The assessment of psychological variables. In Institute of Medicine, *Research Issues in the Assessment of Birth Settings* (pp. 102–148). Washington, DC: National Academy Press.

Wright, J. M. (1981). Fetal Alcohol Syndrome: The social work connection. *Health and Social Work, 6*(1), 5–10.

York, G. Y. (1987). Religious-based denial in the NICU: Implications for social work. *Social Work in Health Care, 12*(4), 31–45.

Young, A. T. (1987). A delicate balance: Teenage and parent rights and responsibilities. In D. H. Rodman & A. Murphy (Eds.), *Adolescent Issues: Pregnancy-Parenting-Health* (DHHS Grant No. MCJ-009060–3) (pp. 11–15). Proceedings of a course sponsored by the University Affiliated Training Program, Shriver Center, Waltham, Massachusetts.

Young, A. T., Berkman, B., & Rehr, H. (1973). Women who seek abortions: A study. *Social Work, 18*, 60–65.

Young, A. T., Berkman, B., & Rehr, H. (1975). Parental influence on pregnant adolescents. *Social Work, 20*, 387–391.

Young, C. L., Hall, W. T., & Collins, J. (1979). Providing health and social services to illegal alien families: A dilemma for community agencies. *Social Work In Health Care, 4*, 309–318.

Zabin, L. S., & Clark, S. D. (1981). Why they delay: A study of teenage family planning clinic patients. *Family Planning Perspectives, 13*, 205–217.

Zabin, L. S., Kantner, J. F., & Zelnik, M. (1979). The risk of adolescent pregnancy in the first months of intercourse. *Family Planning Perspectives, 11*, 215–222.

Zahourek, R., & Jensen, J. S. (1973). Grieving and the loss of the newborn. *American Journal of Nursing, 73*, 836–839.

Zakus, G. & Wilday, S. (1987). Adolescent abortion option. *Social Work in Health Care, 12*(4), 77–91. [reference to anniversary reaction?].

Zellman, G. L. (1982). Public school programs for adolescent pregnancy and parenthood: An assessment. *Family Planning Perspectives, 14*, 15–21.

Zelnik, M. (1980). Second pregnancies to premaritally pregnant teenagers, 1976 and 1971. *Family Planning Perspectives, 12*, 69–76.

Zelnik, M., & Kantner, J. F. (1974). The resolution of teenage first pregnancies. *Family Planning Perspectives, 6*, 74–80.

Zelnik, M., & Kantner, J. F. (1980). Sexual activity, contraceptive use and pregnancy among metropolitan area teenagers: 1971–1979. *Family Planning Perspectives, 12*, 231–238.

Zelnik, M., & Shah, F. K. (1983). First intercourse among young Americans. *Family Planning Perspectives, 15*, 64–70.

Zilbergeld, B. (1975). Men's views of family planning. In S. Plopper, S. Varner, & E. Wagman (Eds.), *The male role in family planning* (pp. 22–31). Conference proceedings from two workshops sponsored by the Office Family Planning, Calirofnia Department of Health, Planned Parenthood of Alameda-San Francisco, and Planned Parenthood Association of Sacramento.

Zimring, F. E. (1982). *The changing legal world of adolescence*. New York: The Free Press.

Index

Index

Abbott, Grace, 25
Abortion, 184–185, 186, 189
  counseling, 214–215
  current services, 213–214
  decision making, 215–217
  follow-up, 218–219
  history of, in the U.S., 210–211
  induced, 97
  involuntary, 89–90
  legalization of, 212
  negative consequences of, 218
  preparation for the procedure, 217–218
  recipients, profile of, 213
  social work involvement, 211–213
  spontaneous, 16, 89, 165
Acquired Immune Deficiency Syndrome (AIDS), 54, 109, 161, 165, 177, 254–255
  in children, 221–223
Adaptive Potential for Pregnancy Scale (TAPPS), 36
Addams, Jane, 193
Adolescent Family Life Act, 172, 238
Adolescent fathers, 159, 160, 166, 168, 172, 182. *See also* Adolescent males
Adolescent health clinics, school-based, 173–174
Adolescent males. *See also* Adolescent fathers
  and abortion, 189
  contraceptives, 162

and pregnancy prevention, 172, 175–177
  prenatal care and services, recruitment into, 180–181
  sexually active, 161
Adolescent mothers, 20, 82
Adolescent pregnancy, 156–190
  consequences of, 165–169
  demographics, 160
Adolescent sexuality, 134, 156–190, 229–251
  demographics, 160–161
  emotional consequences of, 167
Adoption, 106, 157, 185, 236, 237–238, 240
Advocacy, 8–10, 15, 245, 246–251, 257
  case, 8, 74, 247
  class, 8, 247
  defined, 9
  methods, 9
  and the NICU social worker, 68, 74–75
  by parents, 154
  roles for social workers, 50–51
  for special-needs families, 153–155
  strategies, 9–10
Age, maternal, *see* Maternal age
Aid to Families with Dependent Children (AFDC), 28, 39, 40, 41, 50, 54, 73, 118–119, 180, 187, 196, 256